Justice Outsourced

EDITED BY MICHAEL L. PERLIN
AND KELLY FRAILING

Justice Outsourced

The Therapeutic Jurisprudence Implications of Judicial

Decision-Making by Nonjudicial Officers

TEMPLE UNIVERSITY PRESS

Philadelphia • *Rome* • *Tokyo*

TEMPLE UNIVERSITY PRESS
Philadelphia, Pennsylvania 19122
tupress.temple.edu

Library of Congress Cataloging-in-Publication Data

Names: Perlin, Michael L., 1946– editor. | Frailing, Kelly, editor.
Title: Justice outsourced : the therapeutic jurisprudence implications of
   judicial decision-making by nonjudicial officers / edited by Michael L.
   Perlin and Kelly Frailing.
Description: Philadelphia : Temple University Press, 2022. | Includes
   bibliographical references and index. |
Identifiers: LCCN 2022002718 (print) | LCCN 2022002719 (ebook) | ISBN
   9781439921661 (pdf) | ISBN 9781439921647 (cloth) | ISBN 9781439921654
   (paperback)
Subjects: LCSH: Criminal justice, Administration of—United States. |
   Judicial process—United States. | Criminal justice personnel—United
   States. | Therapeutic jurisprudence—United States.
Classification: LCC KF9223 (ebook) | LCC KF9223 .J87 2022 (print) | DDC
   345.73/05 23/eng/20220—dc29
LC record available at https://lccn.loc.gov/2022002718
LC ebook record available at https://lccn.loc.gov/2022002719

Printed in the United States of America

9 8 7 6 5 4 3 2 1

MLP:

To Linda, for her love, her partnership, her spirit of joy, exploration, and creation, and for making every day worth living.

To Alex, Liz, and Sam, and to Julie, Ben, and Sophie, for bringing laughter into my heart, smiles to my face, and happiness to my entire being.

KF:

To Kyle Taylor, who has so thoroughly enriched my life. You are extraordinary, and I love you very much.

MLP and KF would like to recognize and deeply thank Jamara Rowley for her indispensable assistance in creating the index for this book.

Contents

PART II: NONJUDICIAL OFFICERS IN ADMINISTRATIVE SETTINGS

PART III: ETHICAL AND PRACTICAL CONSIDERATIONS IN THE USE OF NONJUDICIAL OFFICERS

PART IV: A WORD FROM THE BENCH

Justice Outsourced

Introduction

Hiding in Plain View

How the Extensive Use of Nonjudicial Officers Corrupts the Criminal Justice System

Michael L. Perlin and Kelly Frailing

In the early 1970s, I was a practicing lawyer in Trenton, New Jersey, just across the Delaware River from Morrisville, Pennsylvania.[1] One of the bridge crossings was a toll bridge with—this being before EZ Pass and other systems—a toll collector.

One day, I got home from work to find a traffic ticket in the mail, the alleged infraction being that I had crossed the bridge without paying the toll. I was puzzled because this was something I would never do. I looked more closely at the ticket and noted that at the time of the alleged infraction, I was actually in court in Trenton at the Mercer County Courthouse. I checked my calendar to verify this. I assumed that a car with a license plate similar to mine (with one different number or letter) did avoid the toll, and that the collector made a transcription era.

I decided that I would fight the ticket. At the time, I was a public defender and represented many defendants in many serious felony cases; going to traffic court on my own behalf thus caused me no concern or apprehension. I looked again at the ticket, and the accompanying letter said, "If you plan to contest, call 215-555-1000 to schedule your hearing."

---

1. This is Michael Perlin's story. Kelly Frailing's comes later. See text that begins "As was Kelly" and ends "a failed drug test cannot provide."

I called that number, and a man answered, "Malinowski Plumbing Company."[2] I immediately said, "Oh, I'm sorry. I must have misdialed." The man at the other end responded, "Wait. Are you calling about a traffic ticket?" I said that I was. He said, "You dialed the right number. I'm Joe Malinowski, the JP[3] in Morrisville. I'll be hearing your case. When would be a good time for you to appear?"

Still surprised, I told him I was a public defender in Trenton and thus was in court almost every day, but I did have some free Friday afternoons. He asked about evenings, and I told him most were free. He then said that he would let me know on which evening the case would be scheduled.

And that was it. I never heard back. A day. A week. A month. A year. Several years. By this time, I was wondering whether the court date notice he had sent me had gone astray, and whether there was a bench warrant out for my arrest for not appearing in court, but I figured that wouldn't be the case because I was pretty easy to find (being in court in Trenton five days a week). I never got a call back.

In retrospect, it became clear to me that the "judge"—who was not a lawyer—had no desire to have a "real lawyer"[4] before him, so he simply dismissed the ticket. And that was, for me, a good thing. But it also made me think—truly for the first time—about what happens when nonlawyers (and non-"real judges") hear cases.[5]

A few years later, I became director of the Division of Mental Health Advocacy in the New Jersey Department of the Public Advocate. We were statutorily tasked with the representation of persons facing civil commitment to the state's psychiatric institutions. These were before "real judges,"

---

2. This wasn't the name, but it was fairly close. In the category of no-one-could-make-this-up, I did some home cleaning during the quarantine and went through a collection of miscellaneous papers that was under a desk in my daughter's room (she has lived away from home for the past twenty years). Among the treasures I found was the traffic ticket I am writing about here!

3. At this time in Pennsylvania, justices of the peace (JPs) heard such cases.

4. There is some irony here, as many people, including many public defender clients, do not think public defenders are actual lawyers. *See, e.g.*, People v. Holliday, 2016 WL 3126467 (Ill. App. Ct. 2016) (the fact that, quoting defense counsel, the jury was advised that "the defendant has a public defender, rather than a 'real lawyer' as most of society puts it," not a reversible error).

5. Of possible interest: At about the same time, the New Jersey Supreme Court had decided that indigent defendants in municipal court (where all cases were heard by judges who were lawyers) had an absolute right to counsel if the disposition of their case could lead to potential incarceration or "any other consequence of magnitude." Rodriguez v. Rosenblatt, 277 A.2d 216, 223 (N.J. 1971).

albeit often bored or disinterested ones,[6] but at the least they were "real judges."

Then I learned some time after I assumed this job how lucky we were in New Jersey to have "real judges" doing these cases, because in many states, it has been held that it is not constitutionally objectionable for an administrative hearing tribunal—composed of nonjudicial officers—to decide such matters.[7] These individuals—including "court clerks"—were vested with the power to commit persons to locked facilities (often including maximum security facilities) for terms often lasting years or decades.[8]

And in all the interim years—the years that I litigated (or supervised litigation) on behalf of psychiatric patients on matters involving their institutional treatment and conditions of confinement[9]—I was always puzzled when decisions that, to my mind, should have been made by judges were made instead by administrative officials (again, often nonlawyers and never judges) in cases involving issues of medication, other treatments, conditions of confinement, release restrictions, and more. I was also struck by the ab-

6. *See, e.g.,* Michael L. Perlin and Deborah A. Dorfman, *Sanism, Social Science, and the Development of Mental Disability Law Jurisprudence,* 11 BEHAV. SCI. & L. 47, 54–55 (1993) ("Mental disability law generally regulates powerless individuals represented by passive counsel in invisible court proceedings conducted by bored or irritated judges").

7. *See* MICHAEL L. PERLIN AND HEATHER ELLIS CUCOLO, MENTAL DISABILITY LAW: CIVIL AND CRIMINAL (3d ed. 2016) (spring 2021 update), §4-2.2.1.3, at 4–33, citing, inter alia, e.g., Doremus v. Farrell, 407 F. Supp. 509, 516 (D. Neb. 1975); State *ex rel.* Hawks v. Lazaro, 202 S.E.2d 109, 127–28 (W. Va. 1974). *See also* N.C. GEN. STAT. § 122C-261 (1997) (authorizing magistrate or court clerk to order emergency evaluation); UTAH CODE ANN. § 62A-12-233 (1997) (court may appoint any attorney as "mental health commissioner" to make commitment recommendations).

8. *See* Salt Lake City v. Ohms, 881 P.2d 844 (Utah 1994), declaring unconstitutional (under state constitutional grounds) state law (UTAH CODE ANN. § 62A-12-233) that had vested court commissioners with the exercise of judicial authority of courts of record.

9. *See, e.g.,* Doe v. Klein, No. L12088-74 P.W. (N.J. Super. Ct. Law Div. 1977) (final order), reprinted in 1 MENT. DIS. L. REP. 475 (1977) (right to treatment); Schindenwolf v. Klein, No. L41293-75 P.W. (N.J. Super. Ct. Law Div. 1975) (right of patients to participate in voluntary, therapeutic compensated work programs as an aspect of the right to treatment); Dixon v. Cahill, No. L30977/y-71 P.W. (N.J. Super. Ct. Law Div. 1973) (implementing Jackson v. Indiana, 406 U.S. 715 [1972], applying Due Process Clause to incompetent-to-stand-trial defendants); Rennie v. Klein, 462 F. Supp. 1131, 1147 (D.N.J. 1978), suppl., 476 F. Supp. 1294 (D.N.J. 1979), modified, 653 F.2d 836 (3d Cir. 1981), vacated, 458 U.S. 1119 (1982) (granting involuntarily committed mental patients a limited right to refuse medication). *See generally,* Michael L. Perlin and John Douard, *"Equality, I Spoke That Word/As If a Wedding Vow": Mental Disability Law and How We Treat Marginalized Persons,* 53 N.Y.L. SCH. L. REV. 9 (2008–09), and Michael L. Perlin, *"John Brown Went Off to War": Considering Veterans' Courts as Problem-Solving Courts,* 37 NOVA L. REV. 445 (2013) (discussing cases).

solute absence of legal academic literature on the role of what we call here nonjudicial officers and the implications of their proliferation.[10]

Then one day in 2019, my son (a public defender in New York state) told me about a New York law[11] that allows judges to outsource certain pretrial motions (including search and seizure hearings) to nonjudges to hold hearings and file reports with the courts. In such cases, the actual judge thus has no opportunity to weigh the credibility or the motivations of the testifying witnesses, always the most critical aspect of a contested search-and-seizure case.[12] Soon after this, I learned about a South Dakota law[13] that was interpreted to allow a "court services officer" (a nonjudicial probation officer) to modify the terms of a sex offender's judicial sentence. When I presented about this issue at a conference at Nova Law School in September 2019,[14] a Broward County (Fort Lauderdale, Florida) judge who was in the audience told me that in her county, sheriff's officers, *sua sponte*, modified court orders in terms of frequency of defendants' meetings with probation officers.[15] I was aghast.

As was Kelly. Here are her thoughts on how her interest in this subject matter evolved.

Sadly, my foray into this area does not involve calling about a ticket and reaching a plumber. Instead, it comes from my second real job after college. I had no idea what I wanted to do when I finished college, so I fumbled around in a variety of social service jobs. That second one had me supervising a group home for people with mental illness who had been justice system–involved. The other staff and I made a variety of decisions for the people in the house, as did their case managers, probation officers, and so on. I got so interested in the nexus of mental health and criminal justice that I went to graduate school

---

10. There is, to the best of our knowledge, only one journal article—Deborah J. Chase and Peggy Fulton Hora, *The Implications of Therapeutic Jurisprudence for Judicial Satisfaction*, 37 CT. REV. 12 (2000)—that discusses the ways that judicial officers and nonjudicial officers in drug courts differ in their attitudes toward court outcomes.

11. NY CRIMINAL PROCEDURE LAW § 255.20(4).

12. *See, e.g.*, Morgan Cloud, *The Dirty Little Secret*, 43 EMORY L.J. 1311 (1994).

13. SDCL § 23A-27-12.1.

14. My substantive chapter in this volume *("But I Ain't a Judge": The Therapeutic Jurisprudence Implications of the Use of Nonjudicial Officers in Criminal Justice Cases)*, addresses the practices in New York and South Dakota and their consequences in more detail.

15. *See, e.g.*, Dan Christensen, *BSO Changes Court's Probation Orders; Broward Judge Blows the Whistle*, MIAMI HERALD (Nov 10, 2014), accessible at https://www.miamiherald.com/news/local/community/broward/article3686226.html. I discuss this in *"But I Ain't a Judge": The Therapeutic Jurisprudence Implications of the Use of Non-Judicial Officers in Criminal Justice Cases*, 64 AM. BEHAV. SCI. 1686 (2020), and am indebted to Judge Ginger Lerner-Wren for bringing this to my attention.

with the idea of studying that very thing. When I started my master's program, I read what seemed like every study on specialty courts and realized just how little scholarship there was that was directly focused on perceptions of people under supervision, both generally and in these courts specifically. When I went to my doctoral program and planned my study on two mental health courts in the United States, I made participant perceptions a central focus of my work. At that time, most studies on mental health courts were focused on criminal justice outcomes, that is, recidivism, almost to the exclusion of anything else.

Since that time, I have worked to better understand the perceptions of people under supervision, including how they feel about their judge, their probation officer, their case manager, the services they are required to engage with, and so on. And I have come to realize that when participants perceive the manifestation of therapeutic jurisprudence across these domains, they are more likely to stay engaged with their programs. Of course, the programming is important, but there is something special about, say, hearing praise from a judge or a probation officer, that the threat of a sanction resulting from a failed drug test cannot provide.[16]

And thus the idea for this book was born. In short, it tackles a topic that has never been written about before: the hidden role of nonjudicial officers (NJOs) in the criminal justice system (defined broadly to include aspects of correctional law and forensic law as well), a role that is sanctioned, variously, by case law, statute, regulations, and customs. What is clear is that nonjudicial officers permeate the criminal justice system (and the forensic mental health system), almost always in hidden ways. When we discussed this book idea with friends, so many said something to the effect of, "Gee, you're right. And I really never thought about that before. Wow!"

It isn't at all clear how this began. In some cases, it appears it was a means of off-loading work of judges with heavy caseloads. In others, it appears that the questions weren't seen as "really" legal.[17] In at least one case, it was done

---

16. The chapter by Kelly and her colleagues in this volume, *Therapeutic Jurisprudence in Swift and Certain Probation*, flows from these experiences.

17. E.g., in Savastano v. Nurnberg, 567 N.Y.S.2d 618 (1990), the court rejected a due process challenge to the nonconsensual transfer of involuntarily committed, mentally ill patients from local acute-care facilities to long-term state institutions without prior judicial approval. The court noted that as the transfers at issue involved primarily medical judgments about the patients' therapeutic needs that, such decisions were better left to psychiatrists. *Id.* at 621. *See* Vincent Martin Bonventre, *Court of Appeals—State Constitutional Law Review, 1990,* 12 PACE L. REV. 1, 36–37 (1992).

ex parte without the knowledge of the presiding court.[18] But what is so striking is how little concern has been shown about this phenomenon—one that, again, pervades the criminal trial process and the forensic mental health system—over the years.[19] The common thread here is that decisions that involve due process rights, decisions that may lead to extended incarceration, and decisions that implicate multiple constitutional rights are being made by those who are not judges (and in many cases, not lawyers).

We also decided that it was mandatory that this book be written from the perspective of therapeutic jurisprudence (TJ).[20] We conclude that often the use of these NJOs—especially, their hidden use—violates every precept of TJ.[21] Professor David Wexler—one of the creators of this school of thought—has clearly identified how the tension inherent in this inquiry must be resolved: "The law's use of "mental health information to improve therapeutic functioning [cannot] impinge upon justice concerns."[22] As one of the coauthors (MLP) has written elsewhere, "An inquiry into therapeutic outcomes does not mean that therapeutic concerns 'trump' civil rights and civil liberties."[23]

TJ "asks us to look at law as it actually impacts people's lives"[24] and "focuses on the law's influence on emotional life and psychological well-

---

18. *See* Christensen, *supra* note 15.

19. It also has a significant impact on the correctional system. *See, e.g.*, Henry Dlugacz, *Correctional Disciplinary Proceedings and Incarcerated People with Mental Disabilities* (this volume); Talia Harmon, Michael Cassidy, and Richelle Kloch, *A Critique of Texas Lethal Injection Cases: An Examination of "Decision-Making" and the Risk of Botches in Texas Lethal Injection Protocols Since 1982* (this volume).

20. We use a standard definition of therapeutic jurisprudence: "The ultimate aim of therapeutic jurisprudence is to determine whether legal rules, procedures, and lawyer roles can or should be reshaped to enhance their therapeutic potential while not subordinating due process principles." *See e.g.*, Michael L. Perlin, *"Who Will Judge the Many When the Game is Through?": Considering the Profound Differences between Mental Health Courts and "Traditional" Involuntary Civil Commitment Courts*, 41 SEATTLE U. L. REV. 937, 957 (2018).

21. *See generally*, Michael L. Perlin, *"Have You Seen Dignity?": The Story of the Development of Therapeutic Jurisprudence*, 27 U.N.Z. LAW REV. 1135 (2017).

22. David B. Wexler, *Therapeutic Jurisprudence and Changing Concepts of Legal Scholarship*, 11 BEHAV. SCI. & L. 17, 21 (1993). On Wexler's role in the creation of the school of thought of therapeutic jurisprudence, *see* Michael L. Perlin, *"Changing of the Guards": David Wexler, Therapeutic Jurisprudence, and the Transformation of Legal Scholarship*, 63 INT'L J. L. & PSYCHIATRY 3 (2019).

23. *See, e.g.*, Michael L. Perlin, *A Law of Healing*, 68 U. CIN. L. REV. 407, 412 (2000) (PERLIN, *Healing*); Michael L. Perlin, *"Where the Winds Hit Heavy on the Borderline": Mental Disability Law, Theory and Practice, Us and Them*, 31 LOY. L.A. L. REV. 775, 782 (1998).

24. Bruce J. Winick, *Foreword: Therapeutic Jurisprudence Perspectives on Dealing with Victims of Crime*, 33 NOVA L. REV. 535, 535 (2009).

being."[25] It suggests that "law should value psychological health, should strive to avoid imposing anti-therapeutic consequences whenever possible, and when consistent with other values served by law should attempt to bring about healing and wellness."[26]

One of the central principles of TJ is a commitment to dignity.[27] Professor Amy Ronner describes the "three Vs" as follows:

- Voice: Litigants must have a sense of voice or a chance to tell their story to a decision maker.
- Validation: The decision-maker needs to take seriously the litigant's story.
- Voluntariness: In general, human beings prosper when they feel that they are making, or at least participating in, their own decisions.[28]

As one of the coeditors (MLP) has written with others, "the *perception of receiving a fair hearing is therapeutic* because it contributes to the individual's sense of dignity and conveys that he or she is being taken seriously."[29] Writing about dignity and the civil commitment process, Professors Jonathan Simon and Stephen Rosenbaum embrace therapeutic jurisprudence as a modality of analysis, and focus specifically on this issue of voice: "When procedures give people an opportunity to exercise voice, their words are given respect, decisions are explained to them their views taken into account, and they substantively feel less coercion."[30]

TJ also focuses on the role of counsel. Again, Professor Ronner, writing with Judge Juan Ramirez, has underscored that the right to counsel is "the

---

25. David B. Wexler, *Practicing Therapeutic Jurisprudence: Psychological Soft Spots and Strategies, in* Practicing Therapeutic Jurisprudence: Law as a Helping Profession 45 (Dennis P. Stolle et al., eds., 2000). *See generally,* Perlin, *Healing, supra* note 23.

26. Bruce J. Winick, *A Therapeutic Jurisprudence Model for Civil Commitment, in* Involuntary Detention and Therapeutic Jurisprudence: International Perspective on Civil Commitment 23, 26 (Kate Diesfeld and Ian Freckelton, eds., 2003).

27. *See* Bruce J. Winick, Civil Commitment: A Therapeutic Jurisprudence Model 161 (2005).

28. Amy D. Ronner, *Songs of Validation, Voice, and Voluntary Participation: Therapeutic Jurisprudence, Miranda and Juveniles,* 71 U. Cin. L. Rev. 89, 94–95 (2002). It is no coincidence that Ronner's "three Vs" are discussed in multiple chapters in this book.

29. Michael L. Perlin, Keri K. Gould, and Deborah A. Dorfman, *Therapeutic Jurisprudence and the Civil Rights of Institutionalized Mentally Disabled Persons: Hopeless Oxymoron or Path to Redemption?,* 1 Psychol. Pub. Pol'y & L. 80, 114 (1995).

30. Jonathan Simon and Stephen A. Rosenbaum, *Dignifying Madness: Rethinking Commitment Law in an Age of Mass Incarceration,* 70 U. Miami L. Rev. 1, 51 (2015).

core of therapeutic jurisprudence."[31] As one of the coauthors (MLP) wrote twenty-five years ago in a consideration of the death penalty (a topic under discussion in this book),[32] "Any death penalty system that provides inadequate counsel and that, at least as a partial result of that inadequacy, fails to insure that mental disability evidence is adequately considered and contextualized by death penalty decision-makers, fails miserably from a therapeutic jurisprudence perspective."[33]

In short, therapeutic jurisprudence values are intertwined with both dignitarian values and effectiveness-of-counsel values.[34] In this book, we explore how the omnipresent use of nonjudicial officers robs the legal processes of this needed dignity in direct violation of therapeutic jurisprudential values.[35] Think of some of the additional questions that are raised. Can we be sure that the nonjudicial officer knows the law? In so many areas of the law that our authors address, the law is ever changing. By way of example, on the same day as we started initial revisions of this chapter, a mail blast arrived with the information that federal executions were being halted because of challenges to the drugs used for the purposes of imposing the death penalty.[36] One of the chapters in this book deals explicitly with this issue as

---

31. Juan Ramirez Jr. and Amy D. Ronner, *Voiceless Billy Budd: Melville's Tribute to the Sixth Amendment*, 41 Cal. W. L. Rev. 103, 119 (2004).

32. *See* Harmon, Cassidy, and Kloch, *supra* note 19; Valerie McClain, *Navigating Judicial Hurdles for Effective Legal Solutions: The Agony and the Ecstasy* (this volume).

33. Michael L. Perlin, *"The Executioner's Face Is Always Well-Hidden": The Role of Counsel and the Courts in Determining Who Dies*, 41 N.Y.L. Sch. L. Rev. 201, 235 (1996). *See also* Michael L. Perlin, *"Merchants and Thieves, Hungry for Power": Prosecutorial Misconduct and Passive Judicial Complicity in Death Penalty Trials of Defendants with Mental Disabilities*, 73 Wash. & Lee L. Rev. 1501, 1542 (2016) (same).

34. *See, e.g.*, Heather Ellis Cucolo and Michael L. Perlin, *Promoting Dignity and Preventing Shame and Humiliation by Improving the Quality and Education of Attorneys in Sexually Violent Predator (SVP) Civil Commitment Cases*, 28 Fla. J. L. & Pub. Pol'y 291 (2017); Michael L. Perlin and Naomi M. Weinstein, *"Friend to the Martyr, a Friend to the Woman of Shame": Thinking About the Law, Shame and Humiliation*, 24 So. Cal. Rev. L. & Soc'l Just. 1 (2014). In this volume, specifically on counsel issues, *see* Heather Ellis Cucolo, *Reconstructing the Ethics Code to Remedy the Failures of Strickland v. Washington*; Bernard Perlmutter, *"Give Me My Allowance or I'll Run!" Everyday Resistance by Foster Children and Justice Outsourced*.

35. *See* David Wexler and Bruce Winick, *Patients, Professionals, and the Path of Therapeutic Jurisprudence: A Response to Petrila*, 10 N.Y.L. Sch. J. Hum. Rts. 907, 914 (1993) (therapeutic jurisprudence calls for a "healthy skepticism toward claims of clinical expertise"). This "healthy skepticism" must make us especially wary of nonjudges exercising judicial power.

36. *See* Bernie Pazanowski, *Federal Executions Again Halted for Challenge to Drug Efficacy*, U.S. Law Week (July 15, 2020), accessible at https://news.bloomberglaw.com/us-law-week/federal-executions-again-halted-for-challenge-to-drug-efficacy.

it is dealt with by the state of Texas;[37] can we be confident that the nonjudicial officers who oversee the administration of such drugs in every state in which the death penalty is being imposed will be familiar with this decision? A recent report by the US Office of Inspector General poignantly described the challenges of meeting the needs of mentally ill migrant children in custody.[38] Can we be confident that this report has been read by all staff at all ICE detention facilities in which such children are housed?[39]

As noted earlier, one of the lodestars of therapeutic jurisprudence is a commitment to dignity. The "track record" has been woefully clear for decades that persons with mental disabilities in jails and prisons are routinely deprived—by administrative staff and officers—of even a modicum of such dignity.[40] Another lodestar is independence.[41] Those in the foster care system often do not reflect this independence in their dealing with youth in foster care.[42]

We have written this book to demonstrate the omnipresence of these issues. We have assembled a cohort of scholars from a full range of disciplines (lawyers (including professors, practitioners and a judge), criminologists, psychologists, sociologists, and several graduate students), all of whom are positioned to offer uniquely expert perspectives on the full range of questions that are raised by our systemic reliance on NJOs, their decision making, consequences for people involved in the criminal justice and mental health systems, and implications for therapeutic jurisprudence.

We have divided this book into four parts, first on nonjudicial officers in the courtroom, second on such officers in administrative settings, third on ethical and practical considerations in the use of nonjudicial officers, and in a brief fourth and final section, a word from the bench.

The courtroom-focused chapters deal with the issues we discuss earlier in this introduction—how nonjudges decide important (often outcome-determinative) Fourth and Fifth Amendment–based motions and make criti-

---

37. *See* Harmon, Cassidy, and Kloch, *supra* note 19.

38. *See* CARE PROVIDER FACILITIES DESCRIBED CHALLENGES ADDRESSING MENTAL HEALTH NEEDS OF CHILDREN IN HHS CUSTODY (Sept. 2019), full report accessible at https://oig.hhs.gov/oei/reports/oei-09-18-00431.pdf.

39. *See* Alison J. Lynch, *The Role of Therapeutic Jurisprudence in Non-Judicial/Administrative Placement of Migrant Children with Mental Illness* (this volume).

40. *See* Deborah A. Dorfman, *Doing Time in "The Devil's Chair": Evaluating Nonjudicial Administrative Decisions to Isolate and Restrain Prisoners and Detainees with Mental Health Disabilities in Jails and Prisons* (this volume); Dlugacz, *supra* note 19.

41. *See, e.g.,* Warren Brookbanks, *Therapeutic Jurisprudence: Conceiving an Ethical Framework*, 8 J.L. & MED. 328 (2001).

42. *See* Perlmutter, *supra* note 34 (this volume).

cal decisions as to defendants' sentences;[43] how such nonjudges, very often untrained in these areas, have the power to make consequential decisions for people with mental illness and people who use substances who are justice system involved;[44] the roles of nonjudges in mental health court decision making;[45] how therapeutic jurisprudence can manifest in specialized probation programs and how that manifestation impacts participants' perceptions;[46] how often perceptions by nonjudicial decision makers as to offenders' remorse is dispositive in the ultimate disposition of their cases;[47] the role of nonjudges in decision-making about whether certain individuals face institutionalization in mental hospitals;[48] the role of nonjudges in decision making related to a wide array of issues including treatment, where one lives, and sexual autonomy in the cases of individuals with dual diagnoses;[49] and the role of nonjudges in decision-making in reentry courts.[50] In many of these areas, the use of nonjudges demeans the "judicial" process and violates the basic precepts of therapeutic jurisprudence.[51]

The chapters whose primary focus is on administrative matters include investigations of the use of nonjudges in isolation and restraint decision-making for inmates and detainees,[52] in disciplinary cases in correctional settings,[53] the role of counsel in cases involving criminal responsibility and persons

---

43. *See* Perlin, *supra* note 14 (this volume).

44. *See* Mehgan Gallagher, *The Role of Nonjudicial Officers and Their Impact on Therapeutic Jurisprudence in the Context of Alcohol and Substance Abuse and Mental Health* (this volume).

45. *See* Karen Snedker, *Therapeutic Jurisprudence in Action: Applying Goffman's Dramaturgical Theory to Mental Health Courts* (this volume).

46. *See* Frailing, Alfonso, and Taylor, *Therapeutic Jurisprudence in Swift and Certain Probation*, *supra* note 16 (this volume).

47. *See* Colleen Berryessa and Ashley Balavender, *The Therapeutic Value of Remorse and Apologies for Probation Decision-Making* (this volume).

48. *See* Shelley Kolstad, *It's Time to Shine: Understanding the Implications of Commitment Decision-Making by Nonjudicial Officers and Embracing Change* (this volume).

49. *See* Naomi Weinstein, *The Role of Nonjudicial Officers in the Disparity of Treatment for Persons with Dual Diagnoses and How TJ Can Improve Outcomes* (this volume).

50. *See* Victoria Rapp, *Therapeutic Jurisprudence in the Jefferson Parish, Louisiana Reentry Court* (this volume).

51. We should note that there are times when non-judges may have a salutary and positive impact on the proceedings in question when they work in authentic partnership with members of the judiciary. *See e.g.*, in this volume, Snedker, *supra* note 45 (discussing mental health courts) Berryessa & Balavender, *supra* note 47 (probation); Frailing, Alfonso & Taylor, *supra* note 46 (same); Rapp, *supra* note 50 (reentry courts).

52. *See* Dorfman, *supra* note 37 (this volume).

53. *See* Dlugacz, *supra* note 19 (this volume).

with intellectual disabilities,[54] cases involving the placement of migrant children with mental disabilities,[55] cases involving children in foster care,[56] and matters related to the selection of drugs used for capital punishment schemes in Texas.[57] Similarly, in each of these instances, there is virtually no attention paid to TJ principles in the processes discussed.

The chapters that deal with ethical and practical considerations assess the role of lawyers in pretrial negotiations,[58] constitutional requirements in the assessment of adequacy of counsel,[59] and the role of nonjudges in the evaluation of custody disputes.[60] Finally, the book ends with a chapter looking at the actions of nonlawyer judges, from both therapeutic jurisprudence and procedural justice perspectives.[61]

We hope that these chapters will explain the relationships between these various uses of nonjudicial officers, how they are alike, how they are different, and how, if crafted carefully and with foresight, they may have positive impacts.[62] This, we also hope, will lead to a greater understanding of this hidden aspect of the law, its practice, and the consequences for people who are justice involved, as well as why, on a daily basis, we—giving this decision little or no thought—outsource important justice decision-making. The extensive involvement of those who are not judges in important human decision-making often leads to the development of a system that is neither just nor fair, especially when it is hidden,[63] and can truly corrupt the adminis-

---

54. *See* Lisa Whittingham and Voula Marinos, *The Complexities of Criminal Responsibility and Persons with Intellectual and Developmental Disabilities: How Can Therapeutic Jurisprudence Help?* (this volume).

55. *See* Lynch, *supra* note 36 (this volume).

56. *See* Perlmutter, *supra* note 34 (this volume).

57. *See* Harmon, Cassidy, and Kloch, *supra* note 19 (this volume).

58. *See* McClain, *supra* note 32 (this volume).

59. *See* Heather Ellis Cucolo, *Reconstructing the Ethics Code to Remedy the Failures of Strickland v. Washington* (this volume).

60. *See* Lenore Walker and Brandi Diaz, *Nonjudicial Influence on Family Violence Court Cases* (this volume).

61. *See* Kevin Burke, *Procedural Fairness Is the Foundation for Making Nonlawyer Judges Effective* (this volume).

62. *See* Perlin, *supra* note 20 (concluding that mental health courts provide more due process using therapeutic jurisprudence principles than do traditional involuntary civil commitment courts). *See also* Meaghan Winter, *Courts of Dignity: Replacing Punishment with Compassion*, Psychotherapy Networker (May/June 2021), accessible at https://www.psychotherapynetworker.org/magazine/article/2547/courts-of-dignity (discussing the work of Judge Ginger Lerner-Wren, pioneering mental health court judge in Broward County, Florida).

63. On how the act of "hiding" demeans all mental disability law, *see* Michael L. Perlin, The Hidden Prejudice: Mental Disability on Trial (2000). On how agendas and doctrines are—and always have been—often hidden in this area of the law, *see, e.g.,* Michael L. Perlin, *Hidden Agendas and Ripple Effects: Implications of Four Recent Supreme Court Deci-*

tration of criminal justice. To counter this, we must consider the extent to which "outsourced" justice can be done—by nonjudicial actors such as specially trained probation officers and mental health court "teams"—in ways that are consonant with therapeutic jurisprudence principles.

Some might think that our approach here is somewhat ironic, as many of the supporters of therapeutic jurisprudence also endorse what some call the nonadversarial approach to justice,[64] and some take the position that "TJ posits that the court system *can be* a non-adversarial setting that addresses specific underlying issues for those engaged in it."[65] A closer look, however, shows that there is no irony in this position.

Over twenty-five years ago, the late Professor Bruce Winick—along with Professor David Wexler, one of the founders of TJ—looked at TJ as a new way to consider the lawyer's role: "a non-adversarial, psychologically beneficial, and humanistic ways to solve legal problems, resolve legal disputes, and prevent legal difficulties."[66] And we agree. But the systems that are described by the authors of chapters in this book—to name a few, isolation and restraint decision-making for inmates and detainees, disciplinary cases in correctional settings, cases involving the placement of migrant children with mental disabilities, cases involving children in foster care, matters related to the selection of drugs used for capital punishment schemes—in no way reflect, in Winick's words, "psychologically beneficial and humanistic ways to solve legal problems." We hope and expect this book will shed light on all of these and additional, equally important issues and prompt new questions about the way forward.

---

sions for Forensic Psychiatrists, 2 J. FORENSIC PSYCHOLOGY PRACTICE 33 (2001); Michael L. Perlin, *The Supreme Court, the Mentally Disabled Criminal Defendant, and Symbolic Values: Random Decisions, Hidden Rationales, or Doctrinal Abyss?* 29 ARIZ. L. REV. 1 (1987).

64. *See, e.g.,* MICHAEL KING ET AL., NON-ADVERSARIAL JUSTICE (2009).

65. Jason Matejkowski, Woojae Han, and Aaron Conrad, *Voluntariness of Treatment, Mental Health Service Utilization, and Quality of Life Among Mental Health Court Participants*, 26 PSYCHOL. PUB. POL'Y & L. 185, 185 (2020) (emphasis added).

66. Bruce J. Winick, *Using Therapeutic Jurisprudence in Teaching Lawyering Skills: Meeting the Challenge of the New ABA Standards*, 17 ST. THOMAS L. REV. 429, 433 (2005).

PART I

Nonjudicial Officers in Courtroom Settings

1

"But I Ain't a Judge"

The Therapeutic Jurisprudence Implications of the Use of Nonjudicial Officers in Criminal Justice Cases*

Michael L. Perlin

Introduction

A core axiom of American political theory is the importance of the separation of powers between executive, legislative, and judicial as a foundational constitutional principle.[1] The constitution's framers regarded this separation as essential to limiting the overall power possessed by the national government and essential to the ability of the people to hold the government politically accountable for its decisions and actions.[2]

But what may be news is the reality that in some very important areas of criminal law, decisions are made by those who are not judges (or nonjudicial officers, as they are known). These decisions can lead to criminal con-

* Earlier versions of this chapter were presented at the International Society for Therapeutic Jurisprudence Scholarship Workshop, held at Nova University Law School (Fort Lauderdale, Florida) on September 13, 2019, and to the American Society of Criminology annual conference (San Francisco, California) on November 15, 2019. Portions appeared in Michael L. Perlin, *"But I Ain't a Judge": The Therapeutic Jurisprudence Implications of the Use of Nonjudicial Officers in Criminal Justice Cases*, 64 AM. BEHAV. SCI. , 1686 (2020).

My thanks to David Shapiro, David Yamada, Lenore Walker, Kathy Cerminara, Shelley Kierstead, and David Wexler for their helpful comments, and my special thanks to Judge Ginger Lerner-Wren for her information about the Broward County Sheriff's Office. My special thanks to my son, Alex Perlin, a staff attorney with the Legal Aid Society of New York, who first made me aware of this issue in that state.

1. For early scholarship on this question, *see* Warren H. Pillsbury, *Administrative Tribunals*, 36 HARV. L. REV. 405 (1923).

2. JAMES MADISON, THE FEDERALIST No. 51 (Jacob E. Cooke ed., 1961).

victions, to enhanced time in correctional facilities, and to stigmatizing labels. And this is truly under the radar for most.

I consider here two disparate statutory grants of authority in two dissimilar states—New York and South Dakota—in which nonjudges are statutorily vested with the jurisdiction to decide certain pretrial motions (motions that may eventually be dispositive of the outcome of the case)[3] and to accept certain guilty pleas, and with determining whether certain criminal defendants have violated their terms of probation and should thus be incarcerated or forced to participate in sex offender treatment[4] (a power markedly different from the traditional role of probation officers who typically present their findings to judges, who make this determination).[5]

These statutes are problematic for multiple reasons. First, they are an impermissible delegation of power in some of the most important matters that courts decide—whether individuals do or do not lose their freedom.[6] Second, with specific reference to pretrial suppression of evidence hearings, the task of weighing and appraising testimony—an especially significant aspect of such hearings[7]—is transferred to those who were never selected to be judges (in New York's case, by the voters).[8] Third, they violate basic tenets of therapeutic jurisprudence that teaches us that "legal rules, proce-

---

3. *See* NY CRIM. PRO. L.§ 255.20(4), discussed *infra* text accompanying notes 14–28.

4. *See* SD CONSOL. L § 23A-27-12.1, discussed *infra* text accompanying notes 39–42.

5. In multiple other areas of the law, nonjudges are given like power, and courts have split in deciding cases challenging this statutory power. Compare, e.g., General Motors, Corp. v. Carter-Wallace, Inc. 553 N.Y.S.2d 983 (Civil Ct. 1990) (judicial hearing officer did not have authority to sign order to show cause in landlord's holdover proceeding), and Seinfeld v. Robinson, 755 N.Y.S.2d 69 (App. Div. 2002) (affidavits should not have been received by Judicial Hearing Officer from witnesses who were not available for cross-examination in court in shareholder derivative action), to Stewart v. Moseley, 958 N.Y.S.2d 598 (App. Div. 2013) (custody determination by judicial hearing officer appropriate).

6. *See* People v. Scalza, 562 N.Y.S.2d 14, 18 (1990) (Titone, J., dissenting). *See also id.* at 19: ("The impairment can hardly be characterized as de minimis, since the vast majority of suppression determinations involve, as the primary fact-finding task, an assessment of the conflicting witnesses' truthfulness").

7. *See infra* notes 16–26.

8. Along with the American Bar Association, I prefer a system of state-level appointed judges (rather than elected ones, the law in about three-quarters of all states), but I recognize at this point in time that this is a losing argument. *See, e.g.*, Heather Ellis Cucolo and Michael L. Perlin, *"They're Planting Stories in the Press": The Impact of Media Distortions on Sex Offender Law and Policy* 3 U. DENV. CRIM. L. REV. 185, 218 (2013). ("Elections have a 'chilling effect' on judicial independence, and even, in the cases of appellate judges, on the issuance of dissents from majority opinions"); *see, e.g.*, Gregory Huber and Sanford Gordon, *Accountability and Coercion: Is Justice Blind When It Runs for Office?* 48 AM. J. POLI. SCI. 247 (2004).

dures, and lawyer roles can or should be reshaped to enhance their therapeutic potential while not subordinating due process principles."[9]

The title of this article comes in part from a relatively obscure Bob Dylan song, "She's Your Lover Now."[10] Notwithstanding its obscurity—it was originally supposed to be on Dylan's *Blonde on Blonde* album—the critic Tony Attwood has noted that most reviewers view it "as an absolute masterpiece, perhaps the greatest Dylan song never to be formally released."[11] The line follows these two: "I already assumed / That we're in the felony room / But I ain't a judge, you don't have to be nice to me."

It may be, as the critic Evan Schlansky has surmised, that in these lyrics, "Dylan spills his vitriol not only over the woman who's done him wrong, but also for the Mr. Jones–type character she's been shacking up since their love affair has ended."[12] Or perhaps, per Paul Williams, a reflection of the "anguish and fury" that underlies the narrator's "pain underneath."[13] But either way, Dylan's metaphor—of being judged for a serious offense (in "the felony room") by one who is not a judge—works equally well for this topic.

Judicial Hearing Officers in New York

New York's Criminal Procedure Law sets out the role of these officers:

> Any pre-trial motion . . . may be referred by the court to a judicial hearing officer [JHO] who shall entertain it in the same manner as a court. In the discharge of this responsibility, the [JHO] shall have the same powers as a judge of the court making the assignment, except that the [JHO] shall not determine the motion but shall file a report with the court setting forth findings of fact and conclusions of law. The rules of evidence shall be applicable. . . . A transcript of any testimony taken, together with the exhibits or copies thereof, shall be filed. . . . The court shall determine the motion on the motion papers, affidavits and other documents submitted by the parties

---

9. *See* Michael L. Perlin and Alison J. Lynch, *"In the Wasteland of Your Mind": Criminology, Scientific Discoveries and the Criminal Process*, 4 Va. J. Crim. L. 304, 348 (2016).

10. *See* Bob Dylan, "She's Your Lover Now," https://www.bobdylan.com/songs/shes-your-lover-now/.

11. Tony Attwood, *Untold Dylan* (Feb. 15, 2016), accessible at https://bob-dylan.org.uk/archives/2042.

12. Evan Schlansky, *The 30 Greatest Bob Dylan Songs: #26 "She's Your Lover Now"* (April 6, 2009), accessible at https://americansongwriter.com/2009/04/the-30-greatest-bob-dylan-songs-26-shes-your-lover-now/.

13. Paul Williams, Bob Dylan, Performing Artist: 1960–1973, The Early Years 181 (1994 ed).

thereto, the record of the hearing before the [JHO], and the [JHO's] report.[14]

Although the final decision here remains vested with a "real judge," that individual only sees the report filed by the JHO (along with exhibits) and thus has no opportunity to weigh the credibility or the motivations of the testifying witnesses. This is of great importance in all criminal pretrial motion practice,[15] but nowhere is it greater than in matters involving Fourth Amendment challenges to searches and seizures, where the evidence of police fabrication—and the frequency of so-called "dropsy cases"[16]—is overwhelming, and where "the determination of the motion to suppress often determines the ultimate question of guilt."[17]

Use of the word "overwhelming" is not an exaggeration. Studying "dropsy" cases in Chicago, Myron Orfield reported that 86 percent of judges, public defenders, and prosecutors questioned (including 77 percent of judges) believed that police officers fabricate evidence in case reports at least "some

---

14. NY CRIMINAL PROCEDURE LAW § 255.20(4). In *Scalza, supra,* the State Court of Appeals (New York's highest court) held that this statute was facially constitutional but was undecided on the issue of whether a defendant can challenge the constitutionality of the statute as applied to his or her particular case. 562 N.Y.S.2d at 17.

15. Note also that JHOs have the statutory authority to accept guilty pleas in certain misdemeanor cases. NY CRIMINAL PROCEDURE LAW [CPL] § 350.20 permits class B and unclassified misdemeanors to be tried and determined by a Judicial Hearing Officer [JHO] "upon agreement of the parties." In such capacity, JHOs act as a court (*see* CPL § 350.20[1]–[3]), and are empowered to "(a) determine all questions of law; (b) act as the exclusive trier of all issues of fact; and (c) render a verdict" (*see* CPL § 350.20[1][a]-[c]).

This procedure was approved of in People v. Abdrabelnaby, 66 N.Y.S. 3d 567 (App. Div. 2017), but was sharply criticized in Issa Kohler-Hausmann, *Managerial Justice and Mass Misdemeanors,* 66 STAN. L. REV. 611, 611 (2014):

> Misdemeanor justice in New York City has largely abandoned what I call the adjudicative model of criminal law administration—concerned with adjudicating specific cases—and instead operates under what I call the managerial model—concerned with managing people through engagement with the criminal justice system over time.

16. *See* Michael L. Perlin, *Pretexts and Mental Disability Law: The Case of Competency,* 47 U. MIAMI L. REV. 625, 626 (1993), discussing "unimpeachable" lies often told in warrantless search and seizure cases. A "dropsy case" is one in which a police officer falsely testifies that the defendant dropped the narcotics in plain view (as opposed to the officer's discovering the narcotics in an illegal search). Gabriel J. Chin and Scott C. Wells, *The "Blue Wall of Silence" as Evidence of Bias and Motive to Lie: A New Approach to Police Perjury,* 59 U. PITT. L. REV. 233, 248–49 (1998).

17. *Scalza,* 562 N.Y.S. 2d at 20. Judicial hearing officers are also vested with determining the admissibility of confessions. *See* People v. Dunbar, 23 N.E.3d 946 (N.Y. 2014), discussed in this specific context in Amanda Miller, Miranda *Or Its Equivalent: The Two "W's" of Reasonable Conveyance Court of Appeals of New York,* 32 TOURO L. REV. 877 (2016).

of the time," and that a staggering 92 percent (including 91 percent of judges) believe that police officers lie in court to avoid suppression of evidence at least "some of the time."[18] A subsequent *New York Times* article called attention to another phenomenon: how police regularly testify that they smelled the odor of marijuana in nearly every traffic stop in the Bronx,[19] a practice decried by a judge who called on other judges across the state "to stop letting police officers get away with lying about it."[20] This has been called "testilying" by leading scholars;[21] it can only be remediated through vigorous cross-examination—before a "real" judge.

The court determines the credibility of witnesses in such cases;[22] the trial judge is expected to be the fact-finder.[23] One of the leading articles thus begins,

> Because law enforcement officers must justify searches and seizures in response to motions to suppress evidence, judges ruling upon these motions often must evaluate the credibility of the officers' testimony.[24]

Yet under New York practice, credibility determinations are passed on to nonjudges, leaving the judges who enter the final order in the case in a kind of legal fantasyland: they must determine whether the search and/or seizure satisfies constitutional standards[25] without ever having seen either the police witness or the defendant subject to cross-examination. The dissenting

---

18. Michael L. Perlin, *"Half-Wracked Prejudice Leaped Forth": Sanism, Pretextuality, and Why and How Mental Disability Law Developed as It Did*, 10 J. CONTEMP. LEG. ISS. 3, 6–7 (1999), quoting, in part, Myron W. Orfield Jr., *Deterrence, Perjury, and the Heater Factor: An Exclusionary Rule in the Chicago Criminal Courts*, 63 U. COLO. L. REV. 75, 100–107, nn.113, 146 (1992).

19. Joseph Goldstein, *Officers Said They Smelled Pot. The Judge Called Them Liars*, N.Y. TIMES (Sept. 12, 2019), accessible at https://www.nytimes.com/2019/09/12/nyregion/police-searches-smelling-marijuana.html.

20. *Id.*

21. *See* Christopher Slobogin, *Testilying: Police Perjury and What to Do About It*, 67 U. COLO. L. REV. 1037 (1996).

22. *See, e.g.*, United States v. Young, 105 F.3d 1, 5 (1st Cir. 1997) (recognizing importance of district court's unique opportunity to observe witness demeanor and determine witness credibility); *see also* United States v. Arvizu, 534 U.S. 266, 276 (2002) (observing importance of district court's access to evidence).

23. JOHN WESLEY HALL, SEARCH AND SEIZURE § 46.5, at 837 (3d ed. 2000).

24. Morgan Cloud, *Judges, "Testilying," and the Constitution*, 69 S. CAL. L. REV. 1341, 1341 (1996). *See generally* Slobogin, *supra* note 21.

25. On "the important function of spelling out police authority under the Fourth Amendment," *see* Wayne R. LaFave et al., 2 CRIM. PROC. § 3.1(c), at 46 (4th ed. Nov. 2018 update).

opinion of Judge Titone in *People v. Scalza* makes the point: this is an "impermissible delegation of the elected County Court Judges' authority."[26]

Some New York authority supports my position. In *People v. Ahmed*, the Court of Appeals reversed a conviction where the trial judge was absent from the courtroom for portion of jury's deliberations and allowed his law secretary to respond to juror questioning, concluding that this deprived defendant of his right to trial by jury.[27] There, the court cited a late nineteenth-century Supreme Court case for the proposition that "The presence and active supervision of a judge constitute an integral component of the... right [to trial by jury]."[28] But at this time, the judicial hearing officers still retain the power to hear pretrial motions and accept guilty pleas.

Court Services Officers in South Dakota

Courts and commentators have long pondered the question of the exact meaning of "core judicial function." In *United States v. York*,[29] the court concluded that the definition encompassed a "significant penological decision," such as deciding whether a probationer must undergo specific types of treatment.[30] Elsewhere, in *United States v. Pruden*,[31] the Third Circuit concluded that a decision as to "nature or extent of the punishment imposed" was nondelegable[32] and thus a core function.[33]

---

26. *Scalza*, 562 N.Y.S. 2d at 18. On how Judge Titone's views are "thoughtfully expressed" in this dissent, *see* Vincent Martin Bonventre, *Court of Appeals—State Constitutional Law Review, 1990*, 12 PACE L. REV. 1, 24 (1992).

27. 496 N.Y.S. 2d 984, 985–86 (1985)

28. *Id.* at 986, quoting Capital Traction Co. v. Hof, 174 U.S. 1, 13 (1899).

29. 357 F.3d 14 (1st Cir. 2004).

30. *Id.* at 21.

31. 398 F.3d 241 (3d Cir. 2005).

32. *Id.* at 250.

33. Core judicial functions also include the "'authority to hear and determine justiciable controversies . . . the authority to enforce any valid judgment, decree, or order . . . (and all powers) necessary to protect the fundamental integrity of the judicial branch.'" Salt Lake City v. Ohms, 881 P.2d 844, 849 (Utah 1994). *Also see id.* (law statutorily empowering nonjudicial officers (commissioners) to enter final orders in criminal cases violated state constitution). *See generally* Heather Brann, *Utah's Medical Malpractice Prelitigation Panel: Exploring State Constitutional Arguments Against a Nonbinding Inadmissible Procedure*, 2000 UTAH L. REV. 359, 405.

See also Mark Thomson, *Who Are They to Judge? The Constitutionality of Delegations by Courts to Probation Officers*, 96 MINN. L. REV. 306, 313–14 (2011). Another commentator has suggested that a "core judicial function" is the "defining [of] constitutional rights." Mary Jean Dolan, *The Constitutional Flaws in the New Illinois Religious Freedom Restoration Act: Why RFRAs Don't Work*, 31 LOY. U. CHI. L.J. 153, 157.

Consider the extensive caselaw and scholarly commentary on the constitutionality of certain sex offender treatment programs. For instance, in *McKune v. Lile*,[34] the Supreme Court ruled that consequences for refusal to participate in a prison sex offender treatment programs did not violate the Fifth Amendment privilege against self-incrimination.[35] Other courts have found, variously, that participation in mandated treatment does not violate free speech,[36] but that a statute prohibiting most registered sex offenders from using social networking websites, instant messaging services, and chat programs was not narrowly tailored to serve a significant governmental interest in shielding children from improper sexual communication, thus violating the First Amendment.[37] A state court found that a defendant's Fifth Amendment rights were not violated by a sexual history therapeutic polygraph examination as part of sex offender treatment, a condition of probation.[38] How do these cases relate to the question at hand?

Under South Dakota law:

> Upon receipt of an order that a defendant has been placed on probation to the court service department, the chief court services officer shall immediately assign the defendant to a court services officer for probation supervision.

---

34. 536 U.S. 24 (2002).

35. *See generally* MICHAEL L. PERLIN AND HEATHER ELLIS CUCOLO, MENTAL DISABILITY LAW: CIVIL AND CRIMINAL (3d ed. 2016; spring 2021 update), § 5-4.10.1.1. On how *McKune* was based on an "unsupported assertion of someone without research expertise who made his living selling such counseling programs to prisons," *see* Heather Ellis Cucolo and Michael L. Perlin, *"The Strings in the Books Ain't Pulled and Persuaded": How the Use of Improper Statistics and Unverified Data Corrupts the Judicial Process in Sex Offender Cases*, 69 CASE W. RES. L. REV. 637, 651–52 (2019), quoting Ira Mark Ellman and Tara Ellman, *"Frightening and High": The Supreme Court's Crucial Mistake About Sex Crime Statistics*, 30 CONST. COMMENT. 495, 499 (2015).

36. Newman v. Beard, 617 F.3d 775 (3d Cir. 2010), *cert. denied sub. nom.* Newman v. Wetzel, 563 U.S. 950 (2011).

37. Doe v. Prosecutor, Marion County, Indiana, 705 F.3d 694 (7th Cir. 2013). *See also* Packingham v. North Carolina, 137 S. Ct. 1730 (2017) (statute banning sex offender registrants from accessing commercial websites that would also allow minors to register and communicate violated First Amendment). On the relationship between sex offender laws and freedom of religion, *see* Christopher Lund, *Sex Offenders and the Free Exercise of Religion*, 96 NOTRE DAME L. REV. 1025 (2021).

38. Com. v. Knoble, 42 A.3d 976 (Pa. 2012). But compare United States v. Von Behren, 2016 WL 2641270 (10th Cir. 2016) (government's threat to seek revocation of defendant's supervised release if he failed to complete sex offender treatment program, which required him to answer incriminating questions, constituted unconstitutional compulsion under the Fifth Amendment).

All such probationers shall cooperate fully with the court services officer and comply with all directives thereby issued in their regard.[39]

It has generally been held that authority to fashion conditions of probation is strictly judicial and may not be delegated,[40] and it must be approved by the court before becoming effective.[41] But only a handful of cases has ever considered this rule of law seriously, and fewer have vacated such conditions.[42] In the most significant of these, *State v. Blakney*,[43] a trial court's sentencing order mandated that the defendant participate in "any" evaluation, counseling, or treatment necessary for him to be successful on probation.[44] This led to a South Dakota "court services officer"[45] ordering that defendant undergo and successfully complete sex offender treatment program in order to be eligible to participate in a Family Violence Program.[46] Although the court noted the constitution is not infringed when courts delegate to nonjudicial officers details with respect to the selection and schedule of a probationary program,[47] this impermissibly delegated a "core judicial function"[48] to a court services officer to make all decisions concerning defendant's probation's conditions and thus not an enforceable condition of probation.[49]

In short, the line between what a nonjudicial court officer may do and what one may not do is a fine one, but it is also one that has not been the topic

---

39. S.D. Consol. L. § 23A-27-12.1.

40. Commonwealth v. MacDonald, 757 N.E. 2d 725 (Mass. 2001) (probation officer's inserting name in preprinted form of person with whom probationer could have "no contact," was not a binding condition because it was not specifically ordered by the court). *See also* State v. Vondal, 585 N.W.2d 129 (N.D. 1998) ("Conditions of probation must be announced by the court and not delegated to other agencies or people.") and United States v. Barany, 884 F.2d 1255 (9th Cir. 1989) (unlawful to delegate to probation officer determination of restitution amount as discussed in Arthur W. Campbell, Law of Sentencing § 5:3 [Sept. 2018 update]).

41. *See, e.g.,* United States v. Bowman, 175 Fed. Appx. 834, 838 (9th Cir.2006).

42. *See also* State v. Putnam, 130 A.3d 836, 858–60 (Vt. 2015) (condition requiring defendant to attend "any counseling or training program" designated by probation officer and to "participate to [probation officer's] satisfaction" unlawful delegation of authority).

43. 851 N.W. 2d 195 (S.D. 2014).

44. *Id.* at 197.

45. *See* SDCL § 23A-27-12.1.

46. *Blakney*, 851 N.W. 2d at 197.

47. *Id.* at 199. *See also* Cohen, *supra* note 38.

48. *Blakney*, 851 N.W. 2d at 200.

49. *Id.* at 199–200. *See also* Jackson v. State, 959 So. 2d 1282 (Fla. Dist. Ct. App. 2007) (only court can impose probation conditions).

of great scholarly (or judicial) attention. It is clear, though, that much authority that should have remained with judges has been offloaded to nonjudges.[50]

A Therapeutic Jurisprudence Analysis[51]

As noted in the introductory chapter in this volume,[52] therapeutic jurisprudence recognizes that as a therapeutic agent, the law can have therapeutic or antitherapeutic consequences,[53] asking whether legal rules, procedures, and lawyer roles can or should be reshaped to enhance their therapeutic potential while not subordinating due process principles.[54]

There is robust literature on the relationship between therapeutic jurisprudence and nonjudges in the context of administrative agencies and other nonjudicial interactions.[55] Some deal with workers' compensation,[56] some

---

50. Omitted because of space constraints is a discussion of the scandal on Florida in which—until stopped by Judge Ginger Lerner-Wren's intervention—county sheriff's officers unilaterally changed terms of probation that were statutorily mandated to be in the discretion of the trial judge. See Michael L. Perlin, *"But, I Ain't a Judge": The Therapeutic Jurisprudence Implications of the Use of Non-Judicial Officers in Criminal Justice Cases,* 64 Am. Behav. Sci. 1686, 1692–93 (2020).

51. This section is largely adapted from Michael L. Perlin, *"I've Got My Mind Made Up": How Judicial Teleology in Cases Involving Biologically Based Evidence Violates Therapeutic Jurisprudence,* 24 Card. J. Equal Rts. & Soc'l Just. 81, 93–95 (2018) (Perlin, *Mind Made Up*), and Perlin and Lynch, *supra* note 9, at 357.

52. See Michael L. Perlin and Kelly Frailing, *Introduction to Justice Outsourced* (this volume).

53. Michael L. Perlin, *"His Brain Has Been Mismanaged with Great Skill": How Will Jurors Respond to Neuroimaging Testimony in Insanity Defense Cases?* 42 Akron L. Rev. 885, 912 (2009).

54. Michael L. Perlin, *"And My Best Friend, My Doctor, Won't Even Say What It Is I've Got": The Role and Significance of Counsel in Right to Refuse Treatment Cases,* 42 San Diego L. Rev. 735, 751 (2005)

55. See, e.g., Bruce J. Winick, *The Expanding Scope of Preventive Law,* 3 Fla. Coastal L.J. 189, 197 (2002):

> *The administrative lawyer or specialist in some area of regulatory law therefore also needs to understand the therapeutic jurisprudence/preventive law model and apply it in client counseling. Many disputes with administrative agencies that are waiting to happen can be avoided or the level and risk of disputatiousness lessened through preventive law.*

56. See, e.g., William E. Wilkinson, *Therapeutic Jurisprudence and Workers' Compensation,* 30 Ariz. Attorney 28 (Apr. 1994); Donald L. Ghareeb, *Life in the Fast Lane of Administrative Law: Workers' Compensation Practice in Arizona,* 30 Ariz. Attorney 10 (Apr. 1994); Katherine Lippel, *Therapeutic and Anti-Therapeutic Consequences of Workers' Compensation,* 22 Int'l J.L. & Psychiatry 521 (1999).

with labor arbitration,[57] some with negotiation theory,[58] some with mediation and alternative dispute resolution,[59] and some with administrative tribunals vested with compensating sexual violence victims.[60] However, with
the important exception of the work done by Professor Lorana Bartels, writing about the HOPE probation program in Hawaii,[61] there is virtually none
on the sort of interstitial,[62] quasijudicial roles I discuss here.[63]

How does this relate to the current questions? Per Professor Michal Albertstein:

> The essential task of therapeutic jurisprudence is to sensitize judges
> to the fact that they are therapeutic agents in the way they play their
> judicial roles and to develop some general principles that might im-
> prove judicial structure, function, and behavior, in a manner that
> allows judges to be more effective therapeutic agents.[64]

Certainly, the roles of judges and attorneys in litigation conducted according to principles of therapeutic jurisprudence are "greatly expanded

---

57. *See, e.g.*, Roger I. Abrams, Frances E. Abrams, and Dennis R. Nolan, *Arbitral Therapy*,
46 RUTGERS L. REV. 1751 (1994).

58. *See* Carol L. Zeiner, *Getting Deals Done: Enhancing Negotiation Theory and Practice
Through a Therapeutic Jurisprudence/Comprehensive Law Mindset*, 21 HARV. NEGOT. L. REV.
279 (2016).

59. *See, e.g.*, David B. Wexler, *Therapeutic Jurisprudence and the Culture of Critique*, 10 J.
CONTEMP. LEGAL ISSUES 265 (1999); Jacqueline M. Nolan-Haley, *Informed Consent in Mediation: A Guided Principle for Truly Educated Decisionmaking*, 74 NOTRE DAME L. REV. 775
(1999).

60. *See, e.g.*, Nathalie Des Rosiers, Bruce Feldthusen, and Oleana A. R. Hankivsky, *Legal
Compensation for Sexual Violence: Therapeutic Consequences and Consequences for the Judi-
cial System*, 4 PSYCHOL. PUB. POL'Y & L. 433 (1998); Bruce Feldthusen, Olena Hankivsky and
Lorraine Greaves, *Therapeutic Consequences of Civil Actions for Damages and Compensation
Claims by Victims of Sexual Abuse—An Empirical Study*, 12 CAN. J. WOMEN & L. 66 (2000)
(discussing the Ontario Criminal Injuries Compensation Board).

61. *See e.g.*, Lorana Bartels, Looking at Hawaii's Opportunity with Probation Enforcement
(HOPE) Program Through a Therapeutic Jurisprudence Lens, 16 QUT L. REV. 30 (206); Lorana Bartels, *HOPE-Ful Bottles: Examining the Potential for Hawaii's Opportunity Probation
with Enforcement (HOPE) to Help Mainstream Therapeutic Jurisprudence*, 63 INT'L J.L. & PSY-
CHIATRY 26 (2019).

62. *See e.g.*, David B. Wexler, *From Theory to Practice and Back Again in Therapeutic Jurisprudence: Now Comes the Hard Part*, 37 MONASH U.L. REV. 33, 38 (2011) (role of judge in such
cases is "interstitial," quoting former Presiding Justice Kevin Bellon).

63. *Also see*, Kelly Frailing, Brandi Alfonso & Rae Taylor. *Therapeutic Jurisprudence in
Swift and Certain Probation* (this volume).

64. Michal Alberstein, *Therapeutic Keys of Law: Reflections on Paradigmatic Shifts and the
Limits and Potential of Reform Movements*, 39 ISR. L. REV. 140, 148 (2006).

from their traditional models,"[65] as therapeutic jurisprudence seeks to "augment current rigid legal processes by taking into account the intangible, emotional states of the parties to the litigation."[66] But there has been absolutely no consideration of the extent to which this expansion has had any impact at all on the topics of this chapter: the use of nonjudges to hear criminal trial motions that are often dispositive of the underlying case, and the authority of the probation department to significantly change the court's orders of probation.

Interestingly and importantly, Professor David Wexler—one of the founders of the school of therapeutic jurisprudence—has underscored that "the sanction of probation, *when legally available for a given offense*, is chock-full of Therapeutic Jurisprudence considerations."[67] The point here is that the South Dakota case of *State v. Blakney*[68] makes clear that some of the probationary sanctions imposed by court services officers were blatantly illegal.

Professor Albertstein's aspirations cannot be fulfilled in cases of nonjudicial officers who decide cases that potentially have such impact on the lives of litigants. Again, such nonjudges (1) make dispositive decisions in cases that turn on search and seizure motions (and other critical pretrial motions as well) and are tasked with accepting pleas in what a scholar has called an "embarrass[ing]" experiment,[69] and (2) are free to *sua sponte* impose potentially onerous conditions of probation on defendants in complex areas of the law in which the Supreme Court continually tinkers and modifies the scope of defendants' rights.[70] There are no checks and no balances.[71]

---

65. Patricia H. Murrell and Philip D. Gould, *Educating for Therapeutic Judging: Strategies, Concepts, and Outcomes*, 78 Rev. Jur. U.P.R. 129, 133 (2009).

66. Philip D. Gould and Patricia H. Murrell, *Therapeutic Jurisprudence and Cognitive Complexity: An Overview*, 29 Fordham Urb. L.J. 2117, 2120 (2002).

67. David B. Wexler, *Therapeutic Jurisprudence and the Rehabilitative Role of the Criminal Defense Lawyer*, 17 St. Thomas L. Rev. 743, 756–57 (2005) (emphasis added). *See also* David B. Wexler, *Therapeutic Jurisprudence and Its Application to Criminal Justice Research and Development*, 7 Irish Probation J. 94 (2010); Faye S. Taxman and Meredith H. Thanner, *Probation from a Therapeutic Perspective: Results from the Field*, 7 Contemp. Issues in L. 39 (2004).

68. 851 N.W. 2d 195 (S.D. 2014). *See supra* text accompanying notes 43–48.

69. Kohler-Hausmann, *supra* note 15, at 611.

70. *See generally* Perlin and Cucolo, *supra* note 35, Chapter 5; Michael L. Perlin and Heather Ellis Cucolo, Shaming the Constitution: The Detrimental Results of Sexual Violent Predator Legislation (2017).

71. *See, e.g.*, Martin Edwards, *Who's Exercising What Power: Toward a Judicially-Manageable Nondelegation Doctrine*, 68 Admin. L. Rev. 61, 65 (2016) ("The very concept of separation of powers is involved intimately with 'checks and balances,' the notion that dividing powers limits the aggregate power of government over the governed").

One of the *sine qua nons* of therapeutic jurisprudence is its refusal to subordinate due process principles.[72] When non-judges make what should be judicial decisions—with perilously little oversight—that may be life-and-death, it is fatuous to even assess whether therapeutic jurisprudence principles are honored. They simply cannot be.

Conclusion

Much of this is truly under the radar for most scholars and most practitioners, and it has also basically escaped the notice of most who write about and care about therapeutic jurisprudence. An article in a bar journal has argued that "the organized bar has a special responsibility to defend the judiciary's proper role as a co-equal branch of government."[73] The Massachusetts constitution sets the issue out clearly and forthrightly: "It is the right of every citizen to be tried by judges as free, impartial and independent as the lot of humanity will admit."[74] Perhaps it was fine for the narrator of the Bob Dylan song that partially gave this chapter its title to not be a "judge," but it is not fine for states to allow nonjudges to make the sorts of what should be judicial decisions. It violates the law, common sense, and the principles of therapeutic jurisprudence.

---

72. *See* Perlin and Lynch, *supra* note 9, at 348.

73. Donald R. Frederico, *Justice Under Fire,* 55 B.B.J.5, 5 (Spring 2011).

74. Mass. Const. art. 29, *Declaration of Rights. See generally* Francis J. Larkin, *The Variousness, Virulence, and Variety of Threats to Judicial Independence,* 36 Judges' J. 4 (Winter 1997).

2

The Role of Nonjudicial Officers and Their Impact on Therapeutic Jurisprudence in the Context of Alcohol and Substance Abuse and Mental Health

Mehgan Gallagher

Introduction

Nonjudicial officers, although not judges—and often not even trained lawyers—make important decisions every day that impact the lives of countless individuals and their families. This is particularly troublesome in the context of criminal law, where the regulations and qualifications of these officers vary among jurisdictions and can lead to criminal trial processes not being followed and even reach the level of deprivation of due process. This chapter explores the evolution of nonjudicial officers and their role and influence in the courts while examining their impact on therapeutic jurisprudence, particularly in the context of individuals with alcohol and/or substance and mental health issues.

Perhaps one of the criminal justice system's best-kept secrets is that life-altering decisions involving mentally ill criminal defendants are being delegated to nonjudges with little to no legal training or education.[1] This is especially concerning due to society's long history of demonizing persons with mental illness and linking mental illness with evil.[2] This is not to say that

---

1. *See* generally Michael L. Perlin, *"But I Ain't a Judge"*: *The Therapeutic Jurisprudence Implications of the Use of Nonjudicial Officers in Criminal Justice Cases*, 64: 12 Am. Behav. Scientist 1686, 1695 (2020).

2. *See* Michael L. Perlin, *"There Are No Trials Inside the Gates of Eden"*: *Mental Health Courts, the Convention on the Rights of Persons with Disabilities, Dignity, and the Promise of Therapeutic Jurisprudence*, in Coercive Care, 19 (1 Ed. 2013); Michael S. Moore, Law

judges and attorneys are exempt from "sanism"—"an irrational prejudice of the same quality and character of other irrational prejudices that cause and are reflected in prevailing social attitudes of racism, sexism, homophobia, and ethnic bigotry"[3]—or treating individuals with mental health issues and or substance abuse issues with less respect than deserved; however, assigning criminal determinations to nonjudges is unethical, is unconstitutional, and goes against the principles of therapeutic jurisprudence.[4]

Despite the fact that the framers of our constitution fought hard for the idea of a separation of powers and to create a constitution that ensures individual rights, including the right to due process,[5] there are jurisdictions in the United States which allow nonjudges to decide pretrial orders which can change the outcome of a trial, a conviction, and ultimately someone's life.[6] Professor Michael L. Perlin, the only scholar who has yet written on the topic of nonjudicial officers within a criminal law context and its impact on therapeutic jurisprudence, argues that the statutes granting nonjudges the jurisdiction to make determinations that may eventually be dispositive of the outcome of the case "violate the basic tenets of therapeutic jurisprudence, that teaches us that 'legal rules, procedures, and lawyer roles can or should be reshaped to enhance their therapeutic potential while not subordinating due process principles.'"[7] I agree.

Throughout most of the world, a law degree is a prerequisite for entry into the judicial profession.[8] In the United States, judges undergo a minimum of three years of law school following four years of university, along with months of studying. They must take and pass a bar exam to be considered qualified to represent a criminal defendant in a courtroom, let alone decide his fate. Moreover, "the professional qualifications now required for the proper exercise of the judicial role go far beyond the basic legal knowledge

---

AND PSYCHIATRY: RETHINKING THE RELATIONSHIP 63 (1984); JUDITH S. NEAMAN, SUGGESTION OF THE DEVIL: THE ORIGINS OF MADNESS, 31, 144 (1975).

3. *See, e.g.,* Michael L. Perlin, *"Striking for the Guardians and Protectors of the Mind": The Convention on the Rights of Persons with Disabilities and the Future of Guardianship Law,* 117 PENN ST. L. REV. 1159, 1180 (2013).

4. Perlin, *supra* note 1, at 1695.

5. *See* JAMES MADISON, THE FEDERALIST, NO. 51. (1961).

6. *See generally* Perlin, *supra* note 1.

7. *Id.* at 1687, citing Michael L. Perlin and Alison J. Lynch, *"In the Wasteland of Your Mind": Criminology, Scientific Discoveries and the Criminal Process,* 4 VA. J. CRIM. L. 304, 348 (2016).

8. United Nations Office on Drugs and Crime, *Resource Guide on Strengthening Judicial Integrity and Capacity, United Nations,* 1, 6 (2011).

and skills of legal interpretation that once were sufficient,"[9] and this is particularly true for criminal defendants with mental health issues. Why is it, then, that we allow individuals who have not fulfilled these requirements to make decisions that could forever alter someone's life? This chapter will explore the role of nonjudicial officers and their impact on individuals with mental health and substance abuse issues within a therapeutic jurisprudence perspective.

Therapeutic Jurisprudence

The concept of therapeutic jurisprudence is vital to the study of law and human rights because it "asks us to look at law as it actually impacts people's lives"[10] by focusing on how the law influences emotional life and psychological well-being of people in the judicial system.[11] Therapeutic jurisprudence is centered around a commitment to dignity.[12] It presents a new model for assessing the impact of case law and legislation, and it recognizes that the law can have therapeutic or antitherapeutic consequences as a therapeutic agent.[13] It is also part of a growing comprehensive movement in the legal field toward handling legal issues in a more humane and psychologically optimal way while focusing on collaboration, creativity, and respect among lawyers and clients with mental disabilities.[14]

Studies show that in cases of judicial review, there are therapeutic jurisprudence benefits in that participation in judicial decisions provides people

---

9. *Id.* at 5; *see also* Kevin Burke, *Procedural Fairness Is the Foundation for Making Non-lawyer Judges Effective* (this volume).

10. Bruce J. Winick, *Foreword: Therapeutic Jurisprudence Perspectives on Dealing with Victims of Crime*, 33 Nova L. Rev. 535, 535 (2009).

11. David B. Wexler, *Practicing Therapeutic Jurisprudence: Psychological Soft Spots and Strategies*, in Practicing Therapeutic Jurisprudence: Law as a Helping Profession 45 (Daniel P. Stolle, David B. Wexler and Bruce J. Winick eds., 2006).

12. *See* Bruce J. Winick, Civil Commitment: A Therapeutic Jurisprudence Model 161 (2005).

13. *See* Michael L. Perlin, *"His Brain Has Been Mismanaged with Great Skill": How Will Jurors Respond to Neuroimaging Testimony in Insanity Defense Cases?* 42 Akron L. Rev. 885, 912 (2009); *see also* Kate Diesfeld and Ian Freckelton, *Mental Health Law and Therapeutic Jurisprudence*, in Disputes and Dilemmas in Health Law 91 (Ian Freckelton and Kate Peterson eds., 2006).

14. Susan Daicoff, *The Role of Therapeutic Jurisprudence Within the Comprehensive Law Movement*, in Daniel P. Stolle, David B. Wexler, and Bruce J. Winick, Practicing Therapeutic Jurisprudence: Law as a Helping Profession 45, 365 (2006).

with mental disabilities opportunities to present their case in a more formal legal setting.[15] Professor Ronner's "3 Vs" argument states:

> Litigants must have a sense of Voice or a chance to tell their story to a decision maker. If that litigant feels that the tribunal has genuinely listened to, heard, and taken seriously the litigant's story, the litigant feels a sense of Validation. When litigants emerge from a legal proceeding with a sense of Voice and Validation, they are more at peace with the outcome. Voice and Validation create a sense of Voluntary participation, one in which the litigant experiences the proceeding as less coercive. Specifically, the feeling on the part of litigants that they Voluntarily partook in the very process that engendered the end result or the very judicial pronunciation that affects their own lives can initiate healing and bring about improved behavior in the future. In general, human beings prosper when they feel that they are making, or at least participating in, their own decisions.[16]

Ensuring people with mental disabilities receive due process provides, at a very minimum, the appearance of fairness. This is therapeutic because it contributes to the individual's sense of dignity and conveys that he or she is being taken seriously.[17]

---

15. *See* Francine Cournos et al., *A Comparison of Clinical and Judicial Procedures for Reviewing Requests for Involuntary Medication in New York*, 39 HOSP. & COMMUNITY PSYCHIATRY 851, 854 (1988); *see also* Paul Sauvayre, *The Relationship Between the Court and the Doctor on the Issue of an Inpatient's Refusal of Psychotropic Medication*, 36 J. FORENSIC SCI. 219, 221 (1991), citing Irwin Hasenfeld and Barbara Grumet, *A Study of the Right to Refuse Treatment*, 12 BULL. AM. ACAD. PSYCHIATRY & L. 65 (1984).

16. *See* Amy D. Ronner, *Songs of Validation, Voice, and Voluntary Participation: Therapeutic Jurisprudence, Miranda and Juveniles*, 71 U. CIN. L. REV. 89, 94–95 (2002) (discussing the positive impact of allowing litigants to play an active role in their treatment and commitment hearings).

17. John Ensimger and Thomas Liguori, *The Role of Counsel in the Civil Commitment Process; A Theoretical Framework, in* THEORETICAL JURISPRUDENCE: THE LAW AS A THERAPEUTIC AGENT (David Wexler ed. 1 1990) 309, 323 n. 83; Tom R. Tyler, *The Psychological Consequences of Judicial Procedures: Implications For Civil Commitment Hearings*, 46 SMU L. REV. 433, 444 (1992) (discussing the therapeutic value of judicial civil commitment hearings, and emphasizing that individuals benefit from hearings in which they are able to take part, are treated with dignity, and are "fair"); Amy D. Ronner, *Punishment Meted Out for Acquittals: An Anti-therapeutic Jurisprudence Atrocity*, 41 ARIZ. L. REV. 459, 472–77 (1999) (discussing how unfair procedures lead to disrespect for the law, disregard for human life, rage and a sense of helplessness).

Substance Abuse and Mental Health Law in
the United States

People with mental disabilities are often stripped of many of their basic human rights,[18] including the right to determine what is done to their bodies.[19] Although as a society we have come a long way in creating protections for these individuals, there is still far to go, and in reality their rights are not always acknowledged or enforced. It is a sad reality that criminal defendants with mental health issues face a double burden of stigma. As a leading scholar on mental disability and the law, Professor Michael L. Perlin, has written, "In the criminal justice system, the mentally disabled were doubly cursed as 'mad' and 'bad,' and were regularly consigned to lifetime commitments in maximum security facilities."[20]

The United States, compared to other nations, is considered "advanced" in terms of accepting people with mental disabilities. Some would go so far to say the United States is at the forefront of disability rights laws and advocacy. Some countries in Latin America were influenced by the Americans with Disabilities Act (ADA)[21] while creating their own mental health legislation.[22] Also, the Convention on the Rights of Persons with Disabilities (CRPD) was partially modeled on the ADA.[23] However, we have a long way to go. Historically, people with mental disabilities in the United States were regularly sent to prisons and shelters, were segregated from society, and were not provided treatment.[24] In the mid-nineteenth century, public asylums opened in pockets of the country to house people with mental disabilities.

---

18. Manfred Nowak, Special Rapporteur of the Human Rights Counsel on torture and other cruel, inhuman or degrading treatment or punishment, transmitted by Note of the Secretary-General, U.N. Doc. A/63/175, 53 (July 28, 2008).

19. Janos Fiala-Butora, *Disabling Torture: The Obligation to Investigate Ill-Treatment of Persons with Disabilities*, 45 COLUM. HUM. RTS. L. R. 214, 216 (2013–14).

20. Michael L. Perlin, *On Sanism*, 46 SMU L. REV. 373, 398–99 (1992), quoting in part Ellen Hochstedler, *Twice-Cursed? The Mentally Disordered Criminal Defendant*, 14 CRIM. JUST. & BEHAV. 251 (1987).

21. The Americans with Disabilities Act of 1990, 42 U.S.C. §§ 12101–213 (codified as amended in scattered sections of 42 U.S.C. and 47 U.S.C.).

22. Christian Courtis, *Disability Rights in Latin America and International Cooperation*, 9 S.W. J.L. & TRADE AM. 109, 115 (2002–3).

23. U.S. International Council on Disabilities, *Disability Advocates Call for Senate Action on Treaty Following Supreme Court Ruling in Bond Case* (June 2014), http://67.199.83.28/detail/news.cfm?news_id=1744&id=216 (last visited Jan. 31, 2021) (discussing how the CRPD is modeled after the Americans with Disabilities Act). Ironically, the United States still has not ratified the CRPD.

24. Stuart Anfang and Paul S. Appelbaum, *Civil Commitment—The American Experience* 43 ISR. J PSYCHIATRY RELATED SCI 209–18 (2006).

Unfortunately, individuals were often subjected to restraint, sedation, and experimental treatments while in these asylums.[25] There is a much longer storied and unfortunate history regarding the rights—or lack thereof—of individuals with mental and physical disabilities and the discrimination they endured and still do endure, but for the purposes of this chapter, I will focus on the ADA and the implications regarding individuals with mental disabilities and due process.

Due process under law is one of the foundations of the constitution and of our society. Procedural due process guarantees that no state nor the federal government "shall . . . deprive any person of life, liberty, or property, without due process of law."[26] For criminal defendants, the due process clause has been interpreted to include that "an accused has a right to be present at all stages of the trial where his absence might frustrate the fairness of the proceedings."[27] Due process may also require an opportunity for confrontation and cross-examination, and for discovery; that a decision be made based on the record, and that a party be allowed to be represented by counsel.[28] Further, the Sixth Amendment grants the accused the right to personally make his defense.[29]

The ADA has been described as "the most innovative and far-reaching federal civil rights legislation—ever—on behalf of disabled persons."[30] Advocates have hailed the ADA as the "Emancipation Proclamation for those with disabilities."[31] The ADA focuses much more on physical rather than mental disabilities[32] but nevertheless is an important piece of legislation

---

25. *See* ROY PORTER, MADNESS: A BRIEF HISTORY (2002); *see also* generally GERALD N. GROB, THE MAD AMONG US: A HISTORY OF THE CARE OF AMERICA'S MENTALLY ILL (1994).

26. U.S. Const. amends. V, XIV

27. Faretta v. California, 422 U.S. 806, 819 n. 15 (1975).

28. Goldberg v. Kelly, 397 U.S. 254, 269 (1970). *See also* ICC v. Louisville and Nashville R.R., 227 U.S. 88, 93–94 (1913). *Cf.* § 7(c) of the Administrative Procedure Act, 5 U.S.C. § 556(d).

29. *Faretta*, 422 U.S. 806 at 819.

30. Michael L. Perlin, *The ADA and Persons with Mental Disabilities: Can Sanist Attitudes Be Undone*, 8 J.L. & HEALTH 15, 15 (1993–94).

31. Americans with Disabilities Act of 1990: Summary and Analysis, Special Supplement (BNA), at S-5, as cited in Kimberly Ackourey, *Insuring Americans with Disabilities: How Far Can Congress Go to Protect Traditional Practices?*40 EMORY L.J. 1183, 1183 n.2 (1991) (statement by bill's sponsors); Bonnie P. Tucker, *The Americans with Disabilities Act of 1990: An Overview*, 22 N.M. L. REV. 13, 16 n. 4 (1992); MICHAEL L. PERLIN AND HEATHER ELLIS CUCOLO, MENTAL DISABILITY LAW: CIVIL AND CRIMINAL (3d ed. 2016, 2020 update), § 11–2, at 11–3 (ADA stands as Congress's "most innovative attempt to address the pervasive problem of discrimination against mentally and physically handicapped citizens").

32. *See, e.g.*, Irwin Shur, *Title III of the Americans with Disabilities Act: Regulations Regarding Modifications New Construction and Alteration of Facilities,*10 ACCA DOCKET 24

protecting the rights of individuals with both physical and mental disabilities. For example, the ADA helps to ensure that individuals with physical disabilities are not excluded from buildings when court proceedings are taking place, therefore protecting against due process violations regarding the right to be present at trial.[33]

However, it is important to note just because regulations are on the books, that does not mean that they are enforced. This is where adequate and dedicated counsel is essential to ensure that important legislative achievements such as the CRPD and ADA are more than mere "paper victories."[34] The right to counsel has been described as "the cornerstone of the American judicial system."[35] It is important to distinguish the right to adequate counsel from simply the right to counsel. Going one step further, counsel should also be dedicated. All too often, there exists what is referred to as the "warm body" problem, in which legal counsel appears to be present in name only.[36]

The CRPD, "the most comprehensive document on international disability law ever created,"[37] mandates "States Parties shall take appropriate measures to provide access by persons with disabilities to the support they may require in exercising their legal capacity."[38] Availability of adequate counsel is so important to protect the rights of all people with mental disabilities because without it, it would be "virtually impossible to imagine the exis-

---

(Summer 1992); Frank Morris, *Americans with Disabilities Act: Overview of the Employment and Public Accommodations Provisions,* C742 ALI-ABA 535 (1992); Brian Poll and John Gose, *The Americans with Disabilities Act of 1990: Impacts on Tenants, Landlords, and Lenders,* C736AU-ABA 179 (1992).

33. *See generally* Tennessee v, Lane, 541 U.S. 509 (2004).

34. *See, e.g.,* Michael L. Perlin, *And My Best Friend, My Doctor, Won't Even Say What It Is I've Got: The Role and Significance of Counsel in Right to Refuse Treatment Cases,* 42: 2 SAN DIEGO L. REV., 735, 737 (2005); Michael L. Perlin, *"Life Is in Mirrors, Death Disappears": Giving Life to* Atkins, 33 N.M. L. REV. 315, 315 (2003); Michael L. Perlin, *"Their Promises of Paradise": Will* Olmstead v. L.C. *Resuscitate the Constitutional "Least Restrictive Alternative" Principle in Mental Disability Law?* 37 HOUS. L. REV. 999, 1049 (2000). *See generally* Michael S. Lottman, *Paper Victories and Hard Realities,* in PAPER VICTORIES AND HARD REALITIES: THE IMPLEMENTATION OF THE LEGAL AND CONSTITUTIONAL RIGHTS OF THE MENTALLY DISABLED 93 (Valerie Bradley and Gary Clarke eds., 1976).

35. 4 APPENDIX, TASK PANEL REPORTS SUBMITTED TO THE PRESIDENT'S COMMISSION ON MENTAL HEALTH 1353, 1366 (1978)

36. *See, e.g.,* Pamela Metzger, *Doing Katrina Time,* 81 TUL. L. REV. 1175, 1198 (2007) ("This right to counsel is not satisfied by the mere appearance of a warm body wearing a business suit and holding a copy of the [statute book].").

37. *See generally* Perlin, *supra* note 3.

38. United Nations Convention on the Rights of Persons with Disabilities, G.A. Res. 61/106, at 27, U.N. Doc. A/Res/61/106 (Dec. 13, 2006) at Article 12.

tence of the bodies of involuntary civil commitment law, [the] right to treatment law, [the] right to refuse treatment law, or any aspect of forensic mental disability law that are now taken for granted."[39]

Unfortunately, data suggests that in many jurisdictions, legal counsel is inadequate, disinterested, ununiformed, and in some cases even hostile toward their clients with mental disabilities.[40] This is why a therapeutic jurisprudence approach is needed to ensure a client-centered model of representation.[41]

Despite these revolutionary documents, individuals with mental disabilities are largely overrepresented in prisons and in the homeless population in the United States.[42] As Professor Perlin aptly notes, "The simple official repudiation of discriminatory practices is not enough to significantly alter the distorted cognitive processes that still frequently dominate our thinking and decision-making."[43] Individuals with mental disabilities tend to be arrested more than individuals with no such diagnosis, and individuals with past civil commitments have a higher likelihood of arrest than individuals who voluntarily sought psychiatric help.[44] Further, individuals with

---

39. MICHAEL L. PERLIN, INTERNATIONAL HUMAN RIGHTS AND MENTAL DISABILITY LAW: WHEN THE SILENCED ARE HEARD 34. (2012).

40. Michael L. Perlin, *Fatal Assumption: A Critical Evaluation of the Role of Counsel in Mental Disability Cases*, 16 LAW & HUM. BEHAV. 37, 47 (1992).

41. *See* Juan Ramirez Jr. and Amy D. Ronner, *Voiceless Billy Budd: Melville's Tribute to the Sixth Amendment*, 41 CAL. W. L. REV. 103, 119 (2004) (recognizing the right to effective counsel as "the core of therapeutic jurisprudence").

42. William H. Fisher, Eric Silver, and Nancy Wolff, *Beyond Criminalization: Toward a Criminologically Informed Framework for Mental Health Policy and Services Research*, 33 AD-MIN. POL'Y MENT. HEALTH & MENTAL HEALTH SERVICES RES., 544, 536 (2006); James A. Wilson and Peter B. Wood, *Dissecting the Relationship between Mental Illness and Return to Incarceration, 42* J. CRIM, JUSTICE 527 (2014); Richard G. Frank and Thomas G. McGuire, *Mental Health Treatment and Criminal Justice Out-comes*, in CONTROLLING CRIME: STRATE-GIES AND TRADEOFFS, 167–207 (Philip J. Cook, Jens Ludwig, and Justin McCrary eds., 2011); Arthur J. Lurigio, *People with Serious Mental Illness in the Criminal Justice System: Causes, Consequences, and Correctives*, 91: 3 THE PRISON JOURNAL, 66S–86S (2011) (Supplement); Jennifer L. Skeem, Sarah Manchak, and Jillian K. Peterson, *Correctional Policy for Offenders with Mental Illness: Creating a New Paradigm for Recidivism Reduction*, 35 LAW & HUM. BE-HAV., 110 (2011).

43. Perlin, *supra* note 30, at 22.

44. Anfang and Appelbaum, *supra* note 24; "Mental Illness and Homelessness," *National Coalition for the Homeless* (July 2009), https://www.nationalhomeless.org/factsheets/Mental_Illness.html (last visited Jan. 30, 2021); H. Richard Lamb and Linda E. Weinberger, Review: *Persons with Severe Mental Illness in Jails and Prisons*, 49 PSYCHIATRIC SERV. 483–92 (1998).

mental illness are likely to reoffend or return to prison at higher rates than individuals without such disabilities.[45]

Likewise, substance disorders may correlate with recidivism. For example, substance use can lead to impaired impulse control and lowered inhibitions and feelings.[46] Studies show that substance use disorders may also affect treatment nonadherence, which may increase the risk of violence among individuals diagnosed with serious mental illness.[47] Further, individuals with substance use disorders may be more likely to trigger parole revocations via failed drug tests or failure to adhere to other conditions of parole.[48] Finally, it is well established that substance use tends to co-occur with mental illness at high rates and has been shown to influence the association between mental illness and crime.[49]

Many individuals with mental health and/or substance abuse issues end up in jails or institutions that are not equipped to provide them with the care and individualized treatment they need. Instead, often these individuals are locked up against their will or become victims to the revolving door of the criminal justice system.[50] The dire circumstances under which persons with serious mental disabilities find themselves in jail are shameful for a civilized society. Prison and jail employees often lack education or training in the appropriate treatment of detainees with a mental illness. They often respond aggressively, thus exacerbating the symptoms exhibited by the detainees in question.[51] Once in jail, individuals with mental health issues are often disciplined or placed in solitary confinement rather than being afforded adequate treatment.[52] Arguably worse, persons with mental disabilities are of-

---

45. James A. Wilson and Peter B. Wood, *Dissecting the Relationship between Mental Illness and Return to Incarceration*, 42 J. Crim. Just. 527, 528 (2014).

46. Steven Belenko and Jordan Peugh, *Fighting Crime by Treating Substance Abuse*, 15 Issues in Science & Technology Online, 53 (1998); Jan Volavka and Jeffrey Swanson, *Violent Behavior in Mental Illness: The Role of Substance Abuse*, 304 JAMA 563 (2010).

47. *See generally* Jan Volavka and Leslie Citrome, *Heterogeneity of Violence in Schizophrenia and Implications for Long-Term Treatment*, 62 Int'l J. Practice, 1237 (2008).

48. *See* Skeem, Manchak, and Peterson, *supra* note 42.

49. *See* James A. Swartz and Arthur J. Lurigio, *Serious Mental Illness and Arrest: The Generalized Mediating Effect of Substance Use*, 53: 4 Crime & Delinq. 581 (2007).

50. *See* Wilson and Wood, *supra* note 45, at 528.

51. Michael L. Perlin and Meredith R. Schriver, *"You Might Have Drugs at Your Command": Reconsidering the Forced Drugging of Incompetent Pre-trial Detainees from the Perspectives of International Human Rights and Income Inequality*, 8 Albany Gov't L. Rev. 381, 396 (2015).

52. *See, e.g.*, Stuart Grassian, *Psychiatric Effects of Solitary Confinement*, 22 Wash. U. J.L. & Pol'y 325, 328–29, 348 (2006); Jeffrey L. Metzner and Jamie Fellner, *Solitary Confinement and Mental Illness in U.S. Prisons: A Challenge for Medical Ethics*, 38 J. Am. Acad. Psychiatry & L. 104, 104–5 (2010). *See also* Michael L. Perlin, *"God Said to Abraham/Kill Me a Son": Why the Insanity Defense and the Incompetency Status Are Compatible with and Required by*

ten forcibly medicated in jails and prisons.[53] Even in the rare circumstances when treatment is administered with good intentions, it leaves a powerful, often lasting effect on the patient. By way of example, psychotropic medications are known to affect the mind, intellectual functions, perception, moods, and emotions and can last for several years after administration.[54]

Nonjudicial Officers and Their Roles in the Courts

Although widely unknown by the general public, decisions regarding important criminal matters—decisions that have traditionally been delegated to judges—which can lead to criminal convictions, enhanced time spent in correctional facilities, and stigmatizing labels are being made throughout the country by nonjudicial officers, individuals who lack the laborious education and training of judges.[55] This impacts whether individuals lose their freedom—one of the most important matters that courts decide—and constitutes an impermissible delegation of power.[56] Professor Perlin, the only scholar who has written on this subject within the perspective of therapeutic jurisprudence, recognizes the sad reality that "when nonjudges make what should be judicial decisions—with perilously little oversight—that may be life-and-death, it is fatuous to even assess whether therapeutic jurisprudence principles are honored. They simply cannot be."[57]

In certain jurisdictions, nonjudicial officers are given a wide range of duties and responsibilities by statute including hearing certain pretrial motions in criminal cases and making decisions as to conditions of probation for sex offenders. These officers are frequently not lawyers, and evidence suggests that many of the basic rudiments of the criminal trial process are often not honored, opening the door to due process violations.[58] This delegation is highly problematic and leaves no room for checks and balances but instead plac-

---

the Convention on the Rights of Persons with Disabilities and Basic Principles of Therapeutic Jurisprudence, 54 AM. CRIM. L. REV. 479, 507–9 (2017).

53. See generally Henry Dlugacz and Christopher Wimmer, Legal Aspects of Administering Antipsychotic Medications to Jail and Prison Inmates, 36 INT'L J.L. & PSYCHIATRY 213 (2013); Henry Dulgacz, Due Process Rights in Inmate Disciplinary Proceedings (this volume); Deborah Dorfman, Doing Time in "the Devil's Chair": Evaluating Nonjudicial Administrative Decisions to Isolate and Restrain Prisoners and Detainees with Mental Health Disabilities in Jails and Prisons (this volume).

54. V. LONGO, NEUROPHARMACOLOGY AND BEHAVIOR 182 (1972); Gerald L. Klerman, Psychotropic Drugs as Therapeutic Agents, 2 HASTINGS CENTER STUD. 81, 82 n.1. (Jan. 1974).

55. See generally Perlin, supra note 1.

56. Id. at 1687.

57. Id. at 1694–95.

58. Id. at 1686.

es nonjudges in roles in which they are not educated or trained to be. In what has been deemed an "embarrass[ing]" experiment,[59] nonjudges accept pleas and are tasked with making dispositive decisions for critical pretrial motions.[60]

As discussed extensively in Chapter 1, in New York, nonjudges are granted the power through statute to decide certain pretrial motions that have potential to determine the outcome of the case.[61] In South Dakota, probation officers now have authority to accept certain guilty plea agreements and determine whether criminal defendants have violated their probation, thereby granting them unprecedented authority to determine whether the defendant should be incarcerated or forced to participate in a sex offender treatment program, a role traditionally delegated to judges.[62]

A state is not prohibited from conferring judicial functions upon nonjudicial bodies, or from delegating powers to a court that are legislative in nature under the Fourteenth Amendment.[63] However, in the criminal law context, this delegation of power violates due process, places far too much power in the hands of probation officers, and takes away the power of judges who are supposed to be impartial.[64] Aside from violating the law and common sense, this delegation of judicial authority to nonjudicial officers violates the principles of therapeutic jurisprudence, which emphasizes that "legal rules, procedures, and lawyer roles can or should be reshaped to enhance their therapeutic potential while not subordinating due process principles."[65]

Conclusion

Individuals with mental illness and substance abuse disorders are disproportionately impacted by the injustice of the criminal justice system. Opening the door to untrained nonjudicial officers to make decisions regarding

---

59. Issa Kohler-Hausmann, *Managerial Justice and Mass Misdemeanors*, 66 STAN. L. REV., 611, 611 (2014).

60. Perlin, *supra* note 1 at 1698.

61. Michael L. Perlin, *"But I Ain't a Judge": The Therapeutic Jurisprudence Implications of the Use of Nonjudicial Officers in Criminal Justice Cases* (this volume); N.Y. CRIMINAL PROCEDURE LAW § 255.20[4]).

62. S.D. CONSOL. L.§ 23A-27-12.1

63. Dreyer v. Illinois, 187 U.S. 71, 83–84 (1902) (state statutes vesting in a parole board certain judicial functions); New York ex rel. Lieberman v. Van De Carr, 199 U.S. 552, 562 (1905) (conferring discretionary power upon administrative boards to grant or withhold permission to carry on a trade or vesting in a probate court authority to appoint park commissioners and establish park districts); Ohio v. Akron Park Dist., 281 U.S. 74, 79 (1930).

64. Perlin, *supra* note 1, at 1687.

65. *Id.*, quoting Perlin and Lynch, *supra* note 7, at 348.

important criminal matters only exacerbates the problem. There is a need for better regulations and procedures to ensure the rights of individuals with mental disabilities are not violated and that they have access to due process, so they do not fall prey to the revolving door of the criminal justice system. Although this is not always guaranteed simply by attorneys and judges with legal background and training, at a bare minimum, judges with adequate education and training—not nonjudicial officers—should be the decision makers. But this alone is not enough. Judges and lawyers need more training to deflect the attitudes of sanism and prejudice toward people with disabilities.

One solution is to utilize existing and implement more mental health courts and drug courts. These problem-solving courts focus on dignity and "acknowledge that the one-size-fits-all structure of the American criminal justice system often leaves much to be desired."[66] There is evidence that demonstrates mental health courts and drug courts are effective in reducing recidivism and positively impacting participant functioning.[67] When mental health courts are structured properly and chaired by a judge who "buys in" to the TJ model, they can be "perfect examples of the practical utility of therapeutic jurisprudence."[68] This will help ensure judges are the decision makers and that therapeutic principles are followed.

We can no longer turn a blind eye to the injustices impacting individuals with mental health and substance abuse issues. Change will likely not happen overnight, but hopefully this chapter will shed light on this hidden space in the criminal justice system and draw attention to the injustices impacting mentally ill and addicted individuals to ensure their dignity and due process rights are not stripped away.

---

66. *See* Perlin, *supra* note 2, at 23.

67. M. Susan Ridgeley et al., *Justice Treatment and Cost: An Evaluation of the Fiscal Impact of Allegheny County Mental Health Court, Santa Monica, CA,* Rand Corporation (2007); Shelli B. Rossman et al., *Criminal Justice Interventions for Offenders with Mental Illness: Evaluations of Mental Health Courts in Bronx and Brooklyn, New York,* Urban Institute (2012).

68. *See* Perlin, *supra* note 2, at 33.

3

Therapeutic Jurisprudence in Action

Applying Goffman's Dramaturgical Theory to Mental Health Courts

Karen A. Snedker

Introduction

The overrepresentation of individuals with mental health diagnoses in U.S. jails and prisons is striking.[1] The development and expansion of specialized mental health courts (MHCs) is one remedy. MHCs are a part of the broader problem-solving movement that addresses the underlying social problems associated with criminal behavior.[2] Beginning in the late 1980s with the drug court model,[3] specialty courts have proliferated.[4] MHCs have grown tremendously since their inception in the late 1990s[5] and gained momentum internationally. They are an attempt to prioritize treat-

1. Jennifer Bronson and Marcus Berzofsky, *Bureau of Justice Statistics (BJS)—Indicators of Mental Health Problems Reported by Prisoners and Jail Inmates, 2011-2012* 1–17 (2017), https://www.bjs.gov/index.cfm?ty=pbdetail&iid=5946.

2. Greg Berman and John Feinblatt, *Problem-Solving Courts: A Brief Primer*, 23 Law Policy 125, 125–27 (2001); Arie Freiberg, *Problem-Oriented Courts: Innovative Solutions to Intractable Problems*, 11 J. Judic. Adm. 8–27 (2001).

3. James L. Nolan Jr., Reinventing Justice: The American Drug Court Movement (2001).

4. Greg Berman and John Feinblatt, Good Courts: The case for Problem-Solving Justice (2005).

5. Gregg Goodale, Lisa Callahan, and Henry J. Steadman, *Law and Psychiatry: What Can We Say about Mental Health Courts Today?* 64 Psychiatr. Serv. 298. 298 (2013); Carol Fisler, *When Research Challenges Policy and Practice: Toward a New Understanding of Mental Health Courts*, 54 Judges. J. 8, 8 (2015).

ment and rehabilitation, moving away from "punitive jurisprudence"[6] to a therapeutic model of justice.

Problem-solving courts represent a type of specialty jurisdiction court[7] reflecting the broader "infusion of the therapeutic ethos into America's criminal justice system."[8] Like all problem-solving courts, MHCs are holistic and are committed to rehabilitative and therapeutic ends with court-ordered and court-supervised treatment.[9] MHCs specifically target defendants with serious mental illness and link them to community-based treatment and services in an attempt to reduce future entanglements in the criminal justice system.[10]

This chapter draws on qualitative data from two MHCs to show how team members translate the tenets of therapeutic jurisprudence into the performance of their social roles in both formal and informal court settings. I argue that the successful operation of teamwork lies at the heart of MHC effectiveness. Judges, acting as both audience and team member, can undermine the work of the team. MHCs clearly rely upon a well-functioning collaborative team, working partially in backstage settings, with a judge willing to alter frontstage performances for the sake of collaboration and therapeutic effects for clients.

Therapeutic Jurisprudence and Collaboration

In MHCs, the court process diverges in many ways from standard criminal justice practices. A philosophy of therapeutic jurisprudence serves as the foundation of the specialty treatment court model.[11] "Therapeutic jurisprudence" entered into the lexicon of the criminal justice system in the late 1980s in the field of mental health law. David Wexler and Bruce Winick defined therapeutic jurisprudence as "the study of the extent to which substan-

---

6. JoANN MILLER AND DONALD C. JOHNSON, PROBLEM SOLVING COURTS: A MEASURE OF JUSTICE (2009).

7. John Petrila, *An Introduction to Special Jurisdiction Courts*, 26 INT. J. LAW & PSYCHIATRY 3, 4–10 (2003).

8. JAMES L. NOLAN , THE THERAPEUTIC STATE: JUSTIFYING GOVERNMENT AT CENTURY'S END (1998).

9. Lauren Almquist and Elizabeth Dodd, *Mental Health Courts: A Guide to Reserach-Informed Policy and Practice* 1–41 (2009); RICHARD D. SCHNEIDER, HY BLOOM, AND MARK HEEREMA, MENTAL HEALTH COURTS: DECRIMINALIZING THE MENTALLY ILL (2007).

10. Goodale, Callahan, and Steadman, *Law and Psychiatry*, 298, 298.

11. SCHNEIDER, BLOOM, AND HEEREMA, *supra* note 9, at 3–4;.Peggy Fulton Hora, William G. Schma, and John T. A. Rosenthal, *Therapeutic Jurisprudence and the Drug Treatment Court Movement: Revolutionizing the Criminal Justice Ssystem's Response to Drug Abuse and Crime in America*, 74 NOTRE DAME L. REV. 439, 442–44 (1999).

tive rules, legal procedures, and the roles of lawyers and judges produce *therapeutic* or *antitherapeutic* consequences."[12] The law as a social force[13] can help heal individual defendants and members of society, or it can lead to greater stress and injury. The principles of therapeutic jurisprudence lead to shifts in the cultural practices of the law. Wexler explicitly links therapeutic jurisprudence to collaboration as opposed to a more traditional adversarialism.[14] These two paradigm shifts—therapeutic jurisprudence and collaboration—work together to inform therapeutic justice.[15]

The mission of MHCs revolves around a less punitive, less adversarial style of criminal justice in a structure of support and accountability. How, then, is therapeutic jurisprudence translated from theory into practice? Drawing on Goffman's dramaturgical theory,[16] I argue that it is through *teamwork* that therapeutic jurisprudence—as a foundational principle of MHCs—is realized. Microlevel interactions between key team members in the court, understood as the stage for the enactment of justice and repair, reveal the level of success of the court's therapeutic reorientation. Qualitative data highlight the importance of Goffman's conceptualization of teams, during both "front" and "back" stages of the judicial process, to produce therapeutic and anti-therapeutic effects on MHC clients.

Goffman's Dramaturgical Approach

Erving Goffman understood everyday situations as theatrical performances in which people enact their claims to social status, produce and reproduce meaning, and create social order. Influenced by sociological theorist Emile Durkheim, one of Goffman's (1959) seminal works, *The Presentation of Self in Everyday Life,* details how actors present themselves to others in various daily social performances and reveals the process by which people act and

---

12. David B. Wexler and Bruce J. Winick, *Therapeutic Jurisprudence as a New Appraoch to Mental Health Law Policy Analysis and Research*, 45 U. Miami L. Rev. 979, 981(1991) (emphasis added);

13. Christopher Slobogin, *Integrating Preventative Law and Therapeutic Jurisprudence: A Law and Psychology Based Approach to Lawyering*, in Practicing Therapeutic Jurisprudence: Law as a Helping Profession 5, 7 (Dennis P. Stolle, David B. Wexler, and Bruce J. Winick eds., 2000, hereafter cited as Stolle).

14. David B. Wexler, *Therapeutic Jurisprudence and the Culture of Critique, in* Stolle, *supra* note 13, at 449, 463.

15. Karen A. Snedker, Therapeutic Justice: Crime, Treatment Courts and Mental Illness (2018).

16. Erving Goffman, The Presentation of Self in Everyday Life (1959).

react in relation to others.[17] Social life is made up of social performances, contending that we are all actors playing roles in a variety of situations and settings. These social roles reflect certain ascribed or achieved status positions and are guided by associated norms inherent in those roles. The performance can include dress (costume), objects (props), and tone of voice and gestures (manner). Actors craft their performances according to the setting or situational context (stage) by engaging in impression management; the effort to deploy appropriate social performances and maintain them in line with roles preserving (or elevating) their status. According to Goffman, actors seek to promote their desired image of self to a relevant audience.

Goffman's dramaturgical analysis focuses on face-to-face interactions. Moreover, Goffman highlights what parts of the self are visible or hidden from the view of the others determines how these social performances play out. Such differences guide successful or failed presentations of the self. Applied to MHCs, I will show how court actors—judges, prosecutors, defense attorneys, probations officers, court liaisons, and social workers—play their role and how well they carry it off.[18]

Three essential concepts—teams, frontstage, and backstage—from Goffman guide my discussion of how therapeutic jurisprudence is enacted through social performances by members of the MHC team. People of like social status may operate as performance teams, sharing a goal and working together to make a favorable impression. Actors engage in teamwork to carry out social roles in such a way as to achieve their ends and preserve social status, including honor, prestige, and self-regard. The "front" refers to the part of a social performance before an audience where impressions must be actively managed. The "back" are settings without an audience.

Data and Methods

I draw on a larger study of MHCs I conducted in a large West Coast city. While there is variation in MHCs[19] and no singular model has been embraced,[20] they all have central features that separate them from the traditional case adjudication process. The courts I studied are typical of other MHCs in many ways, including specialized dockets, a dedicated MHC team, and court-

---

17. For an excellent elaboration of this perspective, *see* RANDALL COLLINS, INTERACTION RITUAL CHAIN (2004).

18. See other applications of Goffman's theory to problem-solving courts. See NOLAN, *supra* note 5. See MILLER and JOHNSON, *supra* note 6.

19. Fisler, *supra* note 5, at 9.

20. *See* Robert Bernstein and Tammy Seltzer, *Criminalization of People with Mental Illnesses: The Role of Mental Health Courts in System Reform*, 7 U. D. C. L. REV. 143 (2003).

supervised treatment.[21] The selection process,[22] including assessments of eligibility and amenability, are comparable to each other and other MHCs.

I use two forms of qualitative data from both MHC sites collected between 2013 and 2016 (details are available elsewhere).[23] First, I draw on my fieldwork data, including detailed court observations of court proceedings. Second, the paper draws upon forty-seven in-depth interviews conducted with MHC professional staff ($n = 41$) and MHC clients ($n = 6$). The interviews probed many aspects of the court process, but here I focus on therapeutic and collaborative goals.

Findings

Therapeutic Jurisprudence in Action

In treatment courts, organizational and cultural priorities actively promote a collaborative framework by placing them in a broader therapeutic orientation. Team members participate in joint decision-making related to treatment, punishment, and therapeutic outcomes.[24] A team of professionals develop an individualized, personal treatment plan for each client, attempting to resolve the root causes of criminal involvement by connecting clients to social services and treatment. These shifts are consistent with notions of "personalized justice" and the individualized nature of the court, "focused more on the person than the crime." Collaboration, central to the team model, is on display in both formal and informal settings. It is during those social interactions that the values of therapeutic jurisprudence become realized.

Teamwork among Therapeutic Agents

Goffman talks about performance teams that are made up of people of similar social status, with a shared set of norms and practices set upon performances and a common task. Members of teams cooperate and have a shared definition of the situation. They collaborate to make favorable impressions

21. Almquist and Dodd, *supra* note 9; Schneider, Bloom, and Heerema, *supra* note 9.

22. Nancy Wolff et al., *Mental Health Courts and Their Selection Processes: Modeling Variation for Consistency*, 35 Law & Hum. Behav. 402, 403–4 (2011).

23. Snedker, *supra* note 15, at 293–96.

24. John S. Goldkamp and Cheryl Irons-Guynn, *Emerging Judicial Strategies for the Mentally Ill in the Criminal Caseload: Mental Health Courts in Fort Lauderdale, Seattle, San Bernardino, and Anchorage* 1–83 (2000), http://www.ncjrs.gov/pdffiles1/bja/182504.pdf; Amy Watson et al., *Mental Health Courts and the Complex Issue of Mentally Ill Offenders*, 52 Psychiatr. Serv. 477, 478 (2001).

upon relevant audiences which can be of higher, lower, similar, or mixed so-
cials statuses. Being a member of the team requires that each claim a role but
also that others recognize that claim and act accordingly in subsequent performances. In MHCs, I found that the underlying expectations about performances by team members are that they should be consistent with a therapeutic orientation. Stability and trust within the team are key factors
related to the functioning and effectiveness of the team model.

The idea of teamwork is baked into the MHC model. From the therapeutic jurisprudence perspective, legal agents and court staff are "therapeutic
agents";[25] team members are working collaboratively with a "mindset" toward therapeutic jurisprudence.[26] This "teamwork" approach includes new
social positions and new social roles as different parties work together across
the traditional demarcations of prosecution and defense. There are both subtle and dramatic changes in social roles in the court with "role refinement."[27]
This requires adjustments in roles, which for some can be substantial.[28]

For lawyers, practicing law as a therapeutic agent embodies lawyering with
an ethic of care[29] and lawyering as a client-centered[30] helping profession, in-
cludng active listening and collaboration.[31] The role of defense attorneys is
crucial for court success[32] because they are advocates aware of the intended
and unintended law-related psychological harm.[33] Judges are central "therapeutic agents" operating in a distinct way in treatment courts such that some
literally "cast their robes" aside.[34] Judicial authority is understood as the "court
room leader"[35] or "coach" as opposed to arbiter[36] characterized as both a

25. Nancy Wolff, *Courts as Therapeutic Agents: Thinking Past the Novelty of Mental Health Courts*, 30 J. Am. Acad. Psychiatry & L. 431, 437 (2002).

26. Schneider, Bloom, and Heerema, *supra* note 9, at 39–56.

27. *Id.* at 53.

28. Nolan, *supra* note 3.

29. Carrie Menkel-Meadow, *Is Altruism Possible in Lawyering?* 8 Ga. State U. L. Rev. 385, 385–86 (1992).

30. Dennis P. Stolle et al., *Integrating Preventative Law and Therapeutic Jurisprudence: A Law and Psychology Based Approach to Lawyering*, in Stolle, *supra* note 13, at 5, 6.

31. Susan Daicoff, *The Role of Therapeutic Jurisprudence within the Comprehensive Law Movement*, in Stolle, *supra* note 13, at 465, 474–75.

32. Michael L. Perlin, *"The Judge, He Cast His Robe Aside": Mental Health Courts, Dignity and Due Process*, 3 Ment. Health L. & Pol'y J. 1, 19,-20 (2013).

33. Bruce J. Winick, David B. Wexler, and Edward A. Dauer, *Preface: A New Model For the Practice of Law.*, 5 Psychol. Public Pol'y & L. 795, 798–99 (1999).

34. Perlin, *supra* note 31, at 5.

35. Miller and Johnson, *supra* note 6.

36. David Rottman and Pamela Casey, *Therapeutic Jurisprudence and the Emergence of Problem-Solving Courts*, Natl. Inst. Justice J. 12–19 (1999).

"cheerleader and stern parent."[37] Judicial temperament, engagement, and buy-in to the court's therapeutic and collaborative mission is important.[38]

Probation officers are also important therapeutic agents whose supervision of clients differs from traditional probation.[39] The probation officers often work behind the scenes in review meeting and follow-ups with social services agencies, and they are balancing accountability and support,[40] working torward perceptions of fairness.[41]

All of these standard judicial actors are part of the MHC, but a working MHC team also includes new members, such as court liaisons/monitors who serve in a "neutral" position acting as a link between defendant and court personnel, as well as "gatekeepers" of the court screening process. There are also defense social workers who work directly with clients to connect them to social services, benefits, and housing. In some felony courts, there are also victim's advocates. Apart from the judge, all of the team members have the same audience. Team members are sometimes performing in front of the judges and at other times the clients. In courts that I studied, the quality of therapeutic performances by lawyers, both defense and prosecution, varied somewhat. Prosecutors were sometimes performing specifically for the judge while the defense attorney was performing for their client.

The underlying therapeutic goals of the court unify team members, facilitating greater compromise. For the prosecution, the goal is to work with defendants, offer recommendations and support for MHC clients, and be cognizant of community safety concerns. In the courts I studied, there was variability in the extent to which prosecutors bought into this model. I witnessed greater therapeutic collaboration between lawyers in nonfelony cases. They are less concerned with their conviction record. Although zealous representation is maintained, for defense counsel the goal is not necessary to get the "best deal" for a defendant but to consider long-term criminal justice entanglements. Probation officers do not respond to violations with automatic revocations, in which clients are thrown out of MHC or into jail as a routine sanction. For judges, there is less discernment over complex legal issues and more time spent communicating (including active listening) with

---

37. Deborah J. Chase and Peggy Fulton Hora, *The Implications of Therapeutic Jurisprudence for Judical Satisfaction*, 37 COURT REV. 12, 12 (2000).

38. Fisler, *supra* note 5, at 9.

39. Jennifer L. Skeem, Paula Emke-Francis, and Jennifer Eno Louden, *Probation, Mental Health, and Mandated Treatment: A National Survey*, 33 CRIM. JUST. & BEHAV. 158, 160 (2006).

40. Jennifer L. Skeem et al., *Assessing Relationship Quality in Mandated Community Treatment: Blending Care with Control*, 19 PSYCHOLOG. ASSESS. 397, 406–7 (2007).

41. Kelly Frailing, Brandi Alfonso, and Rae Taylor, *Therapeutic Jurisprudence in Swift and Certain Probation*, 64 AM. BEHAV. SCI. 1768, 1769–70 (2020).

team members and clients. However, there are also times when judges spend too much time on legal aspects of the process that can detract from the therapeutic goals. Many judges referenced the lack of legal discernment in MHCs with a focus on "trying to decide what's the best way to get to a certain outcome, get them [clients] into treatment, get them on medication, into housing, whatever it might be."

Cooperation among team members is critical, and this often involves a process of socialization whereby individuals become integrated into courts and learn how to perform new therapeutic roles. I found that tensions arise when team members do not fully consider other team members' perspectives. For example, one prosecutor was perceived as holding too much power over the process, leading to an imbalance in the team. This undermined the group's efforts and led to resentment. Carrying over a traditional adversarial criminal justice approach into MHC, this prosecutor explained that "we [the state] lead the meeting, we call the cases, we direct the conversation." One judge called this an example of "entrenched interests" that "interfere with our collaborative approach."

In another instance, a seasoned team member corrected the mistaken performance of a new team member. A probation officer was describing a client's violation of a domestic violence "no contact" order in line with the defense attorney's and the judge's interpretation. However, the new prosecutor disagreed and made the stakes clear that the client "needs to be on notice. She has had her one chance. Will revoke if not in compliance." The tone and firm language were uncharacteristic of MHC hearings, even from a prosecutor. I observed that the judge softened his judgment so as to counteract the prosecution's performance. Over time, as the prosecutor became socialized into the court, he developed a more therapeutic style.

Situational contexts matter in defining the situation and influencing the presentation of self among actors. Teamwork comes together in two different contexts that, in combination, shape therapeutic outcomes for clients. The two settings are the "front" and the "back" of social performances. First, there are precourt meetings that are the "behind the scenes" performances where there is not an audience. Second, the front are the social performances where an audience is present, namely court hearings and reviews. Within both spaces, both "planned" and "ad hoc" interactions can occur.[42] I explore each in turn.

---

42. Simon Lewin and Scott Reeves, *Enacting "Team" and "Teamwork": Using Goffman's Theory of Impression Management to Illuminate Interprofessional Practice on Hospital Wards*, 72. Soc. Sci. Med. 1595, 1598 (2011).

Backstage: Informal Meetings

In Goffman's backstage—"the back region of performances"—actors are closed off to audiences and participation is reserved for team members only. It is a private or semiprivate setting. As such, less impression management is needed. This is where actors can step "out of character" and the presentation of self is more authentic. Goffman understood this backstage region as key places where preparation for frontstage performances happen, which enhances coordination among team members and allows them to "conspire" in devising the most advantageous frontstage performances.

Both courts in my study hold a precourt meeting where team members are in the backstage excluding the judge. Nationally, there is some variability on the presence or absence of the judge in these meetings. During precourt meetings, all team members—except for the judge—are present before court begins (while some eat lunch) to discuss the court calendar and go through each client's case. This is where the teamwork model is most clearly in action, where much of the "work" happens, and where "candid conversations" occur. Team members share recommendations and negotiations precede. Collaboration in precourt meetings routinely result in joint recommendations before the judge, but collaboration need not mean complete agreement. Even if all parties at not in agreement, it is important that "everybody's positions are at least heard before we go to court," according to a prosecutor; this process helps build trust and reinforce the impression that all actors are on the same team and are valued members.

In the MHCs in this study, there was universal agreement among team members that judges be absent from the precourt meetings because it allowed for more "openness," candid sharing of information, and troubleshooting possible responses and court actions without a formal legal proceeding. Team members argued that this benefited clients. A prosecutor summarized, "We all need to hash things out, and he [the judge] is the final decider, and we don't need him in there, going over all the minutiae and the details and high jacking our meeting." Likewise, a defense attorney characterized the meeting as a place where team members are "spitballing ideas that maybe we don't want a judge to hear, we don't want a judge to latch on to." Without the judge, she claimed the "freedom to say those things and get it all out and maybe have a hostile interaction and have that not color the judge's perspective of the client," and the judge's presence would lead to a "chilling effect." Another defense attorney agreed because the judge "changes the dynamics," and "everyone defers to the judge. We can't have that. We can't be deferring to the judge!" This reflects that status differences undermine teamwork.

For Goffman, teams are composed of equal members in terms of status. But judges are superior in professional status. With judicial presence, legal issues tend to me more highly prioritized, and differential status hampers full disclosure in ways that reduce collaboration. Despite absence in the precourt meetings in these two MHCs, often judges were referenced, and the meetings proceeded with full awareness of varying judicial styles. Thus, the shadow of judges was still felt despite their absence, reflecting their power and ultimate control over the court.

Judges whom I interviewed differed in how they felt about not being welcome at the backstage meeting, but all recognized that a lot of work happened behind closed doors without their input. For some, this was a cause of frustration. For others, not being present backstage allowed them to cultivate a more collaborative style and "learn to listen" to the team in service of therapeutic outcomes. Given that team members are mostly in agreement after the precourt discussions, often, this relegates the judge to a "rubber stamp." Some judges appreciated the freedom to prioritize tenets of procedural justice with fairness and dignity at its core in line with therapeutic outcomes. Reimagining the judge's role allows for these principles to be at the forefront. Some judges even acknowledged that in MHCs the status of the team is comparable or even greater than that of the judge.

There are opportunities for judges to engage in the backstage, either before or after the precourt meetings. Some judges actively sought feedback from the team which many noted advanced teamwork. This took different forms. In some cases, judges had an "open-door policy" for any team member to offer reflections. In considering his relationship with probation officers, a judge recalled, "Sometimes they would come in and say, 'Your Honor, I just want to explain a little bit more about this . . . [about] what is going on.'" Similarly, a different judge shared examples from a probation officer warning the judge not to distract a client by talking about a certain subject or using certain words that might "set a client off." This is evidence of judges deferring to team members, a crucial behavior that elevates the status of the team. Similarly, a probation officer identified a willingness of a judge to listen to the team: "You could go back and talk to them beforehand . . . and give the judge a hint on what to do." These types of backstage interventions were "unofficial" or "ad hoc" variants of Goffman's back regions.

Frontstage: Addressing the Court

Once the precourt meeting is over, the actors immediately go to the court setting. Here, formalized exchanges take place in front of the judge in the courtroom drama with idealized "front-stages performances."[43] Before the court is the frontstage, which is the public hearing, both a guarded and restrained setting. Here, one's presentation of self is relevant, and team members from different status positions are performing before an audience. In the frontstage, members of the MHC team work together to create an impression for the client and for the judge. This is important because the judge is outside of the team in the backstage bargaining process. Each court performance depends on all team members playing their role. But team members are trying to perform to both audiences at once—judges and clients—which present problems. These performances have been described as "therapeutic theater."[44]

In the frontstage, there are many examples of the principles of therapeutics jurisprudence at play, including language usage by team members (e.g., "clients" and "we") and reduced formality (e.g., the prosecutor and the defense attorney sat down as opposed to standing before the judge). The social performances that take place inside this formal setting fall into a few categories including opt-in hearings, review hearings, and graduations. Depending on the type of hearing, one audience or another is more prevalent. Many of these court hearings are in fact rituals—especially as clients enter and exit the court—with the therapeutic potential of reducing stigma.[45] In review hearings, when clients are in compliance, team members are therapeutic and full of praise.[46] But in the sanctioning process, when a client is out of compliance, antitherapeutic outcomes are most notable. However, when the team, especially the judge, remains committed to a harm-reduction philosophy, the potential for therapeutic effects increases despite court violations.

Judges, while a part of the team in some ways, have a different role; they preside over the rituals of the court. During the opt-in stage of the selection process, clients go through a brief initiation ritual. A very typical initiation ritual by the judge is, "Welcome to MHC! This is a treatment court. We understand it will be hard. We will ask a lot of you, but the team is here to provide support along the way." Likewise, another judge proclaimed, "This is a treatment court with a team that is going to work with you." If the collaborative and therapeutic orientation was the standard norm of criminal justice, it would not need to be stated so fervently and take center stage in the initiation ritual.

---

43. MILLER AND JOHNSON, *supra* note 6, at 175.

44. NOLAN, *supra* note 3.

45. Karen A. Snedker, *Unburdening Stigma: Identity Repair through Rituals in Mental Health Court*, 6 SOC. MENT. HEALTH 36, 41–47 (2016).

46. Kelly Frailing, *How Mental Health Courts Function: Outcomes and Observations*, 33 INT. J. L. & PSYCHIATRY 207, 209 (2010).

Once in MHC, clients must submit to periodic reviews. During routine status hearings, clients are assessed in terms of their level of compliance with a detailed report from probation. One judge mentioned "signals" embedded in reports to guide judges in the hearing. For example, "One of my probation officers would sometimes write in italics in his reports emphasizing the information that he thought I needed to know but shouldn't be discussing in court." This was an example of an "ad hoc" or "unofficial" interaction in the frontstage that showed deference to the team by the judge. Prosecutors and defense attorney also weigh in during these reviews, often offering joint recommendations evidence of teamwork and the therapeutic orientation. Judges converse directly with clients in a supportive fashion. One judge stated, "The judge's role is really to be a cheerleader [for clients], give positive feedback and give consequences when appropriate, and really just engage."

The positive therapeutic effects of MHCs are most notable in the "graduation" ritual, which is formally exiting the court based on successful completion of the program. During a graduation, a client received a certificate, the judge came down from bench and shook the client's hand—a noticeable reduction of physical and social distance—and the audience applauded. Often, clients hugged MHC professional team members. Team members offered words of praise showing a unified front. Clients are also often joined by family, friends, case managers, and others there to witness the event. Sometimes clients captured the moment with a photograph. Here, performances face mixed audiences. Graduation represents success for the clients, but it is also the culmination performance of the team. At the end of the graduation ritual, one client, "Monique," addressed the judge: "I am really grateful to the court and probation. . . . I did not do this by myself!" Graduations' displays of positive emotion are clearly in line with therapeutic jurisprudence, an affirmation of teamwork, and the social status gained by the client. If team members are not actively engaged in the performance, such as looking at their cell phones or shuffling paperwork, the ritual's effects are lessened. I rarely witnessed this during graduation rituals but did observe such inattention and distracting behavior during routine status hearings, which can diminish therapeutic outcomes.

Asymmetry and Tensions in Teams

I found that one of the biggest barriers in achieving the objectives laid out in the philosophy of therapeutic jurisprudence comes from the bench and less frequently from other team members (e.g., prosecutors). Because of status differences, judges cannot be true team members. Tensions arise when judges are both performer and audience member. Those who insisted on playing both parts—audience and team member—undermined their courts. Judges are both part of the team and outside of the team and afforded higher status. Judges must appear impartial and dedicated to fairness and appropriate procedure. If too closely identified with the team, they surrender that posture. Ironically, it was usually the case that the less active judges were, the more that court process favored therapeutic over antitherapeutic effects. When a judge was acting as a leader, it was to reinforce cultural norms about the fundamental therapeutic focus and notions of procedural justice. For MHCs to fulfill their therapeutic and collaboration goals, status differences need to be reduced. This is particularly true for judges, who may perhaps need to more fully "cast their robes aside,"[47] or even be excluded from parts of the therapeutic teamwork; judges can and need to be symapthetic to therapeutic goals but not necessarily its main practitioners. Judges who embrace therapeutic jurisprudence and procedural justice—giving cleints a "voice"—are the cornerstone of an effective MHC.[48] Furthermore, the judge sets a relatonal tone focused on human dignity, highlighting the court's belief in the client's ability to change.[49]

In some ways, the judge can be seen as the "director" who drives the court performance, but this can be done in a way that allows the team to lead. Judicial demeanor is crucial for therapeutic outcomes and for successful teamwork. The judge sets the tone of the court and needs to develop a "benchside manner" consistent with therapeutic jurisprudence.[50] It matters how a judge translates this in working with the team and in social performances in the court. Judicial temperament that is "welcoming or good-natured"[51] is in line with therepeutic goals. The potential for paternalism[52] leads to antitherapeutic effects. Court observations revealed only rare occasions where judges were overly critical and personally judgmental, as seen in the following dialogue:[53]

> Judge: Why are you hanging around with him? I do not think he is
>   good for you.
> Client: I don't think that my boyfriend choice is a legal issue.

---

47. Perlin, *supra* note 31, at 5.

48. Ginger Lerner Wren, *Mental Health Courts: Serving Justice and Promoting Recovery*, 19 Ann. Health L. 577, 590 (2010).

49. Ginger Lerner Wren, A Court of Refuge: Stories from the Bench of America's First Mental Health Court (2018).

50. Bruce J. Winick, *Therapeutic Jurisprudence and Problem Solving Courts.(Special Series: Problem Solving Courts and Therapeutic Jurisprudence)*, 30 Ford. Urb. L. J. 1055, 1069 (2003).

51. Kathy Mack and Sharyn Roach Anleu, *Performing Impartiality: Judicial Demeanor and Legitimacy* , 35 Law & Soc'l Inq. 137, 148 (2010).

52. John Petrila, *Paternalism and the Unrealized Promise of Essays in Therapeutic Jurisprudence*, in Law in a therapeutic key: Developments in therapeutic jurisprudence 685, 685–88 (Bruce Winick and David Wexler eds., 1996).

53. Snedker, *supra* note 43, at 48–49.

Judge: Well, I am just suggesting that you be more careful about who you choose to spend time with for the sake of your recovery and stability.

After this exchange, the client was clearly offended by the line of questioning and hostile tone from the judge producing an anti-therapeutic outcome.

Asymmetry in the team and status inequalities can undermine the team's effectiveness. MHC teams involve members who are working collaborating but have different claims to status; these are more present during frontstage hearings. This built-in asymmetry makes it harder for a cohesive team to manage impressions before the audience, most notably clients. Judicial behavior sometimes gets in the way of therapeutic outcomes. Team members referenced status and deference by all parties directly attributed to "the black robe" they wear. Many MHCs deal with this asymmetry by the judge not wearing a robe and not being elevated in the courtroom. In fact, a judge suggested that MHCs success is related to relegating judges to a less prominent position: "The reason why they [MHCs] work is because instead of the judge, the prosecutor or the defense attorney is driving a case. It is more so the person being charged with a crime that is driving the case a lot more." Reflecting on this, he further commented that it took time to unlearn what he was taught. Using a sports metaphor, a different judge made a similar point about training for judges: "If you are soccer player, and all of a sudden you are going to play baseball, you need to learn." The implication is clear that legal expertise alone does not make one well equipped to preside effectively over an MHC.

Other judges did not resocialize as successfully, placing themselves firmly in the center of everything. One judge described himself in his judicial role as tending to be "hands-on" as "people look at you and say, 'Solve the problem for us.'" The social status and performance expectations clearly shaped how judges understand their position and influence social performances. However, the majority of judges admitted something like "effective judges are the ones that kind of stay out of the way!"

The consensus among team members was that, with a well-functioning team, judges can be less hands-on. While judges still act as the neutral arbiter of cases, effective judges should "trust the team recommendation" and "listen to the professionals." Part of the frontstage for judges is the recognition of backstage work. Moreover, the most therapeutic judges knew when to assert their authority and when to defer to team expertise in a collaborative manner. While several judges also expressed the view that they could be less directly involved, it was not always consistently practiced. There was often a disconnect between a judge's self-assessment and the team's evaluation. Besides attempts to exert status, multiple team members identified a judge's lack of awareness about mental illness and co-occurring disorders as an impediment to greater therapeutic exchanges. Other judges understood that, in the words of a judge, "it isn't about me." Relying on the team's recommendation and expertise was an adjustment for judges.

Concluding Thoughts

Goffman's understanding about microinteractions and social performances offer insights on how to build effective MHC teams. MHCs work best when team members express consensus on agreed-upon interpretations of the situation and engage in social performances that preserve status of other team members. Disagreement among team members generate the appearance of discord and rivalry. This spoils the collaborative and therapeutic message the that courts means to convey to clients and court participants. Thus, ineffective teams don't collaborate or appropriately defer to another team members status and expertise.

While judges play an important role in the team model, if the judge overshadows other members of the team, the MHC is less likely to deliver therapeutic outcomes. Within a well-functioning team, the judges' role is not at center stage, except in conducting formal judicial process, presiding over decision-making especially with regard to entrees and exits from the court, and presiding over ritual elements. Judges who refuse to defer to teams, accept their offstage advice, or try to join teams impair the performance. The goals of therapeutic jurisprudence lead to a shift in power dynamics, as witnessed through the precourt meeting, as well as judicial deference that is sometimes afforded to team members' expertise. Judges can enhance the standing of the team by deferring to its members' judgments. When this is done in a frontstage setting, it visibly heightens the status of the team and its credibility to clients.

Goffman's dramaturgical approach reveals why the philosophy of therapeutic jurisprudence works in practice. Whether or not MHCs achieve therapeutic outcomes depends on the teams working relationship and internalization of shared therapeutic goals. In sum, MHC teamwork reduces the elevated status of the judge for the benefit of the team and therapeutic outcomes that play out in both the front and back stages of social performances.

4

Therapeutic Jurisprudence in Swift and Certain Probation[1]

KELLY FRAILING, BRANDI ALFONSO, AND RAE TAYLOR

Introduction

As has been well covered elsewhere in this book, the concept of therapeutic jurisprudence (TJ) "focuses on the law's impact on emotional life and on psychological well-being."[2] TJ practices were first conceived and viewed in terms of mental health law. Over time, these practices have evolved to include other types of law and different aspects of the criminal justice system. One such aspect is problem-solving courts. Multiple studies have found participants of drug, mental health, and reentry courts have benefitted from TJ practices.[3] Following the use of TJ practices in problem-solving courts, there has been a push to begin utilizing these practices in more traditional courtroom settings. Some researchers have also discussed the benefits surrounding educating criminal justice professionals on TJ practices. For ex-

1. This study was funded by a Bureau of Justice Assistance Grant, number BJA-2016-SM-BX-0005. Portions appeared in K. Frailing, B. Alfonso, and R. Taylor, *Therapeutic Jurisprudence in Swift and Certain Probation*, 64 AMERICAN BEHAVIORAL SCIENTIST, 1749–67 (2020).

2. David B. Wexler, *Therapeutic Jurisprudence: An Overview*, 17 T. M. COOLEY L. REV. 125, 125 (2000); David B. Wexler and Bruce J. Winick, *Therapeutic Jurisprudence*, in PRINCIPLES OF ADDICTION MEDICINE (A. W. Graham ed., 4th ed. 2008).

3. Shannon Portillo et al., *Front-Stage Stars and Backstage Producers: The Role of Judges in Problem-Solving Courts*, 8 VICTIMS & OFFENDERS 1 (2013); Richard Wiener et al., *A Testable Theory of Problem Solving Courts: Avoiding Past Empirical and Legal Failures*, 33 INT'L J. L. & PSYCHIATRY 417 (2010); Jamey Hueston and Miriam Hutchins, *The Power of Compassion in the Court: Healing on Both Sides of the Bench*, 54 CT. REV. 96 (2018); KAREN SNEDKER, THERAPEUTIC JUSTICE: CRIME, TREATMENT COURTS AND MENTAL ILLNESS (2019).

ample, "compassion training can help judges focus on the humanity of the parties and remain solution focused when they struggle to find patience in contentious matters or seek the right words to explain a decision or ruling."[4] In fact, such education has already been shown to have a positive impact on courtroom proceedings and on participants.[5]

How TJ Can Manifest

A number of studies discuss the TJ techniques utilized by judges in how they address program participants. Judges who utilize TJ practices can communicate directly with defendants, who normally do not have a voice in the courtroom; this direct communication reverses that imbalance. Elements of procedural justice, including voice, validation, and voluntary participation, are essential in the effectiveness of TJ practices.[6] Research has shown that judges who utilize TJ practices judges convey compassion.[7] In order to implement the TJ technique of active listening, "it is important to abandon a paternalistic listening and speaking style in the courtroom and adopt a manner that communicates respect to the litigants and attorneys; this encourages people to feel comfortable speaking in court, giving voice to defendants, victims, and their families."[8] In problem-solving courts in particular, it is often the case that a team or court staff work together to assist in the success of the participant. In these instances, "all team members work collaboratively to eliminate issues (such as drug use) that are related to offending behaviors."[9] TJ practices also encourage the success and compliance of offenders while discouraging noncompliance and continued illicit behaviors. This is accomplished when "judges facilitate the meetings by freely

---

4. Hueston and Hutchins, *supra* note 3, at 99.

5. Risdon N. Slate et al., *Training Federal Probation Officers as Mental Health Specialists*, 68 FED. PROB. 9 (2004); Bruce J. Winick, *Foreword: Therapeutic Jurisprudence Perspectives on Dealing with Victims of Crime*, 33 NOVA L. REV. 536 (2009); Bruce J. Winick and David B. Wexler, *The Use of Therapeutic Jurisprudence in Law School Clinical Education: Transforming the Criminal Law Clinic*, 13 CLINICAL L. REV. 605 (2006); Shannon Portillo et al., *Front-Stage Stars and Backstage Producers: The Role of Judges in Problem-Solving Courts*, 8 VICTIMS & OFFENDERS 1, 1 (2013).

6. Amy D. Ronner, *The Learned-Helpless Lawyer: Clinical Legal Education and Therapeutic Jurisprudence as Antidotes to Bartleby Syndrome*, 24 TOURO L. REV. 601 (2013).

7. Jamey Hueston and Miriam Hutchins, *The Power of Compassion in the Court: Healing on Both Sides of the Bench*, 54 CT. REV. 96 (2018).

8. Michael D. Jones, *Mainstreaming Therapeutic Jurisprudence Into the Traditional Courts: Suggestions for Judges and Practitioners*, 5 PHOENIX L. REV. 753, 756 (2012).

9. Shannon Portillo et al., *Front-Stage Stars and Backstage Producers: The Role of Judges in Problem-Solving Courts*, 8 VICTIMS & OFFENDERS 1, 2 (2013).

interacting verbally with offenders, encouraging them to reach success benchmarks, and sanctioning them when they fail drug tests."[10] Other manifestations of TJ include judicial praise, family and friend attendance, graduation ceremonies, and applause upon achieving success or completion of a program.[11] These acts motivate not only the receiving participant but also participants in attendance, for example during status hearings.

The success these practices have produced in problem-solving courts implies they may also produce successes in more traditional court settings, particularly when the judge can provide time and attention to participants.[12] When courts operate appropriately in this manner, "they are the perfect example of how TJ can be translated into 'real life' in ways that ensure better outcomes for criminal defendants—mostly, but not all, who have been charged with misdemeanor and lower-level felonies—in ways that reduce recidivism and increase safety."[13]

TJ in Probation Programs

While research is limited, a few studies have discussed the presence of TJ practices in probation programs.[14] Compliance with probation conditions plays a large role in the success of TJ practices in probationary settings. As noted earlier in Perlin's conclusion about problem-solving courts, probationers' compliance also relies heavily on the judge's use of TJ practices when determining and setting such conditions.[15] "The way the judge behaves at a sentencing hearing can actually, in and of itself, affect how someone who has been given probation complies with the conditions of that probation."[16] The success of TJ techniques is also dependent on the dedication of the judge and court staff. We turn now to a discussion of a specific probation program and the ways in which we have observed TJ therein.

---

10. *Id.* at 3.

11. *Id.*

12. Michael L. Perlin, *"Have You Seen Dignity?" The Story of the Development of Therapeutic Jurisprudence*, 27 U.N.Z. L. Rev. 1135 (2017).

13. *Id.* at 7; *see* Michael L. Perlin, *"Who Will Judge the Many When the Game is Through?" Considering the Profound Differences between Mental Health Courts and "Tradition" Involuntary Civil Commitment Courts*, 41 Seattle L. Rev. 937 (2018).

14. Max Henshaw, Lorana Bartels, and Anthony Hopkins, *Set Up to Fail? Examining Australia's Approach to Parole Compliance through a Therapeutic Jurisprudence Lens*, 45 U. W. Austl. L. Rev. 107 (2019); J. C. Oleson, *HOPE Spring Eternal*, 15 Criminology & Pub. Pol'y 1163 (2016).

15. Perlin, *supra* note 12.

16. David B. Wexler, *Therapeutic Jurisprudence and Its Application to Criminal Justice Research and Development*, 7 Irish Prob. J. 94, 97 (2010).

The Swift and Certain Probation Program in Jefferson Parish, Louisiana

The Swift and Certain (SAC) probation program in Jefferson Parish, Louisiana,[17] is a HOPE-like[18] probation program that provides enhanced supervision alongside treatment and services for probationers at high risk of revocation. Those referred to SAC are assessed with a risk-assessment tool at the start of the program.[19] This risk-assessment tool is designed to reveal both criminogenic risks and needs, and then conditions of probation are set based on the results of that assessment. These include classes to address criminal thinking, substance abuse treatment, and employment assistance, among others. Like all HOPE-based programs, SAC requires frequent and random drug testing, and there are swift and certain sanctions for failing a drug test, as well as failing to comply with other requirements of probation. The sanctions are arguably proportionate; for example, failing a drug test carries a greater number of jail days as a sanction than does disclosing before the test that it will come back positive. Similarly, being late to court carries a much lighter sanction than does absconding.[20]

Participants are made aware of the details of the program during what is called a warning hearing, the first status hearing they attend once they join the program. During that hearing, they are made aware of the conditions of participation in SAC; this hearing also allows new participants to observe the interactions between the judge and the other participants who have been in the program longer. Participants then engage with the requirements of their probation and have monthly status hearings before the judge, where each participant has a one-on-one interaction with him or her. As noted, violations of the conditions of probation are swiftly and certainly sanc-

---

17. Jefferson Parish surrounds New Orleans, Louisiana, on the east and west.

18. HOPE, which stands for Honest Opportunity Probation with Enforcement, has several key features that distinguishes it from standard probation programs, including (1) frequent and random drug testing; (2) immediate brief jail sentences for failure to show for a drug test, failure of a drug test, or for noncompliance with other program rules; (3) a warning hearing at participants' first court appearance in the program where they are informed of the rules, the resources and supports available, and the sanctions for noncompliance; and (4) jail sentences for violations that are always applied and are applied immediately.

19. From 2016, the year of SAC's inception, until 2019, the program assessed participants after they were enrolled in the program, and the risk-assessment tool used was the COMPAS. In 2019, SAC changed protocol to assess risks and needs for those referred to the program prior to their enrollment, and it switched the tool to the RANT.

20. However, questions remain about proportionality when it comes to substances. A positive test for heroin, for example, carries the same number of jail days as a positive test for marijuana, an arguably much less serious substance.

tioned, but compliance with conditions is rewarded with praise from the judge and more rapid movement through the different phases of the program. Participants are provided with a handbook that provides them with this and other information.[21]

Methodology[22]

Court Observations

Beginning in March 2016, we (the authors) observed SAC monthly status hearings. We arrived before the start of the hearings and sat unobtrusively off to the side of the courtroom. We counted the number of times the judge issues praise to a participant, including phrases such as "keep up the good work," "keep up the hard work," "congratulations," "awesome," "awesome job," "good," "good job," "great," "great job," "way to go," we're proud of you," "way to come back," "keep it up," "keep working hard," "keep pushing," "keep fighting," "I'm impressed," and "you've come a long way." We also counted rounds of applause, which typically accompanied graduation from SAC and successful termination of probation, or phasing up, when a participant had earned enough points through compliance with probation requirements to move to the next of the four phases. Each subsequent phase in SAC is characterized by less intense supervision. Over the course of observing SAC status hearings, we were also able to uncover themes that developed over the course of some status hearing sessions as a result of the judge focusing on the same or similar topics over the course of the session.

Participant Surveys

To assess participant perceptions of SAC, we modified the survey utilized in the Multi Site Adult Drug Court (MADCE) study.[23] This survey was designed to assess participants' perceptions of the judge, their probation officers, and different elements of procedural justice, including voice, understanding,

---

21. SAC, *Swift and Certain Probation program handbook* (2020), https://static1.square space.com/static/5953f48c72af657ab9b59987/t/5e2f1dead995f925d7a1fe86/1580146155836 /SAC+Handbook+Final+Revised.2_2020_01_22.pdf.

22. This study received IRB approval from Loyola University New Orleans in 2016.

23. Kelli Henry, *The Role of Drug Court Participant Attitudes and Perceptions*, 3 MULTI SITE ADULT DRUG CT. EVALUATION (2011), https://www.urban.org/sites/default/files /publication/27376/412356-The-Multi-site-Adult-Drug-Court-Evaluation-The-Drug-Court -Experience.PDF.

neutrality, and dignity/respect.[24] Beginning in 2016, we administered the survey every six months to participants with the help of the social worker who serves as the case manager for participants in the SAC program. Completion of the survey was voluntary, and the SAC case manager assured participants who chose to complete the survey that their responses would remain confidential. We began by administering a pencil and paper version of the survey but switched to an electronic version in 2017. Across both versions, the survey was structured with a Likert scale that ranged from 1 to 5, where 1 was strongly disagree and 5 was strongly agree.

Results

Court Observations

At the beginning of the SAC status hearings, the judge used the opportunity of having most participants in the courtroom to address issues that pertained to the group as a whole. For example, as the program incorporated more online communication requirements, the judge told the group that they needed to register and confirm their email addresses in the program's website. The judge also used the start of the hearings to introduce service providers who were available to meet with participants as needed, such as staff from the parish's Human Service Authority. Another time, a participant had recently been killed while at a bar; the judge used that opportunity to remind participants that court requirements were in place in part to keep participants safe. When a program graduate overdosed and died shortly after graduating, the judge used this incident to encourage participants to reach out to court staff or to service providers when they felt the urge to use.

The judge started his interaction with each participant by asking "How are you?" or "How's it going?" and then moved on to subsequent questions, including those pertaining to work, abstinence from drugs and alcohol, classes, and electronic communication. The judge incorporated information from the staffings held just before the court session into his interaction with participants, for example "I hear you're doing very well," perhaps conveying to participants that information about adherence to court requirements is shared among court staff. Participants were given the chance to respond to

24. The MADCE survey has been successfully modified for previous research on specialty court participant perceptions, e.g., Kelly Frailing and Diana Carreon, *Quiero Hablar Con Usted en Espanol, Juez: The Importance of Spanish at a Majority Hispanic Drug Court*, 27 CRIMINAL JUSTICE POL'Y REVIEW 164 (2016).

the judge's questions and ask questions of their own. When participants were meeting their court requirements, the individual status hearings went very quickly, in less than two minutes in most cases.

However, the individual status hearings went more slowly when participants had not met court requirements, and the judge took that opportunity to remind individual participants of the importance of adhering to requirements. For example, he sternly told a participant to "never ever miss court, never ever miss a drug test." Another participant had yet to start his required classes; the judge told him, "Start immediately; these are not options. Otherwise, you will go in the box," [be held for a jail sanction]. The judge also told another late participant who said he was drug testing when court started, "If you lie to me, you're going to jail immediately." Yet another late participant, who smirked when he was ordered to twenty hours of community service for his tardiness, was told by the judge, "You did very poorly on probation, and now you're backed up on four or five years [in prison]. Would you rather have twenty hours of community service or four to five years at hard labor?" The tone of these interactions may serve as a wider reminder for all participants in the courtroom at the time to adhere to requirements.

For those SAC participants who were meeting their court requirements, the judge issued praise liberally. Examples of this praise include those provided earlier, and Table 4.1 shows how frequently the judge took the opportunity to praise victories both large, such as phasing up or graduating, and small, such as maintaining sobriety, obtaining new employment, or reconnecting with family members. Participants who phased up or who graduated had their achievement recognized with a certificate from and a handshake with the judge, as well as a round of applause from those in attendance. These affirmative displays are a hallmark manifestation of TJ.

Beginning in August 2017, the judge began issuing what can be thought of as soft sanctions to a few participants. These were additional requirements that appeared to be in the interest of promoting participants' sobriety. For example, these included once-a-week Narcotics Anonymous (NA) meetings, immediate drug tests, intensive outpatient treatment, and twice a week drug screens. Soft sanctions were also observed in subsequent status hearings. Beginning in September of that year, the judge began issuing what can be thought of as soft rewards to some participants. The primary soft reward was permission to skip the following month's status hearing because the participants were doing so well in meeting their court requirements; this soft reward was given to six participants in September and to others in subsequent status hearings.

TABLE 4.1 PRAISE AND ROUNDS OF APPLAUSE DURING SAC STATUS HEARINGS

Month and Year	Number of Praises	Number of Rounds of Applause
January 2017	20	0
July 2017	20	3
August 2017	51	7
September 2017	92	13
October 2017	47	3
November 2017	69	16
December 2017	43	4
(PARTIAL) TOTAL FOR 2017	342	46
January 2018	25	8
February 2018	25	8
March 2018	24	1
April 2018	50	6
May 2018	24	0
June 2018	19	2
July 2018	19	0
August 2018	7	0
September 2018	37	0
October 2018	16	0
November 2018	16	0
December 2018	41	0
TOTAL FOR 2018	303	25
January 2019	53	0
February 2019	60	0
March 2019	41	0
April 2019	29	7
May 2019	20	4
June 2019	66	7
July 2019	15	7
August 2019 (substitute judge)	45	2
September 2019 (substitute judge)	61	9
October 2019 (substitute judge)	13	15
November 2019	42	8
December 2019	53	14
TOTAL FOR 2019	498	73

Wittingly or otherwise, a theme seemed to emerge during some of the status hearing sessions. In July 2017, the judge's comments to participants coalesced around changes they may have experienced as a result of participation in the program. He asked questions and made comments such as "How are you thinking?" "Tell me about the first time you saw me versus today," "How does it feel different?" "Tell me about your journey. What have you learned?" "How has your journey been?" "What have you been doing to change things?" and "How is it living clean?" The judge occasionally used participants' responses to emphasize the importance and benefits of change to the larger group, especially earlier on in the SAC status hearing process when more participants were still present in the courtroom. For example, he told one participant, "SAC is to change you, not just keep you out of jail," and he told another, "If we don't start thinking for good, we go back to the old ways."

In August 2017, the judge's comments to participants coalesced around their decision-making and the fact that court staff cares about them and their success in the program. For example, he said to one participant, "I heard you made awesome decisions, that you reached out when you needed help." He told another, "I heard you are making good decisions," and he told another, "Good job reaching out to your probation officer." The judge focused his subsequent comments on the support system that is implied by making the decision to call for help when challenges arise. These comments included "We are here to support you," "Call for help," "Ask for help," "If you have any issues, any indications [of relapsing], call," "Everyone has struggles; it's important you know we are here to support you," and "If you have any issues, call." For one participant whose drug tests had shown traces the last few times, he said, "So do one of two things, reach out for help, or wait until I catch you, and we'll have a very different conversation. You see throughout the hearings that all of us care about you. You want to use, I get it, but call before you use."

In February 2018, the judge began by congratulating participants as a whole for largely staying clean and sober during the Mardi Gras holiday. This set the tone for his subsequent comments to participants, which coalesced around the notion that recovery from drug and alcohol dependence is a struggle and that the SAC Probation Program and all of the services provided through it are there to help participants struggle well. Perhaps to emphasize this point, judge elicited one graduate's story of his time in SAC. The graduate noted, "It was tough, but I stayed focused, I persevered. I stayed clean and sober and focused on the big picture and what's import important to me and my life. I am a changed man, a better man." The judge stayed focused on the idea of struggling well throughout his interactions with subsequent participants. For example, he told one participant, "Don't struggle alone; that's why there's all this [services and resources] around you." He reminded another to reach out for the help he needs because "it's a struggle," but "you're never alone." The judge reminded another participant who was experiencing stress as a result of some life challenges, "The whole point is exactly what you're doing. It's a struggle your whole life." And he encouraged another participant's sobriety when she admitted to being in pain: "But you're not using. You're struggling well."

These themes, all of which focus on longer-term change in some way and confirm court staff's commitment to supporting desirable longer-term change for participants, are another though possibly more indirect manifestation of TJ.

Participant Surveys

Tables 4.2, 4.3, and 4.4 present the results of the participant surveys. Over the various administrations, forty-eight participants completed the survey, which is a response rate of approximately 48 percent.

Perceptions of the judge, of probation officers, and of procedural justice are generally positive and for the most part become more positive over time. It is particularly interesting for the purposes of this chapter that the percep-

TABLE 4.2 ATTITUDES TOWARD THE JUDGE			
	Baseline (N = 7)	Six Months (N = 19)	12 or More Months (N = 15)
The judge is knowledgeable about your case	4.14	4.64	4.75
The judge knows you by name	4	4.84	4.6
The judge helps you to succeed	4	4.55	4.81
The judge emphasizes the importance of treatment and services	4.43	4.59	4.88
The judge is intimidating and unapproachable	3	1.65	1.98
The judge remembers your situation and needs from hearing to hearing	4.14	4.38	4.5
The judge gives you a chance to tell your side of the story	4	4.39	4.21
The judge treats you fairly	4	4.54	4.55
The judge treats you with respect	4.14	4.55	4.75

TABLE 4.3 ATTITUDES TOWARD PROBATION OFFICER

	Baseline (N = 7)	Six Months (N = 19)	12 or More Months (N = 15)
Your probation officer is knowledgeable about your case	4.57	4.77	4.25
Your probation officer knows you by name	4.57	4.89	4.94
Your probation officer helps you to succeed	4.14	4.6	4.88
Your probation officer emphasizes the importance of treatment and services	4.29	4.71	4.94
Your probation officer gives you a chance to tell your side of the story	4.14	4.67	4.88
Your probation officer treats you fairly	4.29	4.72	4.88
Your probation officer treats you with respect	4.43	4.72	4.88

TABLE 4.4 PROCEDURAL JUSTICE

	Baseline (N = 7)	Six Months (N = 19)	12 or More Months (N = 15)
You have the opportunity to express your views in court (V)	4	4.47	4.24
You felt too intimidated or scared to say what you really felt in court (V)	2.71	2.79	2.75
People in the court spoke up on your behalf (V)	3.43	3.29	4.17
The court took account of what you said in its decision (V)	3.86	3.87	3.94
You had a lot of influence over the decision reached in court (V)	3.86	2.49	3.25
You had enough control over the way things went in court (V)	3.14	3.39	3.8
You understood what happened in court (U)	3.86	4.24	4.24
You understood your rights in the case (U)	3.86	4.2	4.02
All sides had a fair chance to bring the facts up in court (N)	3.43	3.74	4.15
You felt that people were treated the same way by the court (N)	3.86	3.68	4.22
You were disadvantaged in court because of your age, income, sex, race or some other reason (N)	1.86	1.02	2.77

TABLE 4.4 PROCEDURAL JUSTICE (CONTINUED)			
	Baseline (N = 7)	Six Months (N = 19)	12 or More Months (N = 15)
You felt pushed around in court by people with more power than you (D/R)	2.14	2.15	3.02
During court, you felt pushed into things you didn't agree with (D/R)	2.14	2.74	3.34
You were treated unfairly by the court (D/R)	1.71	1.6	2.79
People were polite to you in court (D/R)	4.29	4.33	4.5
You were treated with respect in the court (D/R)	3.57	4.11	4.5
Your rights were respected in the court (D/R)	3.57	4.25	4.17
The court got the facts of your case wrong	2.71	2.78	2.67

Note: V is voice, U is understanding, N is neutrality, D/R is dignity/respect.

tions of probation officers are even more positive of those than the judge on the items that are directly comparable. This indicates that both the judge and the probation officers are sources of manifestations of TJ in this probation program.

However, there are some concerning findings when it comes to participant perceptions of procedural justice, particularly across some of the neutrality and dignity/respect items. Participants' perceptions of disadvantage based on demographic factors, of feeling pushed around, pushed into things not agreed to, and being treated unfairly became more negative as their time in SAC progressed. It is reasonable to see these perceptions as potential (or actual) threats to the way TJ is manifested in this court.

Discussion

Observations of SAC status hearings and surveys of participants reveal that TJ is clearly manifest in this particular HOPE-based probation program. The judge's frequent use of praise and the themes that emerge during some of the status hearings are evidence of a patient and caring judge. Judge Steve Alm, the architect of HOPE probation, contends that a successful HOPE program is a "three-legged stool," where probation officers and treatment providers, a patient and caring judge, and sanctions for violations operate in concert to provide a structured program that gives the participants the best chance at successful completion of probation. He emphasizes the equal importance of the three legs and notes that while the sanctions component is indeed critical, the rewards system and consistent encouragement by the judge and probation officers are just as essential.[25]

Interestingly, Bartels notes that some HOPE and HOPE-based probation programs do not utilize status hearings, which would serve to minimize participants' interaction with the judge.[26] The monthly status hearings that are a key part of SAC provide an opportunity for participants to hear from and speak directly to the judge on a regular basis. We believe the status hearings and the participants' experience therein are the basis for participants' generally positive ratings of the judge on the survey.

Status hearings likely have a direct impact on participants' perceptions of the judge, as well as on their perceptions of procedural justice, which are generally positive, but there are some potentially troubling exceptions, as noted earlier. However, TJ is also clearly manifested in participants' interactions with their probation officers. Survey respondents rated their probation officers even more positively than they did the judge on items that were directly comparable. This manifestation of TJ is almost certainly rooted in probation officers' relationships with participants. Though the HOPE model means less discretion in their decision making for those on their caseload, probation officers working in a HOPE model may have the opportunity to "form a therapeutic alliance" with those under their supervision, and that appears to be what is occurring in the SAC program.[27]

In this way, the SAC program has become suffused with TJ and its hallmark aspect of procedural justice. Programs in which TJ is successfully manifested typically have a judge that embodies TJ, but it is unclear what would happen to that embodiment or to those programs if the judge were to leave the bench.[28] In the SAC program, TJ is also clearly manifested in participants' interactions and relationships with their probation officers, which is likely important to the early success of the program[29] and indicates that TJ is now an integral part of SAC.

---

25. Personal communication from Steven S. Alm, Cir. Ct. Judge (July 16, 2018).

26. Lorana Bartels, *HOPE-ful Bottles: Examining the Potential for Hawaii's Opportunity Probation with Enforcement (HOPE) to Help Mainstream Therapeutic Jurisprudence*, 63 INT'L J. L. & PSYCHIATRY 26 (2019).

27. Steven S. Alm, *HOPE Probation: Fair Sanctions, Evidence-Based Principles, and Therapeutic Alliances*, 15 CRIMINOLOGY & PUB. POL'Y 1195, 1677 (2016).

28. Michael L. Perlin, *"The Judge, He Cast His Robe Aside": Mental Health Courts, Dignity, and Due Process*, 3 MENTAL HEALTH LAW & POL'Y J. 1 (2013).

29. Kelly Frailing, Victoria Rapp, and Rae Taylor, *Swift and Certain Probation as a HOPE-like Model: Progress toward Goals and Lingering Challenges*, CORRECTIONS: POL'Y, PRACTICE AND RESEARCH (2020), https://doi.org/10.1080/23774657.2020.1807425.

Conclusion

Participants' experiences with and perceptions of the SAC program appear to be generally positive, in part resulting from the meaningful, deliberate way in which TJ and procedural justice are suffused throughout the program. Of course, this type of intensive supervision where both the judge and probation officer can invest a good deal of time and resources into participants is not scalable for most jurisdictions in the United States, where probation caseloads are notoriously high. However, this approach to TJ is certainly possible in smaller, specialized probation programs like that described here. We are hopeful for the wider adoption of this approach, and we look forward to additional research in this area that empirically examines the value of TJ.

5

The Value of Remorse as a Therapeutic Tool for Probation Officers in Sentencing

COLLEEN M. BERRYESSA AND ASHLEY BALAVENDER

Introduction

Remorse, defined as verbal or nonverbal expressions of regret, communicates "a distressing emotion that arises from acceptance of personal responsibility for an act of harm against another person."[1] The field of psychology has long argued remorse's bearing on rehabilitative potential.[2] Punishment decisions typically involve similar explorations into whether a defendant is capable of and amenable to moral reform.[3] Censuring one's own behavior through remorse is akin to "splitting of the self into a blameworthy part and a part that stands back and sympathizes with the blame giving."[4] In condemning one's own behavior, through remorse, a defendant signals good character and unites with law-abiders in their disapproval.[5] Given what remorse is thought to potentially convey about a defendant's character, expressions of sincere remorse have been suggested to act as effective "therapeutic tools" in the criminal-legal process that signal the po-

---

1. Rocksheng Zhong, *Judging Remorse*, 39 NYU REV. L. & SOC'L CHANGE 137 (2015).

2. Tony Ward, Kathryn Fox, and Melissa Garber, *Restorative Justice, Offender Rehabilitation and Desistance*, 2 RESTORATIVE JUSTICE 36 (2014).

3. Paul H. Robinson, Sean E. Jackowitz, and Daniel M. Bartels, *Extralegal Punishment Factors: A Study of Forgiveness, Hardship, Good Deeds, Apology, Remorse, and Other Such Discretionary Factors in Assessing Criminal Punishment*, 65 VANDERBILT L. REV. 751 (2012).

4. ERVING GOFFMAN, RELATIONS IN PUBLIC 113 (1971).

5. Margareth Etienne and Jennifer K. Robbennolt, *Apologies and Plea Bargaining*, 91 MARQUETTE LAW REVIEW 295–301 (2007).

tential for defendant rehabilitation, as well as community and victim healing.[6] As such, it has been argued that evaluations of remorse should be adopted and integrated into decision-making processes at different stages of the criminal-legal process, and particularly at sentencing.[7]

This chapter examines the therapeutic role of remorse, as well as forgiveness, in the context of probation officer decision-making with particular regard to presentencing reports. We argue that probation officers should evaluate and recognize remorse as a therapeutic tool that can provide genuine evidence of defendants' potential for restoration with victims and reintegration into the community during sentencing. Ultimately, we look to provide three recommendations for probation officers on how to adopt therapeutic jurisprudence (TJ) approaches toward remorse in their interactions with their clients when crafting their presentencing reports and in their sentencing recommendations.

The Therapeutic Role of Remorse for Criminal Justice

In the general sense, displays of true remorse convey responsibility for the harm of one's bad actions and recognition of how such actions impact others.[8] Arguably the most important indicator of sincere remorse is actively changing one's future behavior.[9] Words and verbal expressions of remorse are empty and appear insincere unless they are backed by actions.[10] Thus, one may not be able to evaluate the sincerity or quality of a person's remorse until observing his or her later behavior.[11] Sincere expressions of remorse are at the core of forgiveness; when persons or entities harmed by a person's actions accept his or her displays as an apology, they may wish to show compassion.[12] Together, remorse and forgiveness are considered a two-step "core sequence" of how to resolve conflicts and instill symbolic reparation.[13]

---

6. Susan Daicoff, *Apology, Forgiveness, Reconciliation and Therapeutic Jurisprudence*, 13 Pepperdine Dispute Res. L.J. 131 (2013).

7. Stephanos Bibas and Richard A. Bierschbach, *Integrating Remorse and Apology into Criminal Procedure*, 114 Yale L.J. 98 (2004).

8. Jonathan R. Cohen, *Advising Clients to Apologize*, 72 S. Cal. L. Rev. 1014 (1999).

9. Nick Smith, *Against Court-Ordered Apologies*, 16 New Crim. L. Rev. 43 (2013).

10. *Id. See* Nick Smith, *Just Apologies: An Overview of the Philosophical Issues*, 13 Pepperdine Dispute Res. L. J. 35 (2013).

11. Nick Smith, *Against Court-Ordered Apologies*, 16 New Crim. L. Rev. 43 (2013).

12. Daicoff, *supra* note 6, at 137–38.

13. Thomas Scheff, *Community Conferences: Shame and Anger in Therapeutic Jurisprudence*, 67 Revista Juridica U.P.R. 102 (1998).

In the context of the criminal justice system, the remorse–forgiveness sequence is at the core of criminal cases and is thought to act as a therapeutic tool in the criminal-legal process that signals the potential for community and victim healing, as well as defendant rehabilitation.[14] The utility of remorse falls in line with the goals of TJ as an approach that engages the law, criminal-legal processes, and legal decision-makers as beneficial mechanisms for enhancing well-being, healing, and restoration.[15] It is within this framework that remorse leads to resolution by fostering reconciliation, rehabilitation, and reintegration in two different ways.[16]

First, a defendant's remorse about his or her criminal behavior acts as a moral awakening, including the willingness to follow legal norms, to cooperate with different social groups, and to seek reconciliation with victims and the larger community.[17] In the criminal justice system, the remorse–forgiveness sequence actually occurs between the defendant, victim, and community, as the criminal justice system "speaks for" these parties in its punishment decisions.[18] In criminal contexts, remorse may act as "a vehicle to adjust an imbalance of power in a relationship that occurs when a wrong is committed by a party to the relationship."[19] It does this by helping to diminish shame, guilt, and anger, both in defendants as well as those who have been harmed (i.e. victims and the community), which helps each individual progress past negative, unhealthy, and dysfunctional emotions, including anger, grief, or denial.[20] Further, expressions of remorse help to shift responsibility for harm away from the victim and community to the defendant, which fosters healthier emotional and psychological well-being of those harmed.[21] This aids the defendant's reintegration process back into the community and promotes healing.[22]

Second, remorse represents a therapeutic tool for and signals not only amenability to reconciliation but also rehabilitation and, correspondingly, reintegration into the community.[23] While several factors influence character assessments (i.e., criminal record, social background), remorse is

---

14. *Id. See* Daicoff, *supra* note 6.

15. Daicoff, *supra* note 6, at 153–56.

16. *Id.*

17. Hong Lu and Terance D. Miethe, *Confessions and Criminal Case Din China*, 37 LAW & SOC'Y REV. 551 (2003).

18. Daicoff, *supra* note 6, at 164–66.

19. Daniel W. Shuman, *The Role of Apology in Tort Law*, 83 JUDICATURE 183 (2000).

20. Robin Wellford Slocum, *The Dilemma of the Vengeful Client: A Prescriptive Framework for Cooling the Flames of Anger*, 92 MARQUETTE L. REV. 487–97 (2009).

21. Shuman, *supra* note 19, at 183–84.

22. Scheff, *supra* note 13, at 103–4.

23. Daicoff, *supra* note 6, at 143.

thought to be particularly helpful in illuminating the complex relationships between criminal behavior and character in the criminal-legal process.[24] Remorse signals the degree to which a defendant understands, condemns, and regrets the effects of his or her actions.[25] If a defendant conveys sincere remorse, the implicit or explicit assumption is that his or her criminality is an anomaly that is not reflective of his or her character and that he or she can be successfully reformed to exhibit his or her "true" character.[26]

This suggests that remorse acts as a therapeutic device allowing for "re-integrative shaming,"[27] through which defendants engage with and move past their negative emotions into acknowledging their full responsibility for and denunciation of their bad behaviors, and correspondingly into community reacceptance.[28] Indeed, the remorse–forgiveness sequence is key in assessing the potential for individual rehabilitation, aiding in a defendant's process of community reintegration by allowing victims and the community to feel more positive about a defendant's return and his or her future contributions to the community.[29] However, if the defendant fails to display remorse, or it is thought to be disingenuous, decision-makers involved in the criminal-legal process, as well as victims and members of the community, may assume that the defendant's criminality was a product of his or her true character, meaning he or she represents a risk to safety, may not be amenable to rehabilitation, or may not be able to positively contribute to the community moving forward.[30]

Ultimately, expressions of remorse, as an indicator for both reconciliation (i.e., victim and community healing) and rehabilitation (i.e., reforming a defendant's character) potential, may lead members of the criminal justice system, "speaking for" the community and victims, to rethink a defendant's punishment as recognition and reward for his or her remorse and what it signals about his or her therapeutic potential.[31] Indeed, remorse allows those making decisions regarding a defendant's punishment to see the human side of a defendant, which encapsulates the necessary social bond for

---

24. *See* Richard Weisman, *Being and Doing: The Judicial Use of Remorse to Construct Character and Community*, 18 Soc'l & Leg. Stud. 47 (2009).

25. Etienne and Robbennolt, *supra* note 5, at 295–301.

26. Weisman, *supra* note 24, at 50–52.

27. *See generally* John Braithwaite, *Shame and Criminal Justice*, 42 Canad. J. Criminol. 281 (2000).

28. Daicoff, *supra* note 6, at 144.

29. *Id.*

30. Weisman, *supra* note 24, at 55–57.

31. *See* Bill Wringe, *Collective Agents and Communicative Theories of Punishment*, 43 J. Soc'l Phil. 436 (2012).

both forgiveness and reconciliation with the community.[32] Thus, literature cumulatively suggests that evaluations of remorse, as a therapeutic tool in the criminal-legal process, are likely to be exceedingly relevant, and potentially most influential, when deciding a defendant's punishment at the sentencing stage.[33]

Relevance of Remorse to Probation Officers During Sentencing

Judges are thought to be both consciously and unconsciously influenced by displays of remorse when making sentencing decisions.[34] In fact, the U.S. Sentencing Commission guidelines dedicate its sentencing adjustments section to "Acceptance of Responsibility," which allows judges to weigh a defendant's responsibility and remorse in their potential consideration of whether reduced sentences are merited.[35] The provision itself states that "the sentencing judge is in a unique position to evaluate a defendant's acceptance of responsibility. For this reason, the determination of the sentencing judge is entitled to great deference on review."[36]

Judges can be influenced during sentencing by displays of remorse that they themselves observe in their courtrooms,[37] but arguably it is perhaps more likely that judges' sentencing decisions may be influenced by probation officers' portrayals of defendants' remorse, as written in their presentencing reports.[38] Before sentencing, probation officers are tasked with writing reports that assess the legal and social background of defendants; such reports are used by probation officers to communicate whether there are extenuating circumstances, either positive or negative, that they believe judges should consider when deciding the severity of defendants' sentences.[39] As judges do not have a significant amount of time to assess or interact with defendants and their backgrounds, presentencing reports are usually one of, if not the

---

32. Scheff, *supra* note 13, at 103–4.

33. *See* Steven Keith Tudor, *Why Should Remorse Be a Mitigating Factor in Sentencing?* 2 CRIM. L. & PHIL. 241 (2008).

34. Zhong, *supra* note 1, at 168–71.

35. Christopher Bennett, *The Role of Remorse in Criminal Justice*, in OXFORD HANDBOOKS ONLINE IN CRIMINOLOGY AND CRIMINAL JUSTICE 3 (2016).

36. *Id.* at 3–4.

37. Weisman, *supra* note 24.

38. *See* Kriss A. Drass and J. William Spencer, *Accounting for Pre-Sentencing Recommendations: Typologies and Probation Officers Theory of Office*, 34 SOC'L PROBS. 277 (1987).

39. *See* Caren Wakerman Converse, *Unpoetic Justice: Ideology and the Individual in the Genre of the Presentence Investigation*, 26 J. BUSINESS & TECH. COMMUN. 442 (2012).

main, factors used by the court when determining appropriate sentences.[40] In addition, presentencing reports also serve many other purposes beyond sentencing related to punishment, such as aiding in decisions on which type or level of institution a defendant will serve his or her sentence and in determining a defendant's eligibility for specific rehabilitative and/or correctional programs.[41]

Although probation officers may touch upon defendants' remorse displays in their presentencing reports, remorse is not currently a common factor assessed by probation officers in their interactions with defendants, and more often than not, even if it is expressed, it is not conveyed in presentencing reports.[42] Given that remorse acts as a therapeutic tool in the criminal-legal process that signals the potential for healing, rehabilitation, and reintegration,[43] evaluations of remorse, using a TJ approach, may have immense utility to probation officers in not only improving their interactions and understandings of their clients but also when making their recommendations in their presentencing reports. Thus, as discussed later, we believe that probation officers should actively understand the therapeutic relevance of remorse within the TJ framework, as well as how they might best integrate it into their reports and decision-making moving forward.

Considering Remorse as a Therapeutic Tool: Recommendations for Probation Officers

We argue that probation officers should actively investigate, craft, and integrate "remorse-based narratives" about defendants, as their clients, into their presentencing reports and sentencing recommendations to the court, as well as potential for reconciliation, rehabilitation, and reintegration. To that end, we outline three key recommendations for probation officers: (1) formally assessing for remorse in their clients; (2) reporting on their clients' remorse, or lack thereof, to the court; and (3) leveraging both assessments and reports to facilitate restorative justice and rehabilitation.

---

40. John Hagan, *The Social and Legal Construction of Criminal Justice: A Study of the Pre-Sentencing Process*, 22 Soc'l Probs. 623 (1975).

41. Stephen A. Fennell and William N. Hall, *Due Process at Sentencing: An Empirical and Legal Analysis of the Disclosure of Presentence Reports in Federal Courts*, 93 Harv. L. Rev. 1616, 1627–28 (1980).

42. *See* Ronald S. Everett and Barbara C. Nienstedt, *Race, Remorse, and Sentence Reduction: Is Saying You're Sorry Enough?*, 16 Just. Q. 99 (1999).

43. *See* Daicoff, *supra* note 6.

1. Assessing for Remorse

Probation officers are uniquely positioned to assess for remorse because they have more time to evaluate a defendant than judges do and are likely to have built a relationship with the defendant.[44] However, as with most human emotions, expression of remorse can vary from person to person and is identified subjectively.[45] Remorse can be displayed by a defendant in a number of different ways, from verbal expressions to body language and, most important, rehabilitative or reparative behaviors that often signal desistance.[46] We offer the following categories of displays for probation officers to consider when evaluating their clients for remorse.

- **Verbal Displays:** Gives an apology; discusses the harms caused and to whom; takes responsibility for their actions as voluntary; expresses the desire, or the desire to make a plan, to make things right; expresses the desire for forgiveness.[47]
- **Affective Displays:** Cries; covers face; shows emotional facial expressions and body language. It is important to remember that affective displays need not be overstated and may be subtle.[48]
- **Behavioral Displays:** Makes an apology or reparations (financial or otherwise) to the victim(s); makes attempts to give back to the community; makes efforts to improve oneself or one's situation (e.g., seeking employment, rehabilitative programs); shows sustained behavioral changes over time.[49]

Conversely, identifying a clear lack of remorse can be equally important.

- **Verbal Displays:** Shows denial; makes justifications for the crime (as opposed to contextual explanation); blames the victim; expresses anger about/lack of acceptance of their current legal situations.[50]
- **Affective Displays:** Exhibits "crocodile tears" or false emotion displays; shows overstated, sometimes showy emotional reactions;

---

44. Hagan, *supra* note 40.

45. Zhong, *supra* note 1, at 167.

46. *See generally* Kate Rossmanith, *Affect and the Judicial Assessment of Offenders*, 21 BODY & SOCIETY 167–93 (2015); Shadd Maruna, *Elements of Successful Desistance Signaling*, 11 CRIMINOL. & PUBLIC POL'Y 73–86 (2012).

47. MICHAEL PROEVE AND STEVEN TUDOR, REMORSE: PSYCHOLOGICAL AND JURISPRUDENTIAL PERSPECTIVES 107 (2010).

48. *Id.* at 43.

49. *Id.* at 96–97.

50. *Id.* at 107.

may show emotional displays incongruent to their verbal or behavioral displays.[51]

- **Behavioral Displays**: Shows resistance to apologizing, making reparations, or engaging with rehabilitation; does not show up for assigned programs; does not follow through with commitments to
change; shows repeated or increasingly deviant behavior.[52]

It is worth noting, but outside the scope of this chapter to fully discuss, that
mixed verbal, affective, or behavioral displays do not necessarily negate remorse displays. Behavioral change often takes time, and some people, such as
those with mental illness, may be unable to conventionally express emotions
associated with remorse, such as sadness or regret, in a socially accepted manner.[53] Indeed, through social and cultural experiences, we have been taught to
expect individuals to exhibit certain features or emotions if they feel remorse
and if it is genuine, including "submission, obedience, invisibility, silence, and
the tacit acceptance of blame."[54] However, it is important for probation officers,
as well as other court personnel, to recognize that assessing remorse is a "subjective process that provides fertile ground for cognitive bias"[55] and that all
defendants, even those that are truly remorseful, may not exhibit all or even
some of the expected verbal, affective, or behavioral displays of remorse.[56]
As remorse displays are not one-size-fits all and may be shaped by a client's
age, gender, class, cultural norms, or even manner of speaking,[57] we encourage probation officers to critically think about how a client's social position
and characteristics could influence not only his or her remorse displays but
also how his or her remorse is being understood and assessed by the officer.

For example, if a client is engaged in mental health treatment as a term
of probation that involves taking psychotropic medications, these medications can blunt or disrupt normal functioning of his or her feelings-expres-
sion systems.[58] If a client is taking such medications, he or she may not ex-

---

51. *Id.* at 43–44.
52. *Id.* at 96–97.
53. Zhong, *supra* note 1, at 170–71.
54. Van Cleve Nicole Gonzalez, Crook County: Racism and Injustice in America's Largest Criminal Court 65 (2017).
55. M. Eve Hanan, *Remorse Bias*, 83 Missouri L. Rev. 308 (2018).
56. *Id.*
57. *Id.* at 308–9.
58. *See, e.g.*, Michael L. Perlin, *"Merchants and Thieves, Hungry for Power": Prosecutorial
Misconduct and Passive Judicial Complicity in Death Penalty Trials of Defendants with Mental
Disabilities*, 73 Wash. & Lee L. Rev. 1501, 1531–32 (2016), discussing Justice Kennedy's con-
currence in Riggins v. Nevada, 504 U.S. 127, 144 (1992), relying, on this issue, on the research
reported in William Geimer and Jonathan Amsterdam, *Why Jurors Vote Life or Death: Op-*

hibit traditional, or perhaps any, remorse displays that conform to social expectations due to the effects of drugs on his or her emotional state,[59] and not necessarily due to a lack, or disingenuous feelings, of remorse. Thus, we encourage probation officers to thoroughly look into their clients' records and past experiences to be informed and cognizant of clients' characteristics or circumstances that could potentially affect remorse displays and assessments.

As active behavioral change is perhaps the most potent indicator of sincere remorse, it is also important to remember that assessing for remorse takes time and relationship building.[60] To that end, we recommend officers incorporate assessments of remorse into any initial intake processes and especially in keeping regular case notes. A practice of recording expressions of remorse over time not only may aid in assessing for sincere remorse in one's clients but also will facilitate writing presentencing reports and giving recommendations that effectively articulate a client's level of remorse, or lack thereof. Indeed, given what remorse is thought to potentially convey about character,[61] expressions of sincere remorse over time may help to articulate the therapeutic nature of a client's remorse and whether it may signal potential for rehabilitation and reintegration.[62]

Note-taking practices might also assist officers in observing and combatting their own biases around groups or crimes that may be stereotypically associated with callousness or a general lack of remorse.[63] Ultimately, recording client displays of remorse or remorselessness will assist in more confident and expedient written recommendations that are in alignment with both a TJ framework and public safety.

2. Reporting Remorse

We also recommend that probation officers adopt the practice of formally and explicitly including assessments of clients' remorse in presentencing

---

erative Factors in Ten Florida Death Penalty Cases, 15 Am. J. Crim. L. 1, 51–53 (1988), and Michael L. Perlin and Mehgan Gallagher, *"Temptation's Page Flies out the Door": Navigating Complex Systems of Disability and the Law from a Therapeutic Jurisprudence Perspective*, 25 Buffalo Hum. Rts. L. Rev. 1, 11 n. 57 (2018–19) ("if the medication inhibits the defendant's capacity to react to the proceedings and to demonstrate 'remorse or compassion,' the prejudice suffered by the defendant can be especially acute").

59. Elcin Aydemir, Eda Aslan, and Mustafa Yazici, *SSRI Induced Apathy Syndrome*, 8 Psychiatry & Behav. Sci. 63 (2018).

60. Smith, *supra* note 9; Smith, *supra* note 10.

61. Weisman, *supra* note 24.

62. Maruna, *supra* note 46, at 78. *See generally* Tony Ward and Shadd Maruna, Rehabilitation: Beyond the Risk Paradigm (2007). Shadd Maruna and Hans Toch, Making Good How Ex-Convicts Reform and Rebuild Their Lives (2015).

63. Hanan, *supra* note 55, at 301.

reports and sentencing recommendations. Depending on the client, this might involve creating an individual section specifically for remorse assessments in presentencing reports. Specifically, we suggest what we consider some of the most important details for probation officers to note and include in documenting whether or not individual clients show remorse.

- Note whether remorse or lack of remorse is observed in a client.
- Note how remorse, or a lack of remorse, has been expressed or displayed (i.e., verbal, affective, behavioral) or if it is ambiguous/indeterminate. Particularly, direct quotes from clients showing their remorse or how they generally feel about their charges or current situations are especially beneficial. It is also important to note whether mental health or other issues might play a role in an assessment.[64]
- Note specific statements from clients regarding who has been harmed, what behaviors they are remorseful for, and why they are remorseful (i.e., the impact their actions had on the victim or community).
- Note "corroborating sources," or testimony from family, friends, religious leaders, treatment programs, and more, for these statements.[65]
- Make recommendations that include a client's plan for change or restitution, an assessment of a client's readiness for change, suggested rehabilitative programs or alternative therapeutic sentencing options, and/or perceived risk of violence or reoffending.

As remorse is culturally used to evaluate character and credibility when it comes to criminality, a client who is perceived as remorseful may be described as having experienced "errors in judgement" rather than as having intrinsic defects of character.[66] Conversely, if remorse is believed to be absent or insincere, and that criminality is a product of the client's intrinsic character, he or she may be described as potentially dangerous and recidivistic.[67] As the former could lead to judicial understanding and leniency, while the latter could lead to judicial interest in harsher punishments, we caution probation officers in how they write their "remorse-based narra-

---

64. Zhong, *supra* note 1, at 160–61.
65. *Id.* at 158.
66. Weisman, *supra* note 24. *See* JOHN BRAITHWAITE, CRIME, SHAME, AND REINTEGRATION (1989).
67. *Id.*

tives" and suggest that they recognize the power of their words in presentencing reports and recommendations and their potential significant effects on their clients' outcomes.

Similarly, the act of including assessments of remorse in presentencing reports employs emotion as a therapeutic tool that engages the criminal-legal process and its actors in enhancing well-being, healing, and restoration.[68] This not only empowers probation officers to leverage their expertise and knowledge of clients to assist in appropriate sentencing but also, given the range of purposes that presentencing reports serve in making decisions about correctional placement and eligibility for rehabilitative program options,[69] provides probation officers the opportunity to recommend therapeutic outcomes and strategies for individual clients far beyond sentencing.

3. Facilitating Restitution and Rehabilitation

We recommend that probation officers leverage both their assessments of clients' remorse, as well as communication with other actors in the criminal-legal system, to facilitate restorative justice and rehabilitation. For example, in criminal law, the criminal-legal process can employ the benefits of encouraging a defendant to apologize to a victim, and encouraging a victim to forgive, in a facilitated encounter between them.[70] In addition, lower recidivism rates have been reported as a result of restorative justice processes.[71] Here, we provide examples of recommendations for officers regarding how they can contribute to the therapeutic outcomes of their individual clients:

- Encourage clients to apologize directly to the person or persons harmed by their actions; if a face-to-face encounter cannot be accomplished, encourage them to write a letter or to make a video or public statement.[72]
- Encourage clients to make a public commitment to comply with a behavior plan (e.g., by court order), which research suggests can enhance the likelihood that defendants will comply and change future behavior.[73]

---

68. See generally Daicoff, supra note 6.

69. Fennell and Hall, supra note 41.

70. See Daicoff, supra note 6, at 144, 154.

71. Barton Poulson, A Third Voice: A Review of Empirical Research on the Psychological Outcomes of Restorative Justice, 2003 UTAH L. REV. 199.

72. See Daicoff, supra note 6, at 164–65.

73. David Wexler, Therapeutic Jurisprudence and the Criminal Courts, 35 WM. & MARY L. REV. 157 (1993).

- Utilize alternative sentencing recommendations and/or rehabilitative treatment plans tailored to the charge or specific types of deviant behavior or violence (treatment for mental health, substance abuse, sex offenses, etc.)

Encouraging a client to apologize during the criminal-legal process should help reduce unhealthy shame and anger in both the client and those that he or she has harmed, increasing a client's "therapeutic guilt" and/or "reintegrative shame."[74] These effects, in turn, are likely to reduce his or her recidivism and increase his or her potential for successfully reintegrating into and healing the community.[75]

Conclusion

TJ provides a rich theoretical framework that warrants the integration of remorse, forgiveness, and reconciliation not only into the criminal-legal process[76] but also into the everyday decision-making and practices of probation officers. We argue that probation officers should evaluate and recognize remorse as a therapeutic tool that can provide genuine evidence of clients' potential for restoration with victims and reintegration into the community during the sentencing process.

Thus, our recommendations outline approaches for formalizing remorse assessments and note-taking practices, incorporating detailed accounts of remorse into presentencing reports, and adopting a therapeutic approach when making sentencing recommendations that center around restorative justice and rehabilitation. Such approaches make often subconscious evaluations of clients' remorse more explicit in decision-making and also leverage probation officers' unique expertise and relationships with their clients in order to best and effectively inform the court. At the individual officer level, in addition to encouraging officers to think about their own potential personal biases with regard to their clients' remorse,[77] developing these practices should improve officers' confidence in assessing and evaluating remorse, as well as in weighing and advocating for appropriate sentencing and programming recommendations.

Ultimately, we encourage and recommend that probation officers receive education on and training in identifying remorse, restorative justice,

---

74. Daicoff, *supra* note 6, at 144.

75. Scheff, *supra* note 13, at 102–4.

76. *See generally* Daicoff, *supra* note 6.

77. *See generally* Hanan, *supra* note 55.

and behavior-change facilitation skills (i.e., cognitive behavioral therapy, motivational interviewing). Yet in engaging with and considering the recommendations above, we believe that probation officers are already well positioned to engage in TJ practices in their decision-making and presentencing reports during the sentencing process.

6

It's Time to Shine[1]

Understanding the Implications of Commitment Decision-Making by Nonjudicial Officers and Embracing Change

Shelley Kolstad

Introduction

C hanging a public attitude as entrenched as sanism[2] is a notoriously fraught undertaking. The historical practice in Queensland, Australia, as it was elsewhere, of separating persons with mental illness from the rest of society in custodial settings,[3] coupled with abuses both real[4] and dramatized,[5] has no doubt contributed to this sense of intractability. Although relevant Queensland legislation[6] offers basic statutory safeguards, significant levels of support to decision-makers are necessary to ensure that values at the heart of therapeutic jurisprudence (TJ) such as "participation,

---

1. Queensland Mental Health Commission, *Shifting Minds Queensland Mental Health, Alcohol and Other Drugs Strategic Plan 2018–2023* (2018, cover), accessible at https://www.qmhc.qld.gov.au/sites/default/files/files/qmhc_2018_strategic_plan.pdf.

2. *See* Michael L. Perlin, *On Sanism*, 46 SMU L. Rev. 373 (1992).

3. Queensland Government, *The Road to Recovery—A History of Mental Health Services in Queensland 1859–2009* (undated, 1), accessible at https://www.health.qld.gov.au/__data/assets/pdf_file/0028/444583/qld-mh-history.pdf.

4. *See, e.g.*, Brian Simpson, *Accountability after Ward 10B*, 16 Legal Service Bull. 67 (1991).

5. *See, e.g.*, Kenneth P. Rosenberg, *"Shine" Depicts False View of Mental Illness*, N.Y. Times (1997), accessible at https://www.nytimes.com/1997/03/15/opinion/l-shine-depicts-false-view-of-mental-illness-116394.html.

6. *Mental Health Act 2016* (Qld), hereafter cited as *MHA*.

dignity and trust"[7] bolster the fidelity of involuntary commitment deliberations.

In this chapter, I offer a modest understanding of patients and critical
mental illnesses that sometimes leads to involuntary civil commitment. I
then examine relevant legislation in Queensland, discussing its relationship
to the principles of TJ. In conclusion, I make a case for incorporating TJ in
Queensland mental health law practice to assist in reducing the prevalence
of involuntary commitment.

The Patient

Mental illness is "a condition characterized by a clinically significant dis-
turbance of thought, mood, perception or memory."[8] Conversations and
interactions with patients form the core basis of diagnosis and of treatment.[9]
Suffering, as cautioned by Frances in, for example, a patient with schizophrenia, is not confined to a disease of the brain.[10] Crucially, psychosocial
factors may be indicated in the onset of illness, and a positive environment
including support, housing, work, learning, and social engagement is a key
element in management of mental illness.[11]

How prevalent is mental illness? Statistics indicate a mental or behavioral condition was experienced by one in five Australians in the period
2017–18.[12] It is expected this figure will rise due to impacts of COVID-19.[13]
For context, the UK has modeled the expected impact of their COVID-19
crisis, predicting "up to 10 million people will need either new or addition-

---

7. Michael King, *What Can Mainstream Courts Learn from Problem-Solving Courts?* 32
ALTERNATIVE L. J. 91, 92 (2007).

8. *MHA* § 10(1).

9. The Royal Australian and New Zealand College of Psychiatrists, *The Role of the Psychiatrist in Australia and New Zealand*, accessible at https://www.ranzcp.org/news-policy
/policy-and-advocacy/position-statements/the-role-of-the-psychiatrist-in-australia-and-new
(2013).

10. Allen Frances, *RDoC Is Necessary, but Very Oversold*, 13 WORLD PSYCHIATRY 47, 48
(2014).

11. *Id.*

12. Australian Bureau of Statistics, *Mental Health*, accessible at https://www.abs.gov.au
/statistics/health/health-conditions-and-risks/mental-health/latest-release.

13. UNSW Newsroom, *Australia's Health 2020 Report Shows One in Five Australians Have
a Mental Health Condition*, accessible at https://newsroom.unsw.edu.au/news/health/aus
tralia%E2%80%99s-health-2020-report-shows-one-five-australians-have-mental-health
-condition (2020).

al mental health support."[14] Who develops mental illness? Research in genetics highlights a voluminous number of "small little changes in our DNA makeup that change our risk of disorders, just like they change our risk of height, or obesity," with the key point being this is true for everyone.[15] Brief insights like these refute attitudes of mental illness being the patient's fault, attitudes opposed since the rise of psychiatry that advanced treatment "on medical rather than moral lines."[16] Stigma is still a barrier to social participation, however,[17] and this as well as barriers to finding work[18] causes additional suffering for the patient.

And what of treatment facility options? Early intervention is recognized as important for clinical outcomes and avoidance of social disadvantage.[19] Where a patient's illness is not serious enough for hospitalization and too serious for general practitioner treatment, access to community mental health services is essential.[20] In terms of clinical treatments, modest improvements have been made in medication, with second-generation antipsychotics decreasing risk of tardive dyskinesia and extrapyramidal side effects.[21] Tardive dyskinesia must be carefully monitored for because "the best man-

14. Centre for Mental Health, *Covid-19 and the Nation's Mental Health: October 2020*, accessible at https://www.centreformentalhealth.org.uk/publications/covid-19-and-nations -mental-health-october-2020 (2020).

15. John McGrath, Queensland Mental Health Commission, Media & Events, *Schizophrenia Latest Research and Treatments*, accessible at https://www.qmhc.qld.gov.au/media-events /news/professor-john-mcgrath-schizophrenia-latest-research-and-treatments (2020).

16. William A. Isdale, *The Rise of Psychiatry and its Establishment in Queensland*, 14 J. ROYAL HIST. SOC'Y QUEENSLAND 496 (1992) citing AUBREY LEWIS, THE STATE OF PSYCHIATRY 7 (1967).

17. Queensland Mental Health Commission, *supra* note 1, at 21.

18. Nas Campanella and Celina Edmonds, *Disability Royal Commission Hears about Barriers to Finding Employment Faced by People like Yuri*, ABC NEWS (2020), accessible at https:// www.abc.net.au/news/2020-12-08/disability-royal-commission-schizophrenia-and-finding -work/12961166.

19. Queensland Mental Health Commission, *Awareness & Promotion Early Intervention*, accessible at https://www.qmhc.qld.gov.au/awareness-promotion/early-intervention-initia tives.

20. Zalika Rizmal, *Too Sick for a GP, but Not "Sick Enough for Hospital,"* Patient Tells *Mental Health Royal Commission*, ABC NEWS (2019), accessible at https://www.abc.net.au/news /2019-07-10/patients-falling-through-gaps-mental-health-royal-commission/11295670.

21. Ricardo P. Garay et al., *Therapeutic Improvements Expected in the Near Future for Schizophrenia and Schizoaffective Disorder: An Appraisal of Phase III Clinical Trials of Schizophrenia-Targeted Therapies as Found in US and EU Clinical Trial Registries*, 17 EXPERT OPINION ON PHARMACOTHERAPY 921 (2016).

agement strategy remains prevention."[22] Another study notes the comorbidity of other than serious mental illness, especially cardiovascular diseases, contributes to significant early mortality, with psychotropic medication an independent risk factor.[23] For serious illness such as treatment-resistant schizophrenia, electroconvulsive therapy (ECT) is reported by some to assist in ameliorating neuropsychiatric symptoms,[24] though "its use on those under compulsory mental health treatment orders remains controversial and the United Nations Special Rapporteur on Torture and Other Cruel and Inhuman Treatment or Punishment has called for a ban on its nonconsensual use."[25]

Within this challenging environment, the patient has another hurdle: to choose treatment—or not. Judge Cardozo's statement that "every human being of adult years and sound mind has a right to determine what shall be done with his own body"[26] has been followed in many cases,[27] reflecting Australia's common law position that a competent adult has the right of self-determination.[28] For illnesses such as cancer, the law does not permit treatment to be forced on a patient who is competent to refuse.[29] Only recently in Australia[30] have competent patients been able to refuse treatment for serious mental illness. As signatory to the United Nations Convention on

---

22. Lucia Ricciardi et al., *Treatment Recommendations for Tardive Dyskinesia*, 64 Can. J. Psychiatry 388 (2019); *see* Rennie v. Klein, 462 F. Supp. 1131 (D.N.J. 1978), suppl., 476 F. Supp. 1294 (D.N.J. 1979) and 481 F. Supp. 552 (D.N.J. 1979), modified, 653 F.2d 836 (3d Cir. 1981), vacated, 458 U.S. 1119 (1982), on remand, 720 F.2d 266 (3d Cir. 1983).

23. Victor Mazereel et al., *Impact of Psychotropic Medication Effects on Obesity and the Metabolic Syndrome in People with Serious Mental Illness*, 11 Frontiers In Endocrinology 1 (2020).

24. Amit Singh and Sujita Kumar Kar, *How Electroconvulsive Therapy Works? Understanding the Neurobiological Mechanisms*, 15 Clinical Psychopharmacology & Neuroscience 210 (2017).

25. Bernadette McSherry, *Electroconvulsive Therapy without Consent: The Influence of Human Rights Law*, 26 J. L. & Med. 732 (2019); Janos Fiala-Butora, *Disabling Torture: The Obligation to Investigate Ill-Treatment of Persons with Disabilities*, 45 Colum. Hum. Rts. L. Rev. (2013).

26. Schloendorff v Society of New York Hospital, 105 N.E. 92 (N.Y. Ct. App. 1914).

27. *Hunter and New England Area Health Service v. A by His Tutor T* (2009) 74 NSWLR 88 at [8].

28. *Id.* at [5]; *see MDF v. Central Queensland Network Authorised Mental Health Service and Anor* [2020] QCA 108, in relation to an Examination Authority at [40].

29. Christopher Ryan, *Should We Be Forcing People with Severe Mental Illness to Have Treatment They Don't Want?* SBS Insight (2019). accessible at https://www.sbs.com.au/news/insight/should-we-be-forcing-people-with-severe-mental-illness-to-have-treatment-they-don-t-want.

30. *Id.*

the Rights of Persons with Disabilities[31] (CRPD), Australia made changes to its mental health legislation; I now examine these laws in Queensland.

Queensland's Involuntary Civil Commitment Legislation

Article 25(d) of the CRPD provides:[32]

> Require health professionals to provide care of the same quality to persons with disabilities as to others, including on the basis of free and informed consent by, inter alia, raising awareness of the human rights, dignity, autonomy and needs of persons with disabilities through training and the promulgation of ethical standards for public and private health care.

Free and informed consent is inconsistent with an involuntary treatment regime that Australia retained, "as a last resort and subject to safeguards,"[33] via two CRPD interpretive declarations.[34] The *Mental Health Act 2016* (Qld) (hereafter referred to as the *MHA*) was introduced in Queensland to *inter alia*, "[strengthen] patient rights."[35] The *MHA* is to be interpreted consistent with maintenance and improvement of health and wellbeing, safeguarding rights, promoting treatment least restrictive of rights and liberties and pro-

---

31. United Nations, *Convention on the Rights of Persons with Disabilities*, adopted on December 13, 2006, GA Res 61/106, UN Doc A/Res/61/106 (entered into force May 3, 2008).

32. On the relationship between the CRPD and the right to refuse treatment, *see* Mehgan Gallagher, *No Means No, or Does It? A Comparative Study of the Right to Refuse Treatment in a Psychiatric Institution*, 44 INT'L J. LEGAL INFO. 137 (2016).

33. Queensland Mental Health Commission, *Human Rights Protection Frameworks for People Being Treated Involuntarily for a Mental Illness: Overview, October 2019*, accessible at https://www.qmhc.qld.gov.au/documents/overviewhumanrightsprotectionframeworksfor peoplebeingtreatedinvoluntarilyforamentalillnessoctober201.

34. *See* Australian Law Reform Commission, *International Context United Nations Convention on the Rights of Persons with Disabilities* (May 20, 2014), at 2.17, accessible at https://www.alrc.gov.au/publication/equality-capacity-and-disability-in-commonwealth-laws-dp-81/2-conceptual-landscape-the-context-for-reform/international-context-2/. The CRPD Committee is critical of Australia's substituted decision-making regime; United Nations Convention on the Rights of Persons with Disabilities, Committee on the Rights of Persons with Disabilities, *Concluding Observations on the Combined Second and Third Periodic Reports of Australia* (Oct. 15, 2019), at [23] (*Concluding Observations*).

35. Queensland, *Parliamentary Debates*, Legislative Assembly (Sept. 17, 2015, at 2005, 2006) (Cameron Dick, Minister for Health and Ambulance Services), hereafter cited as Dick statement.

moting recovery and the prospect of life in the community absent involuntary treatment.[36]

With a presumption of competency (decision-making capacity),[37] a person may only be assessed as not having capacity if they are incapable of understanding they have an illness or symptoms and are unable to understand the nature and purpose of treatment or benefits, risks, and alternatives and consequences of no treatment.[38] Further, a person must be deemed incapable of deciding on treatment for themselves and unable to communicate the decision in some way.[39] A decision not to receive treatment does not qualify automatically as an assumption of lack of capacity,[40] even if it is a decision that "the assessor would [not] agree with on rational or moral grounds."[41]

Also affecting autonomy is assessment of risk of serious harm.[42] While improvements are said to have been made to the accuracy of assessing risk of violence to others by identifying high risk groups requiring management, predicting individual acts is subject to inaccuracy given the low prevalence of serious violence.[43] Here, clinicians are urged "not to resort to increased coercion, let alone preventive detention, but to focus attention on greater support and more active follow up and assertive treatment in the community with the possibility of rapid admission, as required, during exacerbations of symptoms or social conflict."[44] Where involuntary commitment is based upon a risk of self-harm, questions are raised by researchers where "long-term consequences of stigma may be particularly harmful for people with mental illness who receive involuntary treatment."[45]

Principles including those relating to human rights, communication and special needs, unique cultural needs of Aboriginal people and Torres Strait

---

36. *MHA* §§ 3(1)(a), 3(2).

37. *MHA* § 5(b).

38. *MHA* § 14(1)(a).

39. *MHA* § 14(1)(b).

40. *MHA* § 14(2).

41. Christopher Ryan et al., *The Capacity to Refuse Psychiatric Treatment: A Guide to the Law for Clinicians and Tribunal Members*, 49 Aust.& N.Z. J. Psychiatry 324, 331 (2015).

42. *MHA* § 12(1)(c)(i).

43. Queensland Health, Final Report, *When Mental Health Care Meets Risk: A Queensland Sentinel Events Review into Homicide and Public Sector Mental Health Services*, 37–38 (2016), accessible at https://www.health.qld.gov.au/__data/assets/pdf_file/0026/443735/sentinel-events-2016.pdf.

44. *Id.* at 38; for a critique on risk management *see* Christopher H. Maylea, *A Rejection of Involuntary Treatment in Mental Health Social Work*, 11 Ethics & Soc. Welfare 336, 341–44 (2017).

45. Ziyan Xu et al., *Involuntary Hospitalization, Stigma Stress and Suicidality: A Longitudinal Study*, 53 Soc. Psychiatry & Psychiatric Epidemiology 309 (2018).

Islanders and minors are required to be upheld.[46] In the context of assessment of decision making capacity for all patients, assessors are encouraged to communicate in an accessible, non-technical way, avoiding stressful environmental factors.[47] Further, recovery-oriented services and reduction of stigma, privacy and confidentiality *must* be recognized and incorporated in the administration of the *MHA*.[48] Treatment and care must only be imposed where a person has a defined mental illness.[49]

Involvement of support persons, providing support and information and helping a person achieve maximum potential and self-reliance, are necessary principles.[50] When discussing involuntary treatment and care, the views, wishes, and preferences of the person are required to be considered where the person can express these or an advance health directive is made.[51] A second opinion cannot be refused.[52] Mandatory checks and balances, supported by penalty provisions, in areas of decision-making that most intrusively affect a patient are provided in the *MHA*;[53] plans that may be approved by the chief psychiatrist to reduce and eliminate seclusion and mechanical restraint are a further protection.[54]

Queensland's Mental Health Review Tribunal (MHRT) mission includes recognizing "the importance of protecting the rights and dignity of persons receiving mental health treatment and care in Queensland."[55] Within its civil commitment jurisdiction, the MHRT reviews treatment authorities[56] and hears applications for examination authorities.[57] Decisions of the MHRT, such as continuation of a treatment authority, are appealable by right to the Mental Health Court.[58] ECT performed on an adult patient unable to give informed consent requires MHRT approval,[59] which in emergency circumstances may occur prior to approval for an involuntary pa-

---

46. *MHA* §§ 5(a), 5(f), 5(g), 5(h), 5(i).

47. Ryan et al., *supra* note 41, at 328.

48. *MHA* §§ 5(k), 5(m).

49. *MHA* §§ 5(l), 10(1), 10(2), 10(4).

50. *MHA* § 5(c), 5(d), 5(e).

51. *MHA* §§ 53(2), 222.

52. *MHA* § 290(3).

53. *MHA*, Chapter 8.

54. *MHA*, Chapter 8, Part 4; Dick Statement, *supra* note 35, at 2007.

55. Queensland Government, Mental Health Review Tribunal, *Strategic Plan* (reviewed May 2020, 1), accessible at https://www.mhrt.qld.gov.au/sites/default/files/2020-08/MHRT%20Strategic%20Plan%202017%20-%202021%20reviewed%20May%202020_0.pdf.

56. *MHA* §§ 28(1)(a), 28(3), 28(4).

57. *MHA* § 28(2)(a).

58. *MHA*, schedule 2.

59. *MHA* § 236(1)(b).

tient.[60] Here, a lawyer must be appointed to represent the patient.[61] While a person has a right to legal representation at hearings,[62] circumstances in which the MHRT in the civil context must appoint a lawyer are limited. They include hearings for minors and where the attorney general is appearing.[63] The MHRT may appoint a lawyer if considered in the patient's best interest.[64]

Research by Gill and his colleagues, which included the prevalence of involuntary civil commitment orders, claims—despite legislative reforms in the *MHA*—the number of orders made is on the rise.[65] Posited reasons "include a lack of systematized voluntary alternatives to compulsory treatment, a paternalistic and restrictive culture in mental health services and risk aversion in clinicians and society."[66] Limited patient attendance at hearings may also affect decisions not to revoke a treatment authority.[67] Another critical contributing factor is limited legal representation. In the comprehensively researched *Shining a Light behind Closed Doors,* legal aid lawyer Eleanor Fritze observed that in comparison to near universal rates of representation in New York and England,[68] Victoria is "out of step with these jurisdictions in terms of both recognizing a formal entitlement to legal representation and providing sufficient resources to meet the demand."[69] Queensland may be similarly out of step. As discussed above, the circumstances in which the MHRT *must* appoint a lawyer in civil commitment proceedings is limited. Legal representative appointments were made in twenty-six treatment authority hearings[70] in the period 2019–20 in the circumstances of a recorded

---

60. *MHA* §§ 237(1)(a), 237(2)(b).

61. *MHA* § 740(3)(b)(ii).

62. *MHA* § 739(1).

63. *MHA* §§ 740(3)(a), 740(3)(c).

64. *MHA* § 740(2).

65. Neeraj S. Gill et al., *Measuring the Impact of Revised Mental Health Legislation on Human Rights in Queensland, Australia,* 73 Int'l. J. L. & Psychiatry 1, 7 (2020).

66. *Id.* at 1; *see id.* at 5, of a patient, advocate, clinician, and stakeholder qualitative study.

67. Jake Buckingham, *A Critical Analysis of Legal Representation in Queensland's Mental Health Review Tribunal,* 6 Griffith J. L. & Hum. Dignity 134, 146 (2019).

68. Eleanore Fritze, Shining a Light behind Closed Doors: Report of the Jack Brockhoff Foundation Churchill Fellowship to Better Protect the Human Rights and Dignity of People with Disabilities, Detained in Closed Environments for Compulsory Treatment, through the Use of Legal Services 32 (2015), noting that in 2014–15, 82% of Victorians did not have legal representation at their MHT hearings.

69. *Id.* at 37.

70. The State of Queensland (Mental Health Tribunal), *2019–2020 Annual Report* (September 2020, 27), accessible at https://www.mhrt.qld.gov.au/sites/default/files/2020-10/MHRT%20Annual%20Report%202019-20%20FINAL.pdf.

10,965[71] treatment authority reviews.[72] This potentially leaves a large gap—a gap that is violative of international human rights law[73]—where a patient who cannot obtain legal support from community-based advocacy groups[74] must fund their own representation. The importance of legal representation is discussed in the context of TJ below, however I note Fritze's concern with not just tribunal representation but also provision of legal advocacy in administrative decision-making. She notes the difficulty for lawyers to advocate[75] in relation to decisions involving, *inter alia,* in-patient's leave, transfers, seclusion, and restraint and whether a patient is forced to accept treatment.[76] Echoing Gill and his colleagues, Fritze observes, "A number of practical operational and attitudinal factors may push against respect for human rights by administrative decision makers and mental health services when a person is detained in a closed environment."[77]

In 1973, Dr. Darold Treffert, a prominent American psychiatrist, expressed the view that "frank abandonment" was as abhorrent as "frank paternalism."[78] Since research indicates coercive treatment may have "powerful negative effects on an individual's health,"[79] is there, or should there be, room for paternalism so as not to "abandon" patients? The CRPD committee insists there is not.[80] Recent mental health law scholarship focuses on how the CRPD model, flowing from a social model of disability where a patient retains legal power, would work in practice, especially in instances of extreme dysfunction.[81] Absent a fully funded state-based system of support or effective mar-

---

71. *Id.* at 23.

72. Note that "the Tribunal may review a number of matters for a patient at the same time"; *id.* at 17.

73. *See* Michael L. Perlin, *"Striking for the Guardians and Protectors of the Mind": The Convention on the Rights of Persons with Disabilities and the Future of Guardianship Law,* 117 PENN ST. L. REV. 1159, 1175 (2013). "One of the most critical issues in seeking to bring life to international human rights law in a mental disability law context is the right to adequate and dedicated counsel."

74. *See, e.g.,* Queensland Advocacy Incorporated, accessible at https://qai.org.au/mental -health-advocacy-practice/.

75. FRITZE, *supra* note 68, at 66.

76. *Id.* at 61.

77. *Id.* at 61.

78. Darold A. Treffert, *Dying with Their Rights on,* 130 AM. J. PSYCHIATRY (1973).

79. Ryan et al., *supra* note 41, at 332, citing Matthew Large et al., *Noscomial Suicide,* 22 AUSTRALASIAN PSYCHIATRY 118–21 (2013).

80. *Concluding Observations, supra* note 35; Maylea, *supra* note 44, at 339.

81. *See* generally Piers Gooding, *Supported Decision-Making: A Rights-Based Disability Concept and Its Implications for Mental Health Law,* 20 PSYCHIATRY, PSYCHOLOGY & L. 431 (2013); Terry Carney, *Prioritising Supported Decision-Making: Running on Empty or a Basis for Glacial-to-Steady Progress?* 6 LAWS 18 (2017).

shalling of community support,[82] a paradigm shift to an enquiry based on a "right to treatment," not the imposition of treatment,[83] will take time. Alongside reform efforts, the principles of TJ can assist in achieving positive outcomes.

Why Therapeutic Jurisprudence?

Dworkin reflects that existence without dignity is merely a blink of time; with dignity we "write a subscript to our mortality. We make our lives tiny diamonds in the cosmic sands."[84] He also urges that life ought to be a successful performance, not a wasted opportunity.[85] Dworkin's philosophy appears compatible with Hennette-Vauchez's elucidation of dignity, which, owing to both modern dignity and medieval *dignitas*, "is marked by an essential duality, for it is always simultaneously public and private."[86] In the debate over involuntary commitment, there exists a tension between the private and public face of dignity: the patient, whose private life performance strives for uniqueness and the public, defining "normative" uniqueness. For the suffering patient whose illness may be debilitating as to interfere with competency, involuntary commitment pulls on the public dignity chord. Here, is treatment justified as the conferral of dignity?[87] Will involuntary commitment obstruct or facilitate the patient's choices in choreographing their own unique performance? TJ can assist in this careful balancing act "in advancing dignity and reducing denials of the same."[88]

Dignity, the Core of the TJ Enterprise[89]

Procedural justice is an important aspect of TJ in granting dignity center stage. If patients perceive they are treated with dignity and respect, they are

---

82. Carney, *supra* note 80, at 2.

83. Maylea, *supra* note 44, at 340. For an early U.S.-based perspective, *see* Bruce J. Winick, *The Right to Refuse Mental Health Treatment: A First Amendment Perspective*, 44 U. MIAMI L. REV. 1 (1989).

84. Stuart Jeffries, *Ronald Dworkin: "We Have a Responsibility to Live Well,"* THE GUARDIAN (2011), accessible at https://www.theguardian.com/books/2011/mar/31/ronald-dworkin -morality-dignity-hedgehogs, citing RONALD DWORKIN, JUSTICE FOR HEDGEHOGS (2011).

85. *Id.*

86. Stéphanie Hennette-Vauchez, *A Human Dignitas? Remnants of the Ancient Legal Concept in Contemporary Dignity Jurisprudence*, 9 INT'L J. CONST. L. 32, 40 (2011).

87. David C. Yamada, *On Anger, Shock, Fear, and Trauma: Therapeutic Jurisprudence as a Response to Dignity Denials in Public Policy*, 63 INT'L J. L. & PSYCHIATRY 35, 40 (2019).

88. *Id.*

89. Michael L. Perlin, *"Have You Seen Dignity?": The Story of the Development of Therapeutic Jurisprudence*, 27 U.N.Z. L. REV. 1135, 1137 (2017).

more likely to feel fairly treated.[90] Procedural justice gives patients an opportunity to understand issues, to consider and discuss them, to voice their views, and to be assisted in feeling comfortable with decisions.[91] Here, we need to consider the dynamics of power and communication.

While we see power utilised in involuntary commitment manifested in locked doors and mechanical restraints, power also functions within a relational context and, as explained by Foucault, in society and in the lives of humans in and through communication.[92] If communication is one-way, concentrated on a decision-maker's opinion of the illness and recommended treatment, the patient is likely to feel "trapped within a specific stereotyping scheme of people with mental health problems" and feel more coerced.[93] If however, a patient feels what they say is being listened to and seriously considered, they will feel a sense of validation and more at peace with the outcome.[94] Giving primacy to the narrative of the patient and valuing aspects of the narrative beyond mental illness ought to give rise to a feeling of voluntary participation. Despite a decision to commit, actively promoting voice, validation, and voluntariness in communication with patients can "initiate healing and bring about improved behavior in the future. In general, human beings prosper when they feel that they are making, or at least participating in, their own decisions."[95]

In this context, Perlin is critical of the limited legal representation granted in Australia,[96] arguing that to ensure patients are afforded dignity,

---

90. Michael L. Perlin, *Dignity and Therapeutic Jurisprudence: How We Can Best End Shame and Humiliation*, in HUMAN DIGNITY: PRACTICES, DISCOURSES, AND TRANSFORMATIONS 113, 118 (Chipamong Chowdhury and Michael Britton eds., 2019), citing Tom R. Tyler, *The Psychological Consequences of Judicial Procedures: Implications for Civil Commitment Hearings*, 46 SMU L. REV. 433, 442 (1992).

91. *Id.*

92. Evi Verbeke et al., *Coercion and Power in Psychiatry: A Qualitative Study with Ex-Patients*, 223 SOC. SCI. & MED. 89, 90 (2019).

93. *Id.* at 91.

94. Michael L. Perlin, *"There Are No Trials Inside the Gates of Eden": Mental Health Courts, the Convention on the Rights of Persons with Disabilities, Dignity, and the Promise of Therapeutic Jurisprudence*, in COERCIVE CARE: RIGHTS, LAW AND POLICY 193, 200 (Bernadette McSherry and Ian Freckelton eds., 2013), citing Amy D. Ronner, *The Learned-Helpless Lawyer: Clinical Legal Education and Therapeutic Jurisprudence as Antidotes to Bartleby Syndrome*, 24 TOURO L. REV. 601 (2008). On how individuals with mental illness have the same procedural justice values as do all others, *see* Tom R. Tyler, *The Psychological Consequences of Judicial Procedures: Implications for Civil Commitment Hearings*, 46 SMU L. REV. 433 (1992).

95. Perlin, *supra* note 93, at 200.

96. Michael L. Perlin and Mehgan Gallagher, *"Temptation's Page Flies out the Door": Navigating Complex Systems of Disability and the Law from a Therapeutic Jurisprudence Perspective*, 25 BUFFALO HUM. RTS. L. REV. 1, 41–42 (2018–19).

"TJ demands the presence of active, trained lawyers"[97] and that "hearings conducted without . . . counsel are utterly contrary to the rationales of any coherent, mature system of justice."[98] According to Winick, "patients would find more acceptable informal administrative models in which they have an opportunity to participate through counsel or a counsel substitute, compared to systems that involve exclusively managerial review."[99]

Assessment of Structural Considerations

TJ analyzes the structure of settings in which decisions are made to understand whether therapeutic or antitherapeutic consequences flow. Both the text of the law and institutional commitment policies and practices must be analyzed.

Commitment decisions are made and reviewed at first instance by nonjudicial decision makers. Steve Wexler argues a difference in decisions made by nonjudicial bodies is that decisions are mass produced; they are not "the result of a deliberative process that goes on in someone's mind."[100] Nonjudicial decision-making is "affected by distant occurrences in the decision making institution" including its recruitment, training, and evaluation of employees; its administration of cases; and its relations with other institutions, "by a host of factors which one does not have to worry about in institutions which make decisions one-by-one."[101]

Consider further the order in which discussions are held and the style of tribunal meetings: does this advance therapeutic outcomes?[102] Freckelton suggests that number of reviewees released before a hearing and rate of subsequent admission, satisfaction rates among participants, quality of legal analysis, and rates at which decisions are set aside should be evaluated.[103] In the context of an initial decision to commit, consider Vine's opinion: the "availability of resources is probably one of the most potent influences on the decision to recommend involuntary detention."[104] It should be noted

---

97. Fritze, *supra* note 68, at 53.

98. *Id.* at 37.

99. Bruce J. Winick, The Right to Refuse Mental Health Treatment 383 (1997).

100. Steve Wexler, *Non-Judicial Decision-Making*, 13 Osgoode Hall L. J. 839, 844 (1975).

101. *Id.*

102. Terry Carney, *Australian Mental Health Tribunals—"Space" for Rights, Protection, Treatment and Governance?* 35 Int'l J. L. & Psychiatry 1, 6 (2012).

103. Kate Diesfeld and Ian Freckelton, *Introduction*, in Involuntary Detention and Therapeutic Jurisprudence 12 (Kate Diesfeld and Ian Freckelton eds., 2017).

104. Ruth Vine, *Decision-Making by Psychiatrists about Involuntary Detention*, in Involuntary Detention and Therapeutic Jurisprudence 12 (Kate Diesfeld and Ian Freckelton eds., 2017), at 127.

that where the unavailability of publicly funded services (such as recently recognized in Victoria where demand has overtaken capacity[105]) is beyond the control of decision-making bodies, TJ must advocate at a system or government level for change.

Mental health practice may also benefit from innovation and change. In the area of advance health care directive planning, how might the form of such directives enhance therapeutic outcomes? Technological tools can help to promote value-concordant care as has been experienced in the context of "many COVID-19 patients losing decision making capacity."[106] Specifically, video recorded instructions and "visually sophisticated decision aids" might assist in helping a patient understand treatment options and outcomes.[107]

TJ Follows the Law but Maintains an Ethic of Care[108]

Ethics guides decision-makers toward choices within a consciously chosen framework. A key value of TJ is that of psychological health, with the goal of facilitating healing and wellness where this is consistent with and does not subordinate other values such as that of "due process" and justice values.[109] If a patient is involuntarily committed due to risk of harm to others, then an ethic of care motivates continued enquiry and concern over the well-being of the patient. Put another way, it militates against detention solely on the basis of risk of harm to another. David Wexler's assertion that "the law's use of mental health information to improve therapeutic functioning [cannot] impinge upon justice concerns"[110] is continuously quoted and affirmed in TJ scholarship. That is not to say TJ endorses legal outcomes

105. Richard Willingham and Zalika Rizmal, *Victorian Mental Health Royal Commission Final Report Finds System Operates in Crisis Mode*, ABC News (2021), accessible at https://www.abc.net.au/news/2021-03-02/victorian-mental-health-royal-commission-final-report/13203938.

106. Thaddeus Mason Pope, *Patient Rights and Healthcare Decision-Making after COVID-19*, QUT Global Law, Science and Technology Seminar Series, accessible at https://blogs.qut.edu.au/law-research/patient-rights-and-healthcare-decision-making-after-covid-19-transformations-and-future-directions/ (2020).

107. *Id.*

108. Michael L. Perlin, *The Judge, He Cast His Robe Aside: Mental Health Courts, Dignity and Due Process*, 3 Mental Health L. & Pol'y J. 1, 11 (2013).

109. Bruce Winick, *A Therapeutic Jurisprudence Model for Civil Commitment*, in Involuntary Detention and Therapeutic Jurisprudence, *supra* note 102, at 26.

110. Michael L. Perlin, *"You That Build the Death Planes": Bob Dylan, War and International Affairs*, 37 Ariz J. Int'l & Comp. L. 305, 325 (2020), citing David B. Wexler, *Therapeutic Jurisprudence and Changing Concepts of Legal Scholarship*, 11 Behav. Sci. & L. 17, 21 (1993).

that are antitherapeutic. Rather, decision-makers ought to explicitly recognize and aim to consciously reduce antitherapeutic outcomes.

Conclusion

In a recent MHRT decision regarding an ECT application, many of the values discussed earlier are present. Here, the tribunal noted the evidence of the patient was "highly regarded" and that while the patient lacked capacity, he was able to give "cogent insight into what his current circumstances were and how he felt" and it was his wish for further treatment.[111] At the hearing, the patient was supported by a peer and had legal representation.

In an environment where pragmatic decisions sometimes must be made quickly, Vine describes the challenge of good practice of a psychiatrist as being "able to enter another person's world, to understand why the person thinks and feels as he or she does, and yet remain objective."[112] While the intention to "bring relief to suffering through the initiation of treatment and provision of support and empathy"[113] is wholeheartedly endorsed, if decision-makers put into practice the principles of TJ, we may improve the chances of assisting our most vulnerable to shine.

---

111. MHRT Statement of Reasons, Published SOR 020, ECT Approved (Sept. 15, 2020), at 5, accessible at https://www.mhrt.qld.gov.au/sites/default/files/2020-09/Published%20 SOR%20-%20020%20-%20ECT%20Approved.pdf.

112. Vine, *supra* note 103, at 132.

113. *Id.*

7

The Role of Nonjudicial Officers in the Disparity of Treatment for Persons with Dual Diagnoses and How TJ Can Improve Outcomes

Introduction

Persons with mental illness who also have an intellectual or developmental disability (ID/DD) face a double prejudice. This double prejudice causes serious disparities in treatment and issues regarding appropriate community treatment and placement. For these persons with dual diagnoses,[1] their care can often be relegated to a tug-of-war between agencies who are supposed to be providing services and arguments over what constitutes a "primary" diagnosis.

Many states, including New York, have separate statutes and regulations that govern persons with mental illness versus persons with ID/DD.[2] These statutes are differentiated only by diagnosis of the person. In most states, there are separate agencies that provide services for persons with mental illness and persons with ID/DD.[3] For example, in New York, the Office of Mental Health (OMH) is responsible for providing services for persons with mental illness while the Office of Persons with Developmental Disabilities (OPWDD) is responsible for providing services for persons with ID/DD.

---

1. Dual diagnosis in the context of mental illness often refers to mental illness and substance use disorders, however for the purposes of this chapter, the term "dual diagnosis" will refer only to persons with mental illness and an intellectual or developmental disorder.

2. *Compare*, e.g., MHL Art. 9 vs. MHL Art. 15; 14 NYCRR 595 vs. 14 NYCRR 633.

3. An internet search of the fifty states shows that most states have separate agencies or completely separate departments that serve persons with mental illness versus persons with ID/DD.

Decisions regarding who provides care to persons with dual diagnoses are often made by nonjudicial officers, comprising of state administrative officials or mental health providers. These nonjudicial officers are responsible for determining what constitutes the primary diagnosis and therefore which agency should be responsible for treatment, housing, and collateral services.

The treatment of persons with dual diagnoses is completely contrary to the principles of therapeutic jurisprudence (TJ). Making decisions based solely on diagnosis and behavior leads to antitherapeutic consequences. Allowing this population to languish in hospitals and suffer in inappropriate settings deprives them of their dignity.

Illustrating the Problem

Sanism is an irrational prejudice, the same quality and character of other prevailing prejudices such as racism, sexism, heterosexism, and ethnic bigotry that is reflected in the legal system and permeates throughout society.[4] Persons with mental illness are perceived as dangerous, scary, and violent. Persons with mental illness are often presumed to lack capacity and deemed incapable of making autonomous decisions regarding their lives.[5]

Similarly, persons with ID/DD are often infantilized and also presumed to be incapable of making any autonomous decisions. When someone has dual diagnoses, the prejudice they face is compounded. These people who suffer from "invisible" disabilities may have different ways of communicating and processing information that might not be as well understood by the nonjudicial officers making determinations as to their needs, which can hinder their ability to obtain the services to which they are entitled.[6]

For persons with both mental illness and ID/DD, the interplay between both conditions is sometimes not well understood or even conflated as being the same thing.[7] It is important for anyone working with someone with dual diagnoses to understand the nuances between the conditions.[8] Without doing so, many persons with dual diagnoses end up facing dire consequences including unnecessary hospitalization, incarceration, and homelessness.

---

4. Michael L. Perlin, *On "Sanism,"* 46 SMU L. REV. 373, 374–75 (1992).

5. *Id.* at 394.

6. Ariana Cernius, *Enforcing the Americans with Disabilities Act for the "Invisibly Disabled": Not a Handout, Just a Hand,* 25 GEO. J. ON POVERTY L. & POL'Y 35, 39 (2017).

7. Dillon Minick, *Intellectually or Developmentally Disabled in Jail: The Need for Reform in Texas Jails,* 42 T. JEFFERSON L. REV. 86, 95 (2020).

8. *Id.* at 96.

Determining which agency should provide services for someone with dual diagnoses largely falls upon nonjudicial officers. These state administrators may or may not rely on mental health professionals in ultimately deciding whether someone should receive services. The Diagnostic Statistics Manual (DSM-5), commonly relied upon by mental health professionals in the United States, removed the multiaxial system that had previously separated out mental illness diagnoses from ID/DD.[9] Clinicians are allowed to list diagnoses in order of clinical focus, which can be important for insurance purposes and also in helping determine eligibility for services.[10] This change in coding suggests that there is no differentiation between mental health disorders and ID/DD.[11] However, for persons with dual diagnoses, there are clear differences between persons with dual diagnoses and those with just mental illness or ID/DD.

The privatization of mental health care also has had a direct impact on how persons with dual diagnoses are treated. Medicaid serves as the most important health-related social welfare responsibilities for persons with dual diagnoses.[12] Medicaid provides medical care for persons with dual diagnoses and nearly exclusive access to government-coordinated services that are not supported by the private market or are cost-prohibitive for individuals to afford to pay privately.[13] These programs improve quality of life, facilitate independent living, and preserve dignity.[14] The emergence of Medicaid-managed care systems parallels the use of network-style insurance coverage, requiring consumers to use specified provider networks.[15] Managed care has often led to a decrease on the amount, duration, and scope of treatment authorized.[16] Managed care has also contributed to added bureaucracy that can make it very difficult for persons with dual diagnoses to navigate.

Even with medical insurance and connections to the right state agencies, often there are still insufficient services for persons with dual diagno-

---

9. DIAGNOSTIC AND STATISTICAL MANUAL OF MENTAL DISORDERS (5th ed. 2013).

10. Victoria E. Kress et al., *The Removal of the Multiaxial System in the DSM-5: Implications and Practice Suggestions for Counselors*, PROFESSIONAL COUNSELOR (2014), available at https://tpcjournal.nbcc.org/the-removal-of-the-multiaxial-system-in-the-dsm-5-implications-and-practice-suggestions-for-counselor.

11. *Id.*

12. Sara Rosenbaum, *Medicaid at Forty: Revisiting Structure and Meaning in a Post-Deficit Reduction Act Era*, 9 J. HEALTH CARE L. & POL'Y 5 (2006).

13. Stephanie R. Hoffer, *Making the Law More Able: Reforming Medicaid for Disability*, 76 OHIO ST. L.J. 1255, 1260 (2015).

14. *Id.* at 1317.

15. Rosenbaum, *supra* note 12, at 21–22.

16. April Land, *Dead to Rights: A Father's Struggle to Secure Mental Health Services for His Son*, 10 GEO. J. ON POVERTY L. & POL'Y 279, 303 (2003).

ses. This can result in the unnecessary psychiatric hospitalization of persons with dual diagnoses or for persons to be forced to seek treatment outside their state of residence.[17] This practice isolates persons with dual diagnoses from their communities, keeping them from their families and from contributing to society, further isolating and stigmatizing them.[18] An impediment to supportive housing for persons with dual diagnoses can be as a result of the conflict between social programs and who is responsible for providing services.[19]

A recent case example from New York that illustrates the complications that arise for persons with dual diagnoses involves a client named Jane.[20] Jane was a patient who spent more time hospitalized in acute care psychiatric hospitals than she had in the community.[21] Jane was diagnosed with ID/DD and schizoaffective disorder. She was subject to services by OPWDD and OMH. Jane's continual wish was to live with her mother. However, one of the acute care hospitals that she was frequently admitted to filed for guardianship, citing her multiple hospitalizations and the alleged incapability of Jane's mother to adequately provide care for her. A very limited guardianship was initially granted, but after numerous hearings and court appearances, the guardianship powers were extended. Jane had several past placements in OPWDD licensed residences, but her behavior of running away or acting out made it difficult to find appropriate placement in the New York City area. The guardianship agency was then allowed to place Jane anywhere in New York state without regard to her wish to be close to her mother and was permitted to limit contact between Jane and her mother.

Despite the guardianship agency having full powers to place Jane in a residential setting, Jane continued to languish in an acute care psychiatric hospital.[22] OPWDD is considered a voluntary agency, and Jane's continual position that she wanted to live only with her mother led many agencies that contract with OPWDD to reject her for placement. OPWDD lacks the authority to force an agency to accept anyone—just one example of how priva-

---

17. Matthew Herr, *Outsourcing Our Children: The Failure to Treat Mental Illness In-State*, 36 N.C. Cent. L. Rev. 66 (2013).

18. *Id.* at 92.

19. Henry Korman, *Clash of the Integrationalists: The Mismatch of Civil Rights Imperatives in Supportive Housing for People with Disabilities*, 26 St. Louis U. Pub. L. Rev. 3, 41 (2007).

20. A pseudonym.

21. Part of this was due to the actions of her mother, who was unable to provide adequate care for her in the community and would repeatedly bring her to the emergency room.

22. Several guardianship court conferences were held, as well as hearings pursuant to MHL Art. 9, where it was determined that she was otherwise stable for discharge but would be a danger to herself or others if not found proper placement.

tization of medical care can have antitherapeutic consequences. Eventually, after over a year and a half, Jane was discharged from the acute care hospital and placed in an OPWDD licensed facility far from the NYC area.[23]

Legal Issues Compounded by Decisions Made by Nonjudicial Officers

The issue of capacity and the right to govern one's life arises for anyone who has carries a dual diagnosis of mental illness and ID/DD. This includes the right to make basic decisions regarding treatment, where one lives, sexuality, to broader issues as to whether guardianship is necessary and other forms of substituted decision-making. For persons with dual diagnoses involved in the criminal system, issues related to capacity to stand trial and participating in their own defense arise.

In the legal system, persons with mental illness and persons with ID/DD are often subject to separate laws and legal standards. In New York, there are two separate guardianship statutes: Article 81 of the Mental Hygiene Law (MHL) and the Surrogate's Court Procedure Act (SCPA) Article 17-A, which only applies to persons with ID/DD.[24] SCPA 17-A relies purely on a medical model requiring essentially only a finding an ID/DD diagnosis, the guardianship is plenary with no time limit, no hearing is required, and there is no requirement that a guardian report to the court as to the status of the guardianship or periodic review.[25] SCPA 17-A fails to promote honor or promote autonomy, self-determination, and dignity, and fails to protect persons under guardianship from abuse.[26] Often nonjudicial officers who work within the agencies serving persons with dual diagnoses will push family members to seek guardianship without regard to the negative consequences that can result for the person subject to the guardianship.

Likewise, in New York, civil commitment for persons with mental illness and commitment for persons with ID/DD are governed by separate stat-

---

23. Unfortunately, there has been no "happy ending" for Jane. The OPWDD licensed residence she ended up in was unable to manage her behavior, leading to many emergency room visits and a possible admission to a long-term state facility.

24. *See generally* MHL Article 81; SCPA 17-A.

25. Karen Andreasian et al., *Revisiting SCPA 17-A: Guardianship for People with Intellectual and Developmental Disabilities*, 18 CUNY L. Rev. 287 (2015) (author of chapter a co-author). There are judges who do limit 17-A guardianship; *see, e.g., In re* Mark C.H., 28 Misc.3d 765 (Sur. Ct. N.Y. Cnty. 2010); *In re* Joyce G.S., 30 Misc. 3d 765 (Surr. Ct. Bronx Cty. 2010).

26. *Id.* at 334.

utes. Often persons with dual diagnoses end up at acute care psychiatric hospitals that are not equipped to address their disability. They are subject to treatment that is not tailored to their learning ability and are blamed for behaviors that may not be due to their mental illness but rather a communication issue as a result of their ID/DD diagnosis.[27] Issues surrounding a safe discharge can become very complicated for persons with dual diagnoses even if they are connected to services, if the residence the person came from refuses to take them back, if they lack a specific place to return to, or when a person does not wish to return to the former residence.

For persons with dual diagnoses who become entangled in the criminal justice system, nonjudicial officers directly affect the outcome including alternatives to incarceration programs and length of incarceration. The prevalence of mental illness and ID/DD within the criminal justice system is overwhelming.[28] Jails and prisons have become de facto mental hospitals, which are designed around security, safety, and control and not treatment.[29] Capacity issues can be the first barrier for a favorable disposition for persons with dual diagnoses. Courts rely almost exclusively on reports by mental health professionals in determining issues surrounding capacity. Persons with dual diagnoses are more likely to face longer commitments to competency restoration programs.[30] Once incarcerated, dual diagnosed persons are vulnerable to victimization and may have greater difficulty following the rules resulting in longer sentences and lower likelihood of parole.[31]

Alternatives to incarceration, also known as diversion programs, often depend solely on the discretion of the court and prosecution, who in turn rely on recommendations by nonjudicial officers. These officers must take into account the complexity that dual diagnoses persons face and narrowly tailor plans that allow for success. It often falls on defense counsel to educate the court and others by gathering as much information as possible about a defendant's psychosocial and medical history, request necessary documen-

---

27. Common notes in medical charts for persons with dual diagnoses often describe the person as "acting like a child," having poor impulse control when the person is denied something they are asking for, and being "unreasonable," as just a few examples.

28. Sheila Shea and Robert Goldman, *Ending Disparities and Achieving Justice for Individuals with Mental Disabilities*, 80 ALB. L. REV. 1037, 1043 (2017).

29. Bette Michelle Fleishman, *Invisible Minority: People Incarcerated with Mental Illness, Developmental Disabilities, and Traumatic Brain Injury in Washington's Jails and Prisons*, 11 SEATTLE J. SOC. JUST. 401, 452 (2012).

30. Haleigh Reisman, *Competency of the Mentally Ill and Intellectually Disabled in the Courts*, 11 J. HEALTH & BIOMEDICAL L. 199, 231 (2015). Competency restoration is the process by which a defendant is evaluated and treated, either in an inpatient or outpatient setting, to allow defendants to fully participate in their defense. *Id.* at 221.

31. Shea and Goldman, *supra* note 28, at 1043.

tation, and, with the defendant's permission, consult collateral sources like family members.[32] Current diversion programs are not always successful in keeping persons with dual diagnoses out of prison because supervision and support tends to stop after diversion.[33] Special training regarding the treatment of persons with mental illness and ID/DD for all of those involved in the criminal justice system, including both judicial and nonjudicial officers, should be provided.[34] Psychiatric examiners should engage in a contextual and functional analysis of a person's capacity, taking into account both the specific circumstances and abilities of the defendant and addressing the defendant's ability to take part in their defense.[35]

The interplay between civil and criminal law for persons with dual diagnoses leads to both positive and negative "blurs."[36] Positive blurs include the expansion of mental health courts and the application of the American with Disabilities Act (ADA).[37] Negative blurs include the coercive aspects of mandatory outpatient treatment, the civil commitment of sex offenders after serving criminal sentences, the imprisonment of insanity acquittees, and continuity of care issues for persons who shuttle between hospitals and jails or prisons.[38] Nonjudicial officers may add to the negative blur of civil and criminal law by failing to recognize these complexities and coercing persons with dual diagnoses into unwanted or inappropriate treatment settings.

The right to treatment and the least restrictive alternative for persons with mental illness, including persons with dual diagnoses, has long been established by case law.[39] Yet it still remains difficult for persons with dual diagnoses to receive appropriate treatment and services in the community. Continuity of care issues for persons with dual diagnoses can be improved through the use of mental health courts, diversion practices, and mental health

---

32. Rebecca J. Covarrubias, *Lives in Defense Counsel's Hands: The Problems and Responsibilities of Defense Counsel Representing Mentally Ill or Mentally Retarded Capital Defendants*, 11 SCHOLAR 413, 467 (2009).

33. Nicole Harris, *Evaluating the Effectiveness of Diversion Programs for Justice-Involved Persons with Mental Illness*, 29 ANNALS HEALTH L. ADVANCE DIRECTIVE 145, 161 (2020).

34. Reisman, *supra* note 30, at 234.

35. Shea and Goldman, *supra* note 28, at 1049.

36. Michael L. Perlin, Deborah A. Dorfman, and Naomi M. Weinstein, *"On Desolation Row": The Blurring of Borders between Civil and Criminal Mental Disability Law, and What It Means to All of Us*, 24 TEX. J. ON C.L. & C.R. 59 (2018).

37. *Id.* at 99–100.

38. *Id.* at 76–93.

39. *See, e.g.,* Jackson v. Indiana, 406 U.S. 715 (1972); Wyatt v. Stickney, 325 F. Supp. 781 (M.D. Ala. 1971); Lessard v. Schmidt, 349 F. Supp. 1078 (E.D. Wis. 1972); O'Connor v. Donaldson, 422 U.S. 563 (1975).

screenings.[40] Attorneys need to address continuity of care issues with non-judicial officers who often make the decisions as to what treatment a client receives.

The ADA applies to persons in psychiatric hospitals and correctional facilities as well as persons in the communities and guarantees certain accommodations for persons with dual diagnoses.[41] In *Olmstead v. L.C. ex rel. Zimring*, the Supreme Court has held that unjustified isolation is discrimination based on disability and that Title II of the ADA requires states to provide community-based treatment.[42] Subsequent litigation following the *Olmstead* decision has been essential in ensuring that persons with disabilities receive supports in the community.[43] Nevertheless, litigation has its limitations and cannot be successful without partnering with peer advocates and state leaders, policy makers, the federal government, and the community.[44]

The UN Convention on the Rights for Persons with Disabilities (CRPD) goes beyond the ADA and guarantees the rights of persons with disabilities to equal access to economic, social, and cultural rights and full participation in all aspects of society.[45] The CRPD's focus on stigma and prejudice, its uncompromising adoption of the social model, its reporting requirements, and its identification of specific steps that states must take to ensure human rights for everyone far extends what the ADA mandates.[46] Instead of asking how a person with a disability can manage on their own or what accommodations can be made for that person, the CRPD asks how society can change to ensure that needed accommodations, support, and assistance are provided to a person with disability.[47] The CRPD also offers more protections to persons with ID/DD in allowing for full participation and deci-

---

40. Naomi M. Weinstein and Michael L. Perlin, *"Who's Pretending to Care for Him?" How the Endless Jail-to-Hospital-to-Street-Repeat Cycle Deprives Persons with Mental Disabilities the Right to Continuity of Care*, 8 WAKE F. J.L. & POL'Y 455, 501 (2018).

41. Americans with Disabilities Act, 42 U.S.C. §§ 12101–213 (2012).

42. Olmstead v. L.C. *ex rel.* Zimring, 527 U.S. 581, 597, 607 (1999).

43. Talley Wells, *Lessons Learned from Georgia's 2010* Olmstead *Settlement: The Good, the Bad, and the Limitations of a Justice Department* Olmstead *Settlement*, 40 J. LEGAL MED. 45, 52 (2020).

44. *Id. at* 49–52.

45. G.A. Res. 61/106, United Nations Convention on the Rights of Persons with Disabilities (Dec. 13, 2006), hereinafter cited as CRPD.

46. Michael L. Perlin and Naomi M. Weinstein, *"There's Voices in the Night Trying to Be Heard": The Potential Impact of the Convention on the Rights of Persons with Disabilities on Domestic Mental Disability Law*, 84 BROOK. L. REV. 873, 906 (2019).

47. Arlene S. Kanter, *The American with Disabilities Act at 25 Years: Lessons to Learn from the Convention on the Rights of Persons with Disabilities*, 63 DRAKE L. REV. 819, 880 (2015).

sion-making rights.[48] Although the United States has yet to ratify the CRPD, it can still be used as a model when interacting with nonjudicial officers in the context of obtaining treatment or social services for persons with dual diagnoses.

How TJ Principles Can Improve Outcomes

TJ recognizes that the law, as a therapeutic agent, can have therapeutic or antitherapeutic consequences.[49] TJ involves a client-centered approach that eschews coercion and paternalism.[50] TJ suggests that the law should value psychological health, should avoid imposing antitherapeutic consequences, and should attempt to bring about healing and wellness.[51] Voice, validation, and a sense of voluntariness are core TJ values.[52] TJ is also one of the key paths to create a law of healing, recognizing, and rejecting the roots of sanism.[53]

One of the central principles of TJ is a commitment to dignity. Dignity means that each person possesses an intrinsic worth that should be recognized and respected, as well as a right to be free from treatment by the state that is inconsistent with their intrinsic worth.[54] Human dignity protects individuals from humiliation and other threats and injuries to people's self-worth.[55]

The right to dignity is memorialized in many state constitutions, human rights documents, judicial opinions, and constitutions of other nations. The CRPD calls for "respect and inherent dignity" and characterizes "discrimination against any person on the basis of disability [as a] violation of the inherent dignity and worth of the human person."[56] Human dignity pro-

---

48. Bryan Y. Lee, *The U.N. Convention on the Rights of Persons with Disabilities and Its Impact Upon Involuntary Civil Commitment of Individuals with Developmental Disabilities*, 44 COLUM. J.L. & SOC. PROBS. 393, 444 (2011).

49. Michael L. Perlin, *"His Brain Has Been Mismanaged with Great Skill": How Will Jurors Respond to Neuroimaging Testimony in Insanity Defense Cases?*, 42 AKRON L. REV. 885, 912 (2009).

50. David B. Wexler, *Getting and Giving: What Therapeutic Jurisprudence Can Get from and Give to Positive Criminology*, 6 PHOENIX L. REV. 907, 908 (2013).

51. Bruce J. Winick, *Outpatient Commitment: A Therapeutic Jurisprudence Analysis*, 9 PSYCHOL. PUB. POL'Y & L. 107, 110 (2003).

52. Amy D. Ronner, *Songs of Validation, Voice, and Voluntary Participation: Therapeutic Jurisprudence, Miranda, and Juveniles*, 71 U. CIN. L. REV. 89, 111–13 (2002).

53. Michael L. Perlin, *A Law of Healing*, 68 U. CIN. L. REV. 407, 419 (2000).

54. Carol Sanger, *Decisional Dignity: Teenage Abortion, Bypass Hearings, and the Misuse of Law*, 18 COLUM. J. GENDER & L. 409, 415 (2009).

55. Michael L. Perlin and Naomi M. Weinstein, *"Friend to the Martyr, A Friend to the Woman of Shame": Thinking about the Law, Shame, and Humiliation*, 24 S. CAL. REV. L. & SOC. JUST. 1, 50 (2014).

56. CRPD, *supra* note 45 at art. 3(a); preamble(h).

vides each of us equal moral standing under the law against arbitrary government action that demeans, humiliates, and degrades.[57] Respecting client autonomy is the best way to ensure that the client's dignity is maintained.

TJ principles also coincide with the movement towards supported decision-making, which is also reinforced in both the ADA and the CRPD. While the total abolition of guardianship remains a controversial topic, there has been recognition that guardianships can unnecessarily isolate persons with psychosocial impairments and lead to feelings of helplessness, shame and humiliation.[58] Supported decision-making allows individuals to receive support in order to understand relevant information and available choices in accordance with their wishes, rather than completely take away their right to make any decisions at all.[59]

Application of TJ principles can enhance the effectiveness of treatment and rehabilitation, increase the effectiveness of the legal process, lead to greater independence and quality of life for persons with dual diagnoses, and create opportunities to enhance advocacy and social policy development for persons with dual diagnoses.[60] When interacting with persons with dual diagnoses, it is important to ensure that actions are truly voluntary and that treatment is not coercive, even in cases where the person is under a guardianship order.[61]

When policies and procedures give people an opportunity to exercise their voice in a manner where their words are given respect, and when decisions are explained to them and their views taken into account, then they substantively feel less coercion, making it more likely they will engage in treatment and be able to live as independently as possible in the community.[62] Even for those with dual diagnoses who are subject to involuntary commitment or imprisonment, by adhering to the basic principles of dignity, showing respect, and listening to the individuals, this will result in more positive outcomes for these individuals.[63] It is also important to remember

---

57. Maxine D. Goodman, *Human Dignity in Supreme Court Constitutional Jurisprudence*, 84 NEB. L. REV. 740, 751 (2006).

58. Leslie Salzman, *Guardianship for Persons with Mental Illness—A Legal and Appropriate Alternative?* 4 ST. LOUIS U.J. HEALTH L. & POL'Y 279, 281 (2011).

59. *Id.* at 306.

60. William Spaulding et al., *Applications of Therapeutic Jurisprudence in Rehabilitation for People with Severe and Disabling Mental Illness*, 17 T.M. COOLEY L. REV, 135, 136 (2000).

61. Richard C. Boldt, *The "Voluntary" Inpatient Treatment of Adults under Guardianship*, 60 VILL. L. REV. 1, 52 (2015).

62. Jonathan Simon and Stephen A. Rosenbaum, *Dignifying Madness: Rethinking Commitment Law in an Age of Mass Incarceration*, 70 MIAMI L. REV. 1, 51 (2015).

63. *Id.* at 41. Beyond the scope of this chapter is the treatment of minors with dual diagnoses and how TJ can improve outcomes; *see, e.g.*, Jan. C. Costello, *Why Have Hearings for*

that society as a whole does not benefit from incarcerating individuals with dual diagnoses in an environment that is countertherapeutic and at times dangerous to the mental and physical well-being of these individuals.[64]

Diversion programs, both prebooking and postbooking, benefit from increased linkage and coordination between people in the justice system and service providers.[65] For those with dual diagnoses subject to prolonged hospitalizations, they must be provided the least restrictive environment that is closely linked to normal life in the community while waiting for further treatment or services in the community.[66] Reassessments must also take place on a regular and individualized basis.[67]

There are several strategies that attorneys can employ when interacting with nonjudicial officers making decisions affecting the lives of persons with dual diagnoses. Litigation is of course one strategy, pursuing actions in accordance with state laws and regulations, the ADA, and the CRPD. Bringing state actions may be more effective in some cases in seeking treatment for individuals with dual diagnoses rather than relying on federal law.[68] Another strategy is using administrative remedies within the state agencies pursuant to state regulations. Often due to the complexity of issues that persons with dual diagnoses face, advocacy can take other forms such as reaching out to nonjudicial officers in efforts to educate and collaborate to achieve the best outcomes. If a person with dual diagnoses is stuck in a hospital pending discharge, working with hospital staff and administrators can lead to additional services being provided to the person while in the hospital and can connect the person to more services upon discharge.

Conclusion

It is important to make sure that persons who have both a mental illness and ID/DD receive appropriate support and services and do not get lost in a system that tends to address only part of their needs. As much as possible, attorneys should try to work together with the nonjudicial officers who often

---

Kids if You're Not Going to Listen? A Therapeutic Jurisprudence Approach to Mental Disability Proceedings for Minors, 71 U. Cin. L. Rev. 19 (2002).

64. Fleishman, *supra* note 29, at 453.

65. Harris, *supra* note 33, at 158.

66. Simon, *supra* note 62, at 46.

67. *Id.*

68. Katie Eyer, *Litigating for Treatment: The Use of State Laws and Constitutions in Obtaining Treatment Rights for Individuals with Mental Illness*, 28 N.Y.U. Rev. L. Soc. Change 1, 55 (2003). *See also* Michael L. Perlin, *State Constitutions and Statutes as Sources of Rights for the Mentally Disabled: The Last Frontier?* 20 Loyola L.A. L. Rev. 1249 (1987).

are in positions of power to make decisions regarding the welfare of their clients. Failing collaborative opportunities, attorneys have multiple avenues of litigation involving international, state, and federal law. By adhering to the TJ principles of giving clients voice, validation, and making sure their actions are voluntary, better outcomes can be achieved for this often-overlooked population.

8

Therapeutic Jurisprudence in the Jefferson Parish, Louisiana, Reentry Court

Victoria Rapp

Introduction

Mass incarceration is a prevalent issue throughout the United States.[1] This problem is heightened in states, such as Louisiana, that have some of the nation's highest incarceration rates. As one effort to decrease the prison population, Reentry Court is a program aimed at both lowering the prison population and recidivism.[2] A combined state and local effort, Reentry Court is implemented in multiple Louisiana parishes,[3] including Jefferson Parish,[4] which created its program in 2014.[5] This chapter discusses how Reentry Court differs from traditional incarceration and probation, describes the different components of the Reentry Court, and concludes with the ways that therapeutic jurisprudence is manifested in that court.[6]

---

1. *See, e.g.*, John Pfaff, Locked in: The True Causes of Mass Incarceration and How to Achieve Real Reform (2017); Rachel Barkow, Prisoners of Politics: Breaking the Cycle of Mass Incarceration (2019).

2. Reentry Court (last visited Jan. 28, 2021), https://www.smartsupervision.us/reentry -court.

3. *Id.*

4. Jefferson Parish encompasses the west and east areas around New Orleans, Louisiana.

5. Reentry Court, *supra* note 2.

6. On the need for Reentry Courts to incorporate therapeutic jurisprudence in general, *see* Kelsey Geary, *A Warmer Welcome Home: The Need for Incorporating Therapeutic Jurisprudence in Reentry Courts*, 27 St. Thomas L. Rev. 268 (2015).

Traditional Incarceration and Probation

Conventional incarceration is much different from the incarceration portion of Reentry Court, as described later. Conventional inmates in Louisiana may be required to work, but they do not get to choose a trade to learn and earn applicable certifications for a trade. There are neither educational nor counseling requirements that a conventionally incarcerated person has to meet in order to be released.

Traditional probation also differs notably from Reentry Court probation as described later. Traditional probationers do not have to contact or see their probation or parole officer nearly as frequently.[7] They also do not have to attend frequent court hearings. While it is not uncommon for traditional probationers to be required to take drug tests,[8] the frequency of taking those tests is not high. Rehabilitative resources are not readily available for traditional probationers.[9] Moreover, when traditional probationers do appear in court for violations of their conditions, it is very unlikely to be in front of a judge who knows them and who is aware of the successes and challenges they have had prior to and while on probation. As such, the hearings are likely to be quite adversarial events.

Reentry Court in Louisiana: An Overview

Reentry Court was created in 2010 by two judges in Orleans Parish.[10] Since then, the program has been implemented in eight parishes across the state.[11] The implementation of Reentry Court has been made available by LA. REV. STAT. § 13:5401.[12] It takes several years for participants to fully complete the Reentry Court program. This, along with the date that Reentry Court was established, is important to keep in mind when examining the literature about Reentry Court.[13] An evaluation study of Reentry Court in St. Tammany Par-

---

7. "Traditional probation is spectacularly ineffective." Stephen Cooper, *The Carrot and the Stick*, 82 MICH. B.J. 20, 22 (Jan. 2003).

8. *See, e.g.*, Molly Webster, *Alternative Courts and Drug Treatment: Finding a Rehabilitative Solution for Addicts in a Retributive System*, 84 FORDHAM L. REV. 855 (2015).

9. *See, e.g.*, Jaclyn Kurin, *Indebted to Injustice: The Meaning of "Willfulness" in a Georgia v. Bearden Ability to Pay Hearing*, 27 GEO. MASON U. CIV. RTS. L.J. 265, 284 (2017) ("Many local governments turn externally to probation companies because the local government and courts are cash-strapped and lack the resources to administer probation services").

10. Reentry Court, *supra* note 2.

11. LA. REV. STAT. §13:5401.

12. *Id.*

13. The majority of the scholarly literature about these courts is specifically about the Reentry Court program in St Tammany Parish, Louisiana. *See* J. Mitchell Miller and David N. Khey, *Fighting America's Highest Incarceration Rates with Offender Programming: Process*

ish found that "while participant attitude varied in terms of enthusiasm and perceived endorsement of treatment objectives, participant involvement was observed as constantly strong and, ostensibly, a function of the strict phase conditions and regular reporting required by the Court."[14] Another article, also on Reentry Court in St. Tammany Parish, provides an interesting perspective, as one of the coauthors is the Reentry Court judge for that parish and another is the person who coined the term "therapeutic jurisprudence."[15] These authors emphasize the importance of collaboration among government agencies and community organizations to facilitate the success of participants in the program.[16]

While Reentry Court is available in multiple Louisiana parishes, there are differences in the way that the program is executed, as well as differences that are more apparent in the probation section of Reentry Court.[17] Reentry Court is designed to serve a specific population of offenders. Offenders who have committed sexual offenses or violent offenses are ineligible for the program.[18] In addition, to qualify for the Reentry Court program, offenders cannot have been sentenced to more than ten years of incarceration.[19] The intended population for Reentry Court are individuals whose offense was somehow related to drug use or sales.[20] Those charges must have been brought forth by a Louisiana parish that is participating in the Reentry Court program. There are no limitations in terms of gender or age for Reentry Court eligibility, though this chapter will focus on the Reentry Court program for men because that program is much more robust in many aspects, including the vocational program choices available, the services available, and the number of participants to date.

Evaluation Implications from the Louisiana 22nd Judicial District Reentry Court, 42 AM. J. CRIM. JUST. 574, 577 (2016).

14. *Id.* at 585.

15. *See* William Knight, Caroline Cooper, and David B. Wexler, *Louisiana Reentry Court Promotes Seamless Transition between Sentencing, Incarceration, and Post Release Services— Some Potential Exportable Elements* (2015), accessible at https://ssrn.com/abstract=2926512, manuscript at 2–3; Liz Richardson, Pauline Spencer, and David B. Wexler, *The International Framework for Court Excellence and Therapeutic Jurisprudence: Creating Excellent Courts and Enhancing Wellbeing*, 25 J. JUD. ADMIN. 148 (2016).

16. Knight, Cooper, and Wexler, *supra* note 15, manuscript at 3–4.

17. The following information on Reentry Court is specifically about the Jefferson Parish Reentry Court, however there are certainly many similarities in the way that Reentry Court is run in Jefferson Parish and the way that Reentry Court is run in other parishes.

18. Reentry Court, *supra* note 2.

19. *Id.*

20. Miller and Khey, *supra* note 13, at 574.

The Reentry Court program is heavily structured, and there are multiple requirements that must be fulfilled by participants. These requirements are divided into the two steps of the program, beginning with incarceration and ending with closely supervised probation.[21] Upon being accepted into the Reentry Court program, participants are sent to the Louisiana State Penitentiary, commonly referred as Angola.[22] The incarceration portion of Reentry Court takes at least two years to complete.[23]

The Reentry Court Program in Jefferson Parish, Louisiana

Incarceration

Although the incarceration section of Reentry Court takes place in a conventional correctional facility, the Reentry Court participants have a much different day-to-day life than prisoners under traditional incarceration. At the Louisiana State Penitentiary, the Reentry Court program takes place in a different camp than traditionally incarcerated offenders. Many of these differences have to do with the requirements and resources available to Reentry Court program participants. Participants must complete the High School Equivalency Test (HISET) if they have not completed high school or passed an equivalent test.[24] Participants are also required to choose a vocation to learn while they are incarcerated.[25] There are a variety of trades to choose from, including horticulture, welding, automotive mechanics, small engine mechanics, and HVAC.[26]

Once participants choose a vocation, they receive a vocational program mentor. These mentors are people trained in that vocation, and in most cases, the mentors are people incarcerated at that correctional facility.[27] While learning their trade, participants earn certifications for their trade to make them better job candidates when they reenter society.[28]

---

21. Reentry Court, *supra* note 2.

22. *Id.*

23. *Id.*

24. *Reentry Court Handbook 24th Judicial District Court Parish of Jefferson State of Louisiana* (2020), https://static1.squarespace.com/static/5953f48c72af657ab9b59987/t/5f6a1e3548 58b942367d10ee/1600790070130/REENTRY+COURT+Handbook+Rev+2020_08_28.pdf, hereafter cited as *Reentry Court Handbook*.

25. *Id.* at 2; Reentry Court, *supra* note 2.

26. *Id.*

27. Miller and Khey, *supra* note 13, at 578.

28. Knight, Cooper, and Wexler, *supra* note 15, manuscript at 2.

While incarcerated, the Reentry Court participants are also given a social mentor.[29] Social mentors are incarcerated at Angola and in many cases are serving very long or even life sentences. Their goal is to help the Reentry Court participants, who will be returning to the community, build the skills, knowledge, and confidence necessary to reduce the likelihood they will recidivate and return to prison.[30] The social mentors are carefully selected from a group of applicants.[31] In order to be eligible to be a social mentor, applicants must be graduates of the New Orleans Baptist Theological Seminary, which provides the social mentor training to the selected inmates at Angola.[32] Due to the mandatory education through the seminary required to become a mentor, there is a religious (specifically, a Christian Baptist) aspect to their approach with the Reentry Court participants.[33] The role of the social mentor is to teach their assigned Reentry Court participants how to be productive members of society in a number of ways.[34] At the Louisiana State Penitentiary, the social mentors help with "peer-based drug education, fatherhood skills, anger management, personal finance and personal health," all of which could aid in preparing Reentry Court participants for the close supervision probation part of the program.[35]

Probation

After at least two years spent completing the requirements of the incarceration component of Reentry Court, participants petition the Reentry Court judge in their parish to move on to closely supervised probation.[36] There are four phases in the probation section of Reentry Court.[37] To move from one phase to another, participants must obtain a certain amount of points.[38] There are multiple requirements that participants must complete in the probation part of the Reentry Court program in order to earn those points and then graduate from the program. This includes attending frequent court hearings. In the first phase of probation, participants have to attend a status

---

29. *Id.*

30. *Id.*

31. *Id.*; Perry Stagg, *Louisiana State Penitentiary Corrections Court Reentry Program: Teaching Morality and Change through Inmate Mentors*, CORRECTIONS TODAY 37, 38 (2015).

32. Stagg, *supra* note 31, at 38.

33. Miller and Khey, *supra* note 13, at 578, 583–84. To the best of my knowledge, there has never been a First Amendment–based challenge to the religious aspect of this program.

34. Reentry Court, *supra* note 2.

35. Miller and Khey, *supra* note 13, at 578.

36. Reentry Court, *supra* note 2.

37. *Reentry Court Handbook, supra* note 24, at 5.

38. *Id.* at 6–9.

hearing every week.[39] As the participants progress through the probation part of Reentry Court, the frequency of court hearings declines.[40] In addition, participants must participate in the group counseling sessions and treatment meetings, pass frequent drug tests, and check in with their probation officer often.[41] Group counseling consists of moral reconation therapy to address criminal behavior and thinking.[42]

The courtroom atmosphere of Reentry Court status hearings is an important aspect of the program. The judge who sentences the Reentry Court participants to begin the program is the same judge the participant has while they are in the probation portion of the program (unless the judge is running for office or on vacation).[43] The status hearing atmosphere varies based on how well the participants have been doing in the program recently. Unlike traditional courtroom interactions with the person on the docket, Reentry Court participants have an opportunity to interact with the judge. The judge typically asks how their week has been, how their job is going, and about any issues that they may have experienced. Reentry Court participants graduate when they complete their program.[44]

Therapeutic Jurisprudence[45] in Reentry Court

Therapeutic jurisprudence is evident in many aspects of both the incarceration portion and the probation portion of Reentry Court. At its core, Reentry Court seeks to prevent recidivism through rehabilitation and increasing prosocial behavior among program participants.[46] All of the therapeutic jurisprudence aspects of the Reentry Court work together to help the program participants succeed in these goals. The approach aims to address why

---

39. *Id.* at 6.

40. *Id.* at 6–7.

41. *Id.* at 14.

42. Moral reconation therapy "is a cognitive-behavioral treatment system that leads to enhanced moral reasoning, better decision making, and more appropriate behavior." Greg Little, *About MRT, Moral Reconation Therapy* (last visited Mar. 7, 2021), https://www.moral-reconation-therapy.com/about.html. It was developed in a prison setting in Tennessee in the 1980s and has since expanded to both custodial and community-based entities. *See* Chris Hansen, *Cognitive-Behavioral Interventions: Where They Come from and What They Do*, 72 Fed. Probation 43, 45–46 (2008). It is based on Lawrence Kohlberg's moral development theory. *See* Sean C. McGarvey, *Juvenile Justice and Mental Health: Innovation in the Laboratory of Human Behavior*, 53 Jurimetrics J. 97, 108 (2012).

43. *See* Knight, Cooper, and Wexler, *supra* note 15, manuscript at 2–3.

44. Reentry Court, *supra* note 2; *Reentry Court Handbook*, *supra* note 24, at 10.

45. For more information about the components of therapeutic jurisprudence, *see* Richardson, Spencer, and Wexler, *supra* note 15.

46. Reentry Court, *supra* note 2.

they have committed crimes, prevent what is characterized as "criminal think-ing," learn strategies to address struggles in a more productive manner rath-er than turning to crime, prevent and/or address struggles that formerly incarcerated people face when attempting to reenter society, and aid each program participant's well-being.[47]

In the incarceration portion of Reentry Court, therapeutic jurispru-dence can be manifested in social mentor and group counseling require-ments. The purpose of the social mentors is to help Reentry Court partici-pants learn prosocial ways of dealing with life's challenges.[48] The issues that Reentry Court participants face differ from one another, and therapeutic jurisprudence is reflected in ways that social mentors work to learn and ad-dress each participant's unique issues and needs. Although not technically a form of therapeutic jurisprudence, group counseling nevertheless seems to enhance the therapeutic jurisprudence principles evidenced elsewhere in the Reentry Count program. The group counseling for Reentry Court has an emphasis on substance abuse treatment.[49] Group counseling gives partici-pants the opportunity to share their personal experiences and struggles with others who have experienced similar struggles in life. This form of counseling addresses a participant's individual needs while also showing participants that they are not alone in what they are experiencing or have experienced in their lifetime.

Therapeutic jurisprudence is also observable in the education of Reentry Court participants while they are at Angola. Some Reentry Court partici-pants did graduate high school or pass high school equivalency tests before starting Reentry Court. However, many Reentry Court participants did not; the requirement to complete the high school equivalency test is only for the latter group.[50] Although not as important as vocational training in obtain-ing a job, passing this test could allow more job opportunities for partici-pants once they finish the incarceration section of the Reentry Court pro-gram, as many jobs require a high school diploma or passing a high school equivalency test.

Vocational training is a large component of the incarceration portion of Reentry Court and also has therapeutic jurisprudence aspects to it. Learn-ing a vocation or trade is a requirement for all Reentry Court participants, even if they are already well versed in a trade not available at their correc-

---

47. Such "criminal thinking" is evaluated and measured through the use of an assessment tool. *See* Research and Evaluation Group at PMHC, *RANT, Criminal Justice Tools* (last vis-ited March 8, 2021), https://research.phmc.org/products/criminal-justice-tools.

48. Reentry Court, *supra* note 2; *Reentry Court Handbook, supra* note 24, at 3.

49. *Id.* At 24.

50. *Id.* At 3.

tional facility.[51] By allowing each participant to select their vocation to learn from the available options rather than assigning them a vocation, the program stakeholders are taking each participant's personal preferences, feelings, and needs into account. A participant may select a specific trade for a number of reasons, such as the one that sounds most enjoyable to them, the trade that they believe will be easiest to obtain a job in when they are released, or the vocation that would be easiest to manage with other life obligations such as fatherhood.

A risk/needs assessment is given to each program participant to aid in determining what the participant's specific needs are.[52] Reentry Court personnel work in a variety of ways either directly or indirectly to address the participants' individual risks and needs. Reentry Court staff include the judge, probation officers, social worker/counselor, an assistant district attorney, a public defender, and community organizations.[53] Most of the court personnel meet in the courthouse (or, since the COVID-19 pandemic, over video chat) to discuss participants prior to each Reentry Court status hearing.[54]

When examining how therapeutic jurisprudence manifests in court personnel roles and in interactions with participants, it is crucial to remember this manifestation is specific to this Reentry Court. If there were a different judge running the program, therapeutic jurisprudence may manifest differently.[55] The same can be said about probation officers working with Reentry Court participants.[56] The availability of services and the quality of those services that can aid Reentry Court participants vary from parish to parish. Thus, the information about the Jefferson Parish Reentry Court personnel likely cannot be generalized to Reentry Court personnel in other parishes, and insofar as court personnel and services impact outcomes for participants, those could not be widely generalized either.[57]

---

51. *Id.*; Reentry Court, *supra* note 2.

52. *See* Miller and Khey, *supra* note 13, for similar assessment details in 22nd Judicial District Court.

53. *Reentry Court Handbook, supra* note 24, at 4–5; Reentry Court participants may obtain private counsel, but it is recommended that such counsel step down upon the participant starting probation because the status hearings are so frequent.

54. *Id.* at 13.

55. Michael L. Perlin, *The Judge, He Cast His Robe Aside: Mental Health Courts, Dignity, and Due Process*, 3 MENTAL HEALTH & L. POL'Y J. 1, 1–2, 27 (2013); Richardson, Spencer, and Wexler, *supra* note 15, at 158.

56. Kelly Frailing, Brandi Alfonso, and Rae Taylor, *Therapeutic Jurisprudence in Swift and Certain Probation*, 64 AM. BEHAV. SCI. 1768, 1781–82 (2020).

57. It appears that participation in reentry courts in other Louisiana parishes, particularly Orleans and St. Tammany, is associated with reduced recidivism. *See* Justice and Ac-

Therapeutic jurisprudence is reflected in the role of the judge in Reentry Court. There is one judge who presides over the Reentry Court in Jefferson Parish, Louisiana.[58] Unlike what is more typical in traditional courts, the Reentry Court judge knows quite a bit about the Reentry Court participants, including information not directly related to their offenses. In the weekly status hearings, the judge asks participants about their lives, including any good news they have as well as any struggles with which they have been dealing.[59] Reentry Court participants have individual interactions with the judge at each status hearing. Thus, the participants are able to freely discuss in their own words any struggles or successes, as well as to ask the judge questions. In the status hearings, therapeutic jurisprudence is manifested by allowing participants to have their own voices heard in court. Discussing the participants' lives helps the judge understand all participants and their unique needs. Further, the judge is able to see the prosocial changes in the individual participants as they progress through the program. These interactions also help future Reentry Court participants because if the judge determines if there are struggles that are more common, he can work with other court personnel to figure out the best ways to address those struggles. Reentry Court hearings are not necessarily negative for participants in the ways that traditional court proceedings often are. If the participant is doing well, then the conversation between the judge and the participant is positive, and the judge may issue praise.[60] When the participants complete the Reentry Program, their final hearing is very positive and is considered a graduation.[61]

The probation officers who manage the Reentry Court cases play an important role in terms of therapeutic jurisprudence.[62] In addition to seeing the participants at each hearing, the probation officers communicate with them throughout the week.[63] If a participant is having trouble with some-

---

countability Center of Louisiana, *Re-Entry Legal Services* (last visited March 8, 2021) https://www.jaclouisiana.org/re-entry.

58. *Reentry Court Handbook, supra* note 24, at 4.

59. Cindy B. Dollar et al., *Examine Changes in Procedural Justice and Their Influence on Problem-Solving Court Outcomes,* 36 BEHAV. SCI. & L. 32, 37 (2018); Kelly Frailing, *How Mental Health Courts Function: Outcomes and Observations,* 33 INT'L J. L. & PSYCHIATRY 207, 208–9, 211–13 (2010).

60. On the role of praise in problem solving courts, *see* Carol Fisler, *Building Trust and Managing Risk: A Look at a Felony Mental Health Court,* 11 PSYCHOL. PUB. POL'Y & L. 587, 597 (2005).

61. Frailing, *supra* note 59, at 211–12.

62. Frailing, Alfonso, and Taylor, *supra* note 56, at 1779.

63. *Reentry Court Handbook, supra* note 24, at 6–7.

thing or has an accomplishment,[64] the probation officer is generally the first court personnel member to know both about it and the details surrounding that issue or accomplishment. The probation officer can notify the judge about recent accomplishments of a Reentry Court participant in the meeting that precedes each status hearing. The frequent communication between participants and their probation officer allows participants more of an opportunity to freely express their feelings, thoughts, and opinions with their probation officer. The close relationship between the probation officers and their Reentry Court participants allows the probation officer to make recommendations to judge as to how to praise a participant in the case of an accomplishment or sanction a participant in the case of a violation. Given the specific circumstances related to an individual participant and their violation of a Reentry Court probation condition, the probation officer may feel that individual would be better suited serving their sanction through community service or writing an essay rather than serving the sanction in jail.

Two probation officers work with Reentry Court participants in Jefferson Parish. Having a small number of probation officers assigned to Reentry Court can be beneficial for multiple reasons. The first of these is related to efficiency. The small number of probation officers may be more efficient because the probation officers are more easily able to attend the hearings. The second reason is related to therapeutic jurisprudence. In a similar way that the judge may notice common issues among Reentry Court participants, the probation officers can as well. Due to the frequent communication with participants, probation officers may be able to detect the underlying issues causing or exacerbating a struggle that one or more participants may be experiencing. Although the individual needs for participants certainly vary, determining common issues and the most effective ways to solve them is important. A probation officer will likely be the first one to hear how well proposed solutions to participants' issues are working for them.

The social worker/counselor is arguably the court personnel member in whom therapeutic jurisprudence is most clearly manifested. The purpose of this person's role is to work with each Jefferson Parish Reentry Court participant in both the incarceration and probation portions of Reentry Court to determine the risks and needs of the participants, how these risks and needs may be changing, and how best to address them. She meets with the Reentry Court participants individually, as well as runs the aforementioned group counseling during the probation portion of Reentry Court. Discus-

---

64. Accomplishments include obtaining a new job, getting a job promotion, reconnecting with family members, using prosocial behaviors to manage a substantial life challenge, and being sober for a prolonged period of time.

sion of accomplishments, struggles, risks, and needs of participants is a manifestation of therapeutic jurisprudence because these discussions often take a psychological and rehabilitative approach.

Finally, there are multiple organizations involved in the Jefferson Parish, Louisiana, Reentry Court. These organizations provide several resources such as drug tests, job placement, and transportation assistance. These organizations are crucial to the probation portion of Reentry Court because they provide services that address risks and needs of program participants and give them the opportunity to successfully meet their probation requirements. Transportation to status hearings or to work could be an issue for some participants that do not have a car and do not live or work near those locations.[65] Some organizations provide bus passes and/or ride-sharing app credits. Also, obtaining a job is one of the requirements in order to move on to the probation section of Reentry Court. Even with the certificates earned while in the vocation program at Angola, jobs can fall through for multiple reasons. Sometimes an employer backs out on the job offer. In addition, the COVID-19 pandemic has caused some job-placement issues. Organizations focused on job placement that work with Reentry Court can help find participants another job.

Conclusion

The Jefferson Parish, Louisiana, Reentry Court takes a unique approach to sentencing by working to provide each participant with individual tools and resources to thoroughly address criminogenic risks and needs. This approach begins at Angola and continues into the probation portion of the program. Concern for participants' well-being is observable throughout the Reentry Court program.[66] Although there have previously been no published studies on Reentry Court in Jefferson Parish, the resources available, as well as the commitment and collaboration of court personnel, indicate that the Jefferson Parish Reentry Court may be promising in terms of criminal justice outcomes for participants, including reduced recidivism. As more participants graduate from this Reentry Court and evaluative studies are conducted on the program, it will be interesting to see the impact of the therapeutic jurisprudence approach to Reentry Court on the recidivism rate and on the lives of Reentry Court participants and graduates.

---

65. Miriam N. Bohmert and Alfred DeMaris, *Cumulative Disadvantage and the Role of Transportation in Community Supervision*, 64 CRIME & DELINQ. 1033, 1033–38, 1047–48, 1050 (2018).

66. *See* Richardson, Spencer, and Wexler, *supra* note 15, at 165.

PART II

Nonjudicial Officers in Administrative Settings

9

Doing Time in "the Devil's Chair"

*Evaluating Nonjudicial Administrative Decisions to
Isolate and Restrain Prisoners and Detainees with
Mental Health Disabilities in Jails and Prisons**

Deborah A. Dorfman

Introduction

People with mental illness often enter the criminal justice system through the forensic mental health system, which in turn involves a range of judicial decisions including bail, competency to stand trial, and other trial issues (e.g., competency to represent oneself or enter a plea, and sentencing). At the same time, most of these individuals are subjected to a parallel process involving a series of nonjudicial administrative decisions that often have profoundly antitherapeutic, devastating, and traumatic effects on their lives. This is particularly true for those who are incarcerated. These decisions include housing assignments, solitary confinement, use of force, and imposition of restraints and other restrictive interventions, among other related decisions.

Not every administrative decision made with respect to mentally ill prisoners is antitherapeutic. There are many daily decisions that prison administrators and staff make that affect the lives of prisoners that are necessary and appropriate. The focus of this article, however, is on those administrative decisions that commonly lead to negative outcomes for prisoners[1] with mental illness. These decisions are often made with broad discretion and little oversight or accountability and result in antitherapeutic effects.[2] The vast and growing numbers of individuals with mental illness confined to jails and prisons, and the concomitant harm resulting from these decisions, make the need to remedy these issues urgent.[3]

Here, I address the antitherapeutic jurisprudential implications of non-judicial administrative determinations on people with mental health illness in jails and prisons, particularly emphasizing decisions made by correctional staff about the use of segregation/isolation and physical restraints. The first part of this chapter provides a brief overview of the historical bias and discrimination against people with mental illness, concentrating on those in the forensic mental health system. The second part addresses the therapeutic jurisprudential implications for people with mental illness as a result of nonjudicial/administrative decision-making in jails and prisons.[4] The final part proposes remedies to address the antitherapeutic effects of nonjudicial/administrative decision-making on incarcerated people with mental illness.

---

1. The term "prisoners" includes individuals incarcerated in jail and in prisons, regardless of their legal status.

2. Kimberly A. Houser et al., *Mental Health Risk Factors and Parole Decisions: Does Inmate Mental Health Status Affect Who Gets Released?*, 16 INT'L J. ENVIRON. RES. & PUBLIC HEALTH 2950, 2963 (2019) ("Decision making takes place at every step of the criminal justice system, with discretion being an inevitable part of the decision-making process.").

3. The number of individuals with mental illness incarcerated in American jails and prisons is substantial and growing. Jamie Fellner, *A Corrections Quandary: Mental Illness and Prison Rules*, 41 HARVARD CIV. R.-CIV. LIB. L.R. 391, 392 (2006) (number of prisoners with mental illness is increasing); *see also* Jennifer Bronson and Marcus Berezofsky, U.S. Department of Justice, Office of Justice Program, *Bureau of Statistics Special Report, "Indicators of Mental Health Problems Reported by Prisons and Jail* (2011–12) at 1 (reporting that more than half of people in jails in the United States and more than one-third of those in prisons had mental health disabilities); *see also* Kenneth L. Appelbaum, *The Use of Restraint and Seclusion in Correctional Mental Health*, 35 J. AM. ACAD. PSYCHIATRY & L. 431 (2007).

4. Administrative decisions in facilities including forensic mental health facilities, juvenile detention, and other institutions are beyond the scope of this article.

Overview of Historical Bias and Discrimination Against Individuals with Mental Health Disabilities

Sanism in Mental Disability Law Decision-Making

Before exploring the therapeutic jurisprudential implications for administrative decision-making, it is important to examine the historical perceptions, and discriminatory treatment of, people with mental health disabilities. While people with disabilities have historically been subject to discrimination,[5] people with mental illness in particular have endured a history of virulent discrimination, despise, and fear—and they continue to do so.[6] For centuries, people with mental health disabilities were regarded as "monsters," subhuman, and possessed by the devil.[7] Consequently, they were often locked up and hidden away from society in institutions or prisons. Today, treatment of people with mental health disabilities has improved, yet stigma and disdain of people with mental illness persists.[8] Many remain relegated to institutions, including jails and prisons, and face discrimination and rejection throughout society.[9]

These fears and stigma are similarly pervasive in almost every aspect of the legal system, including the criminal justice system. As Professor Michael Perlin has written, these unfounded fears of people with disabilities are a result of what he refers to as sanism—"the irrational prejudice and biases that

---

5. As Congress recognized in enacting the Americans with Disabilities Act, "individuals with disabilities are a discrete and insular minority who have been faced with restrictions and limitations, subjected to a history of purposeful unequal treatment, and relegated to a position of political powerlessness in our society, based on characteristics that are beyond the control of such individuals and resulting from stereotypic assumptions not truly indicative of the individual ability of such individuals to participate in, and contribute to, society." 42 U.S.C. § 12101(a)(7).

6. Michael L. Perlin, *On Sanism*," 46 SMU L. REV. 373, 394–97 (1992) (discussing commonly held myths that people with mental health disabilities are dangerous).

7. *See* Michael L. Perlin, *Unpacking the Myths: The Symbolism Mythology of Insanity Defense Jurisprudence*, 40 CASE W. RES. L. REV. 599, 626 (1989–90).

8. Wulf Rossler, *The Stigma of Mental Disorders: A Millennia-Long History of Social Exclusion and Prejudice*, 17 SCI. & SOCIETY 1250 (2016); *see also* Angela M. Parcesepe and Leonardo Cabassa, *Public Stigma of Mental Illness in the United States: A Systematic Literature Review*, 40 ADMIN. POLICY MENT. HEALTH 1 (2013); Houser *et al.*, *supra* note 2, at 2–3 (discussing stereotypes that people with mental illness are violent are "deeply rooted in public opinion" and that this view is exacerbated and perpetuated by the media and others including mental health professionals themselves).

9. E.g., housing and employment discrimination.

permeates our legal system, particularly in the area of mental disability law."[10] Sanism routinely infects decision-making throughout all aspects of forensic mental disability law.[11] Professor Perlin has described a myriad of ways sanism often manifests itself by courts through rejections of defendants' claims of incompetency to stand trial,[12] use of the insanity defense,[13] and other similar issues.[14]

Sanist Nonjudicial Administrative Decision-Making

Sanist decision-making is not confined to the judicial arena. It pervades all aspects of the forensic mental health system, including nonjudicial administrative decisions made affecting prisoners with mental illness in jails and prisons. These decisions are largely discretionary with little or no judicial oversight or due process protections. For example, prisoners who do not comply with the rules are subject to punishment without judicial review.[15] Even where the mental illness plainly contributed to the alleged infraction, correctional staff may punish the person for sanist, or at least partially sanist reasons, such as blaming them for their mental health conditions[16] or the erroneous belief that people with mental illness are exceptionally dangerous.[17] In another example, the decision whether, and when, a prisoner with a mental illness may see a mental health professional is often made by correctional staff and may be denied or extensively delayed due to false beliefs that the person is "manipulating" or "faking" their symptoms.[18]

Even determinations of whether a person has a mental health diagnosis can factor into whether and when the individual receives mental health treatment. For example, diagnoses can be inaccurate or "contested" because

---

10. Perlin, *supra* note 6, at 374; MICHAEL L. PERLIN, THE HIDDEN PREJUDICE: MENTAL DISABILITY ON TRIAL 48–58 (2000) 8.

11. *Id.* at 374.

12. *Id.*

13. *Id.* at 223–44; Perlin, *supra* note 7, at 626.

14. PERLIN, *supra* note 10, at 205–21(competency to plead guilty and competency to waive counsel), 245–58 (sentencing guidelines).

15. *See* Henry A. Dlugacz, *Correctional Disciplinary Proceedings and Incarcerated People with Mental Disabilities* (this volume).

16. MICHAEL L. PERLIN, A PRESCRIPTION FOR DIGNITY: RETHINKING CRIMINAL JUSTICE AND MENTAL DISABILITY LAW 67 (2013) (discussing "The Role of Blame" in the demonization of mental illness and stating that "our need to blame individuals with mental disabilities for their mental disability as our 'culture of punishment'").

17. Deborah A. Dorfman, *Through a Therapeutic Jurisprudence Filter: Fear and Pretextuality in Mental Disability Law*, 10 N.Y.L. SCH. J. HUM. RIGHTS 805 (1993).

18. Perlin, *supra* note 6, at 374.

"judgments about the acuity of a prisoner's mental health problems carry enormous implications for the allocation of resources, and prison systems with too few treatment beds and inadequate mental health staff present clinical decision-makers with ethical dilemmas and a built-in conflict of interest."[19] Such a conflict of interest can further lead to sanist decision-making.

Therapeutic Jurisprudence Implications of Nonjudicial Decision-Making in Jails and Prisons

Therapeutic jurisprudence (TJ) examines the law as a therapeutic agent.[20] In the context of mental disability law, TJ offers a means by which to assess the law and its application to determine whether it is therapeutic, antitherapeutic, or atherapeutic.[21] TJ can also be used to evaluate the efficacy of rules and administrative decision-making in jails and prisons. Viewing these decisions through a TJ lens, it is necessary to consider the context in which these administrative decisions are commonly made. Specifically, it is important to understand that a confluence of factors influence decisions that can result in antitherapeutic outcomes. These factors, as discussed below, include broad discretion afforded to correctional administrators by courts, overall lack of accountability or oversight of these decisions, and pervasive sanism.

Broad Discretion by Courts Afforded to Jail and Prison Administrators

The wide discretion afforded to correctional administrators by courts to manage the operations of correctional facilities, particularly regarding security, significantly contributes to antitherapeutic outcomes for inmates with mental illness.[22] As discussed later, this broad discretion often negatively affects

19. Craig Haney, *"Madness" and Penal Confinement: Some Observations on Mental Illness and Prison Pain*, 19 PUNISHMENT & SOCIETY, 311, 316–17 (2017).

20. THERAPEUTIC JURISPRUDENCE: THE LAW AS A THERAPEUTIC AGENT (David B. Wexler ed., 1990), hereafter cited as THERAPEUTIC AGENT (essays discussing therapeutic jurisprudence); ESSAYS IN THERAPEUTIC JURISPRUDENCE (David Wexler and Bruce Winick eds., 1991) (essays discussing therapeutic jurisprudence).

21. *Dorfman, supra* note 7, at 806, n. 6, citing David B. Wexler, *Therapeutic Jurisprudence and Changing Conceptions of Legal Scholarship*, 11 BEHAV. SCI. & L. 17 (1993); David B. Wexler, *Putting Mental Health into Mental Health Law: Therapeutic Jurisprudence*, 16 LAW & HUM. BEHAV. 27 (1992); THERAPEUTIC AGENT, *supra* note 20.

22. *See* Turner v. Safely, 482 U.S. 78, 89 (1987); Florence v. Board of Chosen Freeholders of County of Burlington, 566 U.S. 318 (2012) (correctional administrators have broad discretion to conduct strip and body searches to ensure institutional safety); KENNETH L. FAIVER, COR-

prisoners with mental illness, particularly regarding their conditions of confinement, and related issues of punishment and use of force.[23]

Lack of Oversight and Accountability: Prison Litigation Reform Act

Because of wide discretion afforded to corrections officials, many administrative decisions go without oversight or accountability. Most are not subject to judicial review unless a prisoner can successfully litigate their claims. But there are significant barriers that make such litigation exceedingly difficult, particularly for prisoners with mental illness.[24]

One major barrier is the Prison Litigation Reform Act (PLRA).[25] The PLRA was enacted in 1996 in response to what some people believed was a flood of "meritless" claims filed by prisoners[26] to impose significant hurdles to prisoner litigation[27] seeking to challenge conditions of confinement, or almost anything pertaining to prisoners' daily lives while incarcerated.[28]

RECTIONAL HEALTH CARE SERVICES: MENTAL HEALTH, INFECTIOUS DISEASE, DENTAL CARE, ADDICTION TREATMENT 40 (2019).

23. David M. Shapiro and Charles Hogle, *The Horror Chambers: Unqualified Impunity in Prison* 93 NOTRE DAME L. REV. 2036, 2036–42 (2018) (discussing deference to correctional officials in excessive force and conditions of confinement cases).

24. Some prisoner litigation is successful, but resources are limited, particularly access to qualified counsel. *See* Michael L. Perlin, *Fatal Assumption: The Critical Evaluation of the Role of Counsel in Mental Disability Law Cases*, 16 LAW & HUM BEHAV. 39 (1992); Shapiro and Hogle, *supra* note 23, at 2048–49. Furthermore, PLRA barriers are often insurmountable, even where a prisoner has counsel. In addition, the United States Department of Justice and protection and advocacy systems have the legal authority to exercise oversight of jail and prison conditions and use of excessive force on prisoners with disabilities. *See* Civil Rights of Institutionalized Persons Act, 42 U.S.C. §1997a; Violent Crime Control and Law Enforcement Act, 42 U.S.C. § 14141; the Protection and Advocacy for Individuals with Mental Illness Act, 42 U.S.C. § 10801, *et seq.* These resources, however, are also limited.

25. Provisions of the PLRA are spread among several titles of the U.S. Code. *E.g.,*18 U.S.C. §3626, 28 U.S.C. § 1932, and 42 U.S.C. § 1997e.

26. For a review of the political and policy considerations leading to the enactment of the PLRA, *see* Adam Slutsky, *Totally Exhausted: Why a Strict Interpretation of 42 U.S.C. § 1977E(A) Unduly Burdens Courts and Prisoners*, 73 FORDHAM L. REV. 2289, 2298–303 (2005).

27. Under PLRA, the term "prisoner" is broadly defined to include convicted prisoners, pretrial detainees, juveniles in juvenile justice, and adult detention facilities. And, in some cases—people found incompetent to stand trial and committed to state hospitals and parolees in "half-way" houses—people have been deemed by courts to be "prisoners" subject to the requirements of the PLRA. *See* 42 U.S.C. §1997(e)(h).

28. Porter v. Nussle, 534 U.S. 516, 524 (2002) (citations omitted) ("all available" remedies must be exhausted in all cases, including § 1983 and state tort damages claims); *see also* Booth v. Churner, 532 U.S. 731, 740 (2001) ("inmate must exhaust irrespective of the forms of relief sought and offered through administrative avenues").

"Prison conditions" covered by the PLRA is broadly interpreted by courts to include "all inmate suits about prison life, whether they involve general circumstances or particular episodes, and whether they allege excessive force or some other wrong."[29] Some courts have also required exhaustion in disability discrimination cases.[30]

Among the PLRA's barriers to prisoners litigating prison conditions claims is the statute's strict requirement that prisoners fully exhaust administrative remedies through a correctional grievance process before filing suit in federal court.[31] The PLRA also requires strict adherence to the facility's grievance procedure.[32] Prisoners must, for example, use required facility grievance forms and exhaust all levels of grievance policy before exhaustion will be deemed complete, even if no response is received.[33] Prisoners themselves must file these grievances, even those with mental or intellectual disabilities. Parents, guardians, and attorneys may not file grievances on behalf of a prisoner to satisfy PLRA exhaustion. A prisoner's failure to adhere to grievance requirements will likely result in loss of their legal claims because there is almost no circumstance excusing exhaustion.[34]

While PLRA restrictions apply to all prisoners, these restrictions are effectively more onerous on a people with mental illness who may, because of their disability, be unable to navigate the grievance process or otherwise comply with rigid PLRA requirements.

---

29. Wood v. Ngo, 548 U.S. 81(2006); *Porter*, 534 U.S. at 532.

30. *See, e.g.*, O'Guinn v. Lovelock Correctional Center, 502 F.3d 1056, 1061–62 (9th Cir. 2007) (although ADA and Section 504 do not require exhaustion, because the PLRA applies to such claims brought by inmates, exhaustion of facility grievance procedures is mandatory before such claims can be pursued).

31. "No action shall be brought with respect to prison conditions under section 1979 of the Revised Statutes of the United States (42 U.S.C. §1983), or any other Federal law, by a prisoner confined in any jail, prison, or other correctional facility until such administrative remedies as are available are exhausted." 42 U.S.C. § 1997(e).

32. Ross v. Blake, 136 S.Ct. 1850 (2016).

33. *See, e.g.*, Beatty v. Goord, 210 F. Supp. 250, 255–56 (S.D.N.Y. 2000) (inmate failed to exhaust administrative remedies where he failed to follow the jail grievance procedures with particularity and instead attempted to exhaust his remedies outside of the specifically defined process.).

34. Courts have refused to excuse prisoners from complying with PLRA requirements due to their psychiatric and/or intellectual disabilities. *See, e.g.*, Williams v. White, 724 F. App'x 380, 383 (6th Cir. 2018) ("there is no mental-capacity exception to the PLRA"); *see also* Johnson v. District of Columbia, 869 F.Supp.2d 34. 39 (D.D.C. 2012) (cataloging numerous cases rejecting mental ability to understand grievance process as basis to excuse exhaustion.). The only narrow exception when PLRA exhaustion not required is when administrative remedies are not available; *Ross*, 136 S. Ctat 1859.

Sanism

Sanism also contributes to negative administrative decisions and antitherapeutic outcomes for prisoners with mental illness. Sanist attitudes are often
revealed through the imposition of what at first seem to be ordinary, everyday correctional administrative decisions. Such decisions include where prisoners with a mental disability are housed, whether they will have an opportunity to participate in prison activities, or whether, and when, they will receive
medical or mental health care. Sanism also permeates other decisions including whether to impose punishment on a mentally ill prisoner for rule infractions, when to use force, when to restrain (and how, and for how long), and
how to manage their mental health symptoms, among others.[35] For example, lack of training for correctional staff often leads to punishment based
upon sanist beliefs that people with mental illness are dangerous and/or that
they are faking their symptoms to manipulate "the system."[36]

Antitherapeutic Outcomes Resulting from Administrative Decision-Making

Such broad, often unchecked discretion, combined with the legal barriers to
redress and sanism, can result in antitherapeutic outcomes for prisoners
with mental illness. Consider these negative outcomes.

Segregated Restrictive Housing, Solitary Confinement, and Overall Isolation

Prisoners with mental illness commonly experience antitherapeutic outcomes relating to housing in correctional facilities. They are assigned to restrictive and segregated units designated for people with mental illness, in a
single cell, in which they are confined for twenty-two to twenty-three hours
per day.[37] They have almost no social interaction and little or no access to em-

---

35. Houser et al., *supra* note 2, at 3 (lack of correctional officers training exacerbates problems managing maladaptive behaviors of prisoners with mental illness; very little training is
offered to help correctional officers understand and identify behavior that is a result of mental illness).

36. *Id.*

37. Office of the Inspector General, U.S. Department of Justice, "Review of the Federal
Bureau of Prisons' Use of Restrictive Housing for Inmates with Mental Illness," *Evaluation
and Inspection Division*, 17–05, July 2017 ("2017 OIG Report"), available at https://oig.justice
.gov/reports/2017/e1705.pdf (last visited March 3, 2022) (although the Federal Bureau of Prisons technically abolished solitary confinement, prisoners were still subjected to isolation).

ployment, education, and other prison programs.[38] Confinement to restrictive housing units is often indefinite—sometimes for weeks, months, and even years at a time.[39] Suicidal prisoners are often placed naked in cells commonly referred to as "strip cells"[40] and subjected to physical restraints such as metal shackles and other restraint devices while in isolation.[41]

Prisoners with mental illness are commonly isolated in solitary confinement as a result of rule infractions. There is a substantial body of research documenting the deleterious effects of solitary confinement and isolation on prisoners generally and particularly for people with mental illness.[42] Their isolation can lead to trauma, anxiety, depression, psychosis, and other problems.[43] Isolation of prisoners with mental illnesses is contraindicated because it can exacerbate already existing mental health symptoms[44] including self-harm[45] and further behavioral problems that in turn often lead to longer periods of isolation.[46] Despite these risks and known negative outcomes, prisoners with mental illness are disproportionately isolated for often dangerously long periods either as a result of administrative or punitive segregation.[47]

Restraints and Other Restrictive Interventions

Administrative decision-making regarding restraint usage to control the behavior of prisoners with mental illness can also result in antitherapeutic

---

38. *Id.*

39. *See, e.g.,* DOJ VA findings letter (2019) at 22, available at https://www.justice.gov/crt/case-document/file/1121176/download.

40. FAIVER, *supra* note 22, at 28 (describing tilting device attached to some restraint chairs used to force prisoner compliance).

41. *See* Discussion in Section IV.A.2, *infra.*

42. 2017 OIG Report, *supra* note 37 ("isolation can by psychologically harmful to any prisoner").

43. *Id.,* citing Jeff Metzner and Jamie Felner, *Solitary Confinement and Mental Illness in United States' Prisons: A Challenge for Medical Ethics,,* 38 J AM. ACAD. PSYCHIATRY & L. 104 (2010).

44. Houser et al., *supra* note 2, at 3 ("the isolation effect of segregation may worsen clinical condition").

45. Hayden P. Smith et al., *Self-Harming Behaviors in Prison: A Comparison of Suicidal Processes, Self-Injurious Behaviors, and Mixed Events.* 32 CRIM. JUST. STUD. 3 (2019) (correctional mental health providers reported that "primary method of institutional response to self-injurious behavior" was the imposition of isolation).

46. Michael K. Champion, *Seclusion and Restraint in Corrections—A Time for Change,* 35 J. AM. ACAD. PSYCHIATRY & LAW 426, 427 (2007) (describing the harmful effects of solitary confinement on prisoners with mental illness).

47. Metzner and Felner, *supra* note 43.

results, including extreme physical or psychological harm and sometimes death.[48] As with isolation, the professional literature has well documented the harm caused resulting from the use of restraints to manage the behaviors of mentally ill prisoners.[49] Consequently, mental health professionals widely concur that restraints should be avoided in a nontherapeutic setting such as jails or prisons.[50]

Different types of restraints commonly used as behavioral interventions in jails and prisons that are not generally used in psychiatric facilities, but that are particularly dangerous and anti-therapeutic,[51] include restraint boards; metal arm, leg, and body restraints; and notoriously dangerous prone restraints, among others.[52] Prone restraints are particularly dangerous because they involve restraining the individual face down, which creates a high risk of death by asphyxiation.[53]

The use of the restraint chair—referred to by some as "the Devil's chair"[54]— is an all-too-common dangerous restraint intervention used in correctional facilities to manage the behavioral problems of inmates with mental health disabilities. Some view the restraint chair as convenient because it is portable and because it is believed, inaccurately, that a person can be left unattended in a restraint chair. However, it is well documented that use of restraint chairs is extremely dangerous because it can lead to serious physical and psychological harm and even death.[55] The extreme risks of harm to prisoners subject to the restraint chair include strangulation, asphyxiation,

---

48. Appelbaum, *supra* note 3.

49. Metzner and Felner; *supra* note 43; Appelbaum, *supra* note 3.

50. Appelbaum, *supra* note 3, at 434–35; FAIVER, *supra* note 22, at 27–28 (describing different types of restraints used in correctional facilities).

51. Appelbaum, *supra* note 3, at 433 (discussing the dangers of restraints in prisons).

52. Champion, *supra* note 46, at 426 (describing different types of restraints used in correctional facilities, including "steel handcuffs, leg irons, waist restraints, and in some jurisdictions, restraint chairs"); FAIVER, *supra* note 22, at 29 (describing how prone restraint is used in correctional facilities, and the associated harm to mentally ill prisoners resulting from their use).

53. FAIVER, *supra* note 22, at 29.

54. *See* Radley Balko, *Death in the Devil's Chair: Florida Man's Pepper Spray Death Raises Questions about Jail Abuse*, HUFFINGTON POST, Jan. 11, 2012, http://www.huffingtonpost .com/2012/01/11/jail-abuse-nick-christie-pepper-spray-florida_n_1192412.html. George Annas has called the chairs the "functional equivalent of strait jackets." George J. Annas, *The Legacy of the Nuremberg Doctors' Trial to American Bioethics and Human Rights*, 10 MINN. J.L. SCI. & TECH. 19, 36 (2009). *See also* Radley Balko, *Opinion: Death by the Devil's Chair*, WASHINGTON POST (AUG. 25, 2017), accessible at https://www.washingtonpost.com/news/the -watch/wp/2017/08/25/death-by-the-devils-chair/.

55. *See* Jeffery L. Metzner, *Resource Document on the Use of Restraint and Seclusion in Correctional Mental Health Care*, 35 J. AMER. ACAD. OF PSY. & L. ONLINE 417 (2007).

blood clots, cardiac arrest, and exacerbation of mental health symptoms, among other life-threatening conditions.[56] Even some manufacturers of restraint chairs acknowledge the serious risks associated with the use of such devices, warning its users not to use it as a punishment or for more than two hours at a time, and to constantly monitor the health of the person while in the chair.[57] The extreme dangers of the restraint chair have also been recognized by the American Bar Association, which bans the practice in its official criminal justice practice standards.[58] Despite these serious dangers, the use of restraint chairs continues throughout correctional facilities and some psychiatric facilities.[59]

The decision whether to confine a prisoner to a restraint chair is often made by correctional staff with little or no administrative or judicial review or oversight.[60] Consequently, individuals with mental illness often find themselves strapped to these chairs for perilously long periods of time—sometimes for days on end—in direct contradiction to the manufacturer's warnings.[61] A recent report issued by the Marshall Project found that numerous prisoners have been injured or died in correctional facilities—particularly jails—due to being placed in restraint chairs.[62] Many not only suffer physical harm and risk of death but also experience exacerbation of their mental health symptoms as a result of being confined in the restraint chair. Some are placed in restraint chairs while simultaneously being subjected to

---

56. William P. Angrick II, *Investigation of Restraint Device Use in Iowa's County Jails* (released Feb. 2009), available at https://www.legis.iowa.gov/DOCS/CAO/Invstgtv_Reports /2009/CIWPA001.PDF (prepared by the Iowa Citizens' Aide/Ombudsman).

57. *See, e.g.,* Sureguard Safety Restraint Chair, available at https://restraintchair.com/su reguard-restraint-chair.php (last visited June 28, 2020); *see also* RestraintChair.com, available at https://restraintchair.com/pdfs/2020/SoftGuard-Instructions_REVISED.pdf (last visited July 8, 2020) (warning customers that "the SoftGuard Safety Restraint Chair should never be used as a means of punishment" and warning against using the chair for prolonged periods).

58. American Bar Association "Standards on Treatment of Prisoners" ("ABA Standards"), https://www.americanbar.org/groups/criminal_justice/publications/criminal_justice_sec tion_archive/crimjust_standards_treatmentprisoners/#23-4.3

59. MARSHALL PROJECT REPORT, *They Went Jail. Then They Say They Were Strapped to a Chair for Days* (Feb. 2020), available at https://www.themarshallproject.org/2020/02/07/they -went-to-jail-then-they-say-they-were-strapped-to-a-chair-for-days (last visited on June 28, 2020).

60. *Callous and Cruel: Use of Force against Inmates with Mental Disabilities in U.S. Jails and Prisons,* HUMAN RIGHTS WATCH (May 12, 2015), available at https://www.hrw.org/re port/2015/05/12/callous-and-cruel/use-force-against-inmates-mental-disabilities-us-jails -and#_ftn2 (last visited July 8, 2020).

61. SAFETY RESTRAINT CHAIR, available at https://restraintchair.com/pdfs/2020/Soft Guard-Instructions_REVISED.pdf (last visited July 8, 2020) (warning against using the restraint chair for prolonged periods).

62. MARSHALL PROJECT REPORT, *supra* note 59.

other restrictive measures such as being doused with pepper spray or having a bag placed over their heads.[63]

Remedying Antitherapeutic Effects of Administrative Decision-Making on Prisoners with Mental Illness

The antitherapeutic effects of harmful administrative decision-making in correctional facilities regarding the use of isolation and restraints on mentally ill prisoners can be remediated. One remedy is to develop rehabilitative mental health units in correctional facilities that focus on the provision of active treatment rather than punishment.[64] Relatedly, trauma-informed care should be provided to prisoners,[65] and training should be provided for corrections officers on mental health and trauma.[66] A process for timely return to the general population should also be adopted.[67]

Creation of a corrections' ombudsman with resources and authority to investigate and remediate conditions of care complaints would help address the problems of almost unfettered discretion and lack of oversight of administrative decisions relating to the use of isolation and restraints.[68]

Policy changes to eliminate, or at least sharply reduce, the use of isolation and restraints to manage prisoners' mental health symptoms are also neces-

---

63. *See, e.g.,* FAIVER, *supra* note 22, at 28 (describing tilting device attached to some restraint chairs used to force prisoner compliance); Shapiro and Hogle, *supra* note 23, at 2036, citing Christie v. Scott, 923 F. Supp.2d. 1308, 1314 (M.D. Fla. 2013) (prisoner died after being doused repeatedly with pepper spray and tied naked to a restraint chair).

64. *See* Elizabeth B. Ford et al., *Clinical Outcomes of Specialized Treatment Units for Patients with Mental Illness in the New York City Jail System*, 71 PSYCHIAT. SERVS. 547 (2020) (mentally ill prisoners who received rehabilitative treatment in jail had better outcomes, including lower rates of injury due to violence and medication non-compliance); *see also* ABA Standards, *supra* note 58.

65. Dana DeHart and Aidyn Iachini, *Mental Health and Trauma among Incarcerated Persons: Development of a Training Curriculum for Correctional Officers*, 44 AM. J. CRIM. JUST. 457 (2019) (describing the large and growing numbers of prisoners who need trauma–informed care and training for corrections officers).

66. *Id.*

67. *See* Matthew Lowen et al., *The Safe Alternatives to Segregation Initiative: Findings, Recommendations, and Reforms for the Nevada Department of Corrections*, Vera Institute of Justice (September 2019) (many people wait long periods to be transferred from restrictive housing units to general population and recommending implementation of a process to avoid such delays).

68. Washington created the Office of the Corrections Ombudsman responsible for investigating and resolving prisoner conditions of care complaints. *See* State of Washington Department of Corrections, Office of the Corrections Ombuds, available at https://oco.wa.gov /complaints-investigations (last visited on July 8, 2020).

sary. Some prisons have eliminated the use of solitary confinement for all prisoners, or at least for prisoners with mental illness. If implemented with fidelity, such policies would eliminate harm resulting from isolation.[69] Adoption of policies removing certain administrative decisions about isolation and restraints from correctional officers and placing them in the hands of qualified clinicians would also likely reduce anti-therapeutic outcomes for mentally ill prisoners.[70]

Finally, cross-system collaboration among service providers and expanded community-based services are essential to avoiding incarceration of and recidivism. These services include housing, employment, and social services, among other community-based services.[71]

Conclusion

Nonjudicial administrative decisions regarding isolation and physical restraint of prisoners are often antitherapeutic. The decision to isolate or restrain mentally ill prisoners is often done with broad discretion, with little oversight, and for sanist reasons. Consequently, these decisions routinely lead to physical and psychological harm and even death of prisoners with mental illness. Nevertheless, corrections administrators and staff routinely continue to use these dangerous interventions. It is essential that corrections administrators, clinicians, lawyers, and other stakeholders collaborate to implement alternative, safe therapeutic ways to treat mentally ill prisoners. The immediate adoption of remedial measures is urgent particularly given the vast and growing numbers of mentally ill prisoners.

69. 2017 OIG Report, *supra* note 37.

70. *See* Champion, *supra* note 46.

71. Natalie Bonfine, Amy Blank Wilson, and & Mark R. Munetz, *Meeting the Needs of Justice-Involved People with Serious Mental Illness within Community Behavioral Health Systems*, 71 PSYCHIAT. SERVS. 355 (2020).

10

Correctional Disciplinary Proceedings and Incarcerated People with Mental Disabilities*

Henry A. Dlugacz

Introduction

The Supreme Court has long recognized that although many rights are extinguished or severely curtailed by incarceration, prisoners retain basic rights while incarcerated. These include the right to free speech, the right to freedom of religion, and the constellation of rights considered fundamental to American citizenship and recognized under the federal constitution's guarantee of substantive due process.[1] However, this was not always the case, and the degree to which the bill of rights penetrates prison walls has evolved over time. While the details vary across states, in the modern era the convicted prisoner facing prison disciplinary proceedings as a constitutional matter must be provided only rudimentary procedural due process protections. These administrative proceedings typically are conducted by a correctional hearing officer and are not heard before a member of the judiciary. The constitutional requirement is only for an impartial decision-maker who is not so biased against the prisoner as to pose the "hazard of arbitrary decisionmaking . . . violative of due process."[2] This would include

* The author would like to thank Elizabet Leader, a paralegal at Beldock Levine and Hoffman LLP, for her extraordinary assistance in preparing this manuscript.

1. *See* Henry Dlugacz and Christopher Wimmer, *Legal Aspects of Administering Antipsychotic Medications to Jail and Prison Inmates*, 36 Int'l J.L. & Psychiatry 213 (2013).

2. Wolff v. McDonnell, 418 U.S. 539, 571 (1974); *cf. Your Rights at Prison Disciplinary Proceedings*, A Jailhouse Lawyer's Manual (Ch. 18). http://jlm.law.columbia.edu/files/2017/05/30.-Ch.-18.pdf.

a hearing officer who had prejudged the case or was directly involved in the underlying charge.[3] There is no right to counsel,[4] only a right to assistance from another prisoner or a prison employee where the accused is illiterate[5] or where the case is unusually complicated.[6] Some states have expanded this list to include, for example, prisoners with certain disabilities or prisoners who do not speak English, but protections remain limited.[7] Adherence to rules of evidence is lax, complex mental status issues (such as the accused's competence or lack of responsibility) may be poorly addressed if at all, and the road to review by a judicial body is significantly limited by the strictures of the Prison Litigation Reform Act (PLRA) and its requirement that a potential litigant exhaust all available administrative remedies, even futile ones,[8] as well as Supreme Court precedent.[9]

Whatever the precise forum, prison disciplinary proceedings take place in a total, closed institution.[10] State participants—the custody officers, clinical staff, and (typically) hearing officers—are institutional actors or repeat players who are frequently viewed by the population of incarcerated people as part of the same system.[11] They typically depend on one another on an ongoing basis for their security and day-to-day job functioning. The stigma of being a convicted prisoner can be an insurmountable hurdle to having one's version of events taken seriously, especially since the prisoner lives in a distorted correctional environment. Greater still are the systematic obstacles posed by implicit bias and other inequities found across criminal judi-

---

3. Wade v. Farley, 869 F. Supp. 1365, 1376 (N.D. Ind. 1994), citing Underwood v. Chrans, No. 90 C 6713, 1992 U.S. Dist. LEXIS 12616, at *10 (N.D. Ill. Aug. 20, 1992) (unpublished); *cf.* Jailhouse Lawyer's Manual, *supra* note 2.

4. *See* Baxter v. Palmigiano, 425 U.S. 308, 315 (1976).

5. *See* Wolff, 418 U.S., at 570.

6. *Id.*

7. *See* Jailhouse Lawyer's Manual, *supra* note 2.

8. *See* Henry Dlugacz, *Jail and Prison Conditions*, chapter 13 in Representing People with Mental Disabilities: A Criminal Defense Lawyer's Best Practices Manual (Elizabeth Kelley ed., 2018).

9. *See, e.g.,* Edwards v. Balisok, 520 U.S. 641 (1997) (holding, in essence, that the only road to judicial review of a disciplinary proceeding that has an impact on the overall length of confinement is in such cases in which the finding was already overturned by a state proceeding; when a claim is based on an argument that the procedures which resulted in discipline were not valid, then as a predicate to such a claim, the administrative determination must have been previously invalidated).

10. *See* Erving Goffman, Asylums: Essays on the Social Situation of Mental Patients and Other Inmates (1961).

11. *See* Michel Foucault, "Society Must Be Defended": Lectures at the Collège de France, 1975–76 (2003); Henry Dlugacz and Christopher Wimmer, *The Ethics of Representing Clients with Limited Competency in Guardianship Proceedings*, 4 St. L. U. J. Health L. & Pol'y 331, 336 (2011).

cial proceedings. These factors can (unwittingly or otherwise) impact the fairness of the proceedings, tilting the outcome against the accused prisoner.

The results of a "conviction" in disciplinary proceedings can profoundly impact an incarcerated person's conditions of confinement, even when the punishment is not considered "atypical and significant" under the standard laid out in *Sandin v. Conner*.[12] A prisoner may be placed in restricted housing, limiting their access to out-of-cell activities such as treatment for a mental disability, recreation, or education. In addition to reductions in "good time" and reduced eligibility for parole, both of which increase the length of prison confinement, such restrictions may decrease a person's access to services which would enhance their ability to successfully reenter the community as a lawful member of society. This isolation can be especially detrimental for an inmate with a mental disability, which will be addressed later in the chapter. As such, the process can be profoundly untherapeutic on a variety of levels and, in that context, violate the tenets of therapeutic jurisprudence. To the extent that the behavior leading to disciplinary action is a manifestation of an untreated or undertreated mental disability, the person is being punished for actions that may be beyond their control with a sanction that may, by the nature of the setting itself, both exacerbate the problem while also restricting access to needed care. This can create a destructive and dangerous cycle. Viewed from a systemic perspective, the effect can be likewise damaging to desired outcomes. Prisoners, like all people, respond more favorably to positive reinforcement. To the extent that negative reinforcement is to be useful in shaping behavior, the consequence should be close in time to the alleged transgression, and be handled in a fair, nonarbitrary manner. A hearing structure that emphasizes negative reinforcement in what may frequently appear to the incarcerated person as a delayed, arbitrary, and unfair manner will serve to undermine confidence in the result, breeding cynicism and discouraging change. A challenge for many correctional systems is finding acceptable, safe, positive reinforcers that are motivating for the population—that is, something they want. To the extent that such an approach is viewed as "coddling" a "manipulative" "inmate" in a hearing system designed and run by custody professionals, it will likely remain untherapeutic to a large degree.

History

Although the current level of protections is lacking, it appears enlightened when viewed historically. In earlier times, prisoners were widely considered

---

12. Sandin v. Conner, 515 U.S. 472 (1995).

"slaves of the State"[13] to whom the bill of rights did not apply because it was considered "a declaration of general principles to govern a society of freeman, and not of convicted felons and men civilly dead."[14] In more modern times, the lack of judicial appetite to examine conditions within prisons (or psychiatric hospitals) was most clearly expressed by the hands-off doctrine. As asserted by the *Banning* court, "Courts are without power to supervise prison administration or to interfere with the ordinary prison rules or regulations."[15]

Overall, the hands-off doctrine eroded during the 1970s and early 1980s, aided by a variety of social and legal developments. These factors included a small number of pioneering judges who were willing to hold evidentiary hearings on conditions within prison walls,[16] which greatly increased access to representation, along with fee-shifting provisions, access to government-funded legal services, and the powerful shift in thinking among some incarcerated people who began to think of themselves as agents of social change.[17]

Gradually, and to varying degrees depending on context, the Supreme Court began to extend constitutional precepts to different aspects of prison life. For example, the pivotal case in correctional healthcare, *Estelle v. Gamble*, held that "deliberate indifference to serious medical needs of prisoners constitutes the 'unnecessary and wanton infliction of pain,'" proscribed by the Eighth Amendment.[18] *Bowring v. Godwin*[19] extended the definition of medical need to mental health conditions. Almost in parallel to this demise of the hands-off doctrine in the substantive due process arena, the Supreme Court decided a series of cases severely limiting the procedural due process rights of prisoners and people confined in psychiatric hospitals. Perhaps fearing that too easy access to counsel would spur a flood of prisoner's rights cases, decades before the passing of the PLRA, the court issued decision after decision supporting administrative decision-making.[20] At the same time, the Su-

---

13. Ruffin v. Commonwealth, 62 Va. (21 Gratt.) 790, 796 (1871).

14. *Id.*

15. 213 F.2d 771 (10th Cir. 1954), cert. den., 348 U.S. 859 (1954).

16. *See, e.g.,* Newman v. Alabama, 349 F. Supp. 278 (M.D. Ala. 1972) (press and media exposés and congressional hearings about prison conditions, especially following well-published riots; the civil rights movement and anti–Vietnam War movement, which brought more educated, well-connected people into contact with the criminal justice system than at any time since the Civil War; the overall growth of the civil rights laws, including 42 U.S.C. § 1983).

17. *See* Michael L. Perlin and Henry A. Dlugacz, Mental Health Issues in Jails and Prisons 15–16 (2008).

18. Estelle v. Gamble, 429 U.S. 97, 104 (1976).

19. Bowring v. Godwin, 551 F.2d 44 (4th Cir. 1977).

20. *See* Michael L. Perlin and Henry A. Dlugacz, *"It's Doom Alone That Counts": Can International Human Rights Law Be an Effective Source of Rights in Correctional Conditions*

preme Court issued a series of decisions supporting the judgment of professionals, especially physicians, over judicial decision-making.[21] Thus, the
court set practical constraints on procedural due process at the same time
that lower federal courts rejected the hands-off doctrine.

One of the seminal cases reflecting this tension is *Vitek v. Jones*,[22] which
held that due process was required before an incarcerated person determined to be mentally ill could be transferred to a psychiatric hospital. *Vitek*
held that a process approximating that required in *Morrissey*, a parole case,
was sufficient. As such, due process required notice, an administrative hearing, an impartial decision-maker, the right to be present and call witnesses,
and qualified lay assistance, but not an attorney or a judicial hearing.[23]

This same approach was taken in the context of forced medication of a
convicted prisoner in *Washington v. Harper*,[24] where an administrative process modeled after that outlined in *Vitek* passed constitutional muster. In
contrast to doctrine in the civil context, Supreme Court criminal cases regarding forced medication of inmates have taken a circuitous path. Generally, while requiring judicial decision-making for pretrial detainees[25] where
the Sixth Amendment right to a fair trial is at stake, administrative processes for convicted prisoners are considered sufficient where prison security and order are considered paramount. In this context, infringement of
an inmate's constitutional interests is supported where the state can show
that they are "reasonably related to legitimate penological interests."[26]

Washington involved a prison that sought forced medication for a prisoner pursuant to a policy that substantially mirrored that in *Vitek*. Upon
challenge, the Supreme Court found that "the procedural issue is whether
the State's nonjudicial mechanisms used to determine the facts in a particu-

---

Litigation? 27 BEHAV. SCI. & L. 675, 684 (2009). Key examples include Mills v. Rogers, 457 U.S.
291 (1982); Rhodes v. Chapman, 452 U.S. 337 (1981); Vitek v. Jones, 445 U.S. 480 (1980); Bell
v. Wolfish, 441 U.S. 520 (1979); Mathews v. Eldridge, 424 U.S. 319 (1976); and Morrissey v.
Brewer, 408 U.S. 471 (1972).

21. *See, e.g.* Parham v. J.R., 442 U.S. 584, 606–8 (1979), which held that that a statute requiring a neutral fact finder to decide about a child's admission to a state mental health
hospital only after admission was consistent with due process requirements, and most notably
Youngberg v. Romeo, 457 U.S. 307 (1982), which explicitly created the "substantial professional judgment" standard to assess liability in institutional cases.

22. *Vitek*, 445 U.S. at 494.

23. *Id.*; Henry Dlugacz and Christopher Wimmer, *Legal Aspects of Administering Antipsychotic Medications to Jail and Prison Inmates*, 36 INT'L J.L. & PSYCHIATRY 213 (2013).

24. Washington v. Harper, 494 U.S. 210 (1990).

25. Riggins v. Nevada, 504 U.S. 127 (1992); Sell v. United States, 539 U.S. 166 (2003); *cf.*
Dlugacz and Wimmer, *supra* note 23.

26. Turner v. Safley, 482 U.S. 78, 79 (1987); Dlugacz and Wimmer, *supra* note 23.

lar case are sufficient."[27] The court further found, "The extent of a prisoner's right . . . to avoid the unwanted administration of antipsychotic drugs must be defined in the context of the inmate's confinement."[28] In a decision that blurred the lines between Harper's medical needs and those of the institution, the court held that "the Due Process Clause permits the State to treat a prison inmate who has a serious mental illness with antipsychotic drugs against his will, if the inmate is dangerous to himself *or others* and the treatment is in the inmate's medical interest."[29] In so doing, the court rejected the argument that "physicians will prescribe these drugs for reasons unrelated to the needs of the patients," and it construed the policy as permitting forcible medication "only for treatment purposes."[30]

Following, a judicial hearing was not required as the court concluded that "an inmate's interests are adequately protected, and perhaps better served, by allowing the decision to medicate to be made by medical professionals rather than a judge."[31] As long as the physicians engaged in the administrative proceedings were not the same as those conducting the prisoner's current treatment, due process was satisfied. As Justice Stevens's vigorous dissent noted, "The panel members, as regular staff of the Center, must be concerned not only with the inmate's best medical interests, but also with the most convenient means of controlling the mentally disturbed inmate. . . . The prescribing physician and each member of the review committee must therefore wear two hats."[32] Therefore, the interests of the patient's medical needs and those of the institution may often be in opposition.

The Disciplinary Process and Sanctions

The seminal case concerning inmate discipline was *Wolff v. McDonnell*, which involved incarcerated persons challenging the revocation of good time credits without adequate due process protections.[33] The court held that disciplinary hearings were separate from the underlying criminal conviction, inmates were not entitled to the full range of rights afforded to criminal defendants, and the due process clause does not create liberty interest in good time credit for good behavior, but the statute governing it created a cognizable inter-

---

27. *Washington,* 494 U.S. at 221; Dlugacz and Wimmer, *supra* note 23.
28. *Washington,* 494 U.S. at 223.
29. *Id.* at 228.
30. *Id.*
31. *Id.*
32. *Id.*
33. *See Wolff,* 418 U.S. at 566.

est. The state had to follow only its own statute. In so doing, the court shifted the analysis from the deprivation experienced to the specific regulation in question. Required procedural due process rights included written notice provided at least one day prior to a hearing, as well as a written statement of the evidence used and reasons for the hearing. Inmates were afforded a limited right to put forth evidence and call witnesses provided they were not "unduly hazardous to institutional safety or correctional goals."[34] No guidance regarding what constituted an impartial hearing was provided. Consistent with *Vitek*, no right to a counseled hearing or access to a hearing before a judge was afforded.

In *Sandin v. Conner*,[35] the Supreme Court, without overruling *Wolff*, placed significant restrictions on its holding. Recalling once again the hands-off doctrine, *Sandin* noted with disapproval the involvement of "federal courts in the day-to-day management of prisons."[36] The court held that placement in disciplinary segregation did not necessarily constitute the type of atypical, significant deprivation that created a liberty interest.[37] However, loss of good time credit or prolonged placement in segregation could.[38]

Prisoners are subject to a variety of sanctions, most notably placement in disciplinary housing as means to impose order and increase safety, yet the effects of restrictive housing on the individual are varied.[39] The rate of inmate placement in restrictive housing varies by state from 0.5 percent of inmates in isolation in Colorado to 19 percent in Louisiana.[40] Although corrections officers may believe that segregation is effective at increasing safety and control, recent studies have found evidence against a relationship between reductions in prison violence and extensive use of solitary confinement, and the use of disciplinary segregation has been challenged over time.[41]

---

34. *Id.*

35. *Sandin*, 515 U.S. at 484.

36. *Id.* at 473.

37. *Id.*

38. *Id.* at 484.

39. *See* Laura M. Salerno and Kristen M. Zgoba, *Disciplinary Segregation and Its Effect on In-Prison Outcomes*, 100 PRISON JOURNAL 74 (2019).

40. *See Reforming Restrictive Housing: The 2018 ASCA-Liman Nationwide Survey of Time-in-Cell*, Association of State Correctional Administrators-Linman (2018), https://law.yale.edu/sites/default/files/documents/pdf/Liman/asca_liman_2018_restrictive_housing_revised_sept_25_2018_-_embargoed_unt.pdf.

41. *Id.*

Disability Statues and Discipline

The Americans with Disabilities Act was passed in 1990 and was quickly hailed as an emancipation proclamation for people with disabilities.[42] Only five years later, as international invocation of the rights of the disabled grew, two women with mental disabilities filed suit against the State of Georgia challenging their continued involuntary commitment even after the state's own clinicians found them capable of living in the community.[43] In *Olmstead v. L.C. ex rel. Zimring*, the Supreme Court ruled that unjustified segregation of individuals with disabilities violated Title II of the ADA, finding that individuals with mental disabilities are entitled to live in a community-based setting rather than in institutions.[44] The court held that society has historically isolated individuals with disabilities and continues to do so.[45] The court further held that, under the ADA and its implementing regulations, "unjustified institutional isolation of persons with disabilities is a form of discrimination."[46] Following, the Department of Justice issued guidance on the implementation of the Title II mandate for integration, stating that "the ADA and the *Olmstead* decision extend to persons at serious risk of institutionalization or segregation and are not limited to individuals currently in institutions or other segregated settings."[47] Subsequent cases have interpreted the ADA's integration mandate to require public entities to provide individuals with disabilities services in integrated settings in a wide variety of contexts.[48]

The ADA also applies to prisons.[49] Although there are a multitude of obstacles to effectively applying the statute's requirements to aspects of prison life, there is no principled or doctrinal reason it should not apply more robustly to prisoners with mental disabilities accused of prison rules violations who are subject to disciplinary proceedings.

---

42. *See* Michael L. Perlin, *"For the Misdemeanor Outlaw": The Impact of the Ada on the Institutionalization of Criminal Defendants with Mental Disabilities*, 52 Ala L. Rev. 193 (2000).

43. *See* Olmstead v. L.C., 527 U.S. 581 (1999); Henry Dlugacz and Luna Droubi, *The Reach and Limitation of the ADA and Its Integration Mandate: Implications for the Successful Reentry of Individuals with Mental Disabilities in a Correctional Population*, 35 Behav. Sci. & L. 135 (2017).

44. Olmstead v. L.C., 527 U.S. 581 (1999).

45. Dlugacz and Droubi, *supra* note 43.

46. *Olmstead*, 527 U.S. at 601.

47. *Id.*

48. See Dlugacz and Droubi, *supra* note 43.

49. *See* Pennsylvania Department of Corrections v. Yeskey, 524 US 206 (1998).

Mental Illness and Disciplinary Infractions

People with mental disabilities are vastly overrepresented in the prison population and have a particularly difficult time at each stage of the criminal justice process.[50] They are at increased risk for multiple bad outcomes, including suicide, and are disproportionally the subject of disciplinary and other types of segregation during their incarceration.[51] Others have written in the past about the therapeutic jurisprudence implications of such prison conditions,[52] and continue to do so.[53]

In corrections, segregation is imposed for different reasons. Precise conditions and hence the degree of isolation vary across systems. Some segregation units impose near-total isolation and thus sensory deprivation. Inmates are confined to their cells twenty-three hours a day, are fed through food ports, and have severely restricted access to medical or mental health care. Some systems provide recreational opportunities, reasonable access to medical and mental health care, reading materials, and radios or televisions to alleviate boredom. A frequently underestimated variable is how custody staff treat inmates attempting to access treatment or recreational activities. They may remain handcuffed and confined to units known as "therapeutic modules" by their proponents and "cages" by their detractors, or they may use specially adapted desks that confine movement while providing a more

---

50. Henry Dlugacz, *Correctional Mental Health in the USA*, 10 INTERNATIONAL JOURNAL OF PRISONER HEALTH 3 (2014); Henry Dlugacz and Christopher Wimmer, *Legal Aspects of Administering Antipsychotic Medications to Jail and Prison Inmates*, 36 INT'L J.L. & PSYCHIATRY 213 (2013); Jeffrey L. Metzner, *Class Action Litigation in Correctional Psychiatry*, 30 J. AM. ACAD. PSYCHIATRY & L. 29 (2002); Mark R. Munetz and Patricia A. Griffin, *Use of the Sequential Intercept Model as an Approach to Decriminalization of People with Serious Mental Illness*, 57 PSYCHIATRIC SERVS. 544 (2006); Henry J. Steadman, *Prevalence of Serious Mental Illness among Jail Inmates*, 60 PSYCHIATRIC SERVS. 761 (2009).

51. Henry Dlugacz, *Correctional Mental Health in the USA*, 10 INT'L J. PRISONER HEALTH 3 (2014); Henry Dlugacz et al., *Ethical Issues in Correctional Psychiatry in the United States* in ETHICAL ISSUES IN PRISON PSYCHIATRY 49 (Norbert Konrad ed., 2013).

52. *See, e.g.*, Astrid Birgden and Michael L. Perlin, *"Tolling for the Luckless, the Abandoned and Forsaked": Therapeutic Jurisprudence and International Human Rights Law as Applied to Prisoners and Detainees by Forensic Psychologists*, 13 LEGAL & CRIMINOLOGICAL PSYCHOL. 231, 234–35 (2008); Astrid Birgden and Michael L. Perlin, *"Where the Home in the Valley Meets the Damp Dirty Prison": A Human Rights Perspective on Therapeutic Jurisprudence and the Role of Forensic Psychologists in Correctional Settings*, 14 AGGRESSION & VIOLENT BEHAV. 256, 257 (2009); Dirk van Zyl Smit, *Regulation of Prison Conditions*, 39 CRIME & JUST. 503 (2010).

53. For the most recent scholarship, *see* Sahar Takshi, *Behind Bars and in the Hole: Applying Olmstead to Incarcerated Individuals with Mental Illness*, 27 GEO. J. ON POVERTY L. & POL'Y 319 (WINTER 2020), as discussed in Snider v. Pennsylvania DOC, F. Supp. 3d, 2020 WL 7229817, *21 n. 171 (M.D. Pa. 2020).

normalized appearance.[54] Other correctional systems make more individualized assessments before imposing such extreme measures.[55]

Segregation's precise effect on the human psyche and whether it causes a unique identifiable syndrome is the subject of debate in the field. Nonetheless, there is a solid consensus that people with mental illness should not be confined to extreme segregation except under highly unusual circumstances.[56] The United Nations considers the placement of people with serious mental illness in segregation to be a form of torture.[57] Various courts have noted the particular harm of segregation for those with serious mental illness,[58] as well as the constitutional concerns about segregation of inmates with mental illness.[59] In this setting with limited access to treatment, increased time confined to one's cell, and overall limitations on human contact, people with serious mental disabilities will usually deteriorate or at best not improve.[60] They may decompensate in isolation, requiring crisis care or hospitalization.[61] The practice of releasing incarcerated persons from segregation directly to the community is also troubling to most professionals in the field and adds to the already disproportional likelihood of recidivism or even death upon release.[62]

The question of the appropriate role for mental health treatment staff in hearings is a vexing one. There is great variation across the country in the role of mental health personnel in the disciplinary process, and not all states

---

54. *See* Deborah A. Dorfman, *Doing Time in "The Devil's Chair": Evaluating Non-Judicial Administrative Decisions to Isolate and Restrain Prisoners and Detainees with Mental Health Disabilities in Jails and Prisons* (this volume); Dlugacz, *supra* note 51.

55. *See* Dlugacz, *supra* note 51.

56. American Psychiatric Association, *Position Statement on Segregation of Prisoners with Mental Illness*, APA Official Actions (2012); National Commission on Correctional Health Care, *Standards for Mental Health Services in Correctional Facilities*, National Commission on Correctional Health Care (2008).

57. *See Solitary Confinement Should Be Banned in Most Cases, UN Expert Says*, UN News (2011), https://news.un.org/en/story/2011/10/392012-solitary-confinement-should-be-banned-most-cases-un-expert-says.

58. *See, e.g.*, Madrid v. Gomez, 889 F. Supp. 1146 (N.D. Cal. 1995). *See also* Ruiz v. Johnson, 37 F. Supp. 2d 855 (S.D. Tex. 1999), *rev'd on other grounds and remanded sub nom.* Ruiz v. United States, 243 F.3d 941 (5th Cir. 2001). Concerning deliberate indifference and segregation, *see* Palakovic v. Wetzel, 854 F.3d 209, 226, 228–29 (3d Cir. 2017).

59. *See, e.g.*, Feliciano v. Barcelo, 497 F. Supp. 14, 35 (D.P.R. 1979).

60. *See* Henry Dlugacz, *Correctional Mental Health in the USA*, 10 INT'L J. OF PRISONER HEALTH 3 (2014).

61. *See* Jeffrey L. Metzner and Jamie Fellner, *Solitary Confinement and Mental Illness in U.S. Prisons: A Challenge for Medical Ethics*, 38 J. AM. ACAD. PSYCHIATRY & L. 104 (2010).

62. *See* Dlugacz, *supra* note 60; Henry A. Dlugacz, *Introduction*, in 2 REENTRY PLANNING FOR OFFENDERS WITH MENTAL DISORDERS: POLICY AND PRACTICE xv (Henry A. Dlugacz ed., 2015).

have written policy regarding mental health in disciplinary proceedings.[63] Most prisons determine sanctions based on the incident severity and prior disciplinary history, without accommodating mental illness.[64] Custody officials who conduct administrative hearings often have minimal training on mental health and do not understand the effect of mental illness on behavior, such as prisoners who self-mutilate and are punished for "destruction of state property."[65] There can be concerns that inmates will use mental illness as an excuse for misconduct, encourage others, and promote a breakdown in order. Hearings also typically do not allow for an insanity defense or recognize incompetence.[66] Federal Bureau of Prison guidelines report that incarcerated persons who do not appear competent to understand the proceeding may have their proceedings postponed, and incarcerated persons should not be disciplined for conduct if they cannot understand the severity of their actions.[67] Yet courts and attorneys may also not have the knowledge to assess whether a practitioner is well equipped with the necessary expertise to make competency determinations and the role of mental illness in infractions given the unique nature of the correction population.[68] Dual agency is a real risk since correctional clinicians serve the conflicting interests of the correctional institution and their patients, which creates ethical and clinical problems regarding confidentiality, participation in disciplinary proceedings, forced medication, interrogations and torture.[69] A system that ignores input of clinical staff will be untherapeutic on its face. But how to best provide for input is a fraught issue. The mixing of a clinical and advocacy role, while not necessarily inappropriate, can complicate the therapeutic relationship. Some systems address this by having separate clinicians uninvolved with the direct treatment perform evaluations in the context of disciplinary actions, but those staff are typically not forensically trained, and the standards applied to these quasiforensic assessments may vary.

---

63. *See* Michael S. Krelstein, *The Role of Mental Health in the Inmate Disciplinary Process: A National Survey*, 30 J. AM. ACAD. PSYCHIATRY & L. 488 (2002). For a recent and comprehensive review of the mental health assessment associated with disciplinary proceedings in corrections *see*, Joseph H. Obegi, *Disciplinary Responsibility in Prison*, 49 J. AM. ACAD. PSYCHIATRY & L. 316 (2021).

64. *See* Jamie Fellner, *A Corrections Quandary: Mental Illness and Prison Rules*, 41 HARV. C.R.-C.L. L. REV. 391 (2006).

65. *Id.*

66. *Id.*

67. Federal Bureau of Prisons, *Inmate Discipline Program Statement*, U.S. Department of Justice (2011).

68. Dlugacz et al., *supra* note 51.

69. *Id.*

Incarcerated persons subject to these harsh conditions not infrequently resort to extreme behaviors to gain access to needed treatment, animate a change to a more humane housing environment, or engage in some form of human contact, even if that contact is negative, violent, or self-destructive. These efforts may be pejoratively viewed as "manipulative" by staff, further damaging their ability to view the segregated inmate as human and respond compassionately and professionally to their needs. For example, mental health professionals may be limited to administering psychotropic medication, stopping at cell fronts to inquire about the inmate's well-being (mental health rounds), and occasionally meeting in private with the inmate.[70]

Mississippi State Penitentiary, Parchman, is an example of a system that changed how it utilized disciplinary segregation for a more therapeutic jurisprudence approach due to litigation.[71] The department reformulated its mental health programming and developed objective criteria for placement in administrative segregation, such as committing a serious infraction, high-level gang involvement, or history of escape attempts.[72] Mental health staff also worked closely with custody staff to develop an "intermediate-level treatment program, or step-down unit" for mentally ill prisoners, which includes education about their illnesses and coping strategies, implementation of incentive plans for appropriate behavior, greater time allocations in activity rooms, and peer-facilitated programming in open custody. These reforms have alleviated the extremes of administrative segregation, and major assumptions about safety concerns were also challenged.[73] Such reforms reflect the power of therapeutic jurisprudence in this context.

Conclusion

Although the constitutional requirements regarding disciplinary hearings are minimal, a state's statutes or regulations may create more rights. Like most people, people who are incarcerated respond better to consequences perceived to be fairly administered. The line of Supreme Court cases discussed

---

70. *See* Metzner and Fellner, *supra* note 61.

71. *See* Terry A. Kupers et al., *Beyond Supermax Administrative Segregation: Mississippi's Experience Rethinking Prison Classification and Creating Alternative Mental Health Programs*, 36 CRIMINAL JUST. & BEHAV. 1037 (2009); Fred Cohen and Joel A. Dvoskin, *Therapeutic Jurisprudence and Corrections: A Glimpse*, 10 N.Y.L. SCH. J. HUM. RTS. 777 (1993) (discussing the impact of jail and prison reform litigation on institutional conditions); Presley v. Epps, No. 4:05–cv–148–DAS, Doc. # 121–1 (N.D. Miss. June 4, 2010), as cited in Russell v. Fisher, 2015 WL 5693040, *1 n.1 (N.D. Miss. 2015); Russell v. Johnson, 210 F. Supp. 2d 804 (N.D. Miss 2002).

72. *See* Kupers et al., *supra* note 71.

73. *Id.* at 1043–44.

earlier rely heavily on maintenance of prison order, suggesting that those with expertise are better equipped than judicial officers to address the thorny issues that arise. The author's experience is that a robust adversarial process before a tribunal perceived of as impartial promotes acceptance and a willingness to mold future behavior, whereas proceedings perceived of as arbitrary and unfair promote a lack of respect for the entire system and reduced acceptance. Seen in this light, the fact that most participants in the typical disciplinary proceeding are repeat actors with generally intertwined roles is countertherapeutic. Hearings held before a judicial officer, even an administrative law judge with proper training, would be preferable and would more likely conform to therapeutic jurisprudence principles.

11

The Complexities of Criminal Responsibility and Persons with Intellectual and Developmental Disabilities

How Can Therapeutic Jurisprudence Help?*

Lisa Whittingham and Voula Marinos

Introduction

The criminal law presupposes important characteristics about humans, including intentions, legal capacity, autonomy, agency, and criminal responsibility. In Canada and in eighteen U.S. states, the chronological age of twelve is the minimum age for reduced legal capacity in criminal law and the ability to make decisions—both important components of determining moral blameworthiness under the criminal law.[1] There is variation by state or country regarding the exact age; what remains consistent is that

* Portions of this paper were presented at the 36th International Congress of Law and Mental Health, University of International Studies of Rome, Rome, Italy, July 27, 2019. Portions are adapted from Marinos, V., & Whittingham, L. "The Complexities of Criminal Responsibility and Persons with Intellectual and Developmental Disabilities: How Can Therapeutic Jurisprudence Help?," *American Behavioral Scientist* (64:12) pp. 1733–48. Copyright © 2020 by SAGE. Reprinted by permission of SAGE Publications Inc. This material is the exclusive property of the SAGE Publications Inc. and is protected by copyright and other intellectual property laws. User may not modify, publish, transmit, participate in the transfer or sale of, reproduce, create derivative works (including course packs) from, distribute, perform, display, or in any way exploit any of the content of the file(s) in whole or in part. Permission may be sought for further use from SAGE Publications Inc., attn. Rights Department, 2455 Teller Road, Thousand Oaks, CA 91360, email: permissions@sagepub.com. By accessing the file(s), the User acknowledges and agrees to these terms. http://www.sagepub.com.

1. In Canada, the minimum age of responsibility can be found in the Criminal Code, RSC 1985, c C-46 (Can.), s 13. For the eighteen U.S. states, *see* Elizabeth S. Barnert et al., *Setting a Minimum Age for Juvenile Justice Jurisdiction in California*, 13 Int'l J. Prison Health 49 (2017).

we punish individuals differently within systems that have been defined by age—youth or adult.

In addition, most legal systems have constructed a category of reduced moral blameworthiness for adults who are not able to form the requisite mens rea—the element of a crime that requires the defendant know the facts that make one's conduct illegal. In Canada, individuals considered to have a mental disorder may not face the full brunt of the law, either because they cannot participate fully in their defense and found unfit to stand trial, or they are found incapable of understanding their actions at the time of the offense and are given a verdict of *Not Criminally Responsible on Account of Mental Disorder* (NCRMD).[2] There, mental disorder is defined as "disease of the mind" and includes a wide range of mental impairments including mental illness, intellectual/developmental disabilities (IDD), and brain injuries.[3]

For persons with IDD involved with the law, justice may not be served if they are tried on the assumption that they have the same capacity, moral blameworthiness, and criminal responsibility as someone without their cognitive and adaptive functioning impairments. Therapeutic jurisprudence (TJ) may provide an opportunity to increase the flexibility of the law to address their needs since it examines "the extent to which substantive rules, legal procedures, and the roles of lawyers and judges produce therapeutic or antitherapeutic consequences."[4] TJ can sensitize us to the changes needed to address the practices and techniques used by legal actors or the legal rules and procedures governing their behavior.[5] For persons with IDD, TJ may help to reconcile some of the challenges created by the current laws and legal practices by ensuring that lawyers have options that represent the interests of their clients while providing acceptable solutions, or by ensuring that the rules and procedures encoded in the law are broad enough to accommodate the range of conditions that may impact an individual.

This chapter uses legal submissions for a case involving a person with an IDD accused of possession of child pornography to examine how the con-

---

2. For fitness to stand trial, *see* CRIMINAL CODE, RSC 1985, c C-46 (Can.), s 672(22); for *Not Criminally Responsible on Account of Mental Disorder* (NCRMD), *see* CRIMINAL CODE, RSC 1985, c C-46 (Can.), s 16(1). The defense of NCRMD is equivalent to the insanity defense in the United States (18 U.S.C. § 17).

3. *See* CRIMINAL CODE, RSC 1985, c C-46 (Can.), s 2.

4. David B. Wexler and Bruce J. Winick, *Therapeutic Jurisprudence as a New Approach to Mental Health Law Policy Analysis and Research*, 45 U. MIAMI L. REV. 981 (1991).

5. For an effective metaphor of these changes, *see* David B. Wexler, *New Wine in New Bottles: The Need to Sketch a Therapeutic Jurisprudence Code of Proposed Criminal Processes and Practices*, 7 ARIZ. SUMMIT L. REV. 463 (2013–14).

cepts of legal capacity, moral blameworthiness, and criminal responsibility are constructed in legal subjects who are adults with IDD. The case highlights the challenges that are created when legal actors try to "do right" by their clients with IDD by characterizing them "like a child" to argue that they do not have the same legal capacity and criminal responsibility due to cognitive impairments. These legal actors are left with an ethical dilemma or a double-edged sword: How does one argue that the same consequences that apply to adults with "adult" capacities should not be applied to other adults with IDD without reducing their legal capacities, violating their human rights, or promoting an ableist attitude within the law?[6]

Intellectual and Developmental Disabilities

"Intellectual disability" is the clinical diagnosis used to describe impairments in cognitive and adaptive functioning that originates in childhood and/or adolescence (typically before the age of eighteen).[7] In contrast, the term "developmental disabilities" is used to describe an array of disabilities that originate in childhood or adolescence that may or may not have an accompanying intellectual disability (e.g., cerebral palsy). In Ontario legislation (the context of the case), the term "developmental disabilities" is used to describe impairments that share the same criteria as the clinical definition for intellectual disability.[8]

It is important to understand the role that cognitive and adaptive functioning impairments play in the lives of persons with IDD; however, focusing only on them can lead to significant diminution of their human rights, including infantilization and denial of legal capacity.[9] Historically, persons with IDD were assumed to be responsible for many of the societal problems

---

6. Ableism is a complex system of cultural, political, economic, and social practices that facilitate, construct, or reinforce the subordination of people with disabilities in a given society. *See* Jamelia N. Morgan, *Reflections on Representing Incarcerated People with Disabilities: Ableism in Prison Reform Litigation*, 96 Denv. L. Rev. 973, 980 (2019).

7. *See Intellectual Disability*, in Diagnostic and Statistical Manual of Mental Disorders: DSM-5 (2013).

8. *See* Services and Supports to Promote the Social Inclusion of Persons with Developmental Disabilities Act, S. O. 2008, c. 14 (ON, Can.), s. 3(1). For discussion of this definition, *see* Elizabeth Lin et al., *Strengths and Limitations of Health and Disability Support Administrative Databases for Population-Based Health Research in Intellectual and Developmental Disabilities*, 11 J. Policy & Practice in Intell. Disabilities 237 (2014).

9. Anna Arstein-Kerslake and Jennifer Black, *Right to Legal Capacity in Therapeutic Jurisprudence: Insights from Critical Disability Theory and the Convention on the Rights of Persons with Disabilities*, 68 Int'l J.L. & Psychiatry 1 (2020). *See also* Theresia Degener, *Disability in a Human Rights Context*, 5 Laws 1 (2016).

of the time.[10] This biomedical discourse remained dominant until the mid-twentieth century and focused on curing or rehabilitating ailments. This resulted in a suspension of rights for persons with IDD, subsequently leading to their institutionalization, segregation, and even sterilization on the grounds that their cognitive impairments made them childlike and in need of protection.[11]

The rights movements in the 1960s and 1970s identified that both physical and cognitive disabilities were the result of poor accommodations, societal discrimination, and stigma.[12] The social model of disability provided an alternative framework for understanding how the interaction between impairments (i.e., physical or cognitive) and environmental conditions (e.g., societal attitudes) created the experience of disability and led to detrimental outcomes for persons with IDD (e.g., unemployment, social exclusion).[13] In Ontario, it also resulted in new strategies that addressed the environmental and systematic barriers that prevented inclusion (e.g., accessible language within courts).[14]

The current human rights model of disability builds on the social model by highlighting the importance of rights and the need to create mechanisms for monitoring, adapting, and implementing rights. It also emphasizes the need for a universal and holistic approach to being human that transcend the emphasis on anti-discrimination.[15] For countries that ratified the United Nation Convention on the Rights of Persons with Disabilities (CRPD), this means ensuring that persons with disabilities (including IDD) are provided supports and services that guarantee the same opportunities to fully participate in society.[16]

---

10. Ivan Brown and John P. Radford, *The Growth and Decline of Institutions for People with Developmental Disabilities in Ontario: 1876–2009*, 21 J. Developmental Disabilities 7 (2015). *See also* Harvey G. Simmons, From Asylum to Welfare (1982).

11. Brown and Radford, *supra* note 10; Degener, *supra* note 9, at 3.

12. Brown and Radford, *supra* note 10, at 1–3.

13. *Id.*

14. Simmons, *supra* note 10, at 192–251.

15. Brown and Radford, *supra* note 10, at 2–3. *See also* Lucy Series and Anna Nilsson, *Article 12 CRPD: Equal Recognition Before the Law* in The UN Convention on the Rights of Persons with Disabilities: A Commentary (Ilias Bantekas et al. eds, 2018).

16. *Convention on the Rights of Persons with Disabilities*, 24 January 2007, UNGA A/Res/61/106 at 11–12 (entered into force May 3, 2008).

The Legal Framework: Mental Disabilities, Legal Capacity, and Moral Blameworthiness

As a country that has ratified the CRPD, Canada is responsible for ensuring that the rights of persons with disabilities are embedded in social structures and policies, including provisions that acknowledge legal capacity and assume legal personhood.[17] For example, Article 12 of the CRPD states that persons with disabilities need to have "legal capacity on an equal basis with others in all aspects of life"[18] and therefore are assumed to have the capacity and autonomy to make decisions within their own best interests. In addition, the CRPD recognizes persons with disabilities as rights-holders like anyone else, and "neither a person's legal agency nor legal personhood can be denied on the basis of disability."[19] Therefore, legal actors must find ways to convey diminished moral blameworthiness without discrimination or violating an individual's right to equal recognition.

Canadian criminal law, as in other Western legal systems, constructs a relationship between capacity to understand the nature and consequences of one's actions and criminal responsibility. It has set out a system that is age-based and that states, "No person shall be convicted of an offence in respect of an act or omission on his part while that person was under the age of twelve years."[20] The legal doctrine of *doli incapax* guides the criminal law in allocating moral blameworthiness and dictates diminished criminal responsibility based on the presumption that children under the age of twelve have the "incapacity to do wrong."[21] Therefore for youth between the ages of twelve and seventeen, the *Youth Criminal Justice Act*[22] identifies that they can be held criminally responsible due to their reduced capacity and moral blameworthiness.[23] The Supreme Court of Canada further articulated the diminished moral blameworthiness of young people as a principle of fundamental justice.[24] For children under the age of twelve, each Canadian province holds them accountable and addresses their needs through systems of child welfare and mental health services.

---

17. Series and Nilsson, *supra* note 15, at 2.

18. *Convention on the Rights of Persons with Disabilities, supra* note 16 at 10.

19. *Id.* at 3.

20. *See Criminal Code*, RSC 1985, c C-46 (Can.), s 13.

21. *See* the Crown's response: Constitutional Challenge to s. 13 in *R. v. D.S.*, 2017 OCJ (Toronto Region), hereafter cited as *Constitutional Challenge.*

22. *Youth Criminal Justice Act*, SC 2002, c. 1 (Can.).

23. *Id.* at s 2(1).

24. *See, e.g., R. v. D.B.*, 2008 2 SCR 3, SCC 25.

The *Canadian Criminal Code* recognizes that apart from age, other individuals may not have the mental or moral capacity to be held criminally responsible or should be held responsible to lesser degrees. NCRMD[25] is a verdict that is neither a finding of guilt nor an acquittal. It can be handed down when it is proven on a balance of probabilities that an individual did not appreciate the nature and quality of their actions at the time of the offense or did not know it was wrong. For many people with mental disorders (including persons with IDD), this may not be a suitable strategy because their impairment may play a role in their offense but may not alter their ability to appreciate the nature of their actions or knowledge that it was wrong.[26] This oversight in the law leaves a gap for persons with IDD.

The presence of an IDD may be entered into evidence at the sentencing stage in pursuit of reduced blameworthiness and mitigation. However, lawyers may face a double-edged sword because arguments about cognitive impairments as a result of brain damage or cognitive impairment may be misinterpreted as indications that the person is not amenable to improvement through treatment and viewed as a risk of reoffending or dangerousness.[27]

Problem-solving courts have thrived as an alternative to traditional judicial processes over the last two decades in Canada.[28] Founded on the principles of TJ, problem-solving courts aim to redirect individuals to more appropriate community services and reduce the negative effects of a traditional court.[29] Specifically, mental health courts employ dedicated, trained staff to develop a community-based plan for treatment intended to reduce the risk of recidivism in cases of persons with a mental disorder charged with certain offenses. In Canada, these courts are reserved typically for less serious offenses—offenses that are of a violent or a sexual nature are not eligible.[30] Once the terms of the diversion plan are fulfilled, charges are typically withdrawn.

25. CRIMINAL CODE, RSC 1985, c C-46 (Can.), s 16(1).

26. Layla Hall and Jessica Jones, *Offenders with Autism Spectrum Disorder: A Case of Diminished Responsibility*, in INTELLECTUAL AND DEVELOPMENTAL DISABILITIES AND THE CRIMINAL JUSTICE SYSTEM 155 (Voula Marinos et al. eds, 2020).

27. Jennifer A. Chandler, *The Use of Neuroscientific Evidence in Canadian Criminal Proceedings*, 2 J. L. & BIOSCIENCES 550 (2015).

28. RICHARD D. SCHNEIDER ET AL., MENTAL HEALTH COURTS: DECRIMINALIZING THE MENTALLY ILL (2007).

29. Voula Marinos and Lisa Whittingham, *The Role of Therapeutic Jurisprudence to Support Persons with Intellectual and Developmental Disabilities in the Courtroom: Reflections from Ontario, Canada*, 63 INT'L J.L. & PSYCHIATRY 18 (2019).

30. *See* PUBLIC PROSECUTION SERVICE OF CANADA DESKBOOK, March 1, 2014, at 3.2, https://www.ppsc-sppc.gc.ca/eng/pub/fpsd-sfpg/fps-sfp/tpd/p3/ch08.html#section_3, hereafter cited as DESKBOOK.

The Case: Reflections on a Legal and Social Quandary

D.S.,[31] a twenty-eight-year-old male with a moderate intellectual disability, appeared in the Ontario Court of Justice having been charged with four counts of possession of child pornography, punishable by a mandatory minimum sentence of one year imprisonment.[32] Due to the nature of these charges and the mandatory minimum sentence of imprisonment, diversion to a mental health court was not an option in this case.[33] It was alleged that the defendant had posted pictures of a child's genitalia on a social media site. His lawyers brought a constitutional challenge on the grounds that the accused in this case had a mental age of an eight-year-old; therefore, prosecution represented a violation of section 13 of the *Canadian Criminal Code*.[34] The accused argued his prosecution was a violation of his constitutional right to life, liberty, and security of the person and right to be equal before the law under the *Canadian Charter of Rights and Freedoms*[35] because his mental capacity was found to be equivalent to someone under the age of twelve. The crux of this argument was that the doctrine of *doli incapax* should apply not only to chronological age but also to those with intellectual disabilities since it creates a distinction based on mental capacity that widens the gap for persons with intellectual disabilities and other cognitive disorders. Specifically, the defense stated,

> Like children, adults with a mental age under 12 years old are less mature and less capable of moral judgment compared to adults with normal cognitive functioning. Like children, adults with a mental age under 12 years old may not appreciate that their criminal conduct is morally wrong. And like children, adults with a mental age below 12 years old are unable to develop cognitively to such a state in which they can sufficiently appreciate the morality of their conduct.[36]

Defense counsel also submitted that the verdict of NCRMD was not applicable as there is no "cure" for the defendant's cognitive disability. The NCRMD verdict assumes that the individual's state can be improved and their dangerousness to society can be reduced through treatment.

31. The authors have identified the case using initials in order to protect his identity.

32. Criminal Code, RSC 1985, c C-46 (Can.), s 163.1.

33. Deskbook, *supra* note 30.

34. *See* Crown's submission: *Constitutional Challenge, supra* note 20.

35. *Canadian Charter of Rights and Freedoms*, s 7 and s 15, Part 1 of the *Constitution Act, 1982*, being Schedule B to the *Canada Act 1982* (UK), 1982, c 11.

36. *See* Defense's submission: *Constitutional Challenge, supra* note 21 at para 12.

The Crown opposed this submission and argued that there was a binding authority on the court from previous case law[37] addressing these points and that, if the judge agreed with the defense's submission, it would set a problematic standard in future cases of like-situated offenders. Specifically, "To allow him [the accused] to do so [not be charged with a criminal offence] by virtue of s. 13 of the Code . . . essentially absolves him of any criminal liability for any offence that he may commit. Respectfully it is a dangerous precedent to set and may 'open the floodgates' to similar types of frivolous applications."[38] In addition, the Crown prosecutor questioned the assumption made by defense that mental age equivalency is an accurate indicator of diminished capacity, given research findings that maturation and life experience play an important role when assessing capacity.[39] The Crown suggested that it was the defense lawyers' choice to not pursue NCRMD because this was an option and would likely result in the accused being granted an absolute discharge by a forensic review board if there was no risk to the public.[40] The judge in this case was left to determine whether protection against criminal responsibility is limited to chronological age or whether it should be extended to include mental age.

Reflections on Embodiment and the Legal Subject

We were struck here by the issues and dilemmas facing legal professionals who must ethically represent their clients but who may also be forced to rely on an ableist construction of the law in order to address diminished criminal responsibility due to cognitive impairment. We believe it is critical that lawyers are aware of the implications that the different models of disability have on the legal system—that is, the medical model of disability used in healthcare law should not be applied to the criminal justice system.[41]

---

37. *See* Crown's response: *Constitutional Challenge, supra* note 21 at para 14 and 15.

38. *Id.* at para 8.

39. *See* Denise C. Valenti-Hein and Linda D. Schwartz, *Witness Competency in People with Mental Retardation: Implications for Prosecution of Sexual Abuse*, 11 SEXUALITY & DISABILITY 287 (1993). *See also* Voula Marinos et al., *Legal Rights and Persons with Intellectual Disabilities*, in CHALLENGES TO THE HUMAN RIGHTS OF PEOPLE WITH INTELLECTUAL DISABILITIES 169 (Dorothy Griffiths et al. eds., 2009).

40. Marinos and Whittingham, *supra* note 29.

41. *See* Michael L. Perlin and Mehgan Gallagher, *"Temptation's Page Flies Out the Door": Navigating Complex Systems of Disability and the Law from a Therapeutic Jurisdiction Perspective*, 25 BUFF. HUM. RTS. L. REV. 1 (2018).

What we see in this case is a dichotomy between the body and the mind in law, and not simply a distinction between actus reus and mens rea. The relationship between chronological age and legal capacity in assessing blameworthiness is severed within this case. Relying on the doctrine of *doli incapax*, the defense constructed an argument that contradicts the rights laid out in section 12 of the CRPD for his client.[42] The conceptualization of adults with IDD as "eternal children" and therefore not morally responsible is fraught with ableist notions and reflects an outdated discourse.[43] The use of mental age to describe the client's abilities relied on IQ fails to understand the individual holistically, including the crucial role that life experience and adaptive skills play.[44] Further, when legal actors conceptualize IDD this way, there can be a gap in the law for persons with IDD that leave few options for defense. It also highlights the challenges of using the defense of NCRMD for persons with IDD since they may appreciate the nature and quality of their actions at the time of the offence but to a lesser degree than that of a neurotypical peer. Consider the opening words of Justice Stevens's opinion in *Atkins v. Virginia,* banning execution of persons with intellectual disabilities:

> Those mentally retarded persons who meet the law's requirements for criminal responsibility should be tried and punished when they commit crimes. Because of their disabilities in areas of reasoning, judgment, and control of their impulses, however, they do not act with the same level of moral culpability.[45]

Clearly the law currently cannot reconcile rights guaranteed in the CRPD for persons with IDD with the notion of criminal responsibility and placing more emphasis on an impairment may be dangerous. Reinforcing having mental "deficiencies" by justice professionals may result in strengthening biomedical assumptions and increasing the risk that we will return to a time in which these individuals faced undue stigma and discrimination.[46] But lawyers should not have to rely on a characterization of their accused as

---

42. *See* Jill Peay, *Mental Incapacity and Criminal Liability: Redrawing the Fault Lines?*, 40 Int'l J.L.& Psychiatry 25 (2015).

43. David Shoemaker, *Responsibility and Disability*, 40 Metaphilosophy 458 (2009).

44. *Constitutional Challenge, supra* note 38; *see also* Voula Marinos et al., *Victims and Witnesses with Intellectual Disability in the Criminal Justice System*, 61 Crim. L. Q. 517 (2014).

45. *Atkins v. Virginia*, 536 U.S. 304, 307 (2002).

46. Richard Devlin and Dianne Pothier, *Introduction: Toward a Critical Theory of Discitizenship*, in Critical Disability Theory: Essays in Philosophy, Politics, Policy, and Law 1 (Dianne Pothier and Richard Devlin eds., 2006).

childlike, which contravenes the right to be assumed to have legal capacity. That is, consistent with the rights-based accommodations and supports that have developed for persons with disabilities in multiple areas of social life (e.g., education and community access), we need to able to extend the same logic to the law. As Craigie argued, "legal capacity in the context of personal decisions and criminal acts should not be thought of as two sides of the same coin."[47]

Reimagining Options for Persons with IDD Using Therapeutic Jurisprudence

As previously identified, TJ can affect the criminal justice system in two ways: It can alter the ways that the law is constructed to ensure that it is broad enough to accommodate the needs of all citizens, or it can alter the practice and techniques used by legal actors.[48] Ideally, consistent with a rights model of disability and the principles of mainstreaming TJ, modifications would be made to the current *Canadian Criminal Code* to address the structural and attitudinal ableism that is embedded within it, including the assumptions associated with chronological age and moral blameworthiness. However, recognizing the challenges associated with changing a legal framework, we propose that TJ can enhance the ability of law and nonjudicial officers to support the justice needs of persons with IDD. TJ's flexibility may either provide new ways of representing clients with IDD within the traditional adversarial process or increase the opportunities to be diverted or when available, referred to mental health courts (MHC).

TJ is appealing for a number of reasons. First, it opens up new possibilities within the criminal justice system for persons with IDD who warrant consideration of diminished culpability but, due to the nature of the crime, must be held accountable. Counterfeit deviance suggests that offenses (particularly sexual offenses) should be understood as a result of the many other factors that do not absolve the individual of accountability but should be considered in determining whether the individual has diminished capacity.[49] In the case of D.S., an increased focus on TJ would have

---

47. Jillian Craigie, *A Fine Balance: Reconsidering Patient Autonomy in Light of the UN Convention on the Rights of Persons with Disabilities*, 29 BIOETHICS 6 (2015).

48. Wexler, *supra* note 5.

49. Dorothy Griffiths et al.. *"Counterfeit Deviance" Revisited*, 26 J. APPLIED RESEARCH INTELLECTUAL DISABILITIES 472 (2013). For example, structural factors such as increased likelihood of congregate living and staff attitudes toward sexuality and disability need to be considered.

allowed the accused to be diverted to a MHC on the grounds that it would provide accountability without a custodial sentence while reducing the likelihood of reoffending through rehabilitation.

Diversion to MHC also affirms the legal capacity of the accused since that court's structure enables them to be an active participant in the proceedings, by providing staff trained in accommodations and mental health–related matters. There is a focus within the legal process that ensures emphasis is placed on rights, capacities, and voice. Judges will often address the accused in addition to the legal counsel throughout proceedings.[50] For D.S., this would have meant the lawyers including him in decision-making processes and/or consulting him in creating a treatment plan that is oriented toward his needs. These are key components of not only TJ but also the rights promised within section 12 of the CRPD. It is also important to recognize that one of the criticisms of TJ, specifically MHC, is that despite promoting legal capacity in the courtroom, it runs the risk of failing to adequately protect the right to legal capacity during treatment if done without active and fully informed consent. In this way, it risks coercion and further marginalization of the individual and the disability community more broadly.[51]

The solution is not necessarily the abandonment of therapeutic models. Instead, it may be possible to transform therapeutic models into emancipatory tools. However, such a transformation is possible only if both the disabled body and the disabled mind are respected. This respect can only be achieved by viewing the disabled body and mind as inherently whole and making therapeutic resources available based on the desires of disabled people themselves—not as interventions that are imposed on disabled people.[52]

Finally, TJ provides flexibility in interpreting the law to reconceptualize the relationship between the person and moral blameworthiness and to move away from ableist assumptions that dichotomize the mind and the body. TJ principles—paying robust attention to the rights of the individual and human diversity—would negate the need for legal actors to make constitutional arguments and enable them to focus on finding the necessary educative and destigmatizing outcomes for the accused. In D.S.'s case, the defense crafted his argument using the assumption that his client has a mental age equivalent to a child in an attempt to provide an ethical defense,

---

50. Voula Marinos and Devon Gregory, *The Tale of a Youth Guilty Plea Court and a Youth Mental Health Court in Ontario: How Different Are They in Practice*, 2 Int'l J. Therapeutic Juris. 25 (2016).

51. Degener, *supra* note 9, at 3.

52. *Id.* at 3.

to avoid a mandatory minimum sentence of one year, and in the context of no other legal recourse to argue for diminished culpability. This conceptualization of IDD is problematic because IQ is only a factor that can be used to understand the impact of cognitive impairments on an individual and should not be used in a way to limit the individual's autonomy, agency, and legal capacity.[53] In fact, heavy reliance on IQ cut-offs is considered an unethical practice, and as identified in the U.S. Supreme Court decision of *Hall v. Florida*, "intellectual disability is a condition, not a number."[54]

Conclusion

Having heard both sides, the judge in D.S. ruled there was no constitutional violation, stating,

> Parliament clearly expressed the test for criminal accountability in terms of chronological age and there was no basis upon which the Court could import a test based on mental capacity. [The accused] was excluded from the protection afforded by section 13 of the Criminal Code because he was older than 12, not because he had a mental disability. He was in no different position than the many children aged 13 or 14 who were virtually indistinguishable from a 12-year-old in terms of physical, mental, cognitive, moral or emotional development.[55]

The judge appeared to agree with the Crown that it was a dangerous precedent to set: The lawyers' conceptualization of the accused as childlike was troubling for the progress made under the CRPD and other legislative frameworks.

Regardless of the decision, this case reflects a number of important issues regarding persons with IDD and the concept of criminal responsibility. Persons with IDD in the justice system can pose a conundrum for legal professionals given they may appreciate the nature and consequences of their actions but not to the same degree as their neurotypical peers, while being found fit to stand trial and not eligible for verdicts of NCRMD.[56] The

---

53. Stephen Greenspan et al., *Intellectual Disability Is "a Condition, Not a Number": Ethics of IQ Cut-offs in Psychiatry, Human Services and Law*, 1 ETHICS, MEDICINE & PUBLIC HEALTH 312 (2015).

54. *Id.* at 312. *See also Hall v. Florida*, 134 S. Ct. 1986, 2004; *id.*, 2001 n.5. (2014).

55. *See* Judge's response: *Constitutional Challenge* at 2.

56. Jessica Jones, *Persons with Intellectual Disabilities in the Criminal Justice System: Review of Issues*, 51 INT'L J. OFFENDER THERAPY & COMPARATIVE CRIM. 723 (2007).

lawyers in this case were faced with a dilemma: how to assert that the consequences that apply to individuals with adult capacities should not be applied to adults with intellectual disabilities, while at the same time trying not to reduce their legal capacities or human rights and reinforcing ableist legal structures. We suggest that the principles of TJ—with an enhanced emphasis on agency and human rights—would lead to better processes and outcomes for people with IDD facing criminal charges. As a framework, TJ is valuable because it can provide flexible, individualized, and destigmatizing responses to individuals with IDD.

To conclude, our curiosity and concern about D.S.'s final sentence led us to follow up with the Crown prosecutor. Through the process of preparing the case, it was discovered that the photos uploaded onto the social media site, as it turned out, were taken by D.S. of himself. The Crown prosecutor withdrew the charges and was relieved that a miscarriage of justice was averted.

12

The Role of Therapeutic Jurisprudence in Nonjudicial Administrative Placement of Migrant Children with Mental Illness

Alison J. Lynch

Introduction

Since June 2018, several thousand migrant children have crossed the border into the United States, some on their own and some with family members or friends. However, many were separated, placed into the Office of Refugee Resettlement (ORR) system, and assigned to a housing facility. Even before placement in U.S. foster care or institutional settings, these children often had displayed symptoms of mental illness or other disabilities. Many have developed post-traumatic stress disorder (PTSD) as a result of conditions in their home country, their journey to the United States, a traumatic separation from family, or all these events combined. Those children experiencing mental health crises may be marked as behaviorally difficult based on these symptoms. That designation allows them to be placed in higher security facilities, making the process of "stepping down" to lower security housing frustrating and time-consuming for advocates.

Frequently, these children have languished in detention centers and residential treatment centers after separation because they are not able to be reunited with family, or because there are administrative hurdles that first must be bypassed. These children are not guaranteed competent, empathetic advocates who will work with them to mitigate trauma and further mental illness. Because much of this process differs from a more "traditional" approach to the legal framework, there has not been significant consideration of how to create a therapeutic environment during these quasilegal administrative placements. Therapeutic jurisprudence is an important tool that could assist advocates at all levels working within this system.

This article will discuss the history of family separation in the United States, how its racist policies marginalize communities of color and disproportionately affect their mental health, and how advocates can use therapeutic jurisprudence tools to not only provide greater measures of comfort and security to their clients but also advocate in a system that frequently fails to recognize the impact of disability and trauma on behavior.

United States Immigration and Family Separation Policies

Historical Context

The United States has a dark history of family separation policy rooted in racism and bigotry. Beginning in 1501 and lasting through 1865, the United States would split up enslaved black families, sometimes even using this practice as punishment.[1] Legally, enslaved parents did not have rights to their children, and they could be sold without permission or notice.[2] This practice of separation led to loss of culture, intergenerational trauma, and connection to one's heritage.[3] Before the Civil War, the Bible chapter Romans 13 was quoted as a religious and moral justification for practices like family separation. In an unsettling repetition of history, this is the same passage used by former attorney general Jeff Sessions and White House press secretary Sarah Huckabee Sanders in 2018 to justify family separation and enforcement of President Trump's policies at the border.[4]

---

1. The Gathering for Justice, *History of Family Separation*, https://www.gatheringforjustice.org/familyseparation (last visited February 8, 2021).

2. Sylviane Diouf, *Remembering the Women of Slavery*, NEW YORK PUBLIC LIBRARY (2015), https://www.nypl.org/blog/2015/03/27/remembering-women-slavery.

3. Russell Contreras, *Other Times in History When the U.S Separated Families*, CHICAGO TRIBUNE, https://www.chicagotribune.com/nation-world/ct-family-separation-history-20180620-story.html (last visited February 8, 2021).

4. Emily McFarlan Miller and Yonat Shimron, *Why Is Jeff Sessions Quoting Romans 13 and Why Is the Bible Verse so Often Invoked?* USA TODAY (2018), https://www.usatoday.com/story/news/2018/06/16/jeff-sessions-bible-romans-13-trump-immigration-policy/707749002/ (Sessions defended the Trump administration's policy by citing a passage from the Apostle Paul's epistle to the Romans: "I would cite you to the Apostle Paul and his clear and wise command in Romans 13, to obey the laws of the government because God has ordained them for the purpose of order," Sessions said. "Orderly and lawful processes are good in themselves

The United States also made a practice of separating Native American children from their parents, sending them to government-created boarding schools in order to force assimilation; make them take on "American" names, clothing, and hairstyles; and outlaw the language and religious traditions of the Native children.[5] Ultimately, 25–35 percent of Native children were removed from their families during this time, and children of families who refused to comply with assimilation policies were far more likely to be taken from their communities and placed with white families. Even today, Native children are four times more likely to be placed in foster care than white children.[6]

Child separation, as a policy, also has endured separate from deportation-based immigration policy but still remains rooted in xenophobia and bigotry. From the mid-nineteenth through the early twentieth century, local governments and private organizations throughout the United States routinely removed the children of Polish and Irish immigrants. The majority of the approximately two hundred thousand children removed were not orphans but were placed with Protestant and Anglo-American families, with the express aim of removing them from their Catholic, immigrant communities.[7]

Mass deportations, especially to Mexico and Central America, are also not new developments but rather are continuations of racist, anti-immigrant policies that were solidified beginning in the 1930s. Fueled by the Great Depression, anti-immigrant rhetoric about job stealing began in earnest, and the government responded by deporting approximately two million people to Mexico. However, some estimates have found that over half that number were actually American citizens.[8] Here too, families were separated: the American-born children of immigrants were allowed to remain while the parents were deported.[9] The United States practice of mass deportation continued into the 1950s, when 1.1 million individuals, including hundreds of

---

and protect the weak and lawful." Later, Huckabee Sanders summed up the same idea: "It is very biblical to enforce the law.").

5. Becky Little, *How Boarding Schools Tried to "Kill the Indian" through Assimilation* (2017), https://www.history.com/news/how-boarding-schools-tried-to-kill-the-indian-through-assimilation; Contreras, *supra* note 3.

6. *About ICWA*, https://www.nicwa.org/about-icwa/ (last visited February 7, 2021).

7. Anita Sinha, *An American History of Separating* Families, AMERICAN CONSTITUTION SOCIETY (2020), https://www.acslaw.org/expertforum/an-american-history-of-separating-families/.

8. Adrian Florido, *Mass Deportation May Sound Unlikely, but It's Happened Before*, NPR CODE SWITCH (2015), https://www.npr.org/sections/codeswitch/2015/09/08/437579834/mass-deportation-may-sound-unlikely-but-its-happened-before.

9. *Id.*

U.S. citizens, were deported to southern Mexico and were then left with no way to get back to their home cities or countries.[10]

Deportations continued and have been part of U.S. homeland security policy ever since. However, the Trump administration took a more focused approach, honing in again on family separation as a way to deter immigrants and refugees from crossing the southern border.

Family Separation Policies Under the Trump Administration

The Trump-era family separation policies began formally in April 2018, however the administration began planting seeds for the policy as early as February 2017, just weeks after President Trump was inaugurated, and it had already begun implementing separations before a formal announcement was made.[11] In fact, the U.S. House of Representatives Committee on the Judiciary released a report that found that the Department of Health and Human Services (HHS) had already separated "at least 856 children" from their parents, and that "twenty-six percent were under the age of five."[12] This report, a product of a twenty-one-month investigation into the family separation policies enacted by President Trump's administration, "revealed a process marked by reckless incompetence and intentional cruelty."[13] Included in the report is the harrowing finding that at the time separations began, government officials already were acknowledging that there was no system in place to ultimately reconnect children with their families, and they did nothing to rectify this.[14]

The policy was initially presented to the public as a "zero tolerance" approach to illegal immigration, meant to deter immigration and encourage stricter legislation. Although the policy was only publicly in place from April to June 2018, multiple reports have found that separations happened both before and after it was in effect. A pilot program that ran in 2017 was the

---

10. Laura Smith, *"Operation Wetback" Uprooted a Million Lives and Tore Families Apart. Sound Familiar?* TIMELINE (2018), https://timeline.com/mass-deportation-operation-wetback-mexico-eb79174f720b.

11. Sinha, *supra* note 7.

12. United States House of Representatives Committee on the Judiciary, *The Trump Administration's Family Separation Policy: Trauma, Destruction and Chaos.* https://judiciary.house.gov/uploadedfiles/the_trump_administration_family_separation_policy_trauma_destruction_and_chaos.pdf?utm_campaign=4526-519 (report opens by stating that "These preventable tragedies must not be forgotten").

13. *Id.*

14. *Id.*

actual beginning of family separation under President Trump,[15] and in January 2020, the American Civil Liberties Union reported that more than 1,100 families had been separated since June 2018.[16]

As of late 2020, the government has yet to find the parents of over six hundred migrant children.[17] Documents show that sixty of those children were under the age of five when separated.[18] The HHS Office of Inspector General has estimated that the U.S. government has separated almost 2,800 children since the Trump administration policy went into effect, but court documents show that number could be closer to 5,500.[19]

The HHS division that manages children, the Administration for Children and Families (ACF), has stated that they concur with recommendations for mitigating against trauma and had begun implementing them. This includes hiring a board-certified child, adolescent, and adult psychiatrist to serve as a mental health team leader. ACF representatives also stated that "significant factors" beyond its control contributed to the myriad mental health issues raised in reporting, including a surge in children crossing the border, the unique mental health needs of the children, and a shortage of qualified bilingual clinicians.[20]

The measures implemented, and the challenges identified, are important, and the fact that there were no plans in place to address them raises the question of why these were not priorities in setting up programs for migrant youth. A therapeutic jurisprudence (TJ) approach to this issue would certainly not be a cure-all solution, however tenets of integrating psychological

---

15. Lisa Riordan Seville and Hannah Rappleye, *Trump Admin Ran "Pilot Program"' for Separating Migrant Families in 2017*, NBC NEWS (2018), https://www.nbcnews.com/storyline/immigration-border-crisis/trump-admin-ran-pilot-program-separating-migrant-families-2017-n887616.

16. Mary Louise Kelly, *Looking at Lasting Effects of Trump's Family Separation Policy at the Southern Border*, NPR All Things Considered (2020), https://www.npr.org/2020/01/01/792916538/looking-at-lasting-effects-of-trumps-family-separation-policy-at-the-southern-bo.

17. Daniel Gonzalez, *628 Parents of Separated Children Are Still Missing. Here's Why Immigration Advocates Can't Find Them*, USA TODAY (2020), https://www.usatoday.com/story/news/nation/2020/12/11/immigrant-advocates-cant-locate-parents-separated-border-children/3896940001/.

18. Caitlin Dickerson, *Parents of 545 Children Separated at the Border Cannot Be Found*, NEW YORK TIMES (2020), https://www.nytimes.com/2020/10/21/us/migrant-children-separated.html.

19. *Id.*

20. Colleen Long et al., *"I Can't Feel My Heart": Children Separated from Their Parents at US-Mexico Border Showed Increased Signs of Post-traumatic Stress, According to Watchdog Report*, PBS FRONTLINE (2019), https://www.pbs.org/wgbh/frontline/article/children-separated-from-their-parents-at-us-mexico-border-showed-increased-signs-of-post-traumatic-stress-us-report-says/.

well-being with administrative decision-making would likely have informed program directors and encouraged a movement toward a more therapeutic setting.

Psychological Trauma of Separation for Young Migrant Children

It is well-settled that PTSD and trauma are significant concerns for immigrants, especially when they experience trauma not just in their home countries but also in the process of emigrating to a new country. This has an inordinately detrimental impact on children, who may not have a full understanding of the circumstances or may have had no assistance to help them process significant traumatic events to which they were exposed.

However, despite the numbers of youth immigrants and refugees around the world who may be affected by trauma, few quantitative studies have examined the nexus between exposure to traumatic events during immigration and the relation to mental health outcomes.[21] Exposure to trauma may not be immediately obvious; studies that only ask about trauma that occurs during the process of immigration may be missing substantial areas of concern, including traumatic events leading to immigration or the fact that the act of immigration itself served as a trauma without any particular remembered experience.

Even through its repeated denials of mistreatment, the U.S. government was conducting reporting on conditions and had the ability to recognize the harm it was causing these children. In a report issued in 2019 (based on a 2018 investigation) by the DHHS Office of the Inspector General, the government recognized deficiencies in mental health care provided to migrant youth, including understaffing of mental health workers across the system.[22] Facility staff reported that separated children exhibited "fear, feelings of abandonment, and post-traumatic stress." Others exhibited acute symp-

---

21. Michael A. de Arellano et al., *Immigration Trauma among Hispanic Youth Missed by Trauma Assessments and Predictive of Depression and PTSD Symptoms*, 6J. LAT. PSYCHOLOGY 159 (2018). *See also* Sean D. Cleary et al., *Immigrant Trauma and Mental Health Outcomes among Latino Youth*, 20 J. IMMIGR. MINOR HEALTH 1053 (2018); Jennifer L. Steel et al., *The Psychological Consequences of Pre-emigration Trauma and Post-migration Stress in Refugees and Immigrants from Africa*, 19 J IMMIGR MINOR HEALTH 523 (2017).

22. U.S. Department of Health and Human Services, Office of Inspector General, *Care Provider Facilities Described Challenges Addressing Mental Health Needs of Children in HHS Custody* (2019), https://www.documentcloud.org/documents/6380666-Inspector-General -Report-from-HHSOIG.html.

toms of grief such as crying inconsolably.[23] Physicians for Human Rights issued a statement after the report was released, saying in part, "No child belongs in immigration detention, even if they are detained alongside their parents. This administration should immediately adopt community-based alternatives to detention, which are humane and effective, and which lessen trauma experienced by children and families."[24]

A child psychologist who interviewed dozens of children in shelters reported that they may be able to move on with their lives after reunifying with family "but may never get over" the trauma that separation has caused.[25] He described both short- and long-term effects that many children will face, including night terrors, separation anxiety, and trouble concentrating. As adults, they will face greater risks of both mental and physical disabilities. He predicts "an epidemic of physical, psychosomatic health problems that are costly to society as well as to the individual child grown up. I call it a vast, cruel experiment on the backs of children."[26]

One recommendation that has been made is to minimize the time children spent separated and in custody, as there were clear findings that the longer children remain in custody, the more their mental health deteriorates.[27]

While TJ cannot solve the myriad physical and mental health issues that accompany the trauma of separation, its practices can certainly mitigate some of the anxiety that accompanies it. Of particular concern are children who may already have underlying mental illnesses, or whose conditions deteriorate so significantly that they require more intensive psychiatric care, whether through medication or movement to a more restrictive residential treatment facility.

Mental Illness in the Immigration System

Children who have immigrated from traumatic circumstances or endured traumatic experiences during their immigration process are not immune

---

23. *Id.*

24. *U.S. Government Confirms Migrant Children Experienced Severe Mental Health Issues Following Family Separation.* Physicians for Human Rights (2019), https://phr.org/news/u-s-government-confirms-migrant-children-experienced-severe-mental-health-issues-following-family-separation/.

25. Long et al., *supra* note 20.

26. *Id.* Facilities also reported greater difficulty treating separated children, compared with children who may have left their home countries and crossed the border independently. Facilities reported that separated children were generally younger and exhibited more fear, feelings of abandonment, and post-traumatic stress symptoms.

27. *Id.*

from additional, compounding trauma once they have been separated and moved to a facility. In fact, in many cases, they continue to experience extremely problematic conditions that can exacerbate mental illness and underlying medical conditions and can impact developing brain function. In one report, a group of attorneys visiting a Border Patrol Center describe the facility, which houses 250 children including a one-year-old, two two-year-olds, a three-year-old, and "dozens more under 12."[28] They report that "kids are taking care of kids, and there's inadequate food, water and sanitation."[29] One girl interviewed, a fourteen-year-old, had been taking care of two younger girls and told the attorneys, "I need comfort, too. I am bigger than they are, but I am a child, too."[30] Later, U.S. Representatives who were given a tour labeled the facility "a human rights crisis." [31]

Reports out of these facilities also detail wholly inadequate mental health care and accommodations for people with disabilities. Between January 2017 and March 2020, twelve people have died as a result of apparent suicide while in detention.[32] Other reports have surfaced of survivors of torture or sexual assault not being provided timely services.[33] For anyone, this setting would be antitherapeutic, but for children with underlying mental illness or trauma, these conditions can contribute to compounding stress and PTSD which in turn can affect brain development and long-term physical and mental health.

The facilities described in these reports are only the first step for children separated from their parents and are often on the southern border. From there, children can be flown hundreds of miles away, in the dead of night and

---

28. Cedar Attanasio et al., *Attorneys: Texas Border Facility Is Neglecting Migrant Kids*, AP News (2019), https://apnews.com/article/46da2dbe04f54adbb875cfbc06bbc615.

29. *Id.*

30. *Id.* In other reporting, children showed both mental and physical signs of trauma and PTSD. A seven-year-old boy believed that his father had been killed after they were separated, and that he was next. He ultimately needed emergency psychiatric care to address his mental health. Other children reported believing that they had been abandoned by their parents. "You get a lot of 'my chest hurts,' even though everything is fine" medically, a clinician told investigators. The children would describe emotional symptoms: "Every heartbeat hurts," or "I can't feel my heart." Long et al., *supra* note 20.

31. Jaclyn Reiss, *Here's What Mass. Representatives Said about Their Experience Visiting Migrant Detention*, Boston Globe (2019), https://www.bostonglobe.com/news/poli tics/2019/07/01/here-what-mass-representatives-said-about-their-experience-visiting-mi grant-detention-centers/wlQWzuF34cnh0EZ2HCo3OP/story.html.

32. American Civil Liberties Union, *Justice-Free Zones: U.S. Immigration Detention Under the Trump Administration.* https://www.aclu.org/sites/default/files/field_document/justice -free_zones_immigrant_detention_report_aclu_hrw_nijc_0.pdf (last visited February 8, 2021).

33. *Id.*

without having been given any information about their relocation, to residential facilities across the country.[34]

Besides the trauma of relocation, often done without warning to the child or the family, migrant children in detention or in residential facilities may be at an increased risk of being given psychotropic medication as a means of control and convenience, without adequate attention paid to underlying mental illness and treatment. Decisions to medicate are done without the processes familiar to many who practice in "domestic" mental disability law, and the children are not provided advocates who can prepare them for hearings (because none are held) or review their records (because generally none are received from the child's home country). The Office of Inspector General (OIG) report showed that between May and July of 2018, around three hundred children were prescribed antidepressants. Staff "described some concerns that dosages or types of medication may not have been right."[35]

Medication management is not the only significant concern when it comes to the mental health of migrant youth. The OIG report also found that although each child in government custody is supposed to receive one counseling session per week and two group sessions, mental health staff at most facilities were frequently overwhelmed and unable to provide the requisite care. A typical caseload for a clinician in this setting is twelve children; the investigators found that number was closer to twenty-five in the facilities surveyed. This also resulted in children who engaged in self-harm, suicidal behavior, or suicide attempts not receiving the proper treatment within an appropriate amount of time.[36]

Therapeutic Jurisprudence and Its Potential Impact for Advocates, Attorneys, Judges, and Government Officials

There is currently no literature or research that examines the teachings of TJ as it relates to migrant youth. While there are some issues that youth with mental illness face more generally, such as access to counsel, trauma-informed care, and added measures of establishing competency, there are oth-

---

34. Liz Robbins, *Hundreds of Separated Children Have Quietly Been Sent to New York*, New York Times (2018), https://www.nytimes.com/2018/06/20/nyregion/children-separated-border-new-york.html.

35. U.S. Department of Health and Human Services, *supra* note 22.

36. Long et al., *supra* note 20.

ers that stem from the unique situation of migrant children that must be examined in greater detail for TJ practitioners to consider in the realities of their work.

Background[37]

From TJ,[38] we gain "a new and distinctive perspective utilizing socio-psychological insights into the law and its applications."[39] Professor Amy Ronner describes the "three Vs," voice, validation, and voluntariness,[40] arguing:

> What "the three Vs" commend is pretty basic: litigants must have a sense of voice or a chance to tell their story to a decision maker. If that litigant feels that the tribunal has genuinely listened to, heard, and taken seriously the litigant's story, the litigant feels a sense of validation. When litigants emerge from a legal proceeding with a sense of voice and validation, they are more at peace with the outcome. Voice and validation create a sense of voluntary participation, one in which the litigant experiences the proceeding as less coercive . . . In general, human beings prosper when they feel that they are making, or at least participating in, their own decisions.[41]

Having established this as a foundation, advocates for migrant youth must ask themselves whether current practices related to their treatment comport with Professor Ronner's three Vs. Based on what is currently known about how migrant youth move through federal custody and the support they receive throughout nonjudicial administrative processes, that answer is no.

---

37. This section is generally adapted from Michael L. Perlin and Alison J. Lynch, *"She's Nobody's Child / the Law Can't Touch Her at All": Seeking to Bring Dignity to Legal Proceedings Involving Juveniles*. 56 FAM. CT. REV. 79 (2018).

38. *See, e.g.*, Michael L. Perlin and Kelly Frailing, *Introduction* (this volume).

39. Ian Freckelton, *Therapeutic Jurisprudence Misunderstood and Misrepresented: The Price and Risks of Influence*, 30 T. JEFFERSON L. REV. 575, 576 (2008).

40. Amy D. Ronner, *The Learned-Helpless Lawyer: Clinical Legal Education and Therapeutic Jurisprudence as Antidotes to Bartleby Syndrome*, 24 TOURO L. REV. 601, 627 (2008).

41. Amy D. Ronner, *Songs of Validation, Voice, and Voluntary Participation: Therapeutic Jurisprudence, Miranda and Juveniles*, 71 U. CIN. L. REV. 89, 94–95 (2002).

TJ and Juveniles Generally

There is a limited database of TJ literature (and some case law) on the extent of rights to be granted to foster children in juvenile and family court proceedings,[42] the civil commitment trial itself,[43] and the need for coordination between juvenile justice and mental health systems.[44] But there has been nothing written about how to use TJ practices to help migrant youth (or adults) who are entrenched in an immigration system where they need substantial amounts of advocacy and knowledge. In particular, this is relevant for youth with mental illness who are at greater risk of being moved to more restrictive settings, and decreasing their chance of release and reunification with family, if there is significant underlying mental illness.

Most important, it is critical to understand how to create a therapeutic environment in these restrictive settings, where the youth there will likely have a great deal of underlying trauma and untreated mental illness. Differences between juveniles and adults need to be taken into account. Juveniles cannot be treated as smaller adults; advocates need to tailor their advocacy approach, both in and out of the courtroom, to working with a juvenile population. This means learning to work with the individual and providing explanations at the level they are able to understand,[45] as well as recognizing that it may be necessary to work within a family structure, including the child's support system in discussions or decisions. This is even more critical when working with migrant youth. English is likely not their native language, and advocates who are not able to speak their native language or have a translator on-site for meetings need to become comfortable with other

---

42. Bernard Perlmutter, *George's Story: Voice and Transformation through the Teaching and Practice of Therapeutic Jurisprudence in a Law School Child Advocacy Clinic*, 17 St. Thomas L. Rev. 561, 580–81 (2005); Bernard Perlmutter, *"Give Me My Allowance or I'll Run!" Everyday Resistance by Foster Children and Justice Outsourced* (this volume).

43. Jan Costello, *Why Have a Hearing for Kids if You're Not Going to Listen: A Therapeutic Jurisprudence Approach to Mental Disability Proceedings for Minors*, 71 U. Cin. L. Rev. 19 (2002); Janet Gilbert et al., *Applying Therapeutic Principles to a Family-Focused Juvenile Justice Model (Delinquency)*, 52 Ala. L. Rev. 1153 (2001).

44. *See, e.g.*, Gene Griffin and Michael J. Jenuwine, *Using Therapeutic Jurisprudence to Bridge the Juvenile Justice and Mental Health Systems*, 71 U. Cin. L. Rev. 65 (2002).

45. Many juveniles may not have the ability to meaningfully participate proceedings if their advocate does not provide appropriate guidance and explanations about what is happening in the proceedings. *See* Deborah K Cooper, *Juveniles' Understanding of Trial-Related Information: Are They Competent Defendants?* 15 Behav. Sci. & L. 167 (1997); Richard A, Lawrence, *Role of Legal Counsel in Juveniles' Understanding of Their Rights*, 34 Juv. & Fam. Ct. J. 34 (1983).

options, like language lines,[46] that allow the juvenile to communicate in the most comfortable matter, especially since they will likely be speaking about topics that are difficult to discuss even in their native language.

In addition, depending on the stage of proceedings, migrant youth may have family involvement in some form, either in their home country or as sponsors in the United States. Advocates need to be particularly sensitive to working within these family structures because the trauma faced by the juvenile is likely also affecting family members and the larger community.

An example of where TJ could be particularly beneficial is in the reunification process, where family members get involved, and a number of "moving pieces" must come together. In many cases, guidance about reunification that came after a federal judge ordered the process be sped up became complicated and frequently changed, which led to further anxiety and distress.[47]

Recognizing and acknowledging juvenile brain development is a way that advocates can remind themselves to be sensitive to how they interact with this population and how it will differ from many adults, even in the immigration context. It is a well-established fact that juvenile brain development is ongoing until at least age twenty-five.[48] As part of a therapeutic jurisprudence approach to dealing with juveniles, advocates need to be aware of why a more "traditional" route of punishment, such as prison sentences or programs without juvenile-focused therapy or treatment, will be ineffective and potentially detrimental to psychological development. Further, punishment by transferring children to more restrictive environments based on their escalating mental health needs will only create a greater need for intervention and support.[49]

---

46. The term "language line" refers to a service used by many legal offices and nonprofits, whereby an advocate and his/her client can call and get a live translator who can assist in communication during in-person or telephone communications.

47. In one case, a child was moved from a Florida facility to Texas to be reunited with her father. After the child made several trips to the detention center, she was returned to the Florida facility "in shambles," without ever seeing him. Long et al., *supra* note 20.

48. "The brain does not mature until well into adulthood." *See* Mark Fondacaro et al., *The Rebirth of Rehabilitation in Juvenile and Criminal Justice: New Wine in New Bottles*, 41 Ohio N.U. L. Rev. 697, 716 (2015); Michael L. Perlin and Alison J. Lynch, *"Some Mother's Child Has Gone Astray": Neuroscientific Approaches to a Therapeutic Jurisprudence Model of Juvenile Sentencing*, 59 Fam. Ct. Rev. 478 (2021).

49. *See* Craig Haney, *Mental Health Issues in Long-Term Solitary and "Supermax" Confinement*. 49 Crime & Delinquency 124 (2003). While these children are not subject to supermax conditions, there are accounts of similar punishment methods, especially in some of the therapeutic treatment programs. The effect of isolation and punishment for displaying mental health symptoms is generally found by researchers to be negative, contributing only to worsening symptoms and the need for more significant interventions.

In practice, this type of intervention, with emphasis on the therapeutic benefits of assigning counsel and treating juveniles as a discrete category, would likely have a transformative effect on the juvenile immigration system. With less of an emphasis on punishment, and with an eye toward treatment and rehabilitation, TJ-inclined practitioners would have a greater impact in cases where interventional services would potentially benefit the juvenile. Ultimately, assigning advocates that understand both the legal and therapeutic benefits that these types of hearings can have for the juvenile could dramatically change the landscape; such a change in practice would pay due regard to the individual qualities that should be taken into account in each separate case, presented in order to provide the most effective advocacy for each individual.

Conclusion

An immediate benefit of incorporating TJ values into the migrant youth process is to give voice and validation to children who have been thrust into a system that fails to prioritize their well-being. In a recent article about dignity and the civil commitment process, Professors Jonathan Simon and Stephen Rosenbaum focus specifically on this issue of voice: "When procedures give people an opportunity to exercise voice, their words are given respect, decisions are explained to them their views taken into account, and they substantively feel less coercion."[50] If we embrace the dignity-enhancing principles of therapeutic jurisprudence, we enhance the likelihood that shame and humiliation will diminish and that greater dignity will be provided.[51] Given what these migrant youth have survived, the benefits of engaging with them in a way that comports with TJ principles can have lasting consequences, not only affording them an additional layer of support and protection in the moment but also ensuring that they experience the dignity, validation, and zealous advocacy they so deserve.

Recognizing the impact of mental illness, trauma, juvenile brain development, and development of PTSD in this population is also a critical part of advocacy. Migrant youth are routinely punished for showing symptoms of serious mental illness by being moved to more restrictive placements and being designated as risks or behavior problems. In reality, many of these

---

50. Jonathan Simon and Stephen A. Rosenbaum, *Dignifying Madness: Rethinking Commitment Law in an Age of Mass Incarceration*, 70 U. MIAMI L. REV. 1, 51 (2015) ("One of the central principles of therapeutic jurisprudence is a commitment to dignity.").

51. On the relationship between dignity and therapeutic jurisprudence in general, *see* Michael L. Perlin, "*Have You Seen Dignity?*": *The Story of the Development of Therapeutic Jurisprudence*, 27 U.N.Z. LAW REV. 1135 (2017).

children may be experiencing mental health crises, and they may be unable to effectively communicate with staff in facilities where language access is not a priority.[52] This punitive system, pushing children further and further from reunification based on their mental health, is the antithesis of therapeutic.

Many advocates are heartened by recent changes in immigration policy, but as our history has shown time and again, we are not immune from circling back to a xenophobic mentality, in government and society. Meeting sentiments like these with principles of TJ can be a powerful tool for allies and advocates and should be highlighted as a way to protect the voices of some of the most vulnerable members of our nation.

---

52. Tom Jawetz and Scott Shuchart, *Language Access Has Life-or-Death Consequences for Migrants.* Center for American Progress, https://www.americanprogress.org/issues/immigration/reports/2019/02/20/466144/language-access-life-death-consequences-migrants/ (2019).

13

"Give Me My Allowance or I'll Run!"

Everyday Resistance by Foster Children and Justice Outsourced

BERNARD P. PERLMUTTER*

Introduction: Ward of the State

Everyday forms of resistance make no headlines.[1]

This chapter examines different forms of power exerted over foster children, their legal consciousness of the rules that envelop them, and how they assert themselves to seek recognition of their personal identities and human needs.[2] Children in the child welfare system typically lack the experience or capacity to develop a consciousness of the law, especially in early childhood. They do what their caregivers and other adults tell them to do. While growing up in care, they live under rules and laws interpreted by their caseworkers and other state actors.

Many times, these interpretations of the law are wrong, or contrary to the written law. The child's ability to challenge everyday decisions made by caseworkers (or foster parents) is limited, even when she has access to a lawyer, trusted adult, or mentor. Subject to rules and regulations that govern their day-to-day lives, some resort to self-help remedies, such as running

* I would like to thank Kelsey Johnson for her research assistance in preparing this chapter.

1. JAMES C. SCOTT, WEAPONS OF THE WEAK: EVERYDAY FORMS OF PEASANT RESISTANCE 36 (1985).

2. *See generally* Austin Sarat,". . . *The Law Is All Over": Power, Resistance and the Legal Consciousness of the Welfare Poor*, 2 YALE J. L. & THE HUMANITIES 343 (1990).

from care and dealing with nonresponsive or dehumanizing practices on their own.[3]

This chapter fits the overall theme of this book, which looks at the role of nonjudicial officers as a hidden space in the U.S. judicial system through a therapeutic jurisprudence (TJ) lens. It examines relationships between children and their state caregivers through their recorded experiences and testimonial voices, incorporating insights from poverty law and lawyering, child welfare law and policy, administrative law, clinical legal education, and TJ. The chapter builds on Austin Sarat's sociolegal study of the complex relationships between welfare recipients and public assistance systems, and their ambivalent relationships with legal services providers.[4] It integrates metaphors from this field study of the welfare poor into the analysis of formal and informal, abstract and material rules that envelope foster children, illustrated by examples from the University of Miami Children & Youth Law Clinic (CYLC) docket.

Although foster children can challenge decisions by the child welfare bureaucracy in court or fair hearings, many decisions fall beyond the purview of judicial or administrative due process. Less formal client advocacy enables children to resist state control as individuals and as a group and to overcome daily challenges such as getting personal allowances from caregivers.[5]

"The Law Is All Over" Redux

I am caught, you know; there is always some rule that I'm supposed to follow, some rule I don't even know about that they say.[6]

While low-income people may seem to lack the capacity and power to resist oppressive governmental structures, they resist and deviate from rules (including rules that play out in the attorney-client relationship) all the time.[7] Austin Sarat explains that "being on welfare means having a significant part of one's life organized by a regime of rules invoked by officials to claim ju-

---

3. *See generally* Ching-Hsuan Lin, *Children Who Run Away from Foster Care: Who Are the Children and What Are the Risk Factors?* 34 CHILDREN & YOUTH SVCES. REV. 807, 808 (2012) ("Running away is viewed as a strategy or a coping behavior for foster youth when they are facing difficult situations in care, such as inadequate familial relationship and restricted institutional system.").

4. Sarat, *supra* note 2.

5. *See generally* SCOTT, *supra* note 1 at 37–42 (resistance by subordinated groups is "more than a collection of individual acts or behaviors," but a "symbol of conscious meaning").

6. Sarat, *supra* note 2 at 343.

7. *See, e.g.,* Lucie E. White, *Subordination, Rhetorical Survival Skills, and Sunday Shoes: Notes on the Hearing of Mrs. G.,* 38 BUFFALO L. REV. 1 (1990).

risdiction over choices and decisions, which those not on welfare would regard as personal and private."[8] Welfare recipients face wide-ranging rules "repeatedly encountered in the most ordinary transactions and events in their lives."[9] Even though the law may seem to dominate the day-to-day lives of the welfare poor, "resistance exists side-by-side with power and domination."[10]

Spencer, a man in his mid-thirties on general welfare, memorably pronounces, "For me the law is all over."[11] Sarat takes this as a "reference point for understanding the meaning and significance of law in the lives of the welfare poor."[12] The welfare poor "use legal ideas to interpret and make sense of their relationship with the welfare bureaucracy even as they refine those ideas by making claims the meaning and moral content of which are often at variance with dominant understandings."[13]

Foster children living under the surveillance of child welfare bureaucracy similarly experience rules that pervade their lives. Each new placement involves a routine that marks the child as the subject of power and control by the child welfare state. The child must "complete an inventory check, sign paperwork, and be advised of the house rules before settling in."[14] State regulations track the child's safety, educational, health care, food and nutrition, and other needs.[15] Padlocks on kitchen cabinets and refrigerator, timed showers, set bedtimes, and arbitrary curfews impose yet more regulations that depart from norms of family life.[16] They may lack access to the house phone, compromising their personal safety, including calls to trusted family members or friends.[17] Having one's hair done in the foster home may require fingerprinting the visitor or the court's permission.[18]

---

8. Sarat, *supra* note 2 at 343.

9. *Id.* at 344.

10. *Id.* at 346.

11. *Id.* at 343.

12. *Id.*

13. *Id.* at 346.

14. KENISHA E. ANTHONY, LABELED: WARD OF THE STATE (2020) 93. *See also* FLA. ADMIN. CODE. R. 65C-14.040(7) (rules governing child's admission to facility).

15. *See, e.g.,* FLA. ADMIN. CODE R. 65C-30.003 (Safety Planning); FLA. ADMIN. CODE R. 65C-28.018 (Educational Needs); FLA. ADMIN. CODE R. 65C-30.011 (Placement Responsibilities of Child Welfare Professionals); FLA. ADMIN. CODE R. 65C-45.010 (Standards for Licensed Caregivers).

16. ANTHONY, *supra* note 14, at 93.

17. *Id. Cf.* FLA. ADMIN. CODE. R. 65C-14.040(9) (agency policies for family visits, mail, telephone calls, and communication with parents, relatives, friends or other significant relationships).

18. ANTHONY, *supra* note 14, at 93.

Children's public testimony captures unreasonable conditions that they often endure.[19] Deprived of "normalcy," they feel like outsiders and outcasts, bound by rules that confine and confuse them.[20] Some, especially teenagers, leave care or live in unsafe homes with fewer restrictions.[21] Many resign themselves to the transactional rules imposed on them.[22] For a few, foster care in extremis is a piercingly violent, traumatic, and degrading experience at the hands of state-supported caregivers.[23]

Confined in state care and permeated by rules imposed by officialdom, children feel disconnected from family and friends.[24] Some forgo everyday childhood activities, such as participating in team sports, to attend court-ordered therapy appointments.[25] Nothing could be more antitherapeutic for that child.

---

19. *See, e.g.,* Statement of Yasmine Koenig: "I lived in four foster homes. Each one was a safe place to sleep and better than my original situation, but my first three foster parents were very unreasonable. The first had a lock on the pantry and only she had the key." Children's Rights, Fostering the Future (2015), https://www.childrensrights.org/18-and-adopted-3/, hereafter cited as Fostering.

20. *See, e.g.,* Statement of Delena Meyer, in Fostering ("The rules and boundaries of foster care feel more like a cage than a sanctuary. My friends' parents had to be background checked for a sleepover."); Statement of David G. Daniels ("I was treated like a 'throwaway kid'—a burden and prisoner. There was no privacy.").

21. *See, e.g.,* Statement of Ke'onda, in Fostering ("Some girls prostitute for money, others prostitute for food, others prostitute for drugs."); *Foster Shock* (2018), at 17:38 mins., https://www.youtube.com/watch?v=YXCByofJ9D0.

22. *See, e.g.,* Statement of David Inglish, in Fostering ("The state is our parent, yet we are sometimes treated like transactions when we should be given the opportunity to live something like a normal life.").

23. *See, e.g.,* Statement of Valnita Ferguson, in Fostering ("They would beat me and my five adoptive siblings with anything they could get their hands on—belts, baseball bats, two-by-fours, shoes, fists, hammers. We were burned with clothes irons, on the stove, with a curling iron. They would beat us while we were naked, duct tape us to a chair or our beds for days, and hold us over a banister by our feet–then drop us. Sometimes they starved us.").

24. *See, e.g.,* Testimony of Talitha James, in Fostering ("I felt like I was in captivity. Many times I was separated from the things that meant so much to me and the only reasoning that was given to me was, 'It's the County rules' or 'We have to get the County to approve.'"). Committee on Ways and Means. Letting Kids Be Kids: Balancing Safety with Opportunity for Foster Youth (May 9, 2013), https://gop-aysandmeans.house.gov/UploadedFiles/Talitha_James_Testimony_HR050913.pdf.

25. *See, e.g.,* Testimony of Talitha James, in Fostering ("The same County officials who skipped out on mandated monthly visits placed me into foster homes that were unfit for any child and overlooked my plea to play sports because it was more important for me to see a therapist.").

Giving the child opportunities to participate in decisions in and out of court may improve the child's psychological health.[26] TJ in the child welfare context gives the child a sense that her voice is genuinely heard and taken seriously, giving her a sense of validation.[27] As a law reform project grounded in the social sciences,[28] TJ has broad application to juvenile law.[29] Research in the psychology of procedural justice suggests that treating a child with fairness, respect, and dignity improves perceptions of the process, promotes greater respect for the law, and fosters greater sense of personal control over her circumstances as a ward of the state.[30] Attending hearings allows children to heal and move on from the abuse and neglect that they have suffered.[31] Active participation in decisions also enables them take more responsibility for the future.[32]

Unfair Hearings for Foster Children: Justice Curtailed

The State did their job, taking my picture every month to document that I was alive and hosted pointless court hearings to discuss my well-being.[33]

The law is all over foster children. Their lives are suffused by house rules enforced by the foster parent, administrative regulations overseen by case-

---

26. *See generally* Bruce J. Winick, *Redefining the Role of the Criminal Defense Lawyer at Plea Bargaining and Sentencing: A Therapeutic Jurisprudence Preventative Law Model*, 5 PSYCH. PUB. POL'Y & L. 1034, 1039 (1999) (legal system should be sensitive to the law's impact on psychological health of clients, and legal actors should perform their roles with awareness of basic principles of psychology).

27. *See generally* Bruce J. Winick and Ginger Lerner-Wren, *Do Juveniles Facing Civil Commitment Have a Right to Counsel? A Therapeutic Jurisprudence Brief*, 71 U. CIN. L. REV. 115, 117–18 (2002) (child's lawyer "typically will advance the child's views concerning his or her own interests," which "could have positive effects for the psychological functioning" of the child).

28. *See generally* DAVID B. WEXLER & BRUCE J. WINICK, EDS, LAW IN A THERAPEUTIC KEY: DEVELOPMENTS IN THERAPEUTIC JURISPRUDENCE (1996) (describing TJ's use of behavioral science to examine the consequences of law for the psychological functioning and emotional well-being of clients).

29. *See generally* Michael L. Perlin, *Book Review of Re-Understanding the Child's Right to Identity: On Belonging, Responsiveness and Hope, by Ya'Ir Ronen*, 2 INT'L J. THER. JURISP. 95, 96–97 (2016) (summarizing "robust" TJ literature about child welfare, mental health, and juvenile justice proceedings).

30. *See, e.g.,* E. ALLAN LIND AND TOM R. TYLER, THE SOCIAL PSYCHOLOGY OF PROCEDURAL JUSTICE (1988); TOM R. TYLER, WHY PEOPLE OBEY THE LAW (1990).

31. *See* Miriam Aroni Krinsky and Jennifer Rodriguez, *Giving a Voice to the Voiceless: Enhancing Youth Participation in Court Proceedings*, 6 NEV. L. J. 1302, 1303 (2006).

32. *See* Catherine J. Ross, *A Place at the Table: Creating Presence and Voice for Teenagers in Dependency Proceedings*, 6 NEV. L. J. 1362, 1371 (2006).

33. ANTHONY, *supra* note 14 at 101.

workers, and statutes and case precedent applied by judges. Every child in foster care has a case plan designed to achieve placement in the least restrictive, most family-like, and appropriate setting available consistent with the child's best interests and special needs.[34]

The juvenile court reviews the case plan every six months.[35] The review assesses the compliance with the plan and progress in alleviating reasons for continued foster placement.[36] The agency must show that foster parents have provided the child opportunities to engage in age- or developmentally appropriate activities.[37] Decisions rendered in the foster or group home and by agency bureaucrats are subject to continual court oversight. Judges and agency caseworkers coexist in an uneasy, fraught relationship as "institutional co-parents."[38] Executive branch decisions are not subject to conventional judicial constraints.[39]

Other factors impeding children's ability to hold child welfare bureaucrats accountable are the routine exclusion of children from hearings and their lack of access to counsel. Participation in court hearings is the exception rather than the rule.[40] Although children in Florida have party status[41] and can have counsel appear for them,[42] they are not guaranteed the right to court-appointed counsel,[43] unlike the state and their parents. Only a small percentage actually have an attorney to advise and speak for them.[44] Given

---

34. 42 U.S.C. § 675(5)(A).

35. 42 U.S.C. § 675(5)(B).

36. *Id.*

37. *Id.*

38. Bruce A. Boyer, *Jurisdictional Conflicts Between Juvenile Court and Child Welfare Agencies: The Uneasy Relationship Between Institutional Co-Parents*, 54 Md. L. Rev. 377 (1995).

39. *Id.* at 377 ("The nature of this relationship—with juvenile courts and child welfare agencies carrying continuing and overlapping responsibilities . . . renders the application of traditional tools of public and administrative law to the field of child welfare awkward and ineffective.").

40. *See, e.g., Home at Last, My Voice, My Life, My Future, Foster Youth Participation in Court: A National Survey* (2006), www.fostercarehomeatlast.org, at 10 (overwhelming majority of youth respondents reported that they attended court only some of the time).

41. Fla. Stat. § 39.01(58).

42. *See, e.g.,* Fla. Stat. § 39.4085(20) (Legislative goal: "To have . . . an attorney ad litem appointed to represent their legal interests").

43. *See generally* Michael J. Dale and Louis M Reidenberg, *The Kids Aren't Alright: Every Child Should Have an Attorney in Child Welfare Proceedings in Florida*, 36 Nova L. Rev. 345 (2012).

44. Robin L. Rosenberg, *Cost of Providing Counsel to Unrepresented Children in Florida* (2016), on file with the author (only 10% of all children in Florida out-of-home care are represented by counsel).

these barriers, it is no surprise that some children consider judicial hearings to be "pointless."

Federal law establishes a secondary tier for accountability focused on service needs or conditions of care. The Adoption Assistance and Child Welfare Act makes fair hearings available for the nonjudicial resolution of disputes with child welfare agencies.[45] Implementation of this requirement to address services or financial assistance to prevent removal or expedite reunification has been uneven.[46]

Fair hearings follow due process norms established by *Goldberg v. Kelly*, through which welfare recipients can challenge the denial, reduction, or termination of benefits from the state.[47] A pretermination hearing must be afforded before the government discontinues public assistance benefits.[48] This proceeding "need not take the form of a judicial or quasi-judicial trial"; a pretermination hearing to comply with due process need only make an initial determination about the validity of the grounds for discontinuing the assistance.[49] As such, administrative fair hearings feature a different form than judicial hearings.[50]

The on-the-ground reality of constitutionally mandated welfare hearings is that they have "not compelled bureaucrats to treat people with dignity."[51] The paradox of *Goldberg* is that "by proclaiming that the Constitution protects poor people from welfare practices that are fundamentally unfair, the case seems to condone those subtle insults that do not easily translate into constitutional claims."[52] Many who seek an administrative hearing "often experience it as a bewildering ordeal."[53]

These observations align with the (un)fair hearing treatment of children in foster care in Florida. Although Florida law recognizes its duty to protect the procedural due process rights of foster children,[54] the conduct of these

---

45. *See generally* Harold M. Freiman, *"Some Get a Little and Some Get None": When Is Process Due through Child Welfare and Foster Care Fair Hearings Under P.L. 96–272?* 20 COLUM. HUM. RTS. L. REV. 343 (1989).

46. *Id.*

47. Goldberg v. Kelly, 397 U.S. 254 (1970).

48. *Id.* at 263.

49. *Id.* at 266–67.

50. *Id.*

51. Lucie E. White, Goldberg v. Kelly *on the Paradox of Lawyering for the Poor*, 86 BROOK. L. REV. 861, 868 (1990).

52. *Id.*

53. *Id.* at 868–69.

54. *See, e.g.*, Occean v. Kearney, 123 F.Supp.2d 618 (S.D. Fla. 2000) (applying *Goldberg v. Kelly* to youth's summary termination from foster care); J.M. v. Florida Agency for Persons with Disabilities, 938 So. 2d 535, n. 8 (Fla. Ct. App. 2006) (fair hearing must meet the due

hearings is often a bewildering ordeal. This is especially true for youth who pursue hearings to preserve post-foster care benefits,[55] and seek posthearing judicial review.[56]

Florida law refers to fair hearings as appeal hearings.[57] Though they maintain many of the same procedures, formal hearings require that an administrative law judge preside[58] while agency "hearing officers" preside over appeal hearings.[59] Although administrative law judges must possess certain qualifications,[60] no statutory criteria exist for hearing officers.[61] Despite the absence of formal requirements for hearing officers, DCF touts hearing officers as "trained, knowledgeable, independent, and neutral adjudicator[s] who had no involvement in the initial determination."[62] While the qualifications of hearing officers remain unclear, Florida law explicitly requires less of DCF hearing officers than of administrative law judges.

DCF employs approximately twenty-two nonjudicial hearing officers who oversee all of the fair hearings on DCF's vast array of public assistance programs.[63] These programs resulted in over twelve thousand fair hearing requests in 2018 alone.[64] The appeals provide curtailed justice, despite their facial compliance with *Goldberg*, for foster children challenging unjust child welfare decisions.[65]

Caught in a web of legal rules with hearings overseen by nonjudicial officers and lacking access to legal counsel, foster children, like welfare clients, "are more resigned than angry about law's inequities . . . which in their view are built into the very fabric of law's rules and practices."[66]

---

process standards set forth in *Goldberg*, C.F.R. § 431.205(d), mirrored by FLA. ADMIN. CODE R. 65-2.042).

55. *See, e.g.*, Wade v. DCF, 79 So. 3d 946 (Fla. Ct. App. 2012) (denying writ of mandamus to continue foster care Road to Independence payments during judicial review of agency action).

56. Wade v. DCF, 57 So. 3d 869 (Fla. Ct. App. 2011); Wade v. DCF, 98 So. 3d 574 (Fla. Ct. App. 2012).

57. *Appeal Hearings*, DEPARTMENT OF CHILDREN AND FAMILIES (Apr. 28 2020), https://www.myflfamilies.com/about-us/office-inspector-general/appeal-hearings/.

58. FLA. STAT. § 120.57(1).

59. FLA. STAT. § 120.57(2).

60. *See* FLA. STAT. § 120.65.

61. *See* FLA. STAT. § 409.285.

62. *Appeal Hearings*, *supra* note 57.

63. *Id.* at 11–12.

64. *Id.* at 3.

65. White, *supra* note 51 at 886.

66. Sarat, *supra* note 2 at 343.

Personal Allowances: Justice Outsourced

If you did one thing wrong that week, you wouldn't get an allowance.[67]

There is another "space," to use Sarat's term, of rules, beyond these formal statutory or administrative constructions, that affect children's daily lives in care. Every child is supposed to receive a monthly personal allowance, deducted from the provider's board payment.[68] Yet many children are short-changed by foster parents in seemingly arbitrary ways. Children may not know that they are entitled to a monthly allowance or that they have a right to ask for it. Others have "legal consciousness" of their right to allowances to purchase personal hygiene items, school supplies, clothing, or other necessities.[69] Many fear removal from the home if they speak up about the allowance.[70]

A parent's use of the power of the purse to motivate a child to do better in school or obey house rules is a proper exercise of parental authority to nurture, guide, and promote the best interests of their child.[71] Conversations about these matters usually happen in the living room, not the courtroom.[72] When the state assumes legal custody of the child, its parens patriae duties similarly require it to support and nurture the child.[73] If a foster parent withholds an allowance to regulate the child's conduct, the parent is subject to heightened accountability, since these funds do not derive from the parent's private earnings but from taxpayer-generated revenue sources.[74]

---

67. Statement of Janice, *Foster Shock, supra* note 21, at 16:01 mins.

68. *Id.*

69. *See generally* FLA. ADMIN. CODE ANN. R. 65C-14.018(11).

70. *See, e.g.,* FLA. ADMIN. CODE R. 65C-30.007 (11).

71. *See, e.g.,* Haxton v. Haxton, 705 P.2d 721 (Ore. 1985); *see also* Leslie J. Harris et al., *Making and Breaking Connections between Parents' Duty to Support and Right to Control Their Children,* 69 OR. L. REV. 689 (1990).

72. *See, e.g.,* Henry J. Reske, *Paying the Price in Court: Breakdowns in Society Have Legal Impact on Children,* 80-Jul. A.B.A. J. 86 (July 1994) (cautioning children's lawyers against "frivolous lawsuits" over their clients' allowances).

73. *See generally* Vivek S. Sankaran, Parens Patriae *Run Amuck: The Child Welfare System's Disregard for the Constitutional Rights of Nonoffending Parents,* 82 TEM. L. REV. 55, 59–61 (2009–10) (describing historical evolution of "state's newfound role as the protector of all children").

74. *See generally* Smith v. Organization of Foster Families for Equality and Reform, 431 U.S. 816, 845, 844 (1977) (distinguishing foster parent-child relationship with its source in "state law and contractual arrangements" from the "intimacy of daily association" that binds children to natural parents).

Florida's allowance rules are meant to guard against arbitrary withholding or misuse of these funds by foster parents[75] or group homes,[76] but individual case management agencies frequently deviate from the rules and improvise variant local practices.[77] These selective local interpretations (or misinterpretations) of the rules have consequences for children.[78] These practices are akin to the unwritten, ad hoc "they say" deployed by welfare bureaucrats to keep their dependents in line.[79] Many parents pocket the money to supplement their board payment, sometimes leading children to fend for themselves so they can eat.[80] Conspicuously absent are procedures guaranteeing children opportunities for administrative appeals or judicial hearings to review allowance practices.[81]

Responding to these inequities, youth have coalesced as an organized force to reform them. The CYLC has a longstanding relationship with Florida Youth Shine (FYS), a foster care advocacy organization.[82] Collaboration with FYS has been a valuable tactic in CYLC's client advocacy and public education missions.[83]

In 2018, FYS held an "issue processing" session with foster kids on allowances, an area of concern that affected many of them. The kids shared

---

75. FLA. ADMIN. CODE ANN. R. 65C-45.010(4)(g) ("Licensed out-of-home caregivers shall not withhold meals, clothing, allowance or shelter as a form of discipline.").

76. FLA. ADMIN. CODE ANN. R. 65C-14.018(11) (allowance shall be provided "at least monthly" and "not be tied to behavior or completion of chores" or "withheld as punishment").

77. *See* Community-Based Care Lead Agencies and Contract Manager (Mar. 8, 2018) and Group Home Allowance Survey (Apr. 10, 2019) (CYLC), on file with author (no local written policies; policies inconsistent with state rules; inconsistent disbursement practices and eligibility criteria).

78. *See generally* Movement Advancement Project, *The High Stakes in the* Fulton *Case: Undermining the Vital Role of Child Welfare Law and Regulations in Protecting America's Children* (Aug. 2020) ("What would it mean . . . if private agencies receiving taxpayer dollars through government contracts could just pick and choose which laws to follow?").

79. Sarat, *supra* note 2 at 343.

80. *See, e.g.,* Statement of Tiana, *Foster Shock, supra* note 21, at 13:29 mins. ("It's like we're money to them. Like you see like [foster parent] would come to work in his Corvette while all of us don't even have food in our fridges.").

81. *Compare* FLA. STAT. §§ 402.17 and 402.33 (mandating notice and hearings for appeals of adverse decisions regarding fee waivers or personal allowances from state-administered disability master trusts). *See also* Daniel L. Hatcher, *Foster Children Paying for Foster Care*, 27 CARDOZO L. REV. 1797 (2006) (analyzing state recoupment of foster children's SSI benefits).

82. *See* Bernard P. Perlmutter, *"Letting Kids Be Kids": Youth Voice and Activism to Reform Foster Care and Promote "Normalcy,"* in 72 STUDIES IN LAW, POLITICS AND SOCIETY, 121, 150–55 (Austin Sarat ed., 2017).

83. *See generally* Sameer Ashar, *Law Clinics and Collective Mobilization*, 1 CLIN. L. REV. 355 (2007); Jane M. Spinak, *They Persist: Parent and Youth Voice in the Age of Trump*, 56 FAM. CT. REV. 308 (2018).

experiences and frustrations. Many considered the lack of guaranteed allowances not only a personal affront but an injustice. Participants recounted never receiving an allowance, and others reported recurring violations of written policy. They all agreed that allowances teach financial responsibility, which is important to adolescents' decision-making capacities in money management and other domains.[84]

The youth asked for a set base amount, good behavior bonuses, no reductions, and higher amounts for older youth for completing a financial literacy course, for birthdays, and for group home residents to encourage self-sufficiency and deter illegal activities. They also proposed cost-of-living adjustments based on location and prepaid debit cards or other traceable systems to make disbursements easier.

They asked the CYLC to help turn the recommendations into reality through legislation or rulemaking. Youth engagement with the Law Clinic, tapping into its child welfare legal expertise, afforded the young people inside the foster care system a chance to collaborate with "outsider" law students, but their outlooks were often different.[85]

Some law students questioned how much additional regulation foster parents and group homes would tolerate, and what benefits would the children get from more rules. They viewed the problem as children of intact middle-class families rather than as allies of foster children seeking justice.[86] Some urged policy to resolve disputes without causing friction between parent and child. Others saw benefits of helping the organization advocate for systemic reforms "at variance with dominant understandings."[87]

Youth Voice, Validation, and Voluntary Participation

> As with other human beings, juveniles need to be treated with "respect, politeness and dignity" and they need to feel that "their rights as citizens are acknowledged."[88]

When foster parents withhold their allowance, should their decision be the final word, as is the case in "normal" families? The traditional presumption

---

84. *See generally* Elizabeth S. Scott, *The Legal Construction of Adolescence*, 29 HOFSTRA L. REV. 547 (2000).

85. *See generally* Lucie E. White, *To Learn and Teach: Lessons from Driefontein on Lawyering and Power*, 1988 WIS. L. REV. ("outsider" lawyers collaborating with client organizers working inside disempowered communities).

86. *See generally* Jane H. Aiken, *Provocateurs for Justice*, 7 CLINICAL L. REV. 287 (2001).

87. Sarat, note 2 at 346.

88. Amy D. Ronner, *Songs of Validation, Voice, and Voluntary Participation: Therapeutic Jurisprudence, Miranda, and Juveniles*, 71 U. CIN. L. REV. 89, 95 (2002).

that parents act in their children's best interests is a paradigm of justice out-sourced.[89] For children in care, the state's legal rules and regulations subject both parent and child to external oversight. A key paradox of the child wel-fare system is the child's subjugation under "a regime of rules invoked by officials to claim jurisdiction over choices and decisions, which those not on welfare would regard as personal and private."[90]

If the parent withholds the allowance, how does a child contest this de-cision under the regime of existing rules? Would a conversation with the foster parent or case manager be useful? If informal contacts fail to resolve the allowance reduction or termination, does the child turn to the juvenile court or an administrative hearing officer? Just as important, what relief can the child seek or expect from the court or fair hearing?

A brief case example from the CYLC's docket illustrates the multiple tiers of foster care bureaucracy involved in a dispute over this seemingly or-dinary, everyday transaction. It also reveals the confusion and silencing that clients experience from "administrative processes, which are the backbone of due process delivery . . . which many regard as harrowing and Kafkaesque."[91]

In 2015, the clinic filed a motion on behalf of a fifteen-year-old foster child to get his allowance funds restored so he could buy a pair of sneakers. The foster parent had cut off his allowance because of his bad grades.[92] The intervention by the legal interns entailed a series buck-passing and finger-pointing conversations with different actors in the regional and local foster care agencies, and with the foster parent. The students drafted an eight-page motion detailing the convoluted sequence of events; the web of rules, guide-lines, and policies in which the client was trapped;[93] and the different agen-cies' and agency representatives' interpretations of the rules, and they asked the court to resolve, or at least referee, the interagency conflicts.[94]

After the lengthy back-and-forth with the different agency bureaucrats and lawyers, and on the eve of the court hearing, the client told the legal in-

---

89. *See, e.g.,* Parham v. J.R., 442 U.S. 584 (1979).

90. Sarat, *supra* note 2 at 343.

91. Evelyn H. Cruz, *Validation through Other Means: How Immigration Clinics Can Give Immigrants a Voice When Bureaucracy Has Left Them Speechless,* 17 St. Thomas L. Rev. 811, 811–12 (2005).

92. *Child's Motion to Compel FRC to Provide [Child] with Tutoring Services, His Required Allowance, and Proof of Monitoring of the Allowance as Mandated by Our Kids Policy and DCF Administrative Code and Policy,* on file with author.

93. *Compare* Sarat, *supra* note 2 at 345 ("For Spencer and other welfare recipients law is not a distant abstraction; it is a weblike enclosure in which they are 'caught.'").

94. *See generally In re* K.A.B. 483 So. 2d 898, 899 (Fla. Ct. App. 1986) ("The agency is, of course, better equipped to make day-to-day health and welfare decisions which concern the child" than the court).

terns that he did not want to "mess with" his foster mother and asked them to dismiss the motion. The foster parent thereafter resumed giving him his monthly allowance, and she paid it until he left her home on his eighteenth birthday.

The client never had his day in court, but the benefits of having his story told in a legal motion filed with the court gave the client an appreciation of the role of his student lawyers, both in court and outside of the judicial process.[95] This empowered him in his relationship with the child welfare bureaucracy.[96] His voice was heard and validated by the account of his experience as recorded in the motion, within the extrajudicial spaces of the child welfare bureaucracy, even if not in the courtroom. Being heard by agency bureaucrats offers a lesson in one young client's perception of the legal system as a positive, even "therapeutic" event, as opposed to an embittering and futile exercise.[97]

Much of the advocacy by children's lawyers centers on making a difference in everyday events and transactions in the child's life. The lawyer uses persuasion or negotiation within the child welfare bureaucracy, as much as formal courtroom advocacy, to help the child achieve ordinary milestones, such as a personal allowance, or more symbolic rites of passage, such as participation in a high school graduation ceremony.[98]

For a child subject to an elaborate regime of rules administered by bureaucrats, the mere experience of being treated with "respect, politeness and dignity" and feeling that his "rights as a citizen are acknowledged"[99] affirms his ability to resist the power of the child welfare system, where justice is often outsourced.

---

95. *See generally* Emily Buss, *You're My What? The Problem of Children's Misperceptions of Their Lawyers' Roles*, 64 FORDHAM L. REV. 1699 (1996).

96. *See generally* Katherine Hunt Federle, *The Ethics of Empowerment: Rethinking the Role of Lawyers in Interviewing and Counseling the Child Client*, 64 FORDHAM L. REV. 1655 (1996).

97. *See* Bernard P. Perlmutter, *George's Story: Voice and Transformation through the Teaching and Practice of Therapeutic Jurisprudence in a Law School Child Advocacy Clinic*, 17 ST. THOMAS L. REV. 561, 594 (2005) (child's attorney was his law enforcer and therapeutic agent).

98. *Id.* at 603–9.

99. Ronner, *supra* note 88, at 95.

14

A Critique of Texas Lethal Injection Cases

An Examination of Decision-Making and the Risk of Botches in Texas Lethal Injection Protocols Since 1982[1]

Talia Roitberg Harmon, Michael Cassidy, and Richelle Kloch

Introduction

O ver the last two decades, scholars have developed a substantial body of research documenting "botched" executions.[2] Though the definition of botched executions varies across prior work,[3] Professor Austin Sarat

---

1. We acknowledge Courtney Hope Fell and Nicole Perry for their exceptional research assistance in the preparation of this article. Portions of this essay are adapted from Harmon, T. R., Cassidy, M., & Kloch, R. "Examination of Decision Making and Botched Lethal Injection Executions in Texas," *American Behavioral Scientist* (64:12) pp. 1715–32. Copyright © 2020 by SAGE. Reprinted by permission of SAGE Publications Inc. This material is the exclusive property of the SAGE Publications Inc. and is protected by copyright and other intellectual property laws. User may not modify, publish, transmit, participate in the transfer or sale of, reproduce, create derivative works (including course packs) from, distribute, perform, display, or in any way exploit any of the content of the file(s) in whole or in part. Permission may be sought for further use from SAGE Publications Inc., attn. Rights Department, 2455 Teller Road, Thousand Oaks, CA 91360, email: permissions@sagepub.com. By accessing the file(s), the User acknowledges and agrees to these terms. http://www.sagepub.com.

2. Christopher Q. Cutler, *Nothing Less Than the Dignity of a Man: Evolving Standards, Botched Executions and Utah's Use of the Firing Squad*, 50 Clev. St. L. Rev. 335 (2002). *See also* Deborah W. Denno, *Getting to Death: Are Executions Constitutional*, 82 Iowa L. Rev. 319 (1997), hereafter cited as Denno, *Getting to Death*; Deborah W. Denno, *When Legislatures Delegate Death: The Troubling Paradox behind State Uses of Electrocution and Lethal Injection and What It Says about Us*, 63 Ohio St. L.J. 63 (2002), hereafter cited as Denno, *Delegate Death*; Corinna Barrett Lain, *The Politics of Botched Executions*, 49 U. Rich. L. Rev. 825 (2015); Austin Sarat, Gruesome Spectacles: Botched Executions and America's Death Penalty (2014); Stephen Eliot Smith, *Going through All These Things Twice: A Brief History of Botched Executions*, 12 Otago L. Rev. 777 (2012).

3. Denno, *Getting to Death*, *supra* note 2; Herb Haines, *Flawed Executions, the Anti-Death Penalty Movement, and the Politics of Capital Punishment*, 39 Soc. Probs. 125 (1992); Smith, *supra* note 2.

states that botched executions are "those involving unanticipated problems or delays that caused, at least arguably, unnecessary agony for the prisoner or that reflect gross incompetence of the executioner."[4] The most recent and regularly relied upon research shows that 5.4 percent of lethal gassing executions were botched, as were 3.12 percent of hangings, 1.92 percent when the method was electrocution, and no botches have been reported in executions by firing squad.[5] Notably, the botched execution rate is highest for lethal injections at 7.12 percent,[6] a method that has often been viewed as the most humane.[7] Currently, twenty-eight states and the federal government have adopted lethal injection as their method for inmate executions.[8]

As the majority of states have shifted to drugs to carry out executions, death penalty scholars have questioned the constitutionality of lethal injection protocols.[9] In recent years, the U.S. Supreme Court has addressed the issue of whether lethal injection subjects individuals to unnecessary pain and suffering in three cases,[10] ultimately stating that Eighth Amendment claims require identification of an "available alternative method of execution that entails a lesser risk of pain."[11] In 2020, the court rejected an appeal by death row inmates from the U.S. Court of Appeals for the D.C. Circuit, which had ruled that the execution protocol used by the federal government could differ from that of the state in which the prisoner was sentenced.[12]

Yet several states have continually changed their lethal injection protocols during the time the Supreme Court rendered its decisions.[13] Domestic pharmaceutical companies have stopped supplying states with the drugs

---

4. SARAT, *supra* note 2, at 5.

5. *Id.*

6. *Id.*

7. Denno, *Delegate Death, supra* note 2.

8. *State-by-State Lethal Injection Protocols*, DEATH PENALTY INFORMATION CENTER, https://deathpenaltyinfo.org/executions/lethal-injection/state-by-state-lethal-injection-pro tocols (last visited Jan. 29, 2021).

9. Eric Berger, *Lethal Injection Secrecy and Eighth Amendment Due Process*, 55 B.C. L. REV. 1367 (2014); Denno, *Getting to Death, supra* note 2; Deborah W. Denno, *Lethal Injection Chaos Post-Baze*, 102 GEO. L.J. 1331 (2014); *State-by-State Lethal Injection Protocols, supra* note 8; Julia Eaton, *"Warning: Use May Result in Cruel and Unusual Punishment": How Administrative Law and Adequate Warning Labels Can Bring about the Demise of Lethal Injection*, 59 B.C. L. REV. 355 (2018).

10. Baze v. Rees, 553 U.S. 35 (2008); Glossip v. Gross, 135 S. Ct. 2726 (2015); Bucklew v. Precythe, 139 S. Ct. 1112 (2019).

11. Glossip, 135 S. Ct. at 2731. *See also* Bucklew 139 S. Ct. at 1129 (reiterating "claim[s] alleging the infliction of unconstitutionally cruel pain must meet the *Baze-Glossip* test").

12. Bourgeois v. Barr, 141 S. Ct. 180 (2020).

13. Denno, *Getting to Death, supra* note 9; *State-by-State Lethal Injection Protocols, supra* note 8.

needed for lethal injections, and many foreign suppliers have followed suit.[14] As a result, states have been forced to change the number and types of drugs used in their protocols, as well as find new suppliers such as compounding pharmacies, to obtain the drugs.[15] Problems associated with procuring drugs from compounding pharmacies have been well documented, particularly concerns related to the lack of rigorous oversight and regulation.[16]

This chapter examines Texas lethal injection executions from 1982 until 2020. We discuss how nationwide drug shortages have led to the rise of compounding pharmacies as the primary suppliers of lethal injection drugs, and the effect this has had on Texas changing its execution protocols. We also explore differences in the length of time the lethal injection took, and complications reported by media witnesses across the state's three- and one-drug protocols. Identifying the prevalence of botched executions associated with these two protocols is necessary to assess whether the state's switch in protocols, which was never sanctioned by a court, has exposed inmates to an increased risk of pain.

Lethal Injection Drug Shortages and Compounding Pharmacies

Over the last decade, lethal injection drug shortages have plagued death penalty states.[17] With decreasing availability from foreign and domestic manufacturers, states have turned to compounding pharmacies to obtain lethal injection drugs.[18] Compounding pharmacies alter or create drugs to fit the needs of individual patients,[19] but state regulation of small compounding pharmacies raises a number of concerns. Whereas the FDA verifies the safety, effectiveness, and quality of FDA-approved drugs, regulations concern-

---

14. Denno, *Getting to Death, supra* note 9.

15. *Id.*; *Compounding Pharmacies and Lethal Injection*, DEATH PENALTY INFORMATION CENTER, https://deathpenaltyinfo.org/executions/lethal-injection/compounding-pharmacies (last visited Jan. 29, 2021).

16. Chris McDaniel, *Inmates Said the Drug Burned as They Died. This Is How Texas Gets Its Execution Drugs*, BUZZFEED NEWS (Nov. 28, 2018), https://www.buzzfeednews.com/article/chrismcdaniel/inmates-said-the-drug-burned-as-they-died-this-is-how-texas; *Compounding Pharmacies and Lethal Injection, supra* note 15; *Compounding and the FDA: Questions and Answers*, U.S. FOOD AND DRUG ADMINISTRATION (June 21, 2018), https://www.fda.gov/drugs/human-drug-compounding/compounding-and-fda-questions-and-answers.

17. Talia Roitberg Harmon, Michael Cassidy, and Richelle Kloch, *Examination of Decision Making and Botched Lethal Injection Executions in Texas*, 64 AM. BEHAV. SCI. 1715 (2020).

18. *See Compounding Pharmacies and Lethal Injection, supra* note 15.

19. *See Compounding and the FDA: Questions and Answers, supra* note 16.

ing compound drugs from small-scale facilities vary across the states.[20] In addition, states may impose less stringent standards than the FDA and lack the resources needed to enforce regulations.[21] Given lax regulation at the state level, small-scale compounding pharmacies have become attractive options for prison officials seeking lethal injection drugs.[22] For example, the Texas Department of Criminal Justice (TDCJ) employed Greenpark Compounding Pharmacy in Houston to create pentobarbital.[23] Dating back to 2010, Greenpark had amassed forty-eight violations of state pharmacy regulations, resulting in its license being put on probation by the Texas State Board of Pharmacy in 2016.[24]

Texas Execution Protocols and Decision-Making

From December 7, 1982, to February 22, 2011, Texas employed a three-drug protocol including sodium thiopental, pancuronium bromide, and potassium chloride to execute 466 death row inmates.[25] The Supreme Court upheld this protocol in *Baze*, concluding that the petitioners "have not carried their burden of showing that the risk of pain from maladministration of a concededly humane lethal injection protocol, and the failure to adopt untried and untested alternatives, constitute cruel and unusual punishment."[26] Claims brought by Texas inmates concerning the constitutionality of the state's three-drug protocol have also been unsuccessful.[27]

Texas was forced to change its execution protocol in 2011 after U.S. manufacturer Hospira ceased all production of sodium thiopental.[28] The state adopted a different three-drug protocol, replacing sodium thiopental with pentobarbital as the first drug, followed by pancuronium bromide and potassium

---

20. *Id.*

21. *Id.*

22. Denno, *supra* note 9; Eaton, *supra* note 9.

23. McDaniel, *supra* note 16.

24. *Id.*; Hannah Wiley, *Report: Houston-Based Pharmacy Is Supplier of State's Execution Drugs*, THE TEXAS TRIBUNE (Nov. 28, 2018), https://www.texastribune.org/2018/11/28/report-houston-based-pharmacy-supplier-texas-execution-drugs/.

25. *State-by-State Lethal Injection Protocols*, *supra* note 8; Terri Langford et al., *Timeline: A History of Lethal Drug Use in Texas*, THE TEXAS TRIBUNE (July 8, 2014), https://www.texastribune.org/2014/07/08/history-lethal-drug-use-texas/.

26. Baze, 553 U.S. at 41.

27. *See Ex parte* Chi, 256 S.W.3d 702 (Tex. Crim. App. 2008); *Ex parte* O'Brien, 190 S.W.3d 677 (Tex. Crim. App. 2006); Raby v. Livingston, 600 F.3d 552 (5th Cir. 2010); Rivas v. Thaler, 2010 LEXIS 30304 (S.D. Tex. 2010).

28. Corrie MacLaggan, *For Executions, Texas Switches to Drug Used on Animals*, REUTERS (Mar. 16, 2011), https://www.reuters.com/article/us-texas-execution-drug/for-executions-texas-switches-to-drug-used-on-animals-idUSTRE72F71920110316.

chloride.[29] This method was used in sixteen executions from May 3, 2011, to April 26, 2012.[30] In 2012, Texas's supply of the second drug in its three-drug cocktail, pancuronium bromide, expired.[31] Like other states, Texas was forced to change its protocol again due to manufacturers prohibiting states from using their drugs in executions and the FDA banning importation from foreign sources.[32] On July 18, 2012, Texas adopted a one-drug protocol using only pentobarbital, an alternative it continues to use at the present time.[33]

Given concerns with the three-drug cocktail, moving to one drug may have seemed liked a step in the right direction. The Constitution Project, a bipartisan, nonprofit think tank, criticized the use of three-drugs, stating the "three-drug cocktail protocol poses a risk of avoidable inmate pain and suffering."[34] The *Baze* court recognized this as well, noting, "It is uncontested that failing a proper does of sodium thiopental to render the prisoner unconscious, there is a substantial, constitutionally unacceptable risk of suffocation from the administration of pancuronium bromide and of the pain from potassium chloride."[35] Alternatively, the Constitution Project urged states to shift to a one-drug protocol, which is preferred by veterinarians for euthanizing animals.[36] However, there are a number of differences between the protocols and procedures used for lethal injection executions of humans and euthanizing animals.

In Texas, animal euthanasia is subject to rigorous oversight and regulation.[37] In contrast, the Texas Code of Criminal Procedure provides little publicly available information on human execution protocols. Concerning drugs and dosage, the code states, "The sentence shall be executed . . . by intravenous injection of a substance or substances in a lethal quantity sufficient to cause death and until such convict is dead."[38] Further, whereas animal euthanasia procedures are vetted by state agency officials and veterinary

---

29. *Id.*

30. *State-by-State Lethal Injection Protocols, supra* note 8.

31. Brandi Grissom, *Texas Will Change Its Lethal Injection Protocol*, Texas Tribune (July 10, 2012), https://www.texastribune.org/2012/07/10/texas-changing-its-lethal-injection-protocol/.

32. Denno, *supra* note 9.

33. *State-by-State Lethal Injection Protocols, supra* note 8.

34. *Irreversible Error: Recommended Reforms for Preventing and Correcting Error in the Administration of Capital Punishment*, The Constitution Project (2014), at 139, https://archive.constitutionproject.org/wp-content/uploads/2014/06/Irreversible-Error_FINAL.pdf.

35. Baze, 553 U.S. at 37.

36. *Irreversible Error: Recommended Reforms for Preventing and Correcting Error in the Administration of Capital Punishment, supra* note 34.

37. 25 Tex. Admin. Code § 169.84.

38. Tex. Code Crim. Proc. Ann. art. 43.14.

medicine experts,[39] inmate execution procedures are determined by the TDCJ director of the Correctional Institutions Division.[40]

Differences also exist in terms of personnel and training. When euthanizing animals, either a licensed veterinarian or a person who has completed a training course for euthanizing animals must perform the procedure, and the training course must be preapproved by the Texas Department of State Health Services.[41] However, less is known about required training for executioners, as the code simply states, "The director of the Texas Department of Criminal Justice shall designate an executioner to carry out the death penalty provided by law."[42] Though the execution team "may" include individuals with medical backgrounds,[43] it is unlikely their qualifications and level of training are on par with medical doctors.[44] The American Medical Association (AMA) has consistently stated that physician participation in executions violates its code of ethics.[45] Recently, the AMA went one step further by stating it is unethical for physicians to provide expert testimony comparing levels of pain under different execution protocols.[46] Thus, while the one-drug protocol has been deemed humane for euthanizing animals, inmate execution protocols lack adequate preparation, administration, and supervision of lethal injection drugs needed to make an appropriate comparison.[47]

The notion that the one-drug protocol poses fewer risks than the three-drug cocktail also assumes that the drugs are obtained from reputable sources. Yet similar to other states, there has been an ongoing attempt by Texas to

---

39. *Guidelines for the Euthanasia of Animals*, AMERICAN VETERINARY MEDICAL ASSOCIATION (2020), https://www.avma.org/sites/default/files/2020-02/Guidelines-on-Euthanasia-2020.pdf; *Regulating Death in The Lone Star State: Texas Law Prevents Lizards from Needless Suffering, but Not Human Beings*, THE AMERICAN CIVIL LIBERTIES UNION OF TEXAS AND NORTHWESTERN UNIVERSITY SCHOOL OF LAW (Mar. 2011), https://www.aclutx.org/sites/default/files/field_documents/Regulating_Death_in_the_Lone_Star_State_2011-03-31.pdf.

40. TEX. CODE CRIM. PROC. ANN. art. 43.14.

41. TEX. HEALTH AND SAFETY CODE ANN. § 821.055.

42. TEX. CODE CRIM. PROC. ANN. art. 43.18.

43. TEX. CODE CRIM. PROC. ANN. art. 43.20.

44. *See Regulating Death in the Lone Star State: Texas Law Prevents Lizards from Needless Suffering, but Not Human Beings, supra* note 39.

45. Brief for American Medical Association as Amicus Curiae Supporting Neither Party, Bucklew v. Precythe, No. 17-8151, 139 S. Ct. 1112 (2019), hereafter cited as Brief for American Medical Association.

46. *Id.*

47. *See Regulating Death in the Lone Star State: Texas Law Prevents Lizards from Needless Suffering, but Not Human Beings, supra* note 39.

keep the supplier of the drugs secret from the public.[48] For example, in 2015 the state legislature enacted a law to keep the identity of any company that manufactured or sold lethal injection drugs to the TDCJ hidden, but the law was not retroactive.[49] Litigation brought by death penalty defense attorneys ensued to identify the state's supplier of pentobarbital in 2014, but in 2019, the Texas Supreme Court ruled in favor of the TDCJ.[50]

In addition to concerns about where the drugs are coming from, information obtained from public record requests raise questions about the drugs' potency. TDCJ records show that part of the reason Texas has been able to continue carrying out executions despite drug shortages is because the state retested the potency levels of its supply of pentobarbital set to expire in July 2017 and then relabeled the drugs with new dates of July 2018.[51] Death penalty defense attorneys have criticized this practice, suggesting that expired drugs are leading to botched executions.[52] Though inmate claims concerning disclosure of pentobarbital preparation, purity, and potency have been unsuccessful in the courts,[53] Judge James Graves Jr., dissenting in *Whitaker v. Collier*, argued that "Whitaker is arguably subject to a continuing injury based on TDCJ's ability to change its protocol at any given time."[54] The TDCJ has rejected concerns about possible negative effects associated with expired drugs, calling them "speculation upon speculation,"[55] but five of the eleven inmates executed in Texas in 2018 said they felt a burning sensation as they were dying.[56] In 2017, death penalty defense attorneys filed a petition for a writ of certiorari arguing that the Texas protocol using pentobarbital manufactured by compounding pharmacies in secret with expired dates was unconstitutional under the Eighth Amendment, however the U.S. Supreme

---

48. Denno, *supra* note 9; Jolie McCullough, *State Supreme Court Rules Texas Can Hide the Identity of Execution Drug Supplier*, THE TEXAS TRIBUNE (April 12, 2019), https://www.tex astribune.org/2019/04/12/texas-execution-drug-suppliers-identity-can-stay-secret-high -court-say/.

49. TEX. GOV'T CODE § 552.1081.

50. *See* Tex. Dep't of Crim. Justice v. Levin, 572 S.W.3d 671 (Tex. 2019).

51. Jolie McCullough, *Will Texas Have to Push Back the Expiration Dates of Its Lethal Injection Drugs?* THE TEXAS TRIBUNE (May 17, 2018), https://www.texastribune.org/2018/05/17 /texas-lethal-injection-drugs-are-set-expire-upcoming-executions/.

52. *Id.*

53. Campbell v. Livingston, No. 14-70020 (5th Cir. 2014); McGehee v. Tex. Dep't of Crim. Justice, Mis. No. H-18-1546 (S.D. Tex. 2018); Trottie v. Livingston, 766 F.3d 450 (5th Cir. 2014); Whitaker v. Livingston, H-13-2901 (S.D. Tex. 2016).

54. Whitaker v. Collier, 862 F.3d 490, 504 (5th Cir. 2017).

55. McDaniel, *supra* note 16.

56. *Id.*

Court rejected the defendant's petition to challenge the state's execution protocol.[57]

Data and Methods

Between December 7, 1982, and February 6, 2020, Texas executed 569 offenders. Given our interest in differences in lethal injection complications involving the first three-drug cocktail (using sodium thiopental) and the one-drug protocol using only pentobarbital, our study excluded the 16 executions from May 3, 2011, to April 26, 2012, that used the second three-drug protocol. This produced a sample of 553 cases available for analysis, consisting of 466 employing the first three-drug cocktail and 87 using the one-drug protocol.

Data collection began with gathering Texas death row inmates' names from the TDCJ's executed offenders list.[58] Next, we reviewed prior research that documented botched executions,[59] and we supplemented these sources by entering the inmates' names in internet search engines to obtain data from online sources, such as newspaper and archive websites. We drew on this information to create variables for the analysis. We used execution date to identify whether the inmate was given the three- or one-drug protocol, and execution time captures the length of time the lethal injection took (in minutes). After reviewing the complications reported by witnesses who observed the executions, we limited our symptoms variables to those that would most likely reflect pain or discomfort. Symptoms included in the analysis are binary variables that indicate the presence or absence of burning sensation, vein complications, dizziness, hurting/stinging, and whether the inmate claimed they "felt" the drugs. Further, we used the symptoms variables to create two additional measures. The first indicates if the inmate experienced any complications, and the second captures the total number of complications. We employed the Mann Whitney U test to examine differences in the length of time the lethal inject took and the total number of complications between those given the three-drug cocktail compared to pentobarbital alone, and chi-square tests for the remaining variables.[60]

---

57. Whitaker v. Collier,. 138 S.Ct. 1172 (2018).

58. *Executed Offenders*, TEXAS DEPARTMENT OF CRIMINAL JUSTICE, https://www.tdcj.texas .gov/death_row/dr_executed_offenders.html.

59. Denno, *Delegate Death*, *supra* note 2 (2002); *Botched Executions*, DEATH PENALTY INFORMATION CENTER, https://deathpenaltyinfo.org/executions/botched-executions; SARAT, *supra* note 2.

60. The Mann Whitney U test was selected due to the nonnormal distributions of the execution time and total complication variables, both of which were skewed. *See* H. B. Mann

Results

Table 14.1 presents descriptive statistics for cases used in the analyses. The overall sample includes 553 executions, with 466 employing the three-drug cocktail and 87 using the one-drug protocol. With the exception of vein complications, the prevalence of symptoms is higher for those receiving pentobarbital alone compared to those receiving the three drugs. Figure 14.1 displays the average amount of time the lethal injection took across the two protocols. The mean number of minutes using the three-drug cocktail was just under nine minutes, whereas executions involving the one-drug protocol averaged almost nineteen minutes ($W = 1084$, $p < .001$).[61] This finding indicates that the time the execution took when using only pentobarbital was statistically significantly longer than executions employing the three-drug cocktail.

TABLE 14.1 DESCRIPTIVE STATISTICS FOR OVERALL SAMPLE AND THREE- AND ONE-DRUG PROTOCOLS

	Overall		Three-Drug		One-Drug	
	($N = 553$)		($n = 466$)		($n = 87$)	
Variables	Mean/%	SD	Mean/%	SD	Mean/%	SD
Execution Time						
(Minutes)	10.70	8.04	8.94	7.38	18.63	5.83
Symptoms						
Burning Sensation	2.35%		0.64%		11.5%	
Vein Complication	2.89%		3.21%		1.15%	
Dizziness	0.72%		0.43%		2.30%	
Hurting/Stinging	0.94%		0.43%		3.45%	
Felt It	3.07%		1.72%		10.34%	
Any Complication	7.77%		5.58%		19.54%	
Total Complications	0.09	0.37	0.06	0.28	0.29	0.66

and D. R. Whitney, *On a Test of Whether One of Two Random Variables Is Stochastically Larger Than the Other*, 18 ANN. MATH. STATIST. 50 (1947). P-values for chi-square tests were computed using a Monte Carlo test with 2000 replicates; Monte Carlo tests involve the repeated use of random sampling to model phenomena with a great deal of uncertainty. *See* Adery C. A. Hope, *A Simplified Monte Carlo Significance Test Procedure*, 30 J. ROYAL STAT. SOC. 582 (1968).

61. The amount of time the execution took was missing in 74 of the 466 cases using the three-drug cocktail. These cases were excluded from the analysis of execution time but were retained for the remaining analyses.

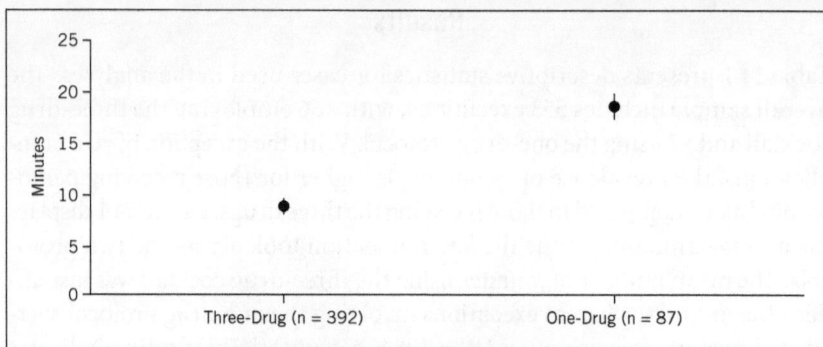

Figure 14.1 Average Execution Time

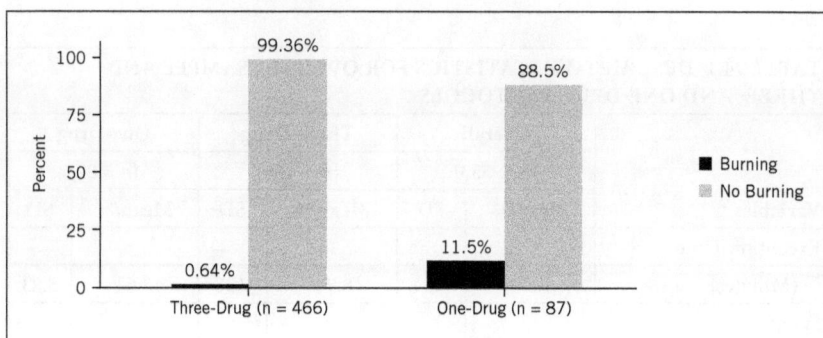

Figure 14.2 Burning Sensation

The next set of figures includes findings for specific complications under the different protocols. Figures 14.2 and 14.3 display the percent of cases with and without burning and hurting or stinging, and Figure 14.4 indicates whether inmates stated they "felt" the drug(s) used in the execution. Overall, a higher percentage of individuals experienced these complications when the one-drug cocktail was administered. All of these findings were statistically significant, indicating individuals who were executed using the one-drug cocktail were more likely to mention they "felt it," X^2 ($N = 553$) = 18.32, $p = .001$, and there is also a higher likelihood of experiencing burning sensations, X^2 ($N = 553$) = 37.60, $p < .001$, and hurting or stinging, X^2 ($N = 553$) = 7.46, $p = .03$, than those executed with the three-drug protocol. No statistically significant relationship was observed for vein complications or dizziness across the two protocols.

The remaining figures display execution complications more broadly. Figure 14.5 shows almost 6 percent of individuals executed using the three-

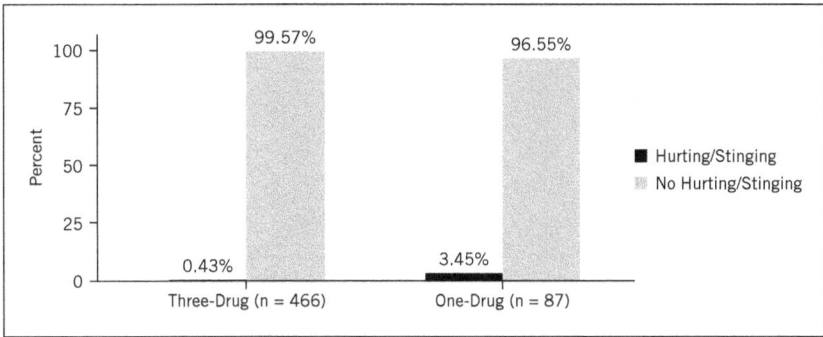

Figure 14.3 Hurting or Stinging

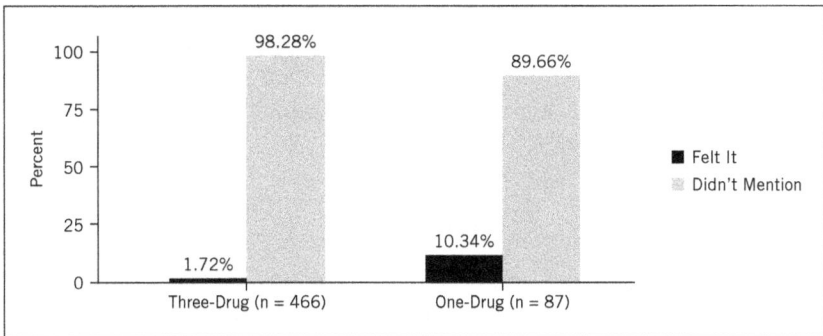

Figure 14.4 "Felt It"

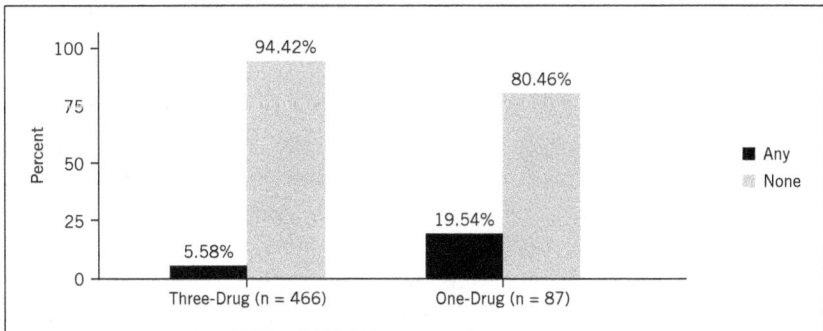

Figure 14.5 Any Occurrence of Complications

drug cocktail experienced at least one of the complications included in the analysis (e.g., burning, vein complications, dizziness, hurting/stinging, "felt it"), compared with nearly 20 percent when pentobarbital alone was administered, $X^2 (N = 553) = 19.93, p < .001$. Figure 14.6 includes the total number of complications under the two protocols. Specifically, fewer individuals had

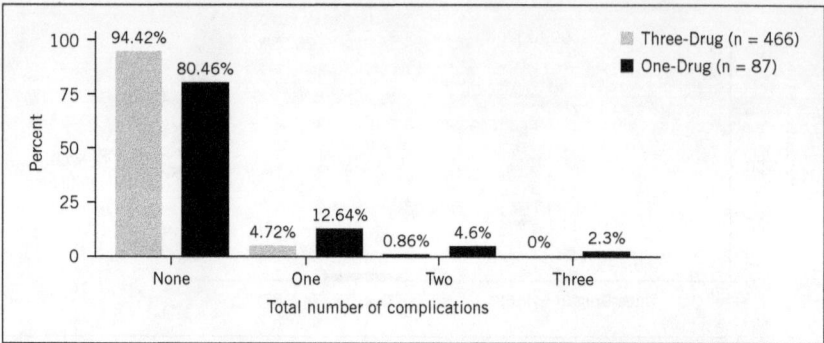

Figure 14.6 Number of Execution Complications

no complications when given only pentobarbital, and more experienced between one and three complications ($W = 17393$, $p = .01$). Taken together, these statistically significant findings suggest complications were more likely when the one-drug protocol is used.

Discussion

We have examined eyewitness accounts of inmates' executions under Texas's three- and one-drug protocols. Findings from the overall sample indicate 7.7 percent of inmates experienced at least one complication, which is consistent with prior research that showed the botched execution rate for lethal injections from 1900 to 2010 was 7.2 percent.[62] However, our results indicate botched lethal injections vary across different protocols, as 19.5 percent of inmates experienced at least one complication when only pentobarbital was used, compared with 5.8 percent who were executed using the three-drug cocktail. We also observed the average length of time the execution took when one drug was administered was almost double that of the three-drug cocktail. It is important to acknowledge that pentobarbital is a slow-acting drug,[63] so longer execution times alone are not evidence of a botched execution. Yet we also found symptoms that do suggest an execution was botched, such as burning, hurting/stinging, and feeling the drugs, were more common when an inmate was executed using the one-drug protocol.

We can only speculate, but the increase in lethal injection execution complications under the one-drug protocol may be associated with Texas's recent reliance on compounding pharmacies to obtain execution drugs.

---

62. Sarat, *supra* note 2.

63. Arielle Duhaime-Ross, *The Big Switch*, Scienceline (Feb. 22, 2013), https://science line.org/2013/02/the-big-switch/.

Texas adopted the one-drug protocol in July 2012 and procured pentobarbital from three different compounding pharmacies in 2013, 2015, and 2016.[64] The risks associated with using compounded drugs have been well documented,[65] and one of the pharmacies Texas employed, Greenpark, had a long history of safety violations dating back to 2010.[66] These included "keeping out-of-date drugs in stock, using improper procedures to prepare IV solutions, and inadequate cleaning of hands and gloves."[67] In addition, the higher prevalence of botched executions under the one-drug protocol may be related to the drug's potency. As noted above, Texas relabeled its supply of pentobarbital set to expire in July 2017 with new expiration dates of July 2018.[68] Though the state retested the potency of the drugs, pentobarbital was not developed to be used as the sole drug in human executions. The drug is used for animal euthanasia, but only after veterinary medicine experts established proper dosage and drug efficacy protocols.[69] Given the medical community's unequivocal stance that it is unethical for physicians to participate in human executions in any way,[70] Texas officials' ability to determine the potency and efficacy of expired pentobarbital is questionable, and its practice of extending expiration dates raises serious concerns about whether executions can be carried out with minimal risk of pain or suffering.

From a legal standpoint, changes in drug protocols, coupled with issues surrounding drug shortages and compounding pharmacies, have rendered much of the court's recent death penalty jurisprudence moot. Addressing the petitioners' claim in *Baze* about the risk of improperly prepared sodium thiopental being used in an execution, Chief Justice Roberts cited the state trial court: "If the manufacturers' instructions for reconstitution of Sodium Thiopental are followed . . . there would be minimal risk of improper mixing."[71] Yet the Court relied on this information during a time when lethal injection drugs were produced by reputable manufactures, not compounding pharmacies operating under lax state regulations. As Denno notes, "compound-

---

64. Eric Nicholson, *Pharmacy Owner Have Second Thoughts about Being Texas' Only Supplier of Execution Drug*, Dallas Observer (Oct. 8, 2013), https://www.dallasobserver.com/news/pharmacy-owner-having-second-thoughts-about-being-texas-only-supplier-of-execution-drug-7109348; McDaniel, *supra* note 16. *See also* Harmon, Cassidy, and Kloch, *supra* note 17 (detailing Texas's use of compounding pharmacies).

65. *Compounding and the FDA: Questions and Answers*, *supra* note 16; *Compounding Pharmacies and Lethal Injection*, *supra* note 15.

66. McDaniel, *supra* note 16.

67. *Id.*

68. McCullough, *supra* note 51.

69. *Guidelines for the Euthanasia of Animals*, *supra* note 39.

70. Brief for American Medical Association, *supra* note 45.

71. *Baze*, 553 U.S. at 54.

ing pharmacies by their very nature run counter to the requirements of *Baze* because the practices they engage in already pose a substantial risk."[72] Moreover, with several states, including Texas, passing legislation to keep the identity of the state's suppliers of lethal injection drugs hidden, "it becomes impossible to subject [lethal injection] protocols to all of the requirements of *Baze*."[73] Thus, instead of requiring the petitioner to identify alternative lethal injection protocols that reduce the risk of pain—a standard that likely cannot be achieved given the AMA's position on capital punishment and state secrecy laws—the burden should be on the state to show its lethal injection drugs have been obtained from reputable sources.

Limitations

Several limitations on our research warrant discussion. First, the data collected concerning complications and symptoms of botched executions come solely from media reports. Yet given the secrecy surrounding execution protocols and procedures, as well as restrictions on the general public viewing executions, no clear alternative exists. Moreover, courts have recognized the importance of having the media present at executions. According to Judge Vaughn R. Walker of the United States District Court for the Northern District of California, "every citizen need not attend an execution in order to be assured that no untoward conduct has occurred; the presence of a group of 'reputable citizens' has traditionally served that purpose."[74] In today's society, "the media almost invariably now serve as the public's surrogate."[75]

We also acknowledge that we cannot say definitively whether the complications we observed in the data are a product of the different drug protocols, or whether they are the result of errors made by the executioner and/or other members of the execution team. Related to this, given the relatively short period of time Texas has been using pentobarbital alone, it is possible that botched executions during this time period are associated with a lack of familiarity with the new protocol. As time passes and more inmates are executed under this protocol, the differences we observed between the protocols may no longer be distinguishable. Finally, this study is limited to lethal injection executions occurring in Texas, using the first three-drug cock-

---

72. Denno, *supra* note 9, at 1366.
73. *Id.*
74. Cal. First Amendment Coal. v. Calderon, 956 F. Supp. 883, 889 (N.D. Cal. 1997).
75. *Id.*

tail and the current one-drug protocol. Thus, these findings may not be generalizable to other death penalty states.

Conclusion: Implications for TJ

In the context of criminal punishment, therapeutic jurisprudence calls for a system that recognizes the human dignity of the offender.[76] One could argue that lethal injection brings the criminal justice system closer to this goal, as this method is often viewed as the most humane form of execution.[77] However, our work provides preliminary evidence that suggests Texas's switch to a one-drug protocol using only pentobarbital is associated with higher botched execution rates, which is antithetical to the tenets of therapeutic jurisprudence. Further, therapeutic jurisprudence scholars posit that the law should minimize antitherapeutic effects.[78] Research on the secondary impacts of the death penalty indicates, "adverse effects from state executions . . . are not limited to the condemned citizen."[79] Adcock provides detailed descriptions of how capital punishment negatively affects judges, prosecutors, defense counsel, jurors, expert witnesses, prison officials, governors, ministers, the inmate's and victim's family and friends, witnesses to the execution, and opponents of capital punishment.[80] To fully understand the secondary impacts of executions on the criminal justice system and society, Dr. Matthew B. Johnson, testifying at a New Jersey Department of Corrections Office of Legal and Legislative Affairs hearing, stated, "Press and public access to the entire state execution process is essential to insure that the full extent of the human costs are known and recorded to fully assess the effects."[81] Yet the extent to which Texas's death penalty decisions have resulted in antitherapeutic consequences is unknown, given the TDCJ's unilateral decision-making concerning execution protocols and state secrecy laws that hide the identity

---

76. Michael L. Perlin, *"Merchants and Thieves, Hungry for Power": Prosecutorial Misconduct and Passive Judicial Complicity in Death Penalty Trials of Defendants with Mental Disabilities*, 73 Wash. & Lee L. Rev. 1501 (2016); Edgardo Rotman, *Therapeutic Jurisprudence, the Death Penalty, and the Significance of Life*, 8 J. Jur. 677 (2010).

77. Denno, *Delegate Death, supra* note 2.

78. Cynthia F. Adcock, *The Collateral Anti-Therapeutic Effects of the Death Penalty*, 11 Fla. Coastal L. Rev. 289 (2010); Rotman, *supra* note 76; Bruce J. Winick, *Therapeutic Jurisprudence and Problem Solving Courts*, 30 Fordham Urb. L.J. 1055 (2003).

79. Amanda Gil, Matthew B. Johnson, and Ingrid Johnson, *Secondary Trauma Associated with State Executions: Testimony Regarding Execution Procedures*, 34 J. Psychiatry & L. 25 (2006).

80. Adcock, *supra* note 78.

81. Gil, Johnson, and Johnson, *supra* note 79 at 33.

of loosely regulated compounding pharmacies that supply lethal injection drugs. Ultimately, the lack of judicial involvement in the TDCJ's decision-making has negative implications for therapeutic jurisprudence, in that it prevents judges from improving individuals' well-being while also minimizing antitherapeutic effects. As such, while future research should continue to document botched executions in Texas and expand this work to lethal injection protocols in other states, it should also further examine the therapeutic and anti-therapeutic impact of the death penalty.

PART III

Ethical and Practical Considerations in the Use of Nonjudicial Officers

15

Navigating Judicial Hurdles for Effective Legal Solutions

The Agony and the Ecstasy

Valerie R. McClain

Introduction

This chapter focuses on judicial decision-making in criminal cases when efforts to negotiate a plea or pretrial resolution are met with either acceptance and or resistance and rejection. Case examples will be used to illustrate the challenges associated with presenting relevant mitigating factors for consideration and the potential pitfalls and obstacles frequently encountered when attempting to resolve cases without further legal proceedings. An analysis of the application of therapeutic jurisprudence (TJ) will be utilized in examining how to facilitate balancing the inherent rights of the defendants and the potential impact on victims.

Specific emphasis will be placed on providing education on relevant mitigating factors and alternative sentencing options to nonjudges including lawyers and mental health experts who play a unique role in resolving legal challenges. The application of TJ principles will be addressed within the context of a full range of cases, from simple misdemeanors such as possession of marijuana to cases involving capital murder. These principles are also applicable within the pretrial litigation period. In all cases, the goal is to balance due process rights with the application of TJ principles when administered by nonjudicial officers or the court.

Therapeutic Jurisprudence and
Problem-Solving Courts

To understand potential options for pretrial resolution, it is important to review historical changes in the structure and function of the court and the judges presiding in the courtroom. The traditional role of the courts as governmental agents for dispute resolution has changed.[1] The role of the courts as neutral arbiters has shifted, in some important instances, to a focus on understanding the underlying psychosocial and psychological issues that cause the disputes so as to optimally decrease or prevent future court involvement.

Courts known as problem-solving courts are designed to deal with specific problems frequently involving individuals with mental health or substance abuse issues in need of treatment[2] as well as other specialized courts.[3] These individuals frequently are brought into criminal courts with legal charges related to both their mental health and substance abuse issues.

Relatedly, family problems and domestic violence issues can occur in the context of the chaos that may arise from untreated substance abuse stemming from a pattern of self-medicating for underlying mental health issues.[4] Juvenile courts were the founding agents for these specialized courts originating in Chicago in 1899 with a focus on rehabilitation as opposed to the punitive focus typically seen in adult court.

Among the descendants of these courts are drug treatment courts evolving from the early nineteenth-century courts. These courts arose out of the recognition that sentencing individuals to prison for nonviolent drug possession in criminal courts failed to change defendants' addictive behaviors.[5] The focus in drug treatment court has been to try to rehabilitate the offender and involve the judge as a member of the treatment team.[6] Typical tasks for the offender involved in the diversion program for drug treatment included pleading guilty and participating in drug treatment, abstinence and random drug testing, and reporting for probation appointments. Statistics provided

---

1. Bruce J. Winick, *Therapeutic Jurisprudence and Problem Solving Courts*, 30 FORD URB L.J., 1054 (2003).

2. Bruce J. Winick and David B. Wexler, *Drug Treatment Court: Therapeutic Jurisprudence Applied*, 18 TOURO L. REV. 481 (2002).

3. John Petrila et al., *Preliminary Observations from an Evaluation of the Broward County Mental Health Court*, 37 CT. REV. 14, 15 (2001).

4. Randall B. Fritzler and Lenore M. J. Simon, *The Development of a Specialized Domestic Violence Court in Vancouver, Washington Utilizing Innovative Judicial Paradigms*, 69 U.MKC L. REV. 139 (2000).

5. Winick and Wexler, *supra* note 2.

6. David B. Wexler, *Robes and Rehabilitation: How Judges Can Help Offenders Make Good*, 38 CT. REV. 18, 18 (2001).

by the U.S. Department of Justice indicate that as of November 2020, there were three thousand drug courts in America.[7] Other problem-solving courts include, but are not limited to, domestic violence, dependency, teen courts, mental health courts, and prison release programs.[8] Domestic violence courts typically focus on protecting the victims, rehabilitating perpetrators, and monitoring compliance with court-ordered intervention. More than three hundred domestic violence courts are currently in place.[9] Dependency courts involving child abuse and neglect also focus on trying to intervene and provide services for rehabilitating the perpetrators through parenting classes, anger management, substance abuse classes, and education regarding special needs children.[10] In teen courts, the focus is on providing peer perspective on juveniles charged with minor offenses to promote prosocial attitudes and build empathy.[11]

Mental health courts began in 1997 in Broward County, Florida, and were designed to accommodate individuals arrested for minor offenses who suffer from serious mental health issues as opposed to criminality. These individuals are typically referred to mental health centers where they can receive treatment including psychiatric stabilization. Individuals with chronic and severe mental health issues may require immediate commitment to a mental hospital for stabilization at the time of arrest if there is concern as to danger to one's self or others. One challenge faced when defendants are not gradually transitioned into the community following secured placement is that they are at risk to decompensate if they do not have the means to obtain housing, the necessary medication (in appropriate cases) and community supports. This can lead to a resumption in minor criminal offenses such as trespassing, resisting arrest without violence, and petit theft,[12] all of which could have possibly been avoided through careful planning for the transition.

The traditional model for judicial approaches to substance abuse, domestic violence, dependency issues, juvenile offenders, and mental illness all fell short of solving the underlying problems; instead, the criminal offenses

---

7. U.S. Department of Justice, *Drug Courts: Special Feature*, Bureau of Justice Assistance https://www.ncjrs.gov (2020).

8. Winick, *supra* note 2, at 1058.

9. Susan Keilitz, *Specialization of Domestic Violence Case Management in the Courts: A National Survey* (2004) accessible at https://citeseerx.ist.psu.edu/viewdoc/download?doi=10 .1.1.521.8992&rep=rep1&type=pdf.

10. Amy K. Brown, *Drug Courts Help Keep Families Together*, F.B. News, 1 (Sept. 15, 2001), available at http://www.flabar.org/the-florida-bar-news/drug-courts-help-keep-families-to getheer/.

11. Winick, *supra note* 1, at 1059.

12. Wexler, *supra* note 6, at 21.

and underlying problems continued and resurfaced through further judicial involvement. Judges in courts of general jurisdiction and other legal personnel lacked the expertise and tools to effectively intervene. This realization led to the evolution of the specialized courts and diversion programs that are designed to facilitate rehabilitation and resolution.[13]

Alternative Judicial Approaches

A collaborative and interdisciplinary approach involving the judge as part of the treatment team emerged as an alternative strategy for problem solving. In this scenario, the judge serves as the facilitator to motivate and direct the roles of the various legal personnel and defendant. This arena permits the parties to identify the underlying psychological and psychosocial factors inherent in the criminal behaviors and address needed rehabilitative strategies to decrease recidivism and promote prosocial behaviors. Inherent in this approach is the need to monitor compliance and progress and measure outcomes. The legal actors serve in a therapeutic capacity to promote mental health and provide adaptive strategies to cope with personal and environmental stressors that may challenge the therapeutic process.[14]

Promoting Awareness and Education

Problem solving necessarily implies that the parties are aware of an underlying issue or challenge which needs to be addressed. The insight and understanding involved in identifying mental health or addiction issues is largely acquired and born both of education and experience. One of the big challenges for judges and other legal personnel is to understand principles of psychology related to the science of behavior and facilitate understanding in defendants. For example, defendants who have a pattern of self-medicating with drugs or alcohol may be unaware of the symptoms associated with a comorbid mental health diagnosis such as bipolar disorder or anxiety. Education provided both in court and through diversion programs can provide options for treatment and cognitive tools for early identification of symptoms which may represent an exacerbation of sign of decompensation related to their mental health disorder.[15] Ultimately, judges cannot make a defendant take responsibility for problem solving through mental health or

---

13. Winick, *supra* note 1, at 1060.

14. *Id.* at 1068.

15. AMERICAN PSYCHIATRIC ASSOCIATION, DIAGNOSTIC AND STATISTICAL MANUAL OF MENTAL DISORDERS, 5th ed. (2013), hereafter cited as DSM-5, at 31.

addiction issues, but certainly they are in a role to facilitate the development of interpersonal strengths and social support to promote recovery.

Pretrial Alternatives and Accompanying Agony

The evolution of specialized courts and sensitivity to underlying mental health issues has facilitated awareness of issues inherent in cases that may permit early resolution to preclude litigation. This not only is cost effective but also saves time and may limit subsequent incarceration.[16] For example, jail diversion programs and mental health courts may permit opportunities for treatment in the community.[17] The referral process is critical and can occur early on in the plea discussions and agreements between the prosecuting attorney and the defense attorney.

In general, the ultimate responsibility for sentence determination lies with the judge or jury. However, the judge and other nonjudicial agents can serve in the role of facilitating discussions between the parties including the attorneys and defendant that may optimally lead to pretrial resolution. This includes possible pleas by the defendant and possible alternative sentences presented as plea bargains, which are negotiated between the prosecutor, defense attorney, and defendant.

The responsibilities of the prosecuting attorney may include abandoning the charges, making a recommendation to agreeing to not oppose the defendant's request for a particular sentence, agreeing to a possible specific sentence and consulting with the victim, investigating officer or other parties, and advising the trial judge of their views during the course of plea negotiations.[18] This becomes particularly important in cases involving defendants with mental health issues who have a long history of being committed to psychiatric hospitals and having criminal offenses related to periods of decompensation with or without medication.[19]

The defense attorney is responsible for informing the defendant of any discussions concerning plea agreement and being certain that any decision to plead guilty or nolo contendere is made voluntarily by the defendant. An

---

16. Catherine Camilletti, *Pretrial Diversion Programs: Research Summary,* Bureau of Justice Assistance U.S. Department of Justice, 1 (2010), accessible at https://bja.ojp.gov/sites/g/files/xyckuh186/files/media/document/PretrialDiversionResearchSummary.pdf.

17. Barry Mahoney et al. *Pretrial Services Programs: Responsibilities and Potential.* National Institute of Justice: Issues and Practices, iii (2001), accessible at https://www.ncjrs.gov/pdffiles1/nij/181939.pdf.

18. Mahoney et al., *supra* note 17, at 9.

19. Christopher Slobogin, *The American Bar Associations Criminal Justice Mental Health Standards: Revisions for the Twenty-First Century,* 44 Hastings Const. Law Q. 1, 20 (2016).

important consideration for the defense attorney is to address issues pertaining to competency that may impede the defendant's ability to comprehend the legal proceedings relevant to the case. The defendant is to be advised of all plea offers and all matters bearing on the choice of which plea to enter and the likely results of any possible alternatives.[20] Whether the defendant faces a misdemeanor or felony charge, TJ principles can be integrated into possible probationary stipulations or sentences being considered.

In cases involving more serious offenses, such as capital cases or homicide cases, it is critical that the attorney representing the defendant be aware of the defendant's life history including mental health, medical, and educational records that have bearing on the criminal offense. Despite the serious nature of the charge, these factors can be tremendously mitigating and lead to a life sentence as opposed to litigation leading to a possible death sentence.[21] This becomes particularly relevant when the defendant is intellectually disabled or on the autism spectrum.[22]

The complexities of presenting mitigating evidence in a jury trial in these types of cases are obstacles to a successful outcome due to the lack of common knowledge in the lay person as to the cognitive and functional deficits associated with mental disabilities.[23] This examiner has been involved in several recent cases in which the defendant in a capital case has been given a life sentence following presentation of past academic records coupled with current testing confirming an intellectual disability.

Most criminal cases are disposed of by pleas of guilty agreed upon by the prosecutor and defense counsel.[24] These plea decisions are too often based upon factors related to the nature of the offense or victim impact without sufficient consideration of the cognitive, emotional, or mental health characteristics of the offender and insufficient documentation of these factors as a basis for the plea. As a result, challenges arise postconviction due to no record being maintained as to plea negotiations, plea bargains, or compromises. This has led to postconviction claims that entail evidentiary hearings and conflicting testimony regarding plea negotiations.[25] For example, if the defendant is actively psychotic or severely depressed, and issues of competency have not been addressed, subsequent postconviction issues may arise. Relatedly, if a defendant is intellectually disabled or autistic, and competency to

---

20. Slobogin. *supra* note 19, at 22.

21. Elliott Atkins et al., *Forensic Psychological Consultation in U.S. Death Penalty Cases in State and Federal Courts.* 25 AM. J. FORENS. PSYCHOL. 10 (2007).

22. DSM-5, *supra* note 15, at 33.

23. Atkins et al., *supra* note 21, at 11.

24. Sherod Thaxton, *Leveraging Death.* 103 J. CRIM L & CRIMINOL. 477 (2013).

25. FLA. R. CRIM. PROC., 3.190(j)(2).

proceed is not raised, the question of the defendant's ability to understand the plea negotiations is frequently raised after the plea agreement. This may result related to other criminal charges in other jurisdictions in which competency is ultimately raised or has been raised previously.

By way of example, in Hillsborough and Pinellas counties in Florida,[26] if a defendant is charged with a nonviolent felony and has no prior criminal record or a minor record, the defendant may qualify for a felony pretrial intervention program (PTI). This program may be offered on a prefile basis before arraignment. In some cases, the prosecutor can elect to file the charge as a misdemeanor or amend the charge to a misdemeanor if a felony charge has already been filed making the defendant eligible for the misdemeanor diversion program.[27] This examiner frequently conducts the evaluations required and has found that there are a number of cases in which no treatment is indicated.

Felony PTI programs may entail completing various evaluations and/or treatment recommendations. For example, the defendant may be required to complete a drug and alcohol evaluation and/or mental health counseling coupled with random urine screens. This program is designed to give first time felony offenders the opportunity to avoid the stigma of a criminal conviction by diverting the case away from the judge and the trial court.[28]

Factors that are considered include the applicant's criminal history, amenability to correction, responsiveness to rehabilitation, and the nature of the offense. Certain criteria are applied concerning details of the criminal activity to include the nature of the offense and the facts of the case.[29]

Plea bargaining in more serious cases, especially in death penalty cases, is an area of controversy.[30] When experienced capital defenders were asked to make estimates, Millard Farmer reported that 75 percent of the defendants who faced the death penalty since 1976 could have avoided the death sentence by accepting a plea offer.[31] Stephen Bright and Michael Burt estimated that half of the defendants executed in America were offered the opportunity to enter a guilty plea precluding the imposition of a death sen-

---

26. Sammis Law Firm, *Felony PTI in Hillsborough County* (last updated July 30, 2020), accessible at https://criminaldefenseattorneytampa.com/statutory-penalties/pre-trial-intervention-pti/.

27. Mahoney et al., *supra* note 17, at 9. For example, in a death penalty case in Tampa, Florida, involving a double homicide, *State of Florida v. Michael Anthony Herald* (2016), the prosecutor agreed to review the mitigation provided concerning his intellectual disability, and the case was resolved with a term of fifty years.

28. Sammis Law Firm, *supra* note 26.

29. Mahoney et al. *supra* note 17, at 6.

30. Thaxton, *supra* note 24, at 480.

31. Albert Alschuler. *Plea Bargaining and the Death Penalty*, 58 DePaul L. Rev. 672 (2008).

tence.[32] Albert Alschuler, in *Plea Bargaining and the Death Penalty* (2008), argues that America executes people not just for the crime of committing an aggravated murder but also for standing trial.[33] For example, consider how the process of trying to negotiate a plea bargain in the death penalty case of John Spenkelink illustrates challenges inherent in negotiations.[34] He was the first person executed involuntarily in the United States after a de facto moratorium on executions beginning in 1967 ended ten years later. His lawyer, Brian T. Hayes, explained why the case was not resolved through a plea bargain. The judge began the process with an indication that he did not want to expend the time in a case where a drifter killed a drifter. The prosecutor offered a guilty plea to a second-degree murder with a recommendation of a life sentence, however Spenkelink turned it down, leading to his death sentence and subsequent execution. In another case, involving a robbery murder (a so-called felony murder case), the defendant was offered a plea bargain for a life sentence, however he turned it down and indicated he believed the attorney did not believe in his case. He was ultimately convicted in less than an hour, and the death penalty was imposed.[35]

Plea bargaining can be viewed as undermining the fundamental reason for imposing the death penalty, namely that the crime is so egregious and heinous that it is necessary. However, American prosecutors seem to convey the message that no lesser punishment is appropriate unless the accused pleads guilty. In other words, the agreement to settle a case in lieu of a costly trial would appear to undermine the intent of the death penalty.[36]

Bargaining tactics involved in death penalty cases may and can include financial arguments of avoiding costly litigation and the hiring of expensive experts. Negotiations with family members of the victims may include promises of no disclosure and meetings to express remorse. The defense attorney and mitigation specialist may also enlist the defendant's family to try to convince the defendant to agree to a plea. The use of TJ strategies promoting dignity and respect between the defendant and the victim and victim's family members is a critical part of the process to facilitate an optimal outcome.

Ultimately, the balance of adhering to due process rights and ethics involved in plea bargaining in death penalty cases must be considered in making decisions to appeal to clients for their consideration of such offers. Ensuring that the defendant is able to comprehend the likely outcomes of a

---

32. *Id.*
33. *Id.*
34. *Id.*
35. *Id.*
36. *Id.* at 680.

jury trial, which can lead to conviction, as well as anticipate the second phase involving sentencing and related awareness of both mitigating and aggravating factors is an important consideration. Examining one's own motives, whether defense counsel or prosecutor, is also relevant in discussing the option of plea bargaining in a death penalty case. While these motives are not always obvious and may been adapted to over time to become the norm, a close internal examination of inherent motives on both sides as well as the defendant's preference and motives can be helpful in making the decision whether to pursue this direction in resolving a case. The quality of the defense attorney and experience in navigating death penalty cases is perhaps the most important contributing factor to ensuring justice is rendered with regard to due process in balance with TJ principles.

Implementing Therapeutic Jurisprudence

There is a delicate balance in ensuring nonjudicial officers assigned to make disposition of legal cases act without impinging on due process rights.[37] The goal is to use mental health principles and education in a way that maintains sensitivity to TJ principles while maintaining and upholding due process rights of defendants. Preservation of civil rights and civil liberties maintains a high priority regardless of whether nonjudicial officers or judicial officers are meting out and making decisions concerning plea deals and sentences for defendants.

Problem solving courts have set precedents for incorporating important psychological principles and education regarding underlying mental health disorders in providing appropriate intervention through plea deals and specialized sentences. The examples provided within these specialized courts are good principles for establishing a foundation from which nonjudicial officers can balance guidelines for probation and sentencing within the parameters of due process.

One of the first steps in accomplishing this task is to provide opportunities to nonjudicial officers for education and training that provides legal guidelines for determining appropriate probation requirements and accompanying monitoring. High priorities include realistic expectations given characteristics of the defendant's mental health issues and intellectual capacity and educational background. The Public Defender's Office handle the majority of criminal cases and represent a potential gateway for providing training. One possibility is to coordinate the education and training through pretrial services

---

37. Michael L. Perlin. *"But I Ain't a Judge": The Therapeutic Jurisprudence Implications of the Use of Nonjudicial Officers in Criminal Justice Cases*, this volume.

and the state attorney and public defender's offices. Public in-services could be offered for nonjudicial officers with an open invitation to probation officers, law enforcement, and local attorneys to help support the initiative.

Pathways for Change and the Ecstasy of Therapeutic Jurisprudence

The goal in pretrial negotiation is targeted at rehabilitation to address underlying psychological problems and to provide services to monitor and provide supervision for defendants involved in the rehabilitative process. Resolution of legal difficulties occurs simultaneously with the process of healing. Nonjudicial officers, treating therapist, and family members provide a support network to facilitate this process.

Inherent in this process is understanding and applying psychological principles designed to facilitate the defendant's ability to comprehend the remedy or prescription for recovery while addressing potential denial that can lead to minimizing responsibility. This is best accomplished in an environment that is empathic and supportive as opposed to punitive.

The foundation of understanding and applying psychological strategies for recovery rests in understanding and education concerning mental health diagnosis as defined in the DSM-5. Recognizing the symptoms common to mental health disorders and the way in which they manifest in criminal behaviors is key to providing alternative strategies to minimize recidivism. Viewing the criminal activity in the context of underlying history provides a context for creating a healing platform. For example, for individuals with bipolar disorder, an untreated manic phase can lead to escalation of impulsive behaviors resulting in drug sprees, domestic violence, and self-injurious behaviors. One remedy that would be appropriate is participation in a dual diagnosis program that can provide stabilization on medication coupled with abstinence from drug use.

Establishing a therapeutic environment consistent with TJ principles includes promoting dignity, providing acceptance and facilitating the defendant's ability to understand and embrace education concerning the relevant mental health issues and relationship to the criminal behaviors. The process of recovery is variable for each individual. Periods of frustration are inevitable, including struggling with relapse, decompensation due to medication adjustments, and situational stressors that can impact progress. Despite the challenges, the overall momentum involved in this approach leads to building a realistic environment to promote problem solving through legal challenges while pursuing rehabilitative strategies.

16

Reconstructing the Ethics Code to Remedy the Failures of *Strickland v. Washington*

Heather Ellis Cucolo

Introduction

Virtue ethics, inspired by Aristotle, acknowledges the complexity of the human condition and that a virtuous moral agent exercises the relevant virtue when appropriate to the circumstances.[1] Simply, an action is right if and only if the action is one that a virtuous moral agent would characteristically perform under the circumstances. St. Thomas Aquinas, the great thirteenth-century theologian, philosopher, and caretaker of the virtue ethics tradition, taught that "the natural law literally commands, in a sense, every act of virtue and prohibits every vice."[2] In legal contexts, the natural law is "law that determines what is right and wrong and that [which] has power or is valid by nature, inherently."[3] Legal ethics refers to the code of conduct that regulates and instructs the behavior of persons within the legal profession.[4] Virtue ethics tells one what kind of person he should be but often fails

---

1. Aristotle and Terence Irwin, Nicomachean Ethics, third Edition (2019).

2. Louis W. Hensler III, *A Modest Reading of St. Thomas Aquinas on the Connection between Natural Law and Human Law*, 43 Creighton L. Rev. 153, 154 (2009).

3. Bryan A. Garner, A Dictionary of Modern Legal Usage 581–82 (2d ed. 1995).

4. James M. Altman, *Considering the ABA's 1908 Canons of Ethics*, 71 Fordham L. Rev. 2395 (2003) (underlying the ABA's efforts was the idea that it is possible to articulate and maintain a level of lawyer conduct that is higher and better than the minimal normative standards imposed by the criminal law).

to provide a clear answer or action in response to a specific moral dilemma.[5] That specific aspect of virtue ethics is similar to the Model Rules of Professional Conduct (hereinafter Model Rules),[6] in that it presents ethical legal practice ideals with limited guidance on their application to a particular legal problem.

This chapter's focus will be on the failure of the enforcement of the Model Rules in order to combat the particular legal problem of ensuring adequacy of counsel. One way to address this failure is through therapeutic jurisprudence (TJ). TJ recognizes that the law can have therapeutic or antitherapeutic consequences and asks whether rules, procedures, and lawyer roles can be reshaped to enhance therapeutic potential without subordinating due process principles.[7] TJ "look[s] at law as it actually impacts people's lives" and supports "an ethic of care."[8] At the end of the chapter, some suggestions for reform, in line with TJ principles, are presented.

Overseeing Legal Ethics

Aquinas's definition of law is "an ordinance of reason for the common good of a [complete] community, promulgated by the person or body responsible for looking after that community."[9] One body responsible for looking after the legal community is the American Bar Association (ABA), authors of the Model Rules. Overseeing organizational ethics and policing within the legal profession is crucial to assuring that lawyers remain diligent in their duties and responsibilities.[10] The ABA and state bar associations promulgate ethical rules to standardize attorney behavior and define an attorney's duties to her clients.[11] The preamble to the Model Rules states in part:

---

5. Rosalind Hursthouse, *Virtue Ethics,* STANFORD ENCYCLOPEDIA OF PHIL., at Pt. 3(i) (Mar. 8, 2012), http://plato.stanford.edu/archives/sum2012/entries/ethics-virtue (the "complaint that virtue ethics does not produce codifiable principles . . . nor provide action-guidance" is a commonly voiced criticism).

6. AMERICAN BAR ASSOCIATION, MODEL RULES OF PROFESSIONAL CONDUCT (2016), hereafter cited as MODEL RULES.

7. Michael L. Perlin, *"His Brain Has Been Mismanaged with Great Skill": How Will Jurors Respond to Neuroimaging Testimony in Insanity Defense Cases?* 42 AKRON L. REV. 885, 912 (2009).

8. Bruce J. Winick, *Foreword: Therapeutic Jurisprudence Perspectives on Dealing with Victims of Crime,* 33 NOVA L. REV. 535, 535 (2009).

9. John Finnis, *Aquinas and Natural Law Jurisprudence,* in THE CAMBRIDGE COMPANION TO NATURAL LAW JURISPRUDENCE 17, 37 (George Duke and Robert P. George eds., 2017).

10. *See* Warren E. Burger, *The Decline of Professionalism,* 63 FORDHAM L. REV. 949, 949 (1995).

11. Each state is free to adopt their own legal ethics code. Almost all states except California have chosen to incorporate the ABA version. *See Alphabetical List of Jurisdictions Adopt-*

The legal profession is largely self-governing. Although other professions also have been granted powers of self-government, the legal
profession is unique in this respect because of the close relationship
between the profession and the processes of government and law
enforcement. This connection is manifested in the fact that ultimate
authority over the legal profession is vested largely in the courts. The
legal profession's relative autonomy carries with it special responsibilities of self-government.[12]

In the United States, each jurisdiction's highest court typically is the
regulatory body that has the overarching responsibility for lawyer regulation.[13] Yet what and who are they regulating? We often think about professional responsibility as something that lawyers owe to their clients, but it in
fact is much greater than that narrow view.[14] There is no consensus on how
to define professional responsibility, but attempts are usually found at the
center of debates on whether the legal profession is adequately meeting its
public purpose and following its core values and ideals.[15] Professional responsibility implies a duty to society at large that is clearly outlined in the
Model Rules: "Lawyers play a vital role in the preservation of society."[16] In
that ultimate objective of playing a vital role in the preservation of society,
overseers of the legal profession have a daunting yet necessary role in protecting the morals of society, some of which can be listed as universal constitutional protections and preventing discrimination on the basis of race,
gender, socioeconomic class, and disability.[17]

---

ing Model Rules, ABA, https://www.americanbar.org/groups/professional_responsibility
/publications/model_rules_of_professional_conduct/alpha_list_state_adopting_model
_rules.html.

12. Model Rules, *supra* note 6 at pmbl. para. 10. *See also* William Shakespeare. The
Second Part of King Henry the Sixth, act 4, sc. 2., when Dick, "the Butcher," says to the
traitorous Jack Cade, "The first thing we do, let's kill all the lawyers" as the first step to over-
throw of the government.

13. Jared K. Carter, *A Reflection on Law, Legal Education, and Pandemic*, Vt. B.J., at 24
(2020).

14. *See, e.g.*, Model Rules *supra* note 6 at pmbl. para. 9 ("Virtually all difficult ethical
problems arise from conflict between a lawyer's responsibilities to clients, to the legal system
and to the lawyer's own interest in remaining an ethical person while earning a satisfactory
living.").

15. Alberto Bernabe, *Ahead of His Time: Cardozo and the Current Debates on Professional Responsibility*, 34 Touro L. Rev. 63, 64 (2018) (professionalism is an elastic concept).

16. Model Rules, *supra* note 6 at pmbl. para. 13.

17. In Theard v. United States, 354 U.S. 278, 281 (1956), the U.S. Supreme Court stated,
"Membership in the bar is a privilege burdened with conditions . . . [it's an] ancient fellowship
for more than private gain." As an officer of the court, appellant is an instrument "to advance

Failure of the Judiciary to Mandate
Competent Counsel

Unfortunately, these ideals are not always maintained and fall particularly short in the area of competency of counsel.[18] One of the most detrimental ethical violations is the failure to provide effective assistance of counsel in criminal cases.[19] Pursuant to the Supreme Court's opinion in *Strickland v. Washington*, a defendant proves an ineffective assistance of counsel claim by establishing (1) that counsel's performance "fell below an objective standard of reasonableness" as measured by "prevailing professional norms," and (2) prejudice, that is, "a reasonable probability that, but for counsel's unprofessional errors, the result of the proceeding would have been different."[20] *Strickland* sets a low bar for attorney competence, and *Strickland* claims are almost always rejected by the courts.[21] Although the court subsequently extended the *Strickland* standard to apply in practically all critical stages of a criminal case, "it has fallen far short of ensuring that counsel is truly adequate: that she investigate the case, provide the defendant with all the information necessary for the defendant to make informed choices, and mount a vigor-

---

the ends of justice." *See also* Hon. Christopher C. Cross, *The Role of an Attorney in Society: A Higher Calling*, 91 Denv. U.L. Rev. Online 75 (2014) (a lawyer must ignite the passion in others to address human rights issues of today and tomorrow).

18. Mark W. Bennett, *Reflections on Judicial Regrets*, Litigation, at 5, 6 (2015) ("I have encountered far too many lawyers who lack the passion for the privilege of representing a client—lawyers who fail to internalize the extraordinary effort it takes to advocate to the best of one's ability.").

19. *See* 1 New York State Judicial Comm'n on Minorities, Report of the New York State Judicial Commission on Minorities (1991).

> *A panel of judges, attorneys, and law professors found that there are two justice systems at work in the courts of New York State; one for whites, and a very different one for minorities and the poor. The panel found inequality, disparate treatment, and injustice based on race. It reported that many minorities received 'basement justice' in that court facilities were infested with rats and cockroaches . . . and racist graffiti appeared on the walls of court facilities. . . . Minority cases often take only 4 or 5 minutes in court, suggesting a form of assembly line justice, and that black defendants outside of [N.Y.C.] frequently have their cases heard by an all-white jury.*

20. 466 U.S. 668, 686 (1984).

21. John M. Burkoff and Nancy M. Burkoff, *Judicial Reluctance to Find Ineffective Assistance—Pervasiveness of Ineffectiveness* Ineffective Assist. of Counsel § 1:7 (2020):

> *Unfortunately, albeit candidly, the reason some judges may be reluctant to find ineffective assistance readily is their belief that if they were totally honest in so finding on every actual occasion of ineffectiveness, too many cases would be reversed.*

ous defense at trial."[22] Courts conducting *Strickland* analyses need not consider both prongs of the inquiry "if the defendant makes an insufficient showing on one."[23] In particular, a court can examine prejudice without first considering counsel's deficient performance.[24] This reflects the court's efficiency concerns: "If it is easier to dispose of an ineffectiveness claim on the ground of lack of sufficient prejudice, which we expect will often be so, that course should be followed."[25]

The failure of the *Strickland* standard, coupled with a lack of reporting and sanctions, has culminated in an overwhelming number of attorneys who are "walking violations of the Sixth Amendment"[26] yet are still allowed to practice in the criminal courts. In fairness, "many ineffective assistance problems are systemic problems: poor appointment systems, weak and underfinanced public defender and defense support systems, a weak defense bar, and undertrained attorneys."[27] But regardless, the excuse of lack of resources can only extend so far and does not negate the contributory role of the courts and the legal oversight committees in furthering ineffective assistance.[28] There are countless examples of cases where lawyers knowingly provided subpar representation and detrimentally impacted the client's case.[29] That failure in criminal cases can be the difference between life or death—literally. There is little evidence disputing *Strickland*'s failure to ensure adequate assistance of counsel for capital defendants.[30] Examples of affirmed trial decisions rejecting *Strickland* arguments are, in some circum-

---

22. Heather Ellis Cucolo and Michael L. Perlin, *"Far from the Turbulent Space": Considering the Adequacy of Counsel in the Representation of Individuals Accused of Being Sexually Violent Predators*, 18 U. Pa. J.L. & Soc. Change 125, 126 (2015).

23. *Strickland*, 466 U.S. at 697.

24. *Id. See also* United States v. Cronic, 466 U.S. 648 (1984). In *Cronic*, the Supreme Court held that in those instances where the absence, actions, or inactions of counsel compromise the very reliability of the trial process, ineffective assistance of counsel may be presumed, requiring a reversal without meeting the prejudice prong of the *Strickland* test.

25. *Id. See* Pamela R. Metzger, *Confrontation Control*, 45 Tex. Tech L. Rev. 83, 92 (2012).

26. David Bazelon, *The Defective Assistance of Counsel*, 42 U. Cin. L. Rev. 1, 2, 22–23 (1973).

27. Gary Goodpaster, *The Adversary System, Advocacy, and Effective Assistance of Counsel in Criminal Cases*, 14 N.Y.U. Rev. L. & Soc. Change 59, 66, 75 (1986).

28. Shaun Ossei-Owusu, *The Sixth Amendment Facade: The Racial Evolution of the Right to Counsel*, 167 U. Pa. L. Rev. 1161, 1223 (2019).

29. Warren E. Burger, *The Special Skills of Advocacy: Are Specialized Training and Certification of Advocates Essential to Our System of Justice?* 42 Fordham L. Rev. 227, 230 (1973) (according to Chief Justice Burger, between one-third and one-half of lawyers in serious trials were not qualified to represent their clients).

30. Michael L. Perlin, *"The Executioner's Face Is Always Well-Hidden": The Role of Counsel and the Courts in Determining Who Dies*, 41 N.Y.L. Sch. L. Rev. 201, 205–6 (1996).

stances, jaw-dropping. In one case, counsel was found to be effective even though he "failed to introduce ballistics evidence to show that the gun taken from [the defendant] when he was arrested was not the murder weapon."[31] In another case, an attorney who had been admitted to the bar for only six months and had never tried a jury case was found constitutionally adequate to provide representation to a death-eligible defendant.[32] Another lawyer found constitutionally adequate was so intoxicated at defendant's trial, he was held in contempt and spent the night in jail.[33]

In 2019, Justice Clarence Thomas held in a dissent in *Garza v. Idaho*[34] that defendants have a right to a lawyer, but not to any degree of reliability in that attorney's performance. Essentially, Thomas said defendants have a right to counsel but not effective assistance from that attorney.[35]

Inherent Failures in Enforcing Ethical Practice and the Interplay between Strickland and the Model Rules

Thus, the *Strickland* standard has neglected to hold lawyers accountable for their detrimental inadequacies, but what about accountability through state sanctioned ethics violations? There are three major barriers that prevent attorneys from being sanctioned for ethics violations. The first barrier to accountability is the lack of reporting, which has serious implications and undercuts the integrity of the legal profession. Rule 8.3, Reporting Professional Misconduct, states, "A lawyer who knows that another lawyer has committed a violation of the Rules . . . that raises a substantial question as to that lawyer's honesty, trustworthiness or fitness as a lawyer in other respects, shall inform the appropriate professional authority."[36] It is commonly accepted that a substantial amount of lawyer misconduct goes unreport-

31. Graham v. Collins, 829 F. Supp. 204, 209 (S.D. Tex. 1993), *vacated on other grounds sub nom.* Graham v. Johnson, 94 F.3d 958 (5th Cir. 1996).

32. Paradis v. Arave, 954 F.2d 1483, 1490–92 (9th Cir. 1992), *vacated,* 507 U.S. 1026 (1993), *aff'd on remand,* 20 F.3d 950 (9th Cir. 1994).

33. Haney v. State, 603 So. 2d 368, 377–78 (Ala. Crim. App. 1991). *See* Cucolo & Perlin, *supra* note 22, at 126.

34. Garza v. Idaho, 139 S. Ct. 738 (2019) (Thomas, C. dissenting).

35. *Id.* at 756.

36. MODEL RULES, *supra* note 6, r. 8.3(a); Lonnie T. Brown Jr., *Ending Illegitimate Advocacy: Reinvigorating Rule 11 through Enhancement of the Ethical Duty to Report,* 62 OHIO ST. L.J. 1555, 1600–1603 (2001) (noting that the ambiguities in reporting and reporting exemptions lead to "a large segment of reportable offenses [that] likely go unreported with the textual blessing of Rule 8.3").

ed to disciplinary authorities.[37] Reasons for such underreporting are directly related to the systemic problems within the self-policing model, such as the following:

1. Those most likely to witness and recognize lawyer misconduct by virtue of their training are the lawyers and judges themselves who have a general reluctance to report despite their ethical duty[38]
2. An "anti-snitch" culture that fosters a societal attitude toward reporting the misconduct of others, "reinforced by the potential negative ramifications of reporting, including soured professional relations and possible retaliatory actions"[39]
3. The standards that impose the duty to report are muddled with discretionary calls and loopholes that, in effect, obviate the requirement to report[40]
4. Lawyer conduct often is seen in isolation[41]
5. Concern that reporting would lead to minimal or no sanctions and thus not worth the time and energy[42]

Even when reporting occurs, there is a strong sentiment among the legal community that no real repercussions or remedies exist against the constitutionally ineffective attorney.[43] As one scholar has noted:

> Assuming the criminal defendant succeeds in securing a new trial, having shown that the lawyer was so negligent that even *Strickland's* presumptions could not whitewash the incompetence, how do the courts deal with the lawyer? Is malpractice presumed? Is the lawyer automatically subject to some disciplinary action? Is the attorney required to undergo continuing peer review and supervision? Is the

---

37. Arthur F. Greenbaum, *The Automatic Reporting of Lawyer Misconduct to Disciplinary Authorities: Filling the Reporting Gap*, 73 Ohio St. L.J. 437, 439 (2012).

38. *Id. See also* Geoffrey C. Hazard Jr. and Dana A. Remus, *Advocacy Revalued*, 159 U. Pa. L. Rev. 751, 774 (2011) (noting that "lawyers rarely report each other's misconduct" and "judges are similarly reluctant").

39. Greenbaum, *supra* note 37 at 440.

40. *See Brown, supra* note 36.

41. *See* Greenbaum, *supra* note 37 at 441.

42. Leslie C. Levin, *The Case for Less Secrecy in Lawyer Discipline*, 20 Geo. J. Legal Ethics 1, 3 (2007) (limited available data suggests "the rate of recidivism among lawyers who receive public sanctions is fairly high").

43. Joseph H. Ricks, *Raising the Bar: Establishing an Effective Remedy Against Ineffective Counsel*, 2015 B.Y.U. L. Rev. 1115, 1122.

lawyer barred from handling criminal cases or required to attend classes? Anything? No.[44]

A second barrier is that the unethical conduct is often hidden and only known to the client during the handling of the case, or it is discovered post-adjudication. The largest category of complaints that disciplinary authorities receive are by clients who often lack the skill to be able to assess the propriety of lawyer conduct and identify when "less than blatantly obvious" misconduct occurs.[45] Failure to comply with certain Model Rules often fall under the radar, such as: Rule 1.1, "Competence," that requires an attorney to have the necessary knowledge of a field of law to represent a client and, if not, to study the field until she can competently represent a client;[46] Rule 1.3, "Diligence," that requires that an attorney diligently advocate for her client's interests despite opposition or inconvenience;[47] and Rule 1.4, "Communication," that requires an attorney to communicate with her client to understand the client's interests, jointly decide how to achieve those interests, and explain legal considerations so that the client can make informed decisions about legal representation and strategy.[48]

A third barrier to holding attorneys accountable is the interplay between *Strickland* and the Model Rules and the classification of trial strategy versus client autonomy. The U.S. Supreme Court has clearly stated that tactical decisions that make up an attorney's trial strategy cannot form the basis for an ineffective assistance of counsel claim.[49] The Model Rules, specifically Rule 1.2(a), provides that a defendant can request counsel to assert a particular defense, but he cannot interfere with how counsel chooses to present

---

44. Susan P. Koniak, *Through the Looking Glass of Ethics and the Wrong with Rights We Find There*, 9 GEO. J. LEGAL ETHICS 1, 9 (1995).

45. *See, e.g.*, DEBORAH L. RHODE AND GEOFFREY C. HAZARD JR., PROFESSIONAL RESPONSIBILITY AND REGULATION 264 (2d ed. 2007) (noting that unsophisticated clients have little way of knowing whether they are victims of incompetence or ethical violations).

46. MODEL RULES, *supra* note 6, r. 1.1.

47. *Id.* r. 1.3. Outside the confines of this chapter is the concern over racial and socioeconomic discrimination that is notoriously known to be hidden and underlies a lawyer's failure to provide competent representation, directly implicating Rule 8.4, Misconduct. In 2016, after twenty years of failed attempts, the ABA moved language prohibiting discrimination from a comment on Rule 8.4 to the rule itself, affirmatively defining professional misconduct as any "conduct that the lawyer knows or reasonably should know is harassment or discrimination on the basis of race, sex, religion, national origin, ethnicity, disability, age, sexual orientation, gender identity, marital status or socioeconomic status in conduct related to the practice of law." *Id.* at r.8.4(g).

48. *Id.* r. 1.4.

49. Wainwright v. Sykes, 433 U.S. 72 (1977). *See Strickland,* 466 U.S. at 690–91 (1984).

the defense.[50] Comment 1 to Rule 1.2(a) explains that the client has the ultimate authority to determine the purposes to be served by legal representation and the right to consult counsel about the means to be used in pursuing those objectives.[51] While Comment 2 also provides that "clients normally defer to the special knowledge and skill of their lawyer with respect to the means to be used to accomplish their objectives, particularly with respect to technical, legal and tactical matters. . . . Because of the varied nature of the matters about which a lawyer and client might disagree and because the actions in question may implicate the interests of a tribunal or other persons, this Rule does not prescribe how such disagreements are to be resolved."[52] As the means used to present a client's theory of defense are the strategic and tactical decisions normally viewed as within the lawyer's control (i.e., what witnesses to call, whether and how to conduct cross-examination, what jurors to accept or strike, what trial motions should be made, and what evidence should be introduced),[53] the Model Rules can be interpreted rather easily to support the attorney who presents the client's theory of defense.[54]

When the *Strickland* test and the Model Rules are viewed in tandem, they can have the effect of cancelling each other out. Under *Strickland*, "breach of an ethical standard does not necessarily make out a denial of the Sixth Amendment guarantee of assistance of counsel."[55] Defendants bear a high burden to prevail on a *Strickland* claim because "judicial scrutiny of counsel's performance must be highly deferential," and "a court must indulge a strong presumption that counsel's conduct falls within the wide range of reasonable professional assistance." The objectively reasonable standard of *Strickland* looks to "prevailing professional norms."[56] With regard to criminal practice, the ABA did promulgate standards specifically for criminal defense attorneys: the Criminal Justice Standards for the Defense Func-

---

50. MODEL RULES r. 1.2 (a) (2016).

51. *Id.* at cm. 1

52. *Id.* at cm. 2.

53. For the interplay between strategy and defendant's autonomy, *see* McCoy v Louisiana, 138 S.Ct. 1500 (2018) (the U.S. Supreme Court held that the Sixth Amendment guarantees criminal defendants the "autonomy to decide . . . to assert innocence" as their defense. This includes the defendant's right to insist that his attorney refrain from admitting guilt, even when counsel's experience advises that confessing guilt provides the best opportunity to avoid the death penalty.).

54. Jean K. Gilles Phillips and Joshua Allen, *Who Decides: The Allocation of Powers between the Lawyer and the Client in a Criminal Case?* 71 J. KAN. B. Ass'N 8, at 28, 33 (2002).

55. Nix v. Whiteside, 475 U.S. 157, 165 (1986)(citing *Strickland*); *see also* Mickens v. Taylor, 535 U.S. 162, 176 (2002) (quoting *Nix*).

56. *Strickland*, 466 U.S. at 688.

tion (hereafter referred to as Standards).[57] The Standards "describe 'best practices,' but are not intended to serve as the basis for the imposition of professional discipline, to create substantive or procedural rights for clients, or to create a standard of care for civil liability."[58]

The Supreme Court in *Strickland* referenced the Standards as reflecting "prevailing norms of practice," emphasizing that they are only guides to determining what is reasonable.[59] Courts continue to use and cite the Standards in determining whether defense counsel has provided effective assistance.[60] However, the procedure to hold lawyers accountable under the Model Rules/Standards can be drastically different from the procedure in *Strickland*. For instance, in some states, the standard of proof at a disciplinary hearing may be higher. In Arizona, the defendant must establish by a preponderance of the evidence that a constitutional defect has occurred, and then the state has the burden of proving that the defect was harmless beyond a reasonable doubt.[61] But Arizona's grounds for discipline require bar counsel to establish allegations by clear and convincing evidence.[62] Thus, if a defendant is unsuccessful in meeting her burden on a *Strickland* ineffective assistance of counsel claim, she will most likely be unable to meet the burden of showing that her attorney's conduct fell below the "prevailing norms of practice" as defined within the Model Rules and Standards.[63]

Despite strong public interest in effectively regulating lawyers, neither state nor federal courts have developed adequate policies and practices to ensure that misconduct during litigation proceedings is consistently reported to state disciplinary agencies. In practice, rarely if ever, are attorneys sanctioned after being found constitutionally deficient.[64] Lawyers can be

---

57. AMERICAN BAR ASSOCIATION, CRIMINAL JUSTICE STANDARDS FOR THE DEF. FUNCTION (2016).

58. *Id.* § 4–1.1(b).

59. *Strickland,* 466 U.S. at 688.

60. *See* Martin Marcus, *The Making of the ABA Criminal Justice Standards: Forty Years of Excellence,* CRIM. JUST., at 10, 14 (2009).

61. ARIZ. R. CRIM. P. 32.8(c).

62. *In re* Wolfram, 847 P.2d 94, 98 n. 4 (Ariz. 1993).

63. *Nix,* 475 U.S. at 165 (1986). *But see In re Warren,* 321 F. App'x 369, 370 (5th Cir. 2009) (the court issued sanctions after granting relief on ineffective assistance of counsel grounds).

64. *See* Stephen B. Bright, *Independence of Counsel: An Essential Requirement for Competent Counsel and a Working Adversary System,* 55 HOUS. L. REV. 853 (2018), discussing violations in Texas:

> [There are] egregious instances of malpractice such as lawyers sleeping during death penalty trials, filing briefs that were incomprehensible or did not apply to the case in which they were submitted, and abandoning clients and turning against them. Neither judges nor the Texas Bar have taken action to prevent such malpractice from occurring

disciplined for any breach of ethical rules, yet only about 5 percent of all complaints result in any sanction against lawyers, and among the 5 percent, the great majority receive private sanctions, the lightest possible punishment.[65] About .08 percent of attorneys are disbarred, and only about 1 percent of lawyers accused of misconduct are suspended from practice.[66] Very few states employ sanctions as a remedy in criminal proceedings, but that does not make them any less effective.[67]

Therapeutic Jurisprudence and Suggestions for Reform

So how might we bolster violation reporting, accountability and remediate ineffective assistance of counsel? As mentioned, TJ may provide some assistance in at least four ways. TJ necessitates the use of the community as a whole in its application and should not be limited to the worlds of the small circle of lawyers and judges. Thus, first we may want to rely on entities outside the legal profession that interact with lawyers in significant ways, to assist in reporting misconduct.[68] Second, TJ requires us to consider the perspective of clients and involve them and their insights into how the therapeutic or antitherapeutic aspects of the justice system actually play out.[69] To make sure that clients are protected and on notice of prior disciplinary conduct, we might want to consider requiring courts to automatically report certain kinds of conduct to disciplinary authorities. Findings of contempt, imposition of significant sanctions, and other matters would be reported automatically to disciplinary authorities. In furtherance of this requirement, it has been suggested that state and federal court systems create electronic databases, accompanied and supported by uniform court procedural

---

again. Judges have continued to appoint those lawyers to represent defendants and the Bar has taken no disciplinary action. The Texas Court of Criminal Appeals has sanctioned lawyers for failing to file pleadings a full seven days before an execution but has not punished those who slept during trials or those who submitted incomprehensible or irrelevant briefs—the convictions and death sentences were upheld in those cases. Id. at 854.

65. Leslie C. Levin, *The Emperor's Clothes and Other Tales about the Standards for Imposing Lawyer Discipline*, 48 Am. U. L. Rev. 1, 8–9 (1998).

66. Richard L. Abel, *United States: The Contradictions of Professionalism*, in Lawyers in Society 186, 219–20 (Richard L. Abel and Philip S. C. Lewis eds., 1988).

67. Altimease Lowe, *Criminal Law—The Call for an Adequate Remedy: The Lack of Deterrence and Judicial Consequences for Prosecutors Who Habitually Violate Batson*, 43 U. Ark. Little Rock L. Rev. 261, 275 (2020) (suggesting imposing monetary sanctions on prosecutors who repeatedly employ racially discriminatory peremptory challenges).

68. *See* Greenbaum, *supra* note 37 at 453. California and Florida require malpractice insurers to report certain actions against lawyers to state officials.

69. Michael L. Perlin, *A Law of Healing*, 68 U. Cin. L. Rev. 407, 413 (2000).

rules and policies, to receive and store judicial reports of litigation-related lawyer misconduct.[70] Third, TJ can be a powerful interpretive tool to make vivid the "stories" of individuals who would otherwise remain anonymous.[71] Requiring attorneys to self-report to disciplinary authorities whether the lawyers were convicted of a crime in any court or had disciplinary penalties entered against them in another state would help achieve that end.[72] The purpose is not to shame or punish the lawyer but to hold her accountable for past violations to prevent further violations going forward. Finally, TJ can be employed as a servant of law reform, by illuminating the therapeutic and antitherapeutic effects of rules that drive behavior.[73] To that end, rigorous legal education must continue to focus on moral and ethical responsibility in practice. Law students are going to become lawyers and will assume the responsibility of the gatekeepers of justice.

Lawyers dominate the public's access to legal services and thus have a responsibility to ensure the fair application of justice to everyone. Every member of the bar must do what he or she can to support and develop solutions that guarantee competent counsel at all stages of all criminal cases, from misdemeanors to death penalty. We—as judges, lawyers, and legal academics—are the caretakers of liberty; to maintain and uphold the integrity of the legal profession, we must combine virtue ethics with action and accountability to better protect the constitutional and human rights of all persons within the criminal justice system.

---

70. Michael S. McGinniss, *Sending the Message: Using Technology to Support Judicial Reporting of Lawyer Misconduct to State Disciplinary Agencies*, PROF. LAW., 2013, at 37.

71. Perlin, *supra* note 69 at 416.

72. *See* Greenbaum, *supra* note 37 at 444 (California adopted much of these recommendations in response to a major scandal concerning the bar).

73. Perlin, *supra* note 69 at 415.

17

Nonjudicial Influence on Family Violence Court Cases

LENORE E. A. WALKER AND BRANDI N. DIAZ*

Introduction

Custody disputes have been recorded since the earliest days of civilization, when King Solomon was tasked with two mothers who both claimed to be the child's "real" parent. Since the king was unable to tell which woman was telling the truth, he suggested cutting the child in half so each woman could have half of the baby. Quickly, the real mother shouted out, "No, don't kill my child. Give it to her, instead." The king recognized that the real mother preferred that her child live rather than be killed by splitting the baby, so he gave the child to her. The king was right: children are not property to be divided. Unfortunately, today in family courts all over the world, many abusive fathers are forcing the courts to split the child, often permitting fathers to continue to control the children and their mothers, placing them both at risk of danger.

* Portions are adapted from Walker, L. E. "Nonjudicial Influence on Family Violence Court Cases," *American Behavioral Scientist* (64:12) pp. 1749–67. Copyright © 2020 by SAGE. Reprinted by permission of SAGE Publications Inc. This material is the exclusive property of the SAGE Publications Inc. and is protected by copyright and other intellectual property laws. User may not modify, publish, transmit, participate in the transfer or sale of, reproduce, create derivative works (including course packs) from, distribute, perform, display, or in any way exploit any of the content of the file(s) in whole or in part. Permission may be sought for further use from SAGE Publications Inc., attn. Rights Department, 2455 Teller Road, Thousand Oaks, CA 91360, email: permissions@sagepub.com. By accessing the file(s), the User acknowledges and agrees to these terms. http://www.sagepub.com.

Historically, mothers were responsible for raising children until they were old enough to work with their fathers. However, in the 1970s, as divorce laws were being reformed, child custody became litigated more frequently. Rather than judges playing King Solomon themselves, they sought assistance from mental health professionals and lawyers to assist in decision-making. But more often than not, families where parents were forced to share custody ended up back in court because those decisions often did not work out.[1]

Over the past forty years, more professionals have been added to assist judges in these cases,[2] however these professionals' credentials rarely include an understanding of what is needed to recognize and stop current abuse and prevent future violence. In many court cases, there were allegations of domestic violence or child abuse that had gone unnoticed or unattended to by the untrained professionals, thus leaving children and mothers unprotected.[3] Or the courts rarely consider how their decisions may perpetuate domestic violence and child abuse in custody disputes. Even when the abuse could no longer be ignored, counterclaims[4] began using newly proposed diagnoses such as "parental alienation syndrome/disorder"[5] or others with questionable scientific validity.[6] Research supports advocates' claims that the current

---

1. D. KELLY WEISBERG, DOMESTIC VIOLENCE: LEGAL AND SOCIAL REALITY 178 (2012).

2. See LESLIE M. DROZD, NANCY W. OLESEN, AND MICHAEL A. SAINI, PARENTING PLAN AND CHILD CUSTODY EVALUATIONS: USING DECISION TREES TO INCREASE EVALUATOR COMPETENCE AND AVOID PREVENTABLE ERRORS (2013).

3. See, e.g., Nicholas M. C. Bala et al., *Sexual Abuse Allegations and Parental Separation: Smoke Screen or Fire?* 13 J. FAM. STUD. 8 (2007); LUNDY BANCROFT AND JAY G. SILVERMAN, THE BATTERER AS A PARENT (2003); Robert E. Emery, Randy K. Otto, and William T. O'Donohue, *A Critical Assessment of Child and Custody Evaluations: Limited Science and a Flawed System*, 6 PSYCHOL. SCI. IN PUB. INTEREST. 5 (2005); Abigail H. Gewirtz and Jeffery L. Edleson, *Young Children's Exposure to Intimate Partner Violence: Towards a Developmental Risk and Resilience Framework for Research and Intervention*, 22 J. FAM. VIOLENCE. 151, 159 (2007); Madelyn S. Milchman, *Misogynistic Cultural Argument in Parental Alienation Versus Child Sexual Abuse Cases*, 14 J. CHILD CUSTODY. 211, 226 (2017); Tracee Parker et al., *Danger Zone: Battered Mother and Their Families in Supervised Visitation*, 14 VIOLENCE AGAINST WOMEN. 1313, 1319 (2008); Daniel G. Saunders, Kathleen C. Faller, and Richard M. Tolman, *Child Custody Evaluators' Belief about Domestic Abuse Allegations: Their Relationship to Evaluator Demographics, Background, Domestic Violence Knowledge and Custody Visitation Recommendations*, U.S. DEPARTMENT OF JUSTICE (2011), https://www.ojp.gov/pdffiles1/nij/grants/238891 .pdf; LENORE E. A. WALKER, THE BATTERED WOMAN SYNDROME (2017).

4. A counterclaim is a claim filed to rebut the initial claim. See FED. R. CIV. PRO. 13.

5. RICHARD A. GARDNER, THE PARENTAL ALIENATION SYNDROME AND THE DIFFERENTIATION BETWEEN FABRICATED AND GENUINE CHILD SEX ABUSE CASES (1987).

6. This particular syndrome has been promoted by some (see DEMOSTHENES LORANDOS, WILLIAM BERNET, AND RICHARD SAUBER, PARENTAL ALIENATION: HANDBOOK FOR MENTAL HEALTH AND LEGAL PROFESSIONALS [2013]) but is strongly disputed by others because of the lack of rigorous, peer-reviewed empirical research (William Bernet, *Parental Alienation and*

way to make contested custody decisions by nonjudicial as well as judges themselves is biased.[7]

This chapter first employs a literature review to examine consequences of decision-making in custody disputes. Main concerns in the literature to be addressed include bias and skepticism toward mothers in the decision-making process and the use of unproven and unscientific alienation theories in custody cases. Based on the literature reviewed, it appears there are deficits in the practical application of mental health in the family court system and how the structure of this system does not effectively protect the children involved. In addition, this chapter deals with some of the current problems and poses a family therapeutic jurisprudence (TJ) court as a possible solution to improving the process for children.

Is the Family Court System Broken?

Family courts are usually considered courts of equity; that is, people are supposed to have their problems solved in a fair and honest way.[8] However, what may feel fair to one member of the family may not be perceived in the same way by others. In 2012, one of the coauthors (LEAW) convened a conference, funded by the Cummings Foundation, in Phoenix, Arizona, to look at the assumption that the family court system was broken. Fifteen invited presenters including lawyers, judges, psychologists, pediatricians, social workers, and advocates met for two days, listened to prepared talks, and discussed with the two hundred people in the audience the premise that family court was broken but possibly could be fixed with a problem-solving court model.[9] The topics covered in that conference remain relevant today, including looking at what were called "deadly sins" that keep family court from truly meeting the child's best interests. As might be expected, postdivorce risk of domestic violence and child abuse were among them. Additional anecdotal concerns raised at the Cummings Foundation conference ten years ago in 2012 include rules of evidence resulting in no limitation on admissibility of

---

Misinformation Proliferation, 58 FAM. CRT. REV., 293, 297 [2020]); *see* Lenore E.A. Walker and David L. Shapiro, *Parental Alienation Disorder: Why Label Children with a Mental Disorder?* 7 J. CHILD CUSTODY 266, 283 (2010).

7. *See* Joan S. Meier, *U.S. Child Custody Outcomes in Cases Involving Parental Alienation and Abuse Allegations: What Do the Data Show?* 42 J. SOCIAL WELFARE & FAM. LAW. 92 (2020).

8. At least one court has defined the court of equity as "a court of conscience." Rayman Investments and Management *v.* Mariner Inn, [1996] B.C.J. No. 1097 at para. 51 (C.A.), online: QL (BCJ).

9. OUR BROKEN FAMILY COURT (Lenore E. A. Walker, Dorothy M. Cummings, and Nicholas A. Cummings eds., 2012).

"junk science" or, for that matter, limited introduction of even reputable science in decision-making; bias against women and toward middle-class professional values; bias against those racially marginalized; admissibility of so-called experts with little or no training in trauma or child development; and the creation of an appeals process with major hurdles for it to be used. However, this chapter deals specifically with the lack of protection to battered women and abused children when they follow untrained judges' advice and orders. While these discussions took place at the Cummings Foundation conference in 2012, they were also the basis for the book *Our Broken Family Court*.[10]

Research has found that ethical violations in the family courts abound, but without the ability to hold judges and other participants accountable[11] for what they permit in their courtrooms, it is difficult to even document them.[12] For an example in a case in which LEAW was personally involved, the judge took my domestic violence clients into his chambers and told them to get down on their knees, pray for forgiveness, and go back to live with each other.[13] Sometimes the ethical violation results in a bad decision for the client like above, and other times it is favorable, like when a judge asked me (LEAW) to come back into his chambers without the lawyers present after my testimony was finished so I could sign a copy of my book *The Battered Woman*[14] for his wife, who had been abused in her previous relationship.[15] Based on subjective experiences, these types of breaches of court ethics and rules are not recorded, and they rarely if ever happen when I have testified in criminal or other civil cases. It is my opinion that few custody evaluators are willing to challenge the prevailing culture in family court, and many well-trained psychologists refuse these difficult and often complex cases, leaving the testimony to "chummy" psychologists. Oversight of a family court judge's abuse of power usually rests with either the appeals court or the various state bar and judicial qualifications committees. There are also significant differences between family and criminal court proceedings/rights that can contribute to lengthy family court proceedings. Despite state laws mandating

---

10. *Id.*

11. Presumptions can be drawn regarding why judges are not held accountable for ethical violations. For example, many of these violations occur off the record or in unofficial discussions.

12. *Id.*

13. Due to ethical considerations and the case being at the trial level in a criminal proceeding, which is not reported publicly, this case cannot be publicly identified.

14. LENORE E. A. WALKER, THE BATTERED WOMAN (1979).

15. Once again, to protect of the confidentiality of the client that was evaluated and the judge's wife mentioned, further details cannot be provided that would lead to identification of involved parties.

speedy trials,[16] some family court cases can take months or even years to resolve while the children and their mothers remain unprotected. Further, many parties do not understand or trust the system and cannot afford the expense associated with a lengthy family court process.

Child custody decisions are "big business" with an entire set of professionals in different disciplines as participants. Many go by different names, but basically they include child custody evaluators who assess the family members' ability to meet a child's best interests, parenting coordinators appointed when parents are unable to share custody on their own, time-sharing professionals who help decide how parents will split time with the baby, guardians ad litem who tell the court what are the child's best interests, children's lawyers who represent their wishes, and even court-appointed therapists who are supposed to use "therapy" to force people to follow court orders even when they disagree with them.[17] Guidelines for conducting child custody and access to children have been published by various groups within professions such as the American Psychological Association, American Bar Association, and National Association of Social Workers, as well as interdisciplinary organizations such as the American Family Courts and Conciliators (AFCC) and the American Professional Society on the Abuse of Children (APSAC). In addition, sometimes governmental groups (e.g., Children's Bureau within the U.S. Department of Health and Human Services and Administration for Children and Family Services) are involved, such as child protective service agencies. Persuading this array of interest groups to function differently in a problem-solving model may be a difficult if not impossible task, but we suggest focusing on several of what were originally called the deadly sins and how a TJ model might work.

Legislative Mandates and Presumptions

Most states have legislated mandates recommended by the Uniform Child Custody Act,[18] some of which have no scientific basis.[19] This includes such

---

16. *See, e.g.,* N.Y. McKinney's Family Court Act § 340.

17. In this article, we use the term "custody evaluators" to refer to any or all of these nonjudicial participants. Toby Kleinman and Daniel Pollack, *How to Select an Expert Witness in a Custody Case (2019),* https://www.law.com/newyorklawjournal/2019/11/18/how-to-select-an-expert-in-a-custody-case/?.&slreturn=20210124094356.

18. National Conference of Commissioners, *The Uniform Child Custody Jurisdiction and Enforcement Act* (1997), www.nccusl.org.

19. Linda D. Elrod, *The Federalization of Family Law,* American Bar Association (2009), https://www.americanbar.org/groups/crsj/publications/human_rights_magazine_home/human_rights_vol36_2009/summer2009/the_federalization_of_family_law/.

statements requiring as the primary goal "keeping the family together"[20] or "reunification," which also may conflict with other principles such as "protection of family members is in the child's best interests."[21] Even though Congress in 2018 passed House Resolution 72, affirming the principle that the child's safety has higher priority than the parent's right of access to their child, only a few states—including California, New Hampshire, and Pennsylvania—have incorporated it into law. In contrast, in other countries that have signed on to the United Nations Convention on the Rights of Children, where similar guarantees are granted,[22] there are models of problem-solving courts using well-trained specialists to try to better prevent or protect child abuse. One example, related to Israel, is discussed later.

Unfortunately, many families seen in both dependency and child custody cases cannot protect their individual members without government assistance. Safety may not be possible in these families when forced to reunify or coparent children as uneven balance of power and control needs are often present. We have seen the rise of domestic violence cases reported during the COVID-19 pandemic across the world as families are locked down together in quarantine.[23] Nonetheless, the custody mechanisms for making decisions designed for the average family are forcing many children into unsafe situations. Their lives are regulated by the court for extended periods of time. Judges are asked to resolve conflicts over problems that the average family usually solves on their own. The judges usually pass these cases on to the assortment of professionals often untrained in assessing the psychological factors that accompany physical and sexual abuse; such individuals may miss appropriate risk assessment cues designed to protect children.[24]

There have been attempts in family law to resolve these problems by creating presumptions by which to make decisions, putting the burden of proof on the party who wishes to remove the presumption. While presumptions are not unusual in the law, the presumptions to decide custody have become a part of the problem, partly because the burden of proof becomes difficult

---

20. *Id.*

21. *Id.*

22. It should be noted that the United States is only one of three countries (Samoa and South Sudan being the other two) that has not signed the UN Convention on the Rights of Children, which provides suggestions for some relief, such as adopting a therapeutic family court. *See* INTERNATIONAL PERSPECTIVES AND EMPIRICAL FINDINGS ON CHILD PARTICIPATION (Tali Gal and Benedetta Duramy eds., 2015), hereafter cited as GAL AND DURAMY.

23. Caroline Bettinger-Lopez, *A Double Pandemic: Domestic Violence in the Age of COVID-19*, COUNCIL ON FOREIGN RELATIONS (2020), https://www.cfr.org/in-brief/double-pandemic-domestic-violence-age-covid-19.

24. Saunders, Faller, and Tolman, *supra* note 3, at 15.

to reach and partly because they are not based on science. In some jurisdictions where there is both a domestic violence court and family court, there are different standards that are used for injunctive relief.[25] For example, in New Jersey, in awarding temporary custody, the domestic violence court "shall presume that the best interests of the child are served by an award of custody to the non-abusive parent."[26] This presumption reflects the science-based Domestic Violence Act's finding "that there exists 'a positive correlation between spousal abuse; and that children, even when they are not themselves physically assaulted, suffer deep and lasting emotional effects from exposure to domestic violence.'"[27] Note, though, that in other courts in the same state, there is a four-prong test for injunctive relief by which the court must find (1) irreparable harm if there is not immediate relief, (2) granting the relief will not do more harm than good, (3) there is likelihood that the issue would be sustained on its merits if heard, and (4) there is settled law on the issue.[28]

Perhaps the most dangerous presumption in family court for a child's safety is that joint custody is always in the best interests of the child.[29] While there are some data to suggest that when both parents can agree on coparenting their child, this may indeed in the best interests of the child,[30] there are also psychological data to show how it is not in their best interests when there is high conflict and abuse.[31] The presumption of joint custody was originally based on a limited sample by Wallerstein and Kelly dealing only with reliable and consistent visitation; its use to support a presumption of joint custody was refuted by the authors fifteen years later.[32]

---

25. For example, a case could be in family court where domestic violence is later discovered in which the injunctive relief would be different than in a domestic violence court. *See* Anna Majestro, *Preparing for and Obtaining Preliminary Injunctive Relief*, AMERICAN BAR ASSOCIATION (2018), https://www.americanbar.org/groups/litigation/committees/woman-advocate/practice/2018/preliminary-injunction-relief.

26. N.J. STAT. ANN. § 9:2-4 (2014).

27. J.D. v. M.A.D., 56 A.3d 882, 887–89 (N.J. App. Div.2012); R.K. v. F.K., 96 A. 2d 291, 294–95 (N.J. App. Div. 2014).

28. *See, e.g.*, Garden State Equity v. Dow, 79 A. 3d 479 (N.J. Law Div. 2013), *stay den.*, 216 N.J. 314 (N.J. 2013).

29. *See* Nancy Gilsan Courley, *Joint Custody: The Best Interest of the Child*, 18 TULSA LAW REV. 159, (1982).

30. JUDITH S. WALLERSTEIN AND JOAN B. KELLY, SURVIVING THE BREAK-UP: HOW CHILDREN AND PARENTS COPE WITH DIVORCE (1979).

31. Vincent J. Felitti, *Reverse Alchemy in Childhood: Turning Gold into Lead*, 8 HEALTH ALERT. 1, 2 (2001); Judith S. Wallerstein and Tony J. Tanke, *To Move or Not to Move: Consideration on Relocation of Children Following Divorce*, 30 FAM L.Q. 305, 309 (1996).

32. Judith S. Wallerstein, *Children of Divorce: Preliminary Report of a Ten-Year Follow-up of Older Children and Adolescents*, 24 J. AM. ACAD. CHILD PSYCHIATRY. 545, 547 (1985).

It has been suggested that legislators were persuaded by this limited data to change the presumption from young children's custody being awarded to their mother, despite the fact that the presumption did not have sufficient psychological data to support the benefits of its widespread application when parents cannot agree and leave the decision to the court.[33] In cases where there are allegations of domestic violence and child abuse, forcing joint custody[34] is actually placing children and their mothers in even more danger.[35] Research shows removal from a parent to whom the child has learned to emotionally attach may harm the child's ability to develop trust and loving feelings for others later in life.[36] Nonetheless, judges can remove the child from their primary parent, sometimes even without a hearing. Circumstances in which a hearing is not required include if the child is placed with a relative, if there is compelling evidence that termination of parental rights would be in the best interest of the child, and if the state agency has not provided the parent with services needed for a safe reunification.[37] In contrast, it is important to remember that there remain no actual empirical data to show that it is beneficial for these children to be forced into contact with a parent. Many children grow up healthy with only one parent during different periods of their lives. An example are children with a parent in the military who is deployed for several years in another country. Today, there are more sophisticated tools to do risk assessment, especially when domestic violence or child abuse is alleged,[38] but these are rarely used in child

---

33. Wendy A. Fitzgerald, *Maturity, Difference, and Mystery: Children's Perspective and the Law*, 36 ARIZ. L. REV. 11, 57 (1994).

34. *See* Meier, *supra* note 7, at 101 (research as to how common the award of forced joint custody or parental responsibility or assigning custody to the alleged abuse is by U.S. courts as described later).

35. BANCROFT AND SILVERMAN, *supra* note 3; OUR BROKEN FAMILY COURT, *supra* note 9; WALKER, *supra* note 3.

36. Jude Cassidy, Jason D. Jones, and Phillip R. Shaver, *Contributions of Attachment Theory and Research: A Framework for Future Research, Translation, and Policy*, 25 DEV. PSYCHOPATHOLOGY. 1415, 10 (2013); E. MAVIS HETHERINGTON AND JOHN KELLY, FOR BETTER OR WORSE: DIVORCE RECONSIDERED (2002).

37. Meier, *supra* note 7, at 96; Children's Bureau, *Grounds for Involuntary Termination of Parental Rights*, CHILD WELFARE INFORMATION GATEWAY (2016), https://www.childwelfare.gov/pubPDFs/groundtermin.pdf.

38. APSAC Taskforce, *Practice Guidelines: Forensic Interviewing in Cases of Suspected Child Abuse*, AMERICAN PROFESSIONAL SOCIETY ON THE ABUSE OF CHILDREN (2012), https://2a566822-8004-431f-b136-8b004d74bfc2.filesusr.com/ugd/4700a8_06b064b4cc304c cc97be55a945acd90d.pdf; G. ANDREW BENJAMIN ET AL., FAMILY EVALUATION IN CUSTODY LITIGATION: PROMOTING OPTIMAL OUTCOMES AND REDUCING ETHICAL RISKS (2018); JACQUELINE CAMPBELL, *Danger Assessment Scale* (2002), www.jacquelinecampbell.com; Emery,

custody evaluations. Further, it is estimated that less than approximately 60 percent of custody evaluators used assessments specific to child custody.[39]

Another presumption in many states is the requirement that the person who can best foster the child's relationship with the other parent should have primary custody.[40] In some states, it is called the "friendly parent." However, in cases where one parent has abused the other parent, it is difficult to expect the victimized parent to be friendly to the other person. This presumption or bias has been used by judges to take custody away from mothers who report abuse by fathers, overruling the joint custody presumption.[41] Many abusers can present as charming and likeable while victims may display their frustration and anger at the unjustness they may accurately perceive occurring. Even when there is no direct presumption, the bias is often in favor of the parent who seems more cooperative, but that parent actually may interfere with the other parent's relationship with the child once the litigation is over. Such postlitigation instances are commonly seen in these highly litigated cases, with judges often refusing to permit admission of the prior history, unless a separate civil personal injury lawsuit or collateral litigation is also filed.[42] Research has shown a bias by evaluators as well as judges against women's attempts to protect their children.[43] Mothers often are held to a higher standard than fathers when a child is abused. In cases where the child is killed by the father (or stepfather), mothers often receive longer sentences for failure to protect the child than the father or father figure who strikes the fatal blows.[44] Even when the mother falsely confesses

---

Otto, and O'Donohue, *supra* note 3, at 7; Michael E. Lamb et al., *Structured Forensic Interview Protocols Improve the Quality and Informativeness of Investigative Interviews with Children: A Review of Research Using the NICHD Investigative Interview Protocol*, 31 Child Abuse and Neglect. 1201, 1210 (2007); Danielle H. Millen et al., *Battered Women Syndrome Questionnaire (BWSQ) Subscales: Development, Reliability, and Validity*, 28 Aggression, Maltreatment, & Trauma. 848, 849 (2019).

39. *See* Emery, Otto, and Donahue, *supra* note 3 at 7.

40. Lawrence v. Lawrence, 20 P.3d 972, 974 (Wash. Ct. App. 2001).

41. Meier, *supra* note 7, at 97.

42. Andrew Cohen, *Influencing and Challenging Judges and Their Decisions in Child Welfare Cases*, American Bar Association (2019), https://www.americanbar.org/groups/pub lic_interest/child_law/resources/child_law_practiceonline/january---december-2019/influ encing-and-challenging-judges-and-their-decisions-in-child-/.

43. Marjorie Fields, *Domestic Violence Cases Are a Major Aspect of the Breakdown of the Family Court*, in Our Broken Family Court, *supra* note 9, at 27; *see* Meier, *supra* note 7; Saunders, Faller, and Tolman, *supra* note 3, at 8.

44. *See, e.g.*, Midyette v. Raemisch, 2018 WL 1961153 (D. Colo. 2018) (denying application for writ of habeas corpus and discussing case); *see also* State v. Edwards, 2018 WL 1477585 (Ariz. Ct. App. 2018) (discussing role of mother, Ashley Buckman).

under the duress of her abuser or the police, these cases rarely get reversed on appeal.[45]

The final presumption to discuss here is that the biological family member will always do what is in the child's best interests (see *Parham v. J.R.*, a US Supreme Court case involving commitment of juveniles to psychiatric institutions, even when the juvenile is a ward of the state).[46] Sometimes splitting up children in the family is in their best interests, especially in families where there has been abuse. Sometimes it is necessary for a child to not be forced to see a parent for a long period until that child's PTSD or other trauma effects have healed and the abusive parent can prove he or she can appropriately parent the child. This puts the burden of proof on the estranged parent to resume access, not on the abuse survivors. A problem-solving court that can hold interim hearings until real changes are measured would eliminate the problems that currently exist with short-term supervised visitation that moves too quickly for the child into unsupervised contact, which can place the child at risk of never healing from the original trauma or developing new psychological problems even if physical or sexual abuse is not present.[47]

Mothers and young children may be disbelieved by child custody evaluators who have not read the literature or been trained to recognize child sexual abuse.[48] Often the mother is accused of "coaching" a child even though

---

45. WALKER, *supra* note 3. The Kelly Savage case, an example of this phenomenon, is discussed in Alisa Bierria and Colby Lenz, *Battering Court Syndrome: A Structural Critique of "Failure to Protect,"* in THE POLITICIZATION OF SAFETY 91, 95–100 (Jane Stoever ed., 2019).

46. Parham v. JR, 442 US 584 (1979). It is also important to note that historically, it has been recognized that "natural bonds of affection lead parents to act in the best interests of their children. *Id.* at 602, citing W. BLACKSTONE, COMMENTARIES *447; J. KENT, COMMENTARIES ON AMERICAN LAW *190. For a sharp criticism of *Parham, see* Michael L. Perlin, *An Invitation to the Dance: An Empirical Response to Chief Justice Warren Burger's Time-Consuming Procedural Minuets Theory in* Parham v. J.R., 9 BULL. AM. ACAD. PSYCHIATRY & L. 149 (1981), reprinted in THERAPEUTIC JURISPRUDENCE: THE LAW AS A THERAPEUTIC AGENT 291 (David B. Wexler, ed. 1990).

47. Stephanie J. Dallam and Joyanna L. Silberg, *Recommended Treatments for "Parental Alimentation Syndrome" (PAS) May Cause Children Foreseeable and Lasting Psychological Harm,* 13 J. CHILD CUSTODY. 134, 141 (2016); *see* DROZD, OLESEN, AND SAINI, *supra* note 2; Felitti, *supra* note 31, at 3; Eli Newberger, *Understanding, Interpreting, and Addressing the Unbelievable in Men's Character and Behavior,* in OUR BROKEN FAMILY COURT SYSTEM, *supra* note 9, at 181; Parker et al., *supra* note 3, at 1321; Joyanna Silberg and Stephanie Dallman, *Abusers Gaining Custody in Family Courts: A Case Series of Overturned Decisions,* 16 J. CHILD CUSTODY 140, 143 (2019); WALKER, *supra* note 3.

48. For example, an evaluator without sufficient training or knowledge may view the reported first "outcry" from a child to their mother as suspicious; however this is often the case based on information reviewed pertaining to attachment theories and child abuse. *See* Cassidy, Jones, and Shaver, *supra* note 36.

it is typical for a child to make the first outcry to her. Or evaluators mistakenly believe that just because a child played without observable fear with the accused father during their evaluation, that play negated the possibility of sexual abuse.[49] Some do not evaluate to see whether "grooming behavior"[50] is present.[51] Nor do they understand that just because the father may hold an important job, that does not mitigate the risk that he possibly could be a pedophile.[52]

Prior research has found that most child custody evaluators, no matter their discipline, were either unimpressed or angered by mother's reports of domestic violence or child abuse.[53] The same skepticism was found in reports of child sexual abuse during separation, despite the findings that many children do not feel safe enough to make a report until the father is out of the home.[54] The only ones in the study[55] who attempted to perform further risk assessment were those who worked at a battered woman shelter or child abuse center, where they saw many cases of children subjected to similar physical, sexual, and psychological abuse as well as power and control issues among fathers and mothers. But not all who worked at child abuse centers were free from bias against mothers' reports of abuse. Marjorie Fields reviewed cases that came before her as chief judge of a busy family court in New York City and found similar abuse that did not concern the professionals tasked with evaluation.[56] These outcomes were not always so in family court prior to the attempts to reform divorce in the late 1970s and early 1980s.[57]

Raising the issue of parent alienation syndrome or disorder (PAS/D) is a problem in protecting children and women from abusive domestic partners. The concept—first put forward by psychiatrist Richard Gardner[58] despite no scientific data to support it—quickly became admissible in family

---

49. Lamb et al., *supra* note 38, at 1202.

50. Grooming behavior is a term used to describe the special attention and love a pedophile gives children to win their trust and affection before slowly engaging in more sexualized behavior. Definitions of grooming are collected in Morris v. State, 361 S.W.3d 649, 661 n. 60 (Tex. Ct. Crim. App. 2011). Children do not want to lose this feeling of special treatment, and unless they are being forced to engage in sexual activity that is painful, they rarely disclose their discomfort to evaluators, especially if they have tried and were not heard.

51. Natalie Bennet and William O'Donohue, *The Construct of Grooming in Child Sexual Abuse: Conceptual and Measurement Issues*, 23 J. CHILD SEXUAL ABUSE. 957, 971 (2014).

52. Milchman, *supra* note 3, at 225.

53. Saunders, Faller, and Tolman, *supra* note 3, at 19; Meier, *supra* note 7, at 101.

54. Bala et al., *supra* note 3, at 3.

55. *See* Saunders, Faller, and Tolman, *supra* note 3.

56. Fields, *supra* note 43.

57. WEISBERG, *supra* note 1.

58. GARDNER, *supra* note 5.

courts and used by custody evaluators to blame mothers for children not wishing to have contact with their often angry and controlling fathers (but see *Mastrangelo v. Mastrangelo*, where testimony on PAS/D was ruled inadmissible).[59] Many of those children saw their fathers abuse their mothers or other family members. Mental health professionals were more inclined to believe mothers were "gatekeeping" by overprotecting children or somehow poisoning them against a relationship with their fathers.[60] Once the "alienation" label was fixed, as noted by Meier,[61] it was almost impossible to protect at-risk children who were forced into shared parental custody against their will. Research shows that without intervention, abusive fathers rarely will stop coercive control or abuse.[62]

Can a TJ Family Court Better Protect Children?

Children in the United States and most other countries do not have legal standing or rights in family court, which they need in order to have a legal voice to state their wishes when their parents separate and divorce. In some cases, they may get representation by a guardian ad litem, who must report on what is in their best interests, not their wishes, if what they wish differs from those of the guardian ad litem. A problem-solving family court based on TJ can help children become a party in their parents' divorce and custody decisions by creating a safe space within the court using trained professionals to participate with them.[63] While the judge and parents still have the final decision-making authority, children participate in family court decisions to the extent their maturity allows.

Arguments against giving children legal rights requiring their participation often focus on a child's "capability" of making rational decisions and

---

59. Mastrangelo v. Mastrangelo, 2012 WL 6901161 (Ct. Super. Ct. 2012).

60. Walker and Shapiro, *supra* note 6, at 276.

61. Meier, *supra* note 7, at 101.

62. Bancroft and Silverman, *supra* note 3; Debra Kalmuss, *The Attribution of Responsibility in a Wife Abuse Context*, 4 Victimology 284, 295 (1979); Walker, *supra* note 3.

63. Penelope E. Bryan, *"Collaborative Divorce: Meaningful Reform or Another Quick Fix?* 6 Pub. Pol'y & L.1001, 1011 (1999); Thomas J. McHahon and Francis D. Giannini, *Substance-Abusing Fathers in Family Court: Moving from Popular Stereotypes to Therapeutic Jurisprudence*, 41 Fam. Ct. Rev. 337, 347 (2003); William J. O'Neil and Barry Schneider, *Recommendations of the Committee to Study the Family Issues in the Arizona Superior Court*, 37 Fam. & Conciliation Cts. Rev. 179, 183 (1999); Andrew Shepard and James Bozzomo, *Efficiency, Therapeutic Justice, Mediation, and Evaluation: Reflections on a Survey of Unified Family Courts*, 37 Fam. L.Q. 333, 338 (2003); Paulin Tesler, *A New Paradigm for Divorce Lawyers*, 5 Pub. Pol'y & L. 967, 997 (1999).

how much weight to give their views.[64] Professionals often fear the child will be harmed by such participation if they do not get their stated wishes, although those who have been implementing new laws of child participation report difficulties in some cases but not actual harm.[65] Having a voice seems to be most important.[66] A third argument often considered is the concern that children should be protected from the confrontational nature of participation, including their ability to be manipulated by parents or other authority figures.[67] Experiments such as children's participation in the divorce courts in Israel have found that in most cases, children's participation led to greater rather than less communication within the family.[68] Even when the decisions did not go in the child's favor, the children felt like having their feelings and opinions respected was empowering.[69] Everyone can come away from the process feeling that whatever the outcome, it was made in a fair way. This might provide the equity family courts are seeking.[70]

It is not new to seek children's views in other areas of legal issues, especially as they gained legal rights in other areas. The Supreme Court's decision in *In re Gault*[71] that extended many adultlike procedural rights to children in juvenile cases also provided the opportunity for children's activists to argue for more legal rights for children in other areas of the law. For example, the same court granted children's rights to speech in public schools in *Tinker v. Des Moines Independent Community School District*.[72] It also grant-

---

64. *See* Gillick v. West Norfolk and Wisbech Area Health Authority [1986] AC 112 regarding children's competency to make decisions in legal and medical decisions.

65. GAL AND DURAMY, *supra* note 22.

66. *See* Kevin Burke, *Procedural Fairness Is the Foundation for Making Nonlawyer Judges Effective*, 64 AM. BEHAV. SCIENTIST. 1786, (2020); Kelly Frailing, Brandi Alfonso, and Rae Taylor, *Therapeutic Jurisprudence in Swift and Certain Probation*, 64 AM. BEHAV. SCIENTIST. 1768 (2020).

67. *See* Elizabeth S. Scott, Dickon Repucci, and Jennifer L. Woolard, *Evaluating Adolescent Decision Making in Legal Contexts*, 19 LAW & HUM. BEHAV. 221 (1995).

68. Tamar Morag and Yoa Sorek, *Children's Participation in Israeli Family Courts: An Account of an Ongoing Learning Process*, in GAL AND DURAMY, *supra* note 22, at 157.

69. Of relevance is the topic of procedural justice, which can be described as the criminal justice system demonstrating a legitimacy to the public in which is serves. Additional facets of procedural justice include an individual's voice, respect, neutrality, understanding, and helpfulness. *See* TOM R. TYLER, WHY PEOPLE OBEY THE LAW (1990). On the relationship between procedural justice and TJ in the context of juvenile law, *see* Carolyn Salisbury, *From Violence and Victimization to Voice and Validation: Incorporating Therapeutic Jurisprudence in a Children's Law Clinic*, 17 ST. THOMAS L. REV. 623, 665 (2005).

70. Morag and Sorak, *supra* note 68, at 157.

71. *In re* Gault, 387 U.S. 1 (1967).

72. Tinker v. Des Moines Independent Community School District, 393 U.S. 503 (1969). The Curt, however, declined to extend *Tinker* in Morse v. Frederick, 551 U.S. 393 (2007), hold-

ed due process protections to school children who were about to be expelled in *Goss v. Lopez*.[73] The following year, the justices went further in granting children access to contraception in *Carey v. Population Services*[74] and later to abortion through judicial bypass if the child did not wish to tell her parents in *Belotti v. Baird*.[75] Researchers describe projects in different countries around the world where these legal rights have been granted successfully to children, although not yet routinely in situations or cases where parents are divorcing.[76]

The legal rights granted to children may be a function of age and maturity, but sometimes the law itself imposes an assumption of dependency that is not necessarily true. If children are not permitted to enter into contracts, consent to medical care, or negotiate wages, they have to rely on adults to perform those functions for them, creating a dependency just because of their legal status. It is important to recognize that even adults are not always independent as they may rely on others to help make decisions for them. For example, there are different ages at which children are considered legal adults capable of entering into marriage, sexual activity, employment, driving, drinking alcohol, voting, and criminal prosecution, and these ages may vary from state to state.[77] Assumptions made about a child's maturity may be influenced by biases around race,[78] class,[79] or gender.[80]

Granting children legal rights remains a controversial area today, with some psychologists and jurists believing that doing so will destroy the family, especially if they are permitted in the courtroom to testify against a par-

---

ing that a principal did not violate a student's right to free speech by confiscating banner she reasonably viewed as promoting illegal drug use.

73. Goss v. Lopez, 419 U.S. 565 (1975).

74. Carey v. Population Services, 431 U.S. 678 (1976).

75. Belotti v. Baird, 443 U.S. 622 (1979).

76. GAL AND DURAMY, *supra* note 22.

77. Asaph Glosser, Karen Gardiner, and Mike Fishman, *Statutory Rape: A Guide to State Laws and Reporting Requirements*, DEPARTMENT OF HEALTH AND HUMAN SERVICES (2004), https://aspe.hhs.gov/system/files/pdf/75531/report.pdf.

78. Nonminority participants were reported to be more mature; Matthew A. Lenard and Pablo A. Pena, *Maturity and Minorities: The Impact of Redshirting on Achievement Gaps*, 26 EDUC. ECON. 593, 602 (2018).

79. *See* Eleanor E Maccoby, *Parenting and Its Effects on Children: On Reading and Misreading Behavior Genetics*, 51 ANNUAL REV. PSYCHOL. 1 (2000).

80. For example, there may be an impact on children's maturity in connection to their need to assume adult responsibilities; Bryan, *supra* note 63 at 1008. For more information on how children progress differently based on gender in their moral development and judgment, *see* Gillian R. Wark and Dennis L. Krebs, *Gender and Dilemma Differences in Real-Life Moral Judgment*, 32 Dev. Psychol. 220 (1996).

ent. Others[81] believe that it is necessary to give children the legal right to contest decisions that will harm them, such as protection against child abuse.[82] Still, some believe that criminalizing child abuse laws that permit children to testify against a parent is particularly destructive to both the child and the family unity.[83] Others say an abusive family is already broken.[84] Obviously, there is not an easy answer to this issue. Estimates are only a small number of false allegations occur, with the highest estimate of false allegations reported at 12 percent in custody disputes.[85]

Parental rights and responsibilities sometimes clash, and these types of laws[86] are needed to protect children, again demonstrating that total autonomy is not possible for adults or children. Currently there are tensions between parents who do not wish to vaccinate their children against measles, for example, and the state laws requiring such immunizations before a child can enter school.[87] So far, refusal to permit the nonvaccinated child to enter school has been the remedy, but then the children are denied their right to an education and freedom from a deadly disease. While these regulations vary by state, most states in some way follow recommendations provided by the Advisory Committee on Immunization Practices.[88]

---

81. Aisling Parkes, *Implementation of Article 12 in Family Law Proceedings in Ireland and New Zealand: Lessons Learned and Messages Going Forward*, in GAL AND DURAMY, *supra* note 22, at 111, 111.

82. Anne Graham, Robyn Fitzgerald, and Judith Cashmore, *Professionals' Conceptions of "Children," "Childhood," and "Participation" in Australian Family Relationship Services Sector Organization*, in GAL AND DURAMY, *supra* note 22, at 257, 273.

83. Parkes, *supra* note 80.

84. *Id.* at 120.

85. Nico Trocme and Nicholas Bala, *False Allegations of Abuse and Neglect When Parents Separate*, 29 CHILD ABUSE & NEGLECT 1333, 1341 (2005).

86. Based on recommendations in House Resolution 72.

87. Like other parental disagreements about vaccination of children, since the COVID-19 vaccine is recommended for children, it is not clear that current legislation will also apply in these instances. For example, the state of Florida asserts that a parent with sole responsibility for healthcare decisions can decide and their unvaccinated children can attend school. In shared custody cases, both parents have the right to decide. However, parents can request a modification of parental responsibly assignments due to substantial changes in circumstances. FLA. STAT. § 61.13 (2010).

88. Advisory Committee on Immunization Practices, *Vaccine-Specific ACIP Recommendations*, CENTERS FOR DISEASE CONTROL AND PREVENTION, https://www.cdc.gov/vaccines/hcp/acip-recs/index.html.

A Model TJ Family Court

Judge Ginger Lerner-Wren, the creator of the first problem-solving mental health court in the United States, suggests building a child-centered, trauma-informed therapeutic family court,[89] where the mission is to take a problem-solving and therapeutic public safety and accountability approach to the court process. To accomplish this, the court must take a multilevel and strategic approach and strive to be healing and restorative to families and children whether they live together or not, through the application of TJ principles. Everyone who comes into contact with this TJ family court will understand the goals and procedures in the court. The safety of the children and each member of the family is paramount. The court will adopt emergency measures to intervene where needed, including adopting risk assessment procedures to protect the people being served.[90] These risk assessment tools will be utilized to assist in the development of a safety plan for each family served by the court and modified as more information about the family needs is learned.

Kleinman[91] describes the importance of communication in the TJ Family Court Model. It is important to not only pay attention to the language each team member uses but also be aware of how the message is being received. Training will need to be ongoing using a team approach. Also problematic is whether family court judges have the expertise to have such a discussion with children of various ages given their own backgrounds and training. Many have little patience, understanding, or tolerance for children, and some are known to say things that can be disturbing to them or violate their confidentiality.

Conclusion

We argued in this article that the current method of resolving child custody disagreements in divorcing parents is broken due to systemic flaws in the law and the ignorance in how it is carried out. There is emphasis on families where there are reports of intimate partner and child abuse because these cases are difficult to resolve in family court with the present laws and meth-

---

89. Ginger Lerner-Wren, *Trauma-Informed Family Court: Lessons Learned from the Mental Health Court*, in Our Broken Family Court, *supra* note 9, at 175.

90. David L. Shapiro and Lenore E. A. Walker, Forensic Practice for the Mental Health Clinician (2019).

91. Toby Kleinman, *Appropriate Language to Use in Family Court to Protect Children*, in Our Broken Family Court, *supra* note 9, at 105.

ods; there are other areas needing reform also.[92] There is hope that change can occur. For that to occur, the following needs to happen:

1. Eliminate bias against women in the courts. Acceptance of the narrative about what has happened should be free of gender bias. Start by believing that someone who reports abuse needs the court's protection, and refer them into a special court that we have described as one designed with the principles of TJ and team-based decision-making. The professionals in that court should be tasked with the responsibility to make sure the woman's narrative should be heard while lowering the risk to her and the child involved by offering immediate protection.

2. Eliminate racial and ethnic bias in making recommendations about access to children. Values of diversity and importance of culture need to be respected to the extent that it protective of women and children and men, in that order, given the privilege accorded to males in most societies. At the same time, assure all who need its services have access without regard for financial resources.

3. Grant children legal rights of representation and participation in custody determinations based on their age, maturity, and wishes. Representation could be provided by appropriately trained guardians ad litem or, even more child-focused, an attorney retained for the child. Provide special protection for gender nonconforming children, including those who identify as LGBTQ even at a young age. This includes young children who may believe they are in the physical body of the wrong gender.

4. Eliminate the presumption of joint custody to a parent who has been found guilty of domestic violence or child abuse in any other court of law. The burden of proof on that person should be to prove his or her ability to parent the child without using coercive methods or harm to the child's mother. Assess that he or she uses positive parenting skills and attitudes. Do not force removal laws on a parent wishing to move away from a convicted batterer, child abuser, or sex offender. Do not accept an alleged batterer's or sex offender's denial without adequate evaluation. Permit adolescent children to make their own decisions about being parented by an abusive parent.

---

92. OUR BROKEN FAMILY COURT, *supra note 9.*

5. Create TJ family courts where equity is based upon a model of protection with encouragement to build the necessary accompanying resources in the community.
6. Ensure methods of accountability are strategically put in place so each change can be measured and adjusted where necessary.

PART IV

A Word from the Bench

18

Procedural Fairness Is the Foundation for Making Nonlawyer Judges Effective

JUDGE KEVIN S. BURKE[1]

Introduction

Although the use of nonlawyer judges may be controversial, their continued existence is a given for the foreseeable future. They are cheaper than lawyers.[2] In areas with few lawyers, using nonlawyer judges can make access to a courthouse more achievable in rural settings.[3] The debate about nonlawyer judges should therefore focus on training. Procedural fair-

---

1. Kevin Burke is a senior judge in Minnesota and founding member of Procedural Fairness for Judges and Courts. Special thanks to Matthew Thom, a University of Minnesota law student who helped with this article. Portions of this essay are adapted from Burke, K. "Procedure Fairness Is the Foundation for Making Nonlawyer Judges Effective," *American Behavioral Scientist* (64:12) pp. 1786–1800. Copyright © 2020 by SAGE. Reprinted by permission of SAGE Publications Inc. This material is the exclusive property of the SAGE Publications Inc. and is protected by copyright and other intellectual property laws. User may not modify, publish, transmit, participate in the transfer or sale of, reproduce, create derivative works (including course packs) from, distribute, perform, display, or in any way exploit any of the content of the file(s) in whole or in part. Permission may be sought for further use from SAGE Publications Inc., attn. Rights Department, 2455 Teller Road, Thousand Oaks, CA 91360, email: permissions@sagepub.com. By accessing the file(s), the User acknowledges and agrees to these terms. http://www.sagepub.com.

2. For example, South Carolina sets the base salary of magistrate judges at 35–55 percent of the circuit judge base salary depending on county population, further reduced during the first three years of the magistrate's term. S.C. CODE ANN. § 22-8-40(B) (West, Westlaw through 2020 session).

3. *See, e.g.,* N.Y. CONST. art. 6, § 20(c) (exempting certain judges outside of New York City from a legal practice requirement).

ness training is a practical and cost-effective method of helping nonlawyer judges serve effectively.

Nonlawyer Judges Are a Long-Standing Part of the American Justice System

Nonlawyer judges date back to the English common law practice of employing nonlawyer gentry as justices of the peace and magistrate judges.[4] Alexis de Tocqueville described the American justice of the peace as a "well informed citizen . . . not necessarily versed in the knowledge of the laws . . . oblige[d] . . . to execute the police regulations of society; a task in which good sense and integrity are of more avail than legal science."[5] The role of nonlawyer judges has expanded and contracted throughout American history, surviving many reform efforts to limit the practice.[6] Though our nation now has many more lawyers, nonlawyer judges remain fixtures of the justice system. The United States Supreme Court has held there is no constitutional prohibition to nonlawyer judges sending people to jail.[7] Twenty-two states allow nonlawyer judges to preside over certain criminal cases that can result in imprisonment.[8]

Generally, nonlawyer judges serve in limited jurisdiction courts located in less populated areas, deciding cases concerning civil suits over smaller sums of money and minor criminal offenses. Some nonlawyer judges are local elected officials.[9] No American jurisdiction allows nonlawyer judges to try felony cases.[10]

Opponents consider the nonlawyer judge to be a relic of the past, now obsolete given the number of American lawyers.[11] Implicit in the oppo-

---

4. Allan Ashman and David L. Lee, *Non-Lawyer Judges: The Long Road North*, 53 CHI. KENT L. REV. 565, 568 (1977).

5. ALEXIS DE TOCQUEVILLE, DEMOCRACY IN AMERICA, VOLUMES ONE AND TWO 92 (Henry Reeve trans., 2002 [1835–40]).

6. *See* Ashman and Lee, *supra* note 4, at 566–68.

7. *See* North v. Russell, 427 U.S. 328, 334–35 (1976).

8. *See generally* Petition for Writ of Certiorari, at app'x I, Davis v. Montana, No. 6-123 (July 22, 2016), 2016 WL 4010822, hereafter cited as Davis Certiorari Petition (providing a fifty-state survey).

9. *See* John Paul Ryan and James H. Guterman, *Lawyer Versus Nonlawyer Town Justices— An Empirical Footnote to North v. Russell*, 60 JUDICATURE 272, 275 (1977).

10. *See* Davis Certiorari Petition, *supra* note 8, at 8.

11. *See New ABA Data Reveals Rise in Number of U.S. Lawyers, 15 Percent Increase Since 2008*, ABA (May 11, 2018), https://www.americanbar.org/news/abanews/aba-news-archives /2018/05/new_aba_data_reveals/.

nent's argument is that nonlawyer judges are incapable of affording procedural fairness or due process.[12] Much of the criticism has focused on states where nonlawyer judges have the power to punish by incarceration.[13]

Incarceration abuse is a legitimate concern, but inequitable enforcement of fines and fees should also be cause for concern. There are legally trained judges who have abused the fine and fee process. There are no empirical studies that support the idea that going to law school makes you more insightful about fine and fee abuse.[14] The municipal court in Ferguson, Missouri, was, after all, presided over by a legally trained judge.[15]

Many courts that utilize nonlawyer judges are funded by the fees they impose,[16] so the temptation to impose fines (or even convict) is real. While de Tocqueville may have thought that America purged the justice of the peace of its aristocratic character,[17] jurisdictions that appoint nonlawyer judges often use opaque appointment processes, opening the door to patronage.[18]

It is plausible that due to the projected record budget shortfalls caused by the COVID-19 pandemic, state and local governments might increase the use of nonlawyer judges, let alone replace them with law trained judg-

---

12. *See* Ryan and Guterman, *supra* note 9, at 276–79 (finding that nonlawyer judges were less skeptical of law enforcement, held more positive perceptions of the local prosecutor, held less favorable attitudes toward indigent persons, and were more likely to have pretrial discussions with only the prosecution than lawyer judges); Joseph Cranney, *These Judges Can Have Less Training Than Barbers but Still Decide Thousands of Cases Each Year*, ProPublica (Nov. 27, 2019, 5 a.m. EST), https://www.propublica.org/article/these-judges-can-have-less-train ing-than-barbers-but-still-decide-thousands-of-cases-each-year (describing South Carolina nonlawyer judges neglecting to appoint public defenders, committing fraud, and threatening litigants).

13. *See, e.g.*, Matt Ford, *When Your Judge Isn't a Lawyer*, Atlantic (Feb. 5, 2017), https://www.theatlantic.com/politics/archive/2017/02/when-your-judge-isnt-a-lawyer/515568/.

14. *Cf.* Doris Marie Provine, Judging Credentials: Nonlawyer Judges and the Politics of Professionalism 104 (1984) (listing empirical research suggesting that nonlawyer judges do not significantly differ from nonlawyers in many areas).

15. Judge Ronald Brockmeyer, first appointed in 2003, was Ferguson's municipal court judge during the civil unrest in response to the police killing of Michael Brown. U.S. Dep't of Just., Civ. Rts. Div., Investigation of the Ferguson Police Department 14 (2015). Brockmeyer attended law school and is licensed to practice in Missouri and Illinois. Ronald J. Brockmeyer, *About Us*, Brockmeyer L. Offs., https://www.brockmeyerlaw.com/about-us/ronald-j-brockmeyer/ (last visited Jan. 14, 2021).

16. *See* Dick Carpenter et al., *Municipal Fines and Fees: A 50-State Survey of State Laws*, Inst. for Just. (2020), https://ij.org/report/fines-and-fees-home.

17. *See* de Tocqueville, *supra* note 5.

18. *See* Cranney, *supra* note 12 (describing the state senate's control over South Carolina's appointment process as lacking meaningful oversight).

es.[19] Moreover, any attempt to eliminate them faces the opposition of thousands of nonlawyer judges, armed with the formidable political clout that helped place them in their positions.[20]

Although many nonlawyer judges attend some training, the amount of required training is often legitimately criticized.[21] But traditional legal education is also criticized by those who argue that law school does not adequately prepare students for practice.[22] The traditional curriculum in a law school is simply not designed to prepare someone to effectively perform the duties of nonlawyer judges.

Sending every nonlawyer judge (most of whom perform their duties part-time) to law school even for a year is not going to happen.[23] Most cannot leave their day jobs or cannot afford law school tuition, assuming they were willing to pay it.[24]

Nonlawyer judges preside in courts with heavy dockets.[25] Rulings are made from the bench. Other than filing out a form order, these courts rarely have written orders. There is little time for or access to legal research. These are courts that may well have no clerk, but even those with clerks are quite lean.[26]

---

19. *Cf.* Alison Felix, *COVID-19 Challenges State and Local Government Finances*, FED. RSRV. BANK KAN. CITY: MAIN ST. VIEWS (May 13, 2020), https://www.kansascityfed.org/en /publications/research/eb/articles/2020/covid-19-challenges-state-local-government-finances.

20. Some jurisdictions have bypassed this problem by exempting incumbents from new legal practice requirements. *See, e.g.*, FLA. STAT. ANN. § 34.021 (West, Westlaw through 2020 Second Regular Session).

21. *See, e.g.*, Cranney, *supra* note 12.

22. *See* Rena I. Steinzor and Alan D. Hornstein, *The Unplanned Obsolescence of American Legal Education*, 75 TEMP. L. REV. 447, 457–59 (2002).

23. Limited jurisdiction court judgeships are often part-time jobs, and this intention is often clear from the structure of the judge's salary and prohibitions on certain forms of employment. For example, MONT. CODE ANN. § 3-10-207(3) (West, Westlaw through 2019 Session) reduces the justice of the peace salary to be commensurate to office hours if the court does not operate full-time, and MONT. CODE ANN. § 3-1-602 (West, Westlaw through 2019 Session) prohibits justices of the peace from practicing law.

24. Yearly in-state tuition at the least expensive public law school in America is $13,134. Ilana Kowarski, *See the Price, Payoff of Law School Before Enrolling*, U.S. NEWS & WORLD REP. (Mar. 18, 2020), https://www.usnews.com/education/best-graduate-schools/top-law-schools /articles/law-school-cost-starting-salary#:~:text=The%20average%20annual%20tuition%20 and,fees%20at%20public%20law%20schools.

25. *See* Ashman and Lee, *supra* note 4, at 568–69; *see also* Ford, *supra* note 13.

26. *Cf.* Ryan Tarinelli, *Hiring Freeze Reduces NY Court Workforce by Hundreds*, LAW.COM: N.Y. L.J. (Dec. 12, 2020 at 6:31 PM), https://www.law.com/newyorklawjournal/2020/12/08 /hiring-freeze-reduces-ny-court-workforce-by-hundreds/.

Nonlawyer Judges Shape Attitudes toward the Justice System

The experience that people have in nonlawyer judge courts is critically important. That experience will shape how people perceive the justice system as a whole. And that is why it is imperative steps are taken to ensure that these courts enhance public trust in the justice system not undermine it.

For a judge of any stripe or jurisdiction, trust is earned, not given. Just as trust can be earned, it can be dissipated. If there ever was an era when people simply trusted the judiciary to do the right thing, it is an era long since passed.[27] Courts depend upon voluntary compliance to enforce the vast majority of their orders. The dispute resolution process courts employ is premised upon the vast majority of people voluntarily participating in the process.

The growing lack of trust in public institutions, although not focused specifically on courts, is especially troublesome for the judiciary.[28] There is no credible evidence that nonlawyer judge courts are any more or less trustworthy than courts where the judge is a lawyer.[29] There is no empirical evidence that law-trained judges are any better at dealing with racial fairness than nonlawyer judges.[30]

The National Center for State Courts regularly conducts a study of public perceptions of courts.[31] The studies do not distinguish between courts presided over by judges with or without legal training. Regrettably, the results are consistently weak. In the original study, only 55 percent of people surveyed described courts as fair and impartial.[32] The 2019 National Center for State Courts study showed the already weak national picture of state courts getting weaker, with confidence in state courts decreasing by 11 per-

---

27. *See* Susan M. Olson and David A. Huth, *Explaining Public Attitudes toward Local Courts*, 20 JUST. SYS. J. 41, 42–43 (1998).

28. *See Public Trust in Government Remains Near Historic Lows as Partisan Attitudes Shift*, PEW RSCH. CTR. (May 3, 2017), https://www.people-press.org/2017/05/03/public-trust-in -government-remains-near-historic-lows-as-partisan-attitudes-shift/; *see also* G. W. Dougherty et al., *Evaluating Performance in State Judicial Institutions: Trust and Confidence in the Georgia Judiciary*, 38 ST. & LOC. GOV'T REV. 176, 176 (2006).

29. *Cf.* Provine, *supra* note 14, at 105 (finding that differences were mainly "stylistic").

30. *Id.* at 114–15.

31. *See The State of State Courts: A 2019 NCSC Public Opinion Survey*, NAT'L CTR. FOR STATE CTS., https://www.ncsc.org/topics/court-community/public-trust-and-confidence /resource-guide/2019-state-of-state-courts-survey (last visited Jan. 15, 2021).

32. GBA STRATEGIES, ANALYSIS OF NATIONAL SURVEY OF REGISTERED VOTERS 1 (Dec. 4, 2014), https://www.ncsc.org/__data/assets/pdf_file/0020/17804/2014-state-of-state-courts -survey-12042014.pdf.

cent from the previous year.[33] Perhaps before we worry about whether or not a judge has a law degree, we should focus on the more fundamental challenge, starting with improving service to those that come to court.

The first National Center for State Courts survey found that 39 percent of the people describe courts as intimidating.[34] Intimidation has a long tradition in courts.[35] Judges usually wear robes, although there are nonlawyer judges who preside over limited jurisdiction courts who may not wear robes.[36] The benches are perched high, and everyone is told to rise when the judge enters the room.[37] The courtrooms of many nonlawyer judges are hardly ornate. A great number of the limited jurisdiction nonlawyer courts have no bench. The courtroom is a multipurpose venue for the city council or some other use.[38] Regardless of the decor of the judge and the courtroom, even the smallest court presided over by a nonlawyer judge has the potential for intimidation.

There is a cost of unchecked intimidation. Intimidation suppresses a willingness to talk or ask questions.[39] Honest misunderstandings about what a judge expects a person to do could easily be corrected, and that does not happen if people are afraid to ask questions. Intimidation is not a prerequisite for dignified court proceedings.[40]

Intimidation may create false impressions or false positives. The judge sternly asks, "Sir, do you understand my order?" "Yes, your honor!" replies the person, even though the person is completely bewildered. The person

---

33. NAT'L CTR. FOR STATE CRTS., STATE OF THE STATE COURTS: 2019 POLL 5, https://www.ncsc.org/__data/assets/pdf_file/0018/16443/ncsc_sosc_2019_presentation.pdf (last visited Jan. 15, 2021).

34. GBA STRATEGIES, *supra* note 32.

35. *See generally* FREE TO TELL THE TRUTH—PREVENTING AND COMBATING INTIMIDATION IN COURT: A BENCH BOOK FOR PENNSYLVANIA JUDGES, PA. COMM'N ON CRIME & DELINQ. (Jan. 2011), https://crimegunintelcenters.org/wp-content/uploads/2017/11/FreetoTelltheTruthPreventingandCombatingIntimidationinCourt_PA2011.pdf.

36. *See, e.g.,* TEX. MUN. CTS. ASS'N, *So, Now You're a Judge!* http://www.tmcec.com/public/files/File/Judges/So%20now%20youre%20a%20judge.pdf (last visited Jan. 15, 2021) (giving municipal court judges the option to wear robes).

37. *See Trauma-Informed Courts*, OFF. FOR VICTIMS OF CRIME TRAINING & TECH. ASSISTANCE CTR., OFF. OF JUST. PROGRAMS, https://www.ovcttac.gov/taskforceguide/eguide/6-the-role-of-courts/63-trauma-informed-courts/ (last visited Jan. 15, 2021).

38. *See, e.g., Municipal Court*, CITY OF GUNNISON, COLO., https://www.gunnisonco.gov/government/municipal_court/index.php (last visited Jan. 15, 2021) (noting that the Municipal Court courtroom is also the city council chambers).

39. *See, e.g.,* Cynthia Gray, *Reaching Out or Overreaching: Judicial Ethics and Self-Represented Litigants*, 27 J. NAT'L ASS'N ADMIN. L. JUD., no. 1, 2007, at 97, 112–16 (describing negative effects that intemperate judges have had on *pro se* litigants).

40. *See Trauma-Informed Courts, supra* note 37.

may have questions about what is expected of them, but intimidation drives them to simply want a way out of the courthouse. Asking a judge why he or she ruled in a certain way, even in a very polite manner, does not happen often. If litigants understand why the decision was made, they may not like the result, but they are more likely to comply with the order.[41] Whether done by a law-trained judge or a nonlawyer judge, intimidation overdone creates real problems.[42]

Procedural Fairness Is Important for All Judges but Especially so with Litigants Who Appear in Courts Presided Over by Nonlawyer Judges

Judges care about fairness, yet far too few courts regularly measure their fairness.[43] Data can improve performance. Analytics is now the buzzword for many major league sports, but with all due deference to sports, courts are more important to how a democracy performs.

Many limited jurisdiction courts presided over by nonlawyers keep very little data.[44] The judges likely know filings—"We had more cases this month than last or fewer cases this year than in the past." By knowing whether the number of filings is up or down, you know the court is busy or not. But if a lot of people in the community get caught speeding and the filings go up, there is not much the courts can do about it. Because the funding of many limited jurisdiction courts is driven by fine and fee revenue, many judges know how much revenue their court generates.[45] But revenue generated will not enhance trust in the justice system.

The mindset of some judges is simple: My job is to apply the rule of law, and that is it. Fairness is not the goal. Although these judges would likely be mortified at the suggestion, they do not care about fairness. Chief Justice Roberts in a sense spoke for that point of view in his confirmation hearing when he said, "Judges are like umpires. Umpires don't make the rules, they

---

41. *See* Tom R. Tyler and Yuen J. Huo, Trust in the Law: Encouraging Public Co-operation with the Police and the Courts, 43–45 (2002).

42. *See* Leon Jaworski, *Judicial Intimidation: A Threat to the Advocate's Independence*, 1 Litigation 11, 13 (1975).

43. *See* Olson and Huth, *supra* note 27, at 48–49.

44. This appears more a symptom of limited jurisdiction courts than a symptom of non-lawyer courts. *See* Kellye Milam Mashburn, Caseload and Warrant Workload Analysis of Courts of Limited Jurisdiction in Arkansas 3 (2004).

45. *See* Mike Maciag, *Addicted to Fines: A Special Report*, Governing (Aug. 21, 2019), https://www.governing.com/topics/finance/fine-fee-revenues-special-report.html.

apply them. The role of an umpire and a judge is critical. They make sure everybody plays by the rules, but it is a limited role."[46]

Fairness is critical to enhance trust in courts. So why are so few courts (regardless of whether the judge has or does not have a law degree) regularly measuring their fairness? Perhaps the reason courts have historically not regularly measured fairness is that we can't agree on a definition of fairness.

There are three possible definitions of fairness in a court: (1) outcome favorability (i.e., did I win), (2) outcome fairness (i.e., did I get what I deserved), or (3) procedural fairness (i.e., was my case handled through fair procedures).[47]

Defining fairness as outcome favorability will not work as a definition of fairness for courts, although it might work if you are a lawyer. Lawyers want to win, and their success is often defined by their history of winning. Law school teaches a young lawyer the importance of winning.

Outcome fairness (i.e., "Did I get what I deserved?") is important and might be a more useful definition of fairness for courts.[48] Outcome fairness is something a judge can have a significant effect upon. The explanation a judge gives provides important context and can enhance a litigant or observer's understanding of the process. When a young black man appears before a white judge in a courtroom full of other white people, there is a decent chance the perception of "Did I get what I deserve?" may not happen unless the judge is insightful and good at explanations. But in the end, outcome fairness as the definition of fairness likely does not fully capture a solid working definition of fairness in court.[49]

For decades, there has been significant social science research regarding procedural fairness in courts. Procedural fairness research shows that what is more important than outcomes is a judicial process that is procedurally fair.[50] People who come to our courts want to win, but almost all of them understand this is a human process with all the frailties humans have. With that caveat, all of the research shows people want to be heard.[51] They want

---

46. *See Confirmation Hearing on the Nomination of John G. Roberts Jr. to Be Chief Justice of the United States: Hearing Before the S. Comm. on the Judiciary*, 109th Cong. 55 (2005) (statement of John Roberts, Judge, D.C. Circuit).

47. *See* Linda J. Skitka et al., *Are Outcome Fairness and Outcome Favorability Distinguishable Psychological Constructs? A Meta-Analytic Review*, 16 Soc. Just. Res. 309, 311 (2003).

48. *Id.*

49. *See* Larry Heuer et al., *The Role of Societal Benefits and Fairness Concerns among Decision Makers and Decision Recipients*, 31 Law & Hum. Behav. 573, 584 (2007).

50. *See* Joel Brockner, *Making Sense of Procedural Fairness: How High Procedural Fairness Can Reduce or Heighten the Influence of Outcome Favorability*, 27 Acad. Mgmt. Rev. 58, 58 (2002).

51. *See* Tom R. Tyler, *Procedural Justice and the Courts*, 44 Ct. Rev. 26, 30 (2007).

to be treated with respect.[52] They want to understand why the decision was made.[53] And people are much more likely to obey court orders if they receive procedural fairness.[54] Even if the compliance with the order is simply going to the clerk's counter and paying a fine because they lost, the imperative is walking out of the courthouse feeling you were treated with respect and trusting the courts at least as much if not more than when you arrived at the courthouse.[55]

Achieving compliance is not just establishing a set of rules we expect people to obey. Litigant compliance with court orders is driven by behavior of the judge as well.[56] If a judge wants to get higher compliance with orders, he or she can try intimidation—even add yelling at the person—but that will not work to achieve long-term compliance, and it may not even work in the very short run. Procedural fairness achieves higher compliance with orders.[57] Procedural fairness enhances trust in courts, and that is exactly what is needed now.[58]

There are some different views of what the key component of procedural fairness are. A simple version of procedural fairness's key components are voice, neutrality, respect, and trust.[59]

People want the opportunity to tell their side of the story, and have the experience of telling that story to a judge who listens carefully. It sounds so simple, but it is not. There are courts with unacceptably high volumes.[60] Just how much time do you give people to speak? There are people who cannot get to their point, including lawyers who do not even know what the point is to which they want to get. Listening isn't easy. A judge can daydream or

---

52. *Id.* at 30–31.

53. *Id.* at 30.

54. *See* Jessica Kay and Emily LaGratta, Talking about Fairness: A Planning Guide for Communities and Justice System Leaders 1 (2019), https://www.courtinnova tion.org/sites/default/files/media/documents/2019-04/guide_pjrountablenewark_04172019.pdf.

55. *See* Heuer et al., *supra* note 49, at 575.

56. *Id.*

57. *See* Kristina Murphy, *Procedural Justice and Its Role in Promoting Voluntary Compliance*, in Regulatory Theory: Foundations and Applications 44 (Peter Drahos ed., 2017).

58. *See* Ramona-Gabriela Paraschiv, *The Importance of Procedural of Justice in Shaping Individuals' Perceptions of the Legal System*, 4 Geopolitics, Hist., & Int'l Rel., no. 2, 2012, at 162, 163.

59. *See* Tyler, *supra* note 51, at 30–31.

60. In 2017, there were 83.2 million reported civil cases in state courts. Crt. Stats. Project, State Crt. Caseload Dig.: 2017 Data 8 (2019), http://www.courtstatistics.org/__data /assets/pdf_file/0021/29820/2017-Digest-print-view.pdf. Roughly 54.2 million cases, or 65 percent, of cases were before courts of limited jurisdiction. When counting only the reported cases in states that have limited jurisdiction courts (69.5 million), courts of limited jurisdiction handled 78 percent of cases. *See id.*

be lulled into thinking, "I've heard it before." Active listening takes energy and is a skill judges are often not taught. If you are a lawyer and are still wed to the idea that to be a judge, you need to go to law school, how many courses did you take in law school specifically designed to teach you how to listen better?

Courts that are interested in collecting meaningful data on fairness collect data from court participants by asking questions like the following: "Did the judge listen to you?" "Did the judge listen to both sides evenly?" "Do you feel there was an adequate time for you to speak?" This type of data collection is possible for a nonlawyer judge. Some may even collect customer satisfaction data in their daytime job or business.

What does the courtroom look like to litigants? How do they perceive the judge? Videotaping proceedings is a great tool to answer those questions.[61] A part-time nonlawyer judge with no local training budget and minimal assistance from the state judicial education office can get pretty good insight by simply videotaping their presence on the bench.

The vast majority of judicial decisions made by nonlawyer judges are oral and made quickly so the judge can move on to the next case in that crowded courtroom.[62] But whether it is an oral order issued in a crowded courtroom or a written decision at any level of the court system, there is no excuse for not being transparent about the decision-making process and explaining why in an understandable way.

Everyone to some degree has implicit biases. We are a nation polarized by race, and as the data show, courts have a problem with the perception of fairness based upon race.[63] Therefore, it is vitally important that the decisions that judges make are reflective enough to overcome implicit bias of the judge and the decision explained to those in the courtroom so they believe the decision was made based upon rules of law not bias.[64]

Neutrality, properly understood, is not masking that the judge cares. The definition of the word "empathy" is essentially the ability to put yourself

---

61. *See* Kevin Burke and Steve Leben, *Procedural Fairness: A Key Ingredient in Public Satisfaction*, 44 CT. REV. 4, 18 (2007).

62. *See, e.g.*, ALISA SMITH ET AL., RUSH TO JUDGEMENT: HOW SOUTH CAROLINA'S SUMMARY COURTS FAIL TO PROTECT CONSTITUTIONAL RIGHTS 21 (2017), https://www.nacdl.org/getattachment/ab9d6b03-2b45-4235-890e-235461a9bb2d/rush-to-judgment-how-south-carolina-s-summary-courts-fail-to-protect-constitutional-rights.pdf.

63. NAT'L CTR. FOR STATE CRTS., *State of the State Courts: 2015 Poll 9*, https://www.ncsc.org/__data/assets/pdf_file/0020/15833/sosc_2015_presentation.pdf (last visited Jan. 15, 2021).

64. *See Preliminary Information*, HARVARD UNIV.: PROJECT IMPLICIT, https://implicit.harvard.edu/implicit/takeatest.html (last visited June 21, 2020) for the Harvard implicit bias test.

in someone else's shoes.[65] It is not the same as sympathy (a tendency to favor or support) or prejudice (a preconceived judgment or opinion).[66] Contrary to sympathy or prejudice, empathy and justice are not mutually exclusive but mutually reinforcing.[67]

Neutrality is being open and transparent about how the decision was made.[68] A procedurally fair decision is one that gives an explanation that is understandable to everyone, not just lawyers or an appellate court.[69] Citing to statutes, rules, or cases helps convey that the judge is not just deciding this case because of a personal whim. But there is more to it. For judges in high-volume courts, the audience needs to understand why. Judges who want to achieve procedural fairness can practice how to explain.

Achieving respect is the third component of procedural fairness.[70] People take cues about respect for them as they encounter court employees throughout the building. The personnel who may provide security at a magnetometer are not as critical as the judge, but they can set a tone.[71] They can start the overdone intimidation in the courthouse, or they can convey a tone of respect. Achieving respect requires judges to be relentlessly proactive. In the courtroom, respect requires taking people's concerns seriously even when that maybe a challenge.[72] People come to court because courts make them, but also come because they care about issues in their cases. "The police officer did not respect me and was rude just because I am a young black man." If you want to be an effective trial court judge, you had better have an answer other than, "Well, young man, were you speeding or not?"

Active listening conveys respect. Active listening requires judges to make clear that they have heard the needs and concerns of those that appear before them.[73] Yes, sometimes there is no good answer to the young black man who felt disrespected by the police, but at a minimum he needs to leave

---

65. *See Empathy*, WIKIPEDIA, https://en.wikipedia.org/wiki/Empathy (last visited June 21, 2020).

66. *See Sympathy*, MERRIAM-WEBSTER, https://www.merriam-webster.com/dictionary/sympathy (last visited June 21, 2020); *Prejudice*, MERRIAM-WEBSTER, https://www.merriam-webster.com/dictionary/prejudice (last visited June 21, 2020).

67. Jean Decety and Jason M. Cowell, *Empathy, Justice, and Moral Behavior*, 6 AJOB NEUROSCIENCE, no. 3, 2015, at 12–13.

68. *See* Tyler, *supra* note 51.

69. *Id.*

70. *Id.* at 30–31.

71. *See generally* Jon B. Gould, *Security at What Cost? A Comparative Evaluation of Court Security*, 28 JUST. SYS. J. 62 (describing court users' irritation with certain security protocols).

72. *See* T. R. S. Allan, *Procedural Fairness and the Duty of Respect*, 18 OXFORD J. LEGAL STUD. 497, 500–501 (1998).

73. *Id.*

the courthouse believing he was heard and that the judge cared about what he had to say.

Procedural Fairness and Therapeutic Jurisprudence Complement Each Other

Professors David Wexler and Bruce Winick are credited with conceiving the field of therapeutic jurisprudence as a system of "law as therapy—of therapy through law."[74] The field's largest achievement has been the creation of problem-solving courts, which seek to help the people that come before them through rehabilitation.[75] The creation of these new courts has been an ambitious and radically different approach that typically concerns limited areas of criminal law and issues viewed through a mental health lens.[76] Given the budgetary problems now faced by state court systems, it is unlikely that the limited misdemeanor jurisdiction of some nonlawyer courts will be wholly transferred to problem-solving courts. Neither is the quintessential jurisdictional issue of the nonlawyer judge court, the disputed traffic ticket, a prime candidate for a holistic therapeutic justice–based reform. However, not all therapeutic justice initiatives need arise from the creation of new courts.

The adoption of procedural fairness principles would be a useful tool to create a more therapeutic jurisprudence in any court. Professor Wexler has recently focused on utilizing therapeutic jurisprudence methods through a procedural fairness framework, suggesting that judges also ask questions that help parties before the court process and learn from their experience.[77] Professor Amy Ronner has utilized the procedural fairness work of Professor Tom Tyler to create her key components of a therapeutic court experience, or three Vs—voice, validation, and voluntary participation.[78] She argues that these procedural fairness inspired concepts are a necessary condition to any therapeutic jurisprudence.[79] An individual who experiences an unjust procedure denying them of any voice is less likely to accept

---

74. See David Wexler, *The Development of Therapeutic Jurisprudence: From Theory to Practice*, 68 Revista Juridica U. P.R. 691, 693 (1999).

75. See Michael Perlin, *"Have You Seen Dignity?": The Story of the Development of Therapeutic Jurisprudence*, 27 N.Z.U. L. Rev. 1135, 1149–55 (2017).

76. *Id.*

77. See David Wexler, *Guiding Court Conversation along Pathways Conductive to Rehabilitation: Integrating Procedural Justice and Therapeutic Jurisprudence*, 1 Int'l J. Therapeutic Juris. 367, 370–72 (2016).

78. See Amy D. Ronner, *Songs of Validation, Voice, and Voluntary Participation: Therapeutic Jurisprudence, Miranda and Juveniles*, 71 U. Cin. L. Rev. 89, 93 (2002).

79. *Id.* at 94–95.

responsibility for their actions and change their behavior.[80] This theory is not necessarily limited to criminal contexts. Even over issues as limited as contested traffic tickets, procedural fairness may facilitate future compliance with the law that was violated.

Judge Learned Hand once said, "The spirit of liberty is the spirit which is not too sure it is right."[81] It is practical to train nonlawyer judges to aspire to have the wisdom of Judge Hand: to not be too sure you are right. It is practical to give nonlawyer judges skills training in procedural fairness. Was the person listened to? Were people treated in the courthouse with respect? Do they understand what the decision was and why the decision was made? The answers to those questions may not always please us, but they are the questions we need to ensure all judges regardless of their legal training ask.

---

80. *Id.*
81. Judge Learned Hand, The Spirit of Liberty Speech (May 21, 1944).

Contributors

Brandi Alfonso earned both her undergraduate and master's degrees in criminology and justice at Loyola University New Orleans, where she also won the prestigious Patrick D. Walsh Integrity Award. During her time at Loyola, she was instrumental as a research intern on two innovations in supervision projects in Jefferson Parish and gained expertise in observing status hearings as a way to measure the presence (or absence) of therapeutic jurisprudence in that setting.

Ashley Balavender is a Ph.D. student at the Rutgers University School of Criminal Justice. Her research interests center on community supervision, correctional system frontline workers, and agency organizational development.

Dr. Colleen M. Berryessa is an assistant professor at the School of Criminal Justice at Rutgers University. Her research, utilizing both qualitative and quantitative methods, considers how psychological processes, perceptions, attitudes, and social contexts affect the criminal justice system, particularly related to courts and sentencing. Dr. Berryessa received her Ph.D. in criminology from the University of Pennsylvania. Before Penn, she graduated from Harvard University with a B.A. in government and mind, brain, and behavior, and she served as a CIRGE research fellow at Stanford University.

Judge Kevin S. Burke served on the bench from 1984 until the fall of 2020. He continues to write, speak. and do mediations. He was named by Politics in Minnesota as one of the one hundred most influential lawyers in the history of Minnesota. He has received numerous awards, including the 2003 William Rehnquist Award given by the National Center for State Courts. In 2005, *Governing Magazine* named him Public Official of the Year. He has spoken in forty states and several counties about procedural fairness and court leadership. He teaches at the University of Minnesota Law School and the University of St. Thomas Law School.

Dr. Michael Cassidy is an assistant professor in the Department of Criminology and Criminal Justice at Niagara University. His research interests include courts and sentencing, community corrections, and evaluation of criminal justice programs.

Brandi N. Diaz is currently a doctoral student at Nova Southeastern University, where she is studying clinical psychology with a concentration in forensic psychology. Brandi's graduate work has included interpersonal violence, therapeutic jurisprudence, and the assessment of malingering.

Deborah A. Dorfman is currently the executive director of Disability Rights Connecticut (DRCT). Prior to working at DRCT, Deborah was the managing attorney for the Everett Field Office of the Northwest Justice Project in Washington state. She has almost thirty years of experience litigating individual and class actions, as well other systemic reform cases, in the areas of disability and related law, with a particular focus on legal issues pertaining to people with intellectual and/or mental health disabilities, including juvenile justice, access to Medicaid and state-funded services and other public benefits, Olmstead and other disability discrimination, special education, prison and jail conditions, abuse and neglect, fair housing, civil commitment, and forensic mental health, among other issues. Deborah has also been an adjunct professor at New York Law School in the Mental Disability Law Online Program and at St. John's School of Law, and she has given numerous presentations nationally and internationally and published a number of articles on disability rights issues.

Henry A. Dlugacz is an attorney and licensed social worker who is a partner at New York law firm Beldock Levine & Hoffman LLP and a clinical assistant professor of psychiatry and behavioral sciences at New York Medical College. He has forty years' experience in corrections as a treatment provider, program director, and court-appointed monitor and expert.

Heather Ellis Cucolo is a distinguished adjunct professor of law and the facilitator of the joint J.D./M.A. program with John Jay College of Criminal Justice, at New York Law School (NYLS). She is also an adjunct professor at Emory University School of Law and a fellowship faculty member at Albert Einstein College of Medicine. In addition to those roles, Professor Cucolo is co-owner of Mental Disability Law and Policy Associates, a legal education and professional training company, and is on the board of trustees for the International Society of Therapeutic Jurisprudence, a nonprofit organization.

Dr. Kelly Frailing is an associate professor of criminology and justice at Loyola University New Orleans. Her areas of expertise include crime and disaster, people with mental illness who are justice system involved, and specialty courts and programs, and she has published dozens of articles on these topics. She is a coauthor of *Toward a Criminology of Disaster, The Criminalization of Mental Illness*, 3rd edition, and *Fundamentals of Criminology*, 2nd edition. She is the coeditor of *Crime and Criminal Justice in Disaster*, 3rd edition, and *The Criminalization of Mental Illness: A Reader.*

Mehgan Gallagher has been advocating on behalf of human rights domestically and internationally for the past fifteen years. She currently practices as a litigator in state and federal court. Mehgan has been published widely on international law and the rights of people with disabilities; the right to refuse treatment; health and justice issues for historically underrepresented populations; and suicide among mental health detainees in prisons, jails, and immigration detention centers. She holds an LL.M. from Georgetown University Law Center, a J.D. from New York Law School, and a B.A. from Clark University.

Dr. Talia Roitberg Harmon obtained her Ph.D. from the School of Criminal Justice at the State University of New York at Albany. She is currently a full professor and chair of the Department of Criminal Justice and Criminology at Niagara University. Her major research focus is on various issues surrounding the efficacy of capital punishment. She has published work on issues surrounding capital punishment including death qualification, capital commutations, wrongful convictions in capital cases, the current decline in death sentences, and ineffective assistance of counsel in capital cases that raised mental health issues.

Richelle Kloch is a summa cum laude graduate of Niagara University, where she majored in criminal justice and minored in prelaw, computer crime, and forensics. She is currently attending SUNY at Buffalo School of Law. She has a position on the editorial board of the Buffalo Law Review, is a member of UB Law's Trial Team, and is a class director for the Student Bar Association. In addition, she is the secretary of the North Tonawanda Housing Development Corporation, a not-for-profit organization that provides financing for improvements in senior low-income housing.

Shelley Kolstad is a sessional academic with the Law Faculty at Queensland University of Technology, where she teaches in criminal law sentencing and tutors in evidence. She is also a unit coordinator in the Data and New Technology Law Graduate Certificate for QUT Online. Her research interests include therapeutic jurisprudence and compassion informed law. Shelley has a bachelor of business (with distinction) from the University of Queensland and a bachelor of laws (first class honours) from Queensland University of Technology.

Alison J. Lynch is an attorney practicing in New York City. She has spent her career representing individuals with mental illness in the criminal and civil systems, and more recently she has begun exploring mental health issues in the U.S. immigration system.

Dr. Voula Marinos is a professor of child and youth studies and the director of the forensic psychology and criminal justice program at Brock University, Ontario, Canada. She holds a Ph.D. in criminology from the Centre of Criminology, University of Toronto. Her interdisciplinary research is currently focused on three primary areas: diversion of youth and adults from the formal court process; mental health, intellectual disabilities, law, and the courts; and plea bargaining and sentencing of youth and adults. Much of her work involves interviews with criminal justice professionals and court observations. She lectures widely to criminal justice professionals, law students, and community-based organizations about her research and criminal justice policy.

Dr. Valerie R. McClain is a licensed psychologist in the state of Florida. She is in private practice and works in the areas of forensic and neuropsychology. She conducts forensic evaluations that are both court ordered and privately retained, and she testifies frequently in both circuit and federal courts. She has authored multiple articles with colleagues that are peer reviewed and published. She graduated from Florida Tech in Melbourne, Florida, with her doctoral degree.

Michael L. Perlin is Professor of Law Emeritus at New York Law School (NYLS), where he was director of NYLS's Online Mental Disability Law

Program and director of NYLS's International Mental Disability Law Reform Project in its Justice Action Center. He is cofounder of Mental Disability Law and Policy Associates and is currently an adjunct professor of law at Emory University School of Law and an instructor at Loyola University New Orleans, Department of Criminology and Justice. Formerly, he was a deputy public defender in charge of the Mercer County (Trenton, NJ) Trial Region of the NJ Public Defender and the director of the Division of Mental Health Advocacy in the NJ Department of the Public Advocate. He has written thirty-three books and over three hundred articles on all aspects of mental disability law. He has litigated at every court level from police court to the U.S. Supreme Court, and he has done advocacy work on every continent. He is the honorary life president of the International Society for Therapeutic Jurisprudence and a member of that society's current board of trustees. He is also a member of the Lawrence Township (NJ) Community Concert Band, the Temple University Night Owls band, and the board of directors of the Washington Crossing (NJ) Audubon Society.

Bernard P. Perlmutter is Professor of Law and Codirector of the Children and Youth Law Clinic at the University of Miami School of Law, where he also teaches Family Law, Transnational Family Law, Children and the Law, and New Directions in Lawyering: Interviewing, Counseling, and Attorney-Client Relational Skills. In the clinic, Professor Perlmutter supervises law students who represent children and adolescents in abuse and neglect, foster care, adoption, public benefits, health care, mental health, disability, education, immigration, and general civil legal matters, in addition to appellate, legislative, administrative, and law reform advocacy.

Victoria Rapp is a Ph.D. student at University of Miami. She received her bachelor of arts and master of criminology and justice degrees from Loyola University New Orleans, where she earned awards for the highest GPA at both levels. She is the coauthor of a number of articles on swift and certain probation. Her research interests include specialty courts, sexual violence, and criminological theory.

Dr. Karen A. Snedker is a professor of sociology at Seattle Pacific University. Her research is interdisciplinary and addresses mental health, homelessness, crime and violence, and neighborhood effects. Her published work has appeared in sociology, geography, demography, public health, and crime academic outlets. Dr. Snedker's recent book, *Therapeutic Justice: Crime, Treatment Courts and Mental Illness*, examines mental health courts within the larger problem-solving court movement. She is currently working on her next book, in collaboration with Dr. Jennifer McKinney (SPU), on home-lessness and tent cities.

Dr. Rae Taylor is an associate professor in the Department of Criminology and Justice at Loyola University New Orleans. Her research and teaching interests include intimate partner violence and other violent crimes, societal and organizational responses to violent crime and social inequalities, and issues pertaining to mass incarceration.

Dr. Lenore E. A. Walker is a clinical and forensic psychologist at Walker & Associates and Professor Emerita from Nova Southeastern University College of Psychology, where she coordinated the forensic psychology master's and doctoral level programs. Her research on battered woman syndrome helped introduce the concept in the courts around the world. She has published over twenty books, including four editions of *The Battered Woman Syndrome*. She is an editor of *The Handbook on Sex Trafficking* and (with David Shapiro) *Introduction to Forensic Psychology and Forensic Practice for the Mental Health Practitioner*. Her mystery novel, *Madness to Murder*, is now available on Amazon. Her many accomplishments are available at www.drlenoreewalker.com.

Naomi Weinstein is an attorney for a state agency representing persons with mental disabilities, persons facing guardianships, and sex offenders facing civil commitment. Naomi was the past chair of the New York City Bar Association Mental Health Law Committee. As chair, Naomi organized events with ThriveNYC and Supported Decision-Making New York, and she hosted guest speakers on a variety of topics including mental health mediation, the use of advance psychiatric directives, and supportive housing, as well as commented on pending legislation. Naomi continues to present at conferences on various topics involving mental health law and has published several articles with Professor Perlin. Naomi also spent a year in Japan teaching English, after graduating from Tufts University. Naomi received a bachelor's degree from Tufts University in clinical psychology.

Lisa Whittingham is a Ph.D. candidate in the Department of Child and Youth Studies at Brock University. Her interdisciplinary research examines the interactions of persons with developmental disabilities with the criminal justice system. She is also a board-certified behavior analyst.

Index